Professional ASP.N

Professional
ASP.NET 2.0 Design

Professional
ASP.NET 2.0 Design

CSS, Themes, and Master Pages

Jacob J. Sanford

Wiley Publishing, Inc.

Professional ASP.NET 2.0 Design: CSS, Themes, and Master Pages

Published by
Wiley Publishing, Inc.
10475 Crosspoint Boulevard
Indianapolis, IN 46256
www.wiley.com

Copyright © 2007 by Wiley Publishing, Inc., Indianapolis, Indiana

Published simultaneously in Canada

ISBN: 978-0-470-12448-2

Manufactured in the United States of America

10 9 8 7 6 5 4 3 2 1

Library of Congress Cataloging-in-Publication Data

Sanford, Jacob J., 1972-
  ASP.net 2.0 design : CSS, themes, and master pages / Jacob J. Sanford.
       p. cm.
  Includes index.
  ISBN 978-0-470-12448-2 (paper/website)
  1. Active server pages. 2. Web sites--Design. I. Title.
  TK5105.8885.A26S25 2007
  006.7'6--dc22

                                 2007026260

I dedicate this, my first book, to my son, Matthew. I am the second-generation "first son" to write a book; you will be the third. I love you, Matt.

About the Author

Jacob J. Sanford is currently a Project Lead with the Rapid Application Development Team at the Florida Department of Children & Families. He began developing web applications more than 10 years ago using primarily classic ASP with various relational databases. Over the years he has dabbled in other web application development languages such as ColdFusion and PHP. However, he has been working almost exclusively with the .NET Framework since its 1.0 release. He is a regular contributor to 2MinuteTips.com and makes frequent presentations at local and regional .NET events. Having worked in all aspects of the SDLC, he has been focusing his recent efforts primarily on accessible web design (especially as it pertains to .NET applications). He also spends an inordinate amount of time "playing" with the latest (alpha and beta) web technologies, especially Microsoft Silverlight. He is married and as of writing this book has one son, but by the time you read it, he will have two. (Welcome to the world, Hayden.)

Credits

Senior Acquisitions Editor
Jim Minatel

Development Editor
Kelly Talbot

Technical Editor
Adam Kahtava

Production Editor
Debra Banninger

Copy Editor
Foxxe Editorial Services

Editorial Manager
Mary Beth Wakefield

Production Manager
Tim Tate

Vice President and Executive Group Publisher
Richard Swadley

Vice President and Executive Publisher
Joseph B. Wikert

Proofreader
Sossity Smith

Indexer
Jack Lewis

Project Coordinator, Cover
Lynsey Osborn

Anniversary Logo Design
Richard Pacifico

Acknowledgments

I was literally sitting at my computer staring at the screen thinking "I can't believe I am finally writing my acknowledgments." This book has been one of the most rewarding experiences of my life, even though it had to accommodate back surgery, pregnancy (my wife's — not mine), work commitments, and a variety of other obstacles. There was at least a time or two when I seriously questioned whether or not I would finish. But I did. And it was due in no small part to a lot of people who I now get the chance to thank.

First, I want to acknowledge the amazing people at Wrox who helped me get here. I recently read a blog entry by Jim Minatel, the senior acquisitions editor who was my first contact at Wrox. He outlined all of the things that a good book submission should have in order to be considered for a book deal. After reading it, I thought "How did I make it through that process?" Jim saw something and gave me a chance, and I will never forget that. He has been involved throughout the entire process and given me a lot of great advice and direction along the way. He also hooked me up with my development editor, Kelly Talbot. Kelly was very gracious and helpful to me throughout the entire book. He was funny, encouraging, insightful, and kept me motivated throughout the chapters and all of the review processes at the end. He kept me on track and was extremely accommodating when I had unexpected delays. I also want to publicly thank my technical editor, Adam Kahtava. I was excited, albeit a bit intimidated, when I found out he was going to be my technical editor. I had read his blogs before ever starting this book and had some specific entries bookmarked for my own reference. He provided even more technical expertise in his editing than I had expected (and I expected a lot). He caught the errors I missed and made a lot of really great suggestions on how to expand or clarify certain points I was trying to make. If this book becomes a success, it is because of these three people.

I also want to thank my family for all of their support and forgiveness. To my wife, Shannan, you rock. You let me spend countless hours on the computer writing, reading, and "playing." You never let me question how much you believed in me, and I know the book happened in large part because of your love and support. To my son, Matthew, you are my constant inspiration. My office is covered with your photos for a reason. I love you and want to be just like you when I grow up. To my son, Hayden, I can't wait to meet you. Even though you aren't here yet, you inspired me in ways that you will never know. Now that I am done with the book, I can finally work on your room. I also want to thank my mother, Peggy, for being my first, and still favorite, tech support customer. And to my brother, Daniel, thank you for keeping me level-headed and "real." My family is more important to me than anything else, and I hope you all know how much I love you.

I would like to acknowledge some of the people who helped me get to the point, technically, where I felt like I could write about web application development. First, to David Drinkwine, who started me on my first classic ASP project. To Telly Buckles for giving me my first real web designer job and starting me on my Photoshop journey. To Marsha Ryan for letting me sit in a locked office for a week to teach myself .NET. And to Kim Brock and Margie France who helped me mature into the professional web developer I have become over the last year or two.

To all of the Gaines Street Saints: I love you like family.

To Roger at No Regrets Tattoo: Thanks for keeping straight lines even if you couldn't keep a straight face.

And, finally, to all of the people who are using this book. I hope you find it as fun to read as it was to write.

Contents

Contents

Contents

Introduction

Welcome to my first book, *Professional ASP.NET 2.0 Design: CSS, Themes, and Master Pages*. This book started off with the goal of telling the world about the business uses and advantages of themes. I had started developing them a bit and was getting further and further into them and kept thinking "this is the coolest thing I have seen in a while". I began telling coworkers and colleagues about the different uses of themes and most of them had not even heard of themes at the time or, if they had, they had no real concept of what they were or how they could be used. I began making Code Camp presentations on themes, and the response was overwhelming. I decided this would be a really great topic for a book.

As I started creating my book submission, though, the topic expanded. Sure, Themes were amazing and their merits should be touted to the world. But is that enough? Meaning, is it enough just to show the basics of creating themes and how to apply them? Or is there a fundamental foundation of web design knowledge that needs to be incorporated into any theme design? Obviously, the latter began to become more and more the focus of the book. While themes are an important part of the concept I have coined as "aesthNETics," which means the art of making powerful .NET pages look as amazing as the technology that drives them, they are only part of the equation. As an aesthNETics developer, you must include consideration of universal web standards like CSS, color, graphics, and accessibility, in the planning of any of your web projects. But more than that, you have to put .NET into the equation. This means using the tools of Visual Studio 2005 to enhance the look, feel, and consistency of the sites you develop. Tools such as menu controls, control adapters, Master Pages, and, yes, themes are critically important if you are to take aesthNETics seriously.

This book sort of chronicles my journey towards accessible web design. I learned web design using tables-based layout design. Anyone who started using HTML ten or more years ago, as I did, would probably say the same thing. There wasn't much discussion of CSS and accessibility standards. This remained true until a year or so ago when I started slowly moving over to begin experimenting with CSS-for-structure design. When I started this book, I hadn't totally made the switch, but by the time it was finished, I had. This is partially because of the research I did for the book but also because of the lessons learned from my own work experience at a State agency. If I had written this book a year ago, it probably would not have been as heavily laden with CSS. If I were to write it a couple of years from now, it probably wouldn't be as open to tables for design in the earlier chapters as it is now. Its funny how time has a way of changing things.

My goal is for you to find the tools and tricks shown in this book useful so you can begin thinking about accessible web design and incorporating it into the projects you develop. I want you to see that you can, and should, use the .NET controls in your projects to create consistent and stylish web applications while still remaining accessible to all. I want you to get as excited about doing the interface piece of your web projects as I do. If you already have a strong handle on the data access and business logic tiers of your projects, this should help round out your skills so that you bring to your organization the "whole package." I hope, when you are done, you will feel like you are a Renaissance man or woman of .NET web design.

Who This Book Is For

This book is for anyone who wants to learn about using .NET for web interface design. Beginner or hobbyist .NET developers can certainly get a good foundation of .NET web interface design by going through this book from cover to cover. However, more seasoned .NET professionals, especially if they tend to steer away from the GUI of their projects, can also pick up a thing or two by focusing on certain chapters that appeal to them. This book is meant to take a reader from the beginning of a project to the completion of the interface design. Along the way, concepts are illustrated to show how the different pieces play together. So, anyone who really wants to understand the concepts presented in this book will be able to do so by reading the entire thing. However, this book should also serve as a good reference after you have read it or, in some cases, in place of reading it.

All of the early chapters provide useful information and examples for any web developer. Many of the concepts presented after Chapter 4 are more specifically targeted at .NET developers. In the later chapters, the target audience is .NET developers or, at least, people who want to become .NET developers. In those chapters, you should probably have at least a basic understanding of the .NET Framework and some experience with Visual Studio 2005 (or possibly Visual Studio 2003). If you are completely new to .NET, you may find it useful to pick up a beginning ASP.NET 2.0 book before delving too deeply into those chapters. If you want to learn about .NET 2.0 web interface design, you are the intended audience.

It should be noted that all of the .NET code samples in this book are in C#. However, this shouldn't limit other developers, such as VB.NET developers, from understanding the concepts or being able to replicate the code in their own projects. The actual managed code examples are pretty limited and, when they are used, they should be fairly easy to port over to VB.NET.

What This Book Covers

This book covers the concepts serious developers need to begin designing cool and consistent web layouts. The early chapters focus on general web design standards that you need to grasp in order to move into the later chapters. Specifically, these concepts are:

- ❑ Basic web design considerations (colors, fonts, images, accessibility, and so on) (Chapter 2)
- ❑ Photoshop basics to get you started making your own graphics and color schemes (Chapter 3)
- ❑ Cascading Style Sheets (CSS) and their use in web design layout (Chapter 4)

When you finish these chapters, you will have the basic shell for the project that you will continue to develop throughout the book. You will have the header graphic, color scheme, and CSS layout that you will begin to incorporate .NET-specific concepts to in the later chapters. This includes:

- ❑ How to make .NET controls render accessible CSS code rather than their default: tables (Chapter 5)
- ❑ Using the built-in controls of .NET to create easily maintainable and consistent site navigation (and how to make them render CSS `divs` instead of tables) (Chapter 6)
- ❑ Creating your web site template with Master Pages (Chapter 7)
- ❑ Creating themes and skins to style your .NET controls (Chapter 8)
- ❑ Applying themes to your projects through various approaches, including base classing (Chapter 9)

The final "regular" chapter ends with you building an entirely new mobile device theme using all of the concepts learned in the previous chapters. In Chapter 10, you will start with modifying your graphic to better fit the resolution of your mobile devices. You will also learn how to modify your stylesheets and apply them programmatically to be used only for this theme. You will have a new Master Page and an entirely new theme. You will also see one way of switching themes based on your criteria (in this example, your criterion will be whether your client browser is a mobile device).

Beyond these chapters, you will get a "forward look" at some of the new technologies coming down the pipeline that affect these some of the material you learned in the preceding chapters. In Appendix A, you will get a glimpse at the upcoming release for Visual Studio, codenamed "Orcas." This will almost exclusively focus on the new CSS features because they are the most relevant to the other chapters of the book, and there are so many new features regarding CSS management in this release that they warrant their own chapter (nested Master Pages are also included, but CSS takes up most of the appendix).

Finally, with Appendix B, the Visual Studio Codename "Orcas" discussion is extended to include Microsoft Silverlight. You will learn how to create drawing objects, incorporate images, animate your objects, and affect the rendered output through your managed code.

If you read this book from cover to cover, you should end up with a really solid understanding of the current technologies for .NET developers to create consistent and accessible web interfaces, as well as a feeling of excitement for the new stuff that should be coming soon to a computer near you.

What You Need to Use This Book

This book is structured in a way that you may not be familiar with. Most chapters begin with a lot of theoretical knowledge that is illustrated through what might be considered a chapter-specific scratch project. These chapter examples are just to show you exactly how different components relevant to that chapter work and how to make them meet the needs of your own projects. The end of the chapter, in most cases, is concerned with updating a single project that spans the entire book, the surfer5 project. This project starts with the graphics and color in Chapter 3. Each chapter then will build on the surfer5 project as it was left at the end of the last chapter. If you do not read the book from cover to cover, you may get confused when you see a surfer5 project update at the end of a chapter you are using for reference. Pieces of this project are in almost every chapter of this book so, if you are not reading the entire book sequentially, you need to be aware of this structure so that you are not surprised when you run into it.

The first real prerequisite for this book is an understanding of the basic structure and tenants of HTML. If something like "`<p><b>Hello</b>, <i>world</i></p>`" looks foreign to you, then you may need to brush up on basic HTML before getting into the chapters of this book. Many examples have HTML components that are barely mentioned if discussed at all. It is assumed in these examples that you have a basic foundation in HTML before beginning this book.

You would also do well to have at least a cursory understanding of Cascading Style Sheets (CSS) and how they work. There is an entire chapter dedicated to CSS and, in that, some of the basics are, in fact, covered. However, many of the basics are not, and it is assumed that you will come into this book with at least some exposure to CSS. Most of the examples in this book are based on CSS examples, and if you are completely new to this standard, you may want to begin with a CSS beginner's book to help get you started.

To follow the examples used throughout the chapters, you should have, at a minimum, some version of Visual Studio 2005 installed and have a basic familiarity with how it works. You should also have at least a basic working knowledge of .NET and be able to follow C# examples (most examples would easily port to VB.NET). You can download versions of Microsoft Visual Studio from the following location:

```
http://msdn2.microsoft.com/en-us/vstudio/default.aspx
```

If you are not ready to pay the full price tag for the Standard, Professional, or Team Suite versions of Visual Studio, you can follow the examples with Microsoft's free offering, Microsoft Visual Web Developer 2005 Express Edition, available here:

```
http://msdn.microsoft.com/vstudio/express/vwd/
```

While it is recommended that you upgrade to one of the paid versions as you mature into a professional developer, you should be able to replicate all of the examples in the chapters using this free version.

When you get into the appendixes, though, you will need to get some version of Microsoft Visual Studio Codename Orcas installed and ready to use, which you can download from here:

```
http://msdn2.microsoft.com/en-us/vstudio/aa700831.aspx
```

You should have the option of downloading self-extracting installation files or Virtual PC images. If you are not comfortable installing the full version on your development environment, you may prefer to use the Virtual PC images. Be warned, though, that you must have at least 1GB of available RAM on the system you will be running the images from. This means if you only have 1GB installed, you will not be able to run the images because some of the memory will be taken up by the background operations of your system. You will probably want to have at least 2GB of RAM installed on any system attempting to run these images.

The final application that you may need is Adobe Photoshop. The version used for this book was Adobe Photoshop CS2. However, this version has been replaced with Adobe Photoshop CS3, which is available here:

```
http://www.adobe.com/products/photoshop/index.html
```

The functionality shown throughout the book (mostly in Chapter 3) will be based on CS2 but should be very similar, if not exactly the same, in other versions of Photoshop, including the new CS3. There are other freely available graphic editors that may provide comparable functionality, and if your funds are limited, these might be viable substitutes for the purpose of recreating the work in the chapters of this book. However, there is no guarantee that they will, in fact, provide similar functionality, so if you wish to use one of these solutions, you may or may not be able to easily follow the examples in the book.

With regard to Photoshop, you are not expected to have a lot of experience using this application. The examples are targeted more towards the beginning Photoshop user and, as such, no real experience is required. Even if you are not a beginner, you should go through the chapter on Photoshop (Chapter 3) so that you have the graphic elements you need for later chapters. If you omit the chapter, you will find that you do not have the graphics referenced in your project as the surfer5 project matures through the other chapters.

It is worth noting that all of the images used to create the graphic headers in Chapter 3 have been licensed from Photos To Go Unlimited (http://unlimited.photostogo.com) to be distributed with this manuscript. If you would like to get the copies of these images, you can download them directly from the book website at the following location:

```
http://www.wrox.com/WileyCDA/WroxTitle/productCd-0470124482.html
```

In addition to these specific applications, you will also need a few plug-ins and integrated toolsets that are also freely available. This will include the CSS Friendly Control Adapters that become a template for Visual Studio 2005 and can be freely downloaded from the following URL:

```
http://www.asp.net/cssadapters/Default.aspx
```

From that location, you can also find out more about the adapters and see other working samples.

For Appendix B of this book, you will also want to install the Microsoft Silverlight 1.1 Alpha for Windows, which is available through this link:

```
http://msdn2.microsoft.com/en-us/silverlight/bb419317.aspx
```

Additionally, you may want to install the Microsoft Silverlight Tools Alpha for Visual Studio Codename "Orcas" Beta 1, which is available here:

```
http://www.microsoft.com/downloads/details.aspx?familyid=
    6c2b309b-8f2d-44a5-b04f-836f0d4ec1c4&displaylang=en
```

These two Silverlight downloads will directly integrate with Visual Studio Orcas so that you can have the experience described in Appendix B.

As both Appendixes A and B are previews of new technologies, it is not expected that you will have any previous experience with either Visual Studio Orcas or Microsoft Silverlight. The examples used in these appendixes are written with the understanding that these technologies are probably new to you.

With the specific technologies and expected level of knowledge expressed in this section, you should be well armed to take on the chapters of this book. The only other requirement, really, is the desire, or maybe even compulsion, to create some of the best web interfaces on the Internet. You should have a desire to learn new concepts and be open to using those new concepts in the projects you develop. If you have that attitude and these tools, you are ready.

Conventions

To help you get the most from the text and keep track of what's happening, we've used a number of conventions throughout the book.

> **Boxes like this one hold important, not-to-be forgotten information that is directly relevant to the surrounding text.**

Tips, hints, tricks, and asides to the current discussion are offset and placed in italics like this.

As for styles in the text:

- ❑ We *highlight* new terms and important words when we introduce them.
- ❑ We show keyboard strokes like this: Ctrl+A.
- ❑ We present code in two different ways:

```
In code examples we highlight new and important code with a gray background.
```

```
The gray highlighting is not used for code that's less important in the
present context, or has been shown before.
```

Source Code

As you work through the examples in this book, you may choose either to type in all the code manually or to use the source code files that accompany the book. All of the source code used in this book is available for download at www.wrox.com. Once at the site, simply locate the book's title (either by using the Search box or by using one of the title lists) and click the Download Code link on the book's detail page to obtain all the source code for the book.

Because many books have similar titles, you may find it easiest to search by ISBN; this book's ISBN is 978-0-470-12448-2.

Once you download the code, just decompress it with your favorite compression tool. Alternately, you can go to the main Wrox code download page at www.wrox.com/dynamic/books/download.aspx to see the code available for this book and all other Wrox books.

Errata

We make every effort to ensure that there are no errors in the text or in the code. However, no one is perfect, and mistakes do occur. If you find an error in one of our books, such as a spelling mistake or faulty piece of code, we would be very grateful for your feedback. By sending in errata you may save another reader hours of frustration and at the same time you will be helping us provide even higher-quality information.

To find the errata page for this book, go to www.wrox.com and locate the title using the Search box or one of the title lists. Then, on the book details page, click the Book Errata link. On this page you can view all errata that has been submitted for this book and posted by Wrox editors. A complete book list including links to each book's errata is also available at www.wrox.com/misc-pages/booklist.shtml.

If you don't spot "your" error on the Book Errata page, go to www.wrox.com/contact/techsupport.shtml and complete the form there to send us the error you have found. We'll check the information and, if appropriate, post a message to the book's errata page and fix the problem in subsequent editions of the book.

p2p.wrox.com

For author and peer discussion, join the P2P forums at p2p.wrox.com. The forums are a web-based system for you to post messages relating to Wrox books and related technologies and interact with other readers and technology users. The forums offer a subscription feature to e-mail you topics of interest of your choosing when new posts are made to the forums. Wrox authors, editors, other industry experts, and your fellow readers are present on these forums.

At http://p2p.wrox.com you will find a number of different forums that will help you not only as you read this book but also as you develop your own applications. To join the forums, just follow these steps:

1. Go to p2p.wrox.com and click the Register link.
2. Read the terms of use and click Agree.
3. Complete the required information to join as well as any optional information you wish to provide, and click Submit.
4. You will receive an e-mail with information describing how to verify your account and complete the joining process.

You can read messages in the forums without joining P2P, but in order to post your own messages, you must join.

Once you join, you can post new messages and respond to messages other users post. You can read messages at any time on the web. If you would like to have new messages from a particular forum e-mailed to you, click the Subscribe to this Forum icon by the forum name in the forum listing.

For more information about how to use the Wrox P2P, be sure to read the P2P FAQs for answers to questions about how the forum software works as well as many common questions specific to P2P and Wrox books. To read the FAQs, click the FAQ link on any P2P page.

1

aesthNETics

Technology has continued to scream past us over the last few decades. What is top of the line now may be completely obsolete in six months. As soon as you begin to understand a new technology, updates to it come out and make the entire learning curve start over. This has certainly been true for .NET developers. When .NET was introduced it was an amazing improvement over previous Microsoft programming languages. The mere fact that VB and C programmers could understand each other's code should say something. But the incredible number of new controls and gizmos could prove daunting to a lot of people. Before anyone could get comfortable with .NET 1.0, 1.1 was released. When people finally started getting comfortable with 1.1, 2.0 was released. And now, barely a year after the 2.0 release, there is a new 3.0 coming out. Some programmers love the flux and constant improvements to the functionality of .NET. They strive to learn all of the new features and enhancements to see how they can improve the projects they produce. Others try to keep up only so that their projects stay current and to see what impact the new frameworks will have on their existing applications. Either way, most folks want to focus on the "under-the-hood" pieces of the framework. They want to determine if the new .NET 2.0 GridView really is that much better than the 1.1 DataGrid (it is). They can immediately see the benefits of implementing `Try...Catch...Finally` statements in their code.

But what seems to happen too often is that these same programmers forget about, or at least put on the back burner, the concept of making these new powerful .NET pages look good; they forget about aesthNETics.

What Is aesthNETics?

aesthNETics simply refers to making .NET pages look good. Okay, that may be a bit simplistic. What does "making .NET pages look good" really mean? Does this simply mean "aesthetically pleasing"? Beauty is in the eye of the beholder, right? The short answer is *no*.

For the longer answer, you have to consider websites you like and don't like. There is probably a consistent theme to those groups among most people. It may be hard to come up with a definitive list of the features you want or expect when you access a website, but here are a few that would probably appear on most people's lists:

❑   You can find what you want easily.

❑   There is a consistent look and feel to every page you visit.

❑   Pages are laid out in an intuitive and logical manner.

❑   Graphics, if used, are not overpowering or obnoxious and not just used for the sake of using graphics.

❑   Colors used don't burn your retinas or make you immediately want to leave the site.

❑   You don't load the page and think "Wow, there is just too much going on here."

❑   The page doesn't take too long to load, even on slower connections.

❑   You don't immediately think "Hey, I've seen this template before. A lot."

In addition to these items, developers might think of how to provide the best experience for their patrons. Things like browser compatibility come in to play. You must at least decide which browsers you want to support and, subsequently, code your site to meet this standard. When thinking of browsers, though, you should remember that large populations of Internet surfers use text-based browsers or readers to access the content of your site. Have you coded your site for these people?

aesthNETics incorporates all of these ideas. aesthNETics means that you don't forget the look and feel of your site. It means that you don't just worry about the business logic and data of your site; you give equal consideration to making the interface user-friendly and pleasant. aesthNETics means that you remember to make the things your site patrons *can* see be as powerful as the things they can't.

The skill set for a good aethNETics programmer includes:

❑   A good understanding of web design and layout basics.

❑   An appreciation of colors and graphics. (Sometimes less really is more.)

❑   A working knowledge of cascading style sheets.

❑   A comprehensive knowledge of the tools in ASP.NET that allow for consistency among pages you create:

   ❑   **Site Navigation** components for intuitive and consistent access to content.

   ❑   **Master Pages** for structural layout.

   ❑   **Themes** for consistent .NET components.

Using this book as a guide, you will learn to appreciate the design element of the websites you produce. You will learn enough about graphics to get you started on your quest to learn more. And, most relevant to .NET programmers, you will learn about the new features of .NET 2.0 that can help you with the aesthNETics of the sites you produce.

Don't misunderstand the scope of this book, though. It does more than outline specific .NET tools available to you as a web application developer. It shows you sound web design principles and tools that are not necessarily limited to .NET programs. This includes a discussion of Cascading Style Sheets and their standards, which are established and maintained by the Worldwide Web Consortium (W3C). You will also be given an overview of colors, images, and other universally relevant web design considerations. As the book progresses, though, you will see how to integrate these philosophies within Visual Studio 2005 and the components offered through the .NET 2.0 Framework. Many of the concepts discussed in this book will not be strictly .NET-specific. The idea of aesthNETics, though, is focusing and applying those concepts in your .NET applications.

Why Is aesthNETics Important?

You might think of aesthNETics as the presentation layer of a typical n-tier application. Many presentations regarding programming, and this is certainly true of .NET, go into great detail on how to make websites powerful and inundate them with the latest and greatest technologies. They introduce topics like AJAX and XML serialization and often go into real-world examples of implementing business logic into web applications you develop. What most presentations seem to lack, though, is a fair discussion of the presentation layer. The risk of this mentality is, quite simply, the perpetuation of really powerful websites that are really powerfully boring to look at.

Does the presentation layer matter? Of course it does. Does it matter as much as the business logic and data access layers in a typical 3-tier application? Well, that depends on who you ask. At one end of the spectrum, you might see the seasoned programmer who reads the most current periodicals and attends technical conferences in an effort to stay on top of the latest technological trends. He might say "no, it's not nearly as important." But what about the customers? Sure, they might be appreciative of a 235-millisecond reduction in access speeds using the new cross-tab functionality of SQL Server 2005. Or maybe you can wow them with the fact that your Social Security field is validated through regular expressions and then encrypted in the database. But what do you think they will say if you are telling them all of this while they are looking at a white page with a couple of text boxes on it? This is often referred to as the "halo effect," whereby initial perceptions are used to judge the other properties of an item. In regard to web design, this means that a potential customer will often make a judgment on an entire web application according to what they see in the browser in its initial load. If you have lost the customer before you begin discussing the behind-the-scenes merits, you will have a tough time getting them back.

To illustrate, assume that you have a client who wants a data dashboard application. They have some data in a spreadsheet that they first want converted to some sort of Enterprise solution. They then want to create functionality to automatically import data into the new database on a daily basis. Finally, they want to present the analysis of the data in a web application viewable on the corporate intranet. This is a high-profile project with a lot of potential accolades and recognition to the team that delivers the new system. As a result, two groups compete for the distinction of designing the new system and presenting it to the Executive Leadership team. The first team spends a lot of time making the data conversions and creating an automatic update system that should work within the parameters of the project requirements. They decide to forego spending much time on the interface of the project and just use some of the Microsoft Office graphing components to represent the data. They present to management the example in Figure 1-1.

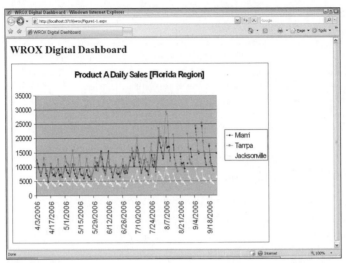

Figure 1-1

The second team also completes the initial data conversion but, in preparing for their presentation proposal, they spend time coming up with an aesthetically and intuitive layout that they hope will please the project management team. They decide to come up with custom graphics using Adobe PhotoShop. They decide to create custom graphing components using the System.Drawing namespace. They pay close attention to the color scheme of the site and make an attempt to have everything flow together. They do not spend the time at this point working on the automatic data upload piece. They present the example in Figure 1-2.

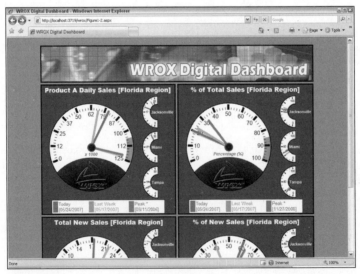

Figure 1-2

Which of these projects do you think, in a real-world situation, would win the nod from management?

Don't misunderstand; the presentation layer is not the only important component of a web project. In the above example, if it turned out that the second team was assigned this project but, soon after starting, it became apparent that they were only capable of making sites look good and had no real concept of how to gather and analyze the data, management would not be happy. Making a site look good is by no means enough. The point of this example, though, is to show that the interface design is important and should not be ignored.

Evolving Expectations of Employers

In today's rapidly evolving technological market, programmers are being asked more and more often to become the "Renaissance men" of programming. This simply means clients and managers want these programmers to be able to handle all aspects of a web project from requirements gathering to application development to coordination of user testing to documentation. And, yes, even graphics and design. How many job postings have you looked at that had a laundry list of requirements that doesn't at least suggest the company wants you to do it all? Programmers already find it completely impossible to say "I don't do database stuff; that is for the DBAs." As time goes on, you will find it increasingly hard to say "I don't do graphics; that is for the designers."

Even if that were not true, there are certainly other reasons to become a better web designer with regard to your .NET applications. For one, it can make you stand out among your peers and coworkers. Say that you are in a programming shop that does a lot of .NET web applications. Most of the programmers are pretty efficient at .NET. You are somewhere in the middle. You aren't the best of the group, but you certainly aren't the worst either. How can you distinguish yourself? You could certainly put the time in and become the best .NET developer in the group. But what else might you do?

Phillip Van Hooser, author of *Willie's Way: 6 Secrets for Wooing, Wowing, and Winning Customers and Their Loyalty* and an expert on leadership and customer service, has a simple and direct method for distinguishing yourself from the crowd. He says that all you have to do is just the smallest bit more than anyone else. You don't have to make huge leaps of improvement over everyone else; you only have to do slightly more. He explains that, if you are doing even slightly more than anyone else, you will be noticed and people will remember you.

So what can you do to be even the smallest bit better than the peers in your group? If you are proficient at web design and layout, and certainly if you can navigate your way around graphics programs like Adobe PhotoShop and create custom graphics, you will stand out. If you create applications that are aesthetically stunning, while others are bland and uninspired, you will be remembered.

Creating a Consistent Look and Feel for Your Website: aesthNETics Essentials

This book will attempt to outline some of the basic tools, primarily available in Visual Studio 2005, that .NET developers can use to make their sites appearance at the same level of the coding behind them. But if there is any hard-and-fast rule for web development, it is this: make the look and feel of your site consistent. There is probably no bigger annoyance than going to a site and having the front page look one way and then a content page look entirely different. This doesn't mean that page layout can't vary from page to page. But it should be the developer's goal to make the user feel that the site is consistent throughout every page. Sure, at times, you will have to stretch the header to accommodate large data tables. Or maybe you will have some sidebar links on some sections of the page and other links for other pages, depending on where the user is on the site, to accommodate a large site with many different sections. But if the position of the links shift five or ten pixels to the left or right as the user navigates or if one page has a blue-based color scheme and another uses shades of brown, it will make the site look sloppy.

Of course, a first step in creating a consistent look and feel to your site is to actually establish the look and feel you want. While it can be argued that having a white page with text and various controls on it is, in fact, a look and feel (one which would be easily carried out through all pages), this doesn't really meet the standards of good aesthNETics. Although it may be hard to define exactly what the standards of good aesthNETics are, you can use the "wow" factor test to see if you are on the right track. If you show your project to your client and he or she says "wow," you know you are probably following the aesthNETics standards. If the client doesn't say this or seems uninterested, you might want to rethink your approach. This can prove to be a challenge, since different clients have different "wow" factor criteria. It is your job, as an aesthNETics developer, to figure out what those criteria are. You should understand who your potential customers will be and how they will access the content you provide. You should have a basic understanding of website design and layout. To stand out from the crowd, you should have a basic understanding of graphics and color use and be familiar with the tools to help you create both. You should pick your colors and create your graphics early in the process so that you can decide the other necessary components of your site. A more detailed explanation of how this is done and what tools are available can be found in Chapter 2.

Once you have decided on a look and feel for your site, you need to figure out a way to carry it out throughout the pages of your site. Most applications have a template tool available to them. For example, you can easily find skins you can apply, or even create yourself, for applications such as Windows Media Player. Some web designer applications include them as well. But historically, .NET has not really had a clean way of making pages using a template.

That changed drastically with the release of the .NET 2.0 Framework. Master Pages are now a part of the Framework and should be a part of every .NET developer's arsenal of web design tools and tricks. Master Pages allow developers to create the structural template for the design of their website. In essence, this means that you can say "I want the header to be at this position and the footer to be at this position and the navigation to go here and the content to go here" and then save that as, for lack of a better word, a project template. Your other pages can then inherit the Master Page, and the content of those pages will fall into the content area created in your Master Page. This will be covered in more detail in Chapter 7. It is enough, for now, to understand that Master Pages can help you create a project template that can be imported into your web pages.

Cascading Style Sheets (CSS), which have been around for over 10 years, are another great way to create consistency throughout your site. With CSS, you can dictate the look and feel not only for the HTML elements on your site but also for XML, XHTML, SVG, XUL, and most derivations of SGML. If, for example, you want to say that the background color of your entire site is gray, you can do that with CSS. With the new Visual Studio 2005, a couple of tools were introduced to help you with creating accurate style sheets for your applications. There are also a couple of cool tricks for applying them to your site, as you will see in Chapter 4.

One shortcoming of using CSS, though, is that you can't use it effectively to create a consistent look and feel to ASP.NET elements. This means that with stylesheets alone you can't say "I want every .NET label dropped on a page to be bold red Arial 12pt font." You can certainly create a CSS class that has that formatting to it and then reference it from the "CssClass" property of the label control. But what happens when you drop another label on the page? If you don't make a similar reference to the CSS class in the `CssClass` property of that label, it isn't applied; the label just uses the default settings for a label.

With the .NET 2.0 Framework, however, you can modify the default behavior for that label. You can tell your application that for every label dropped onto any of your pages, it should apply this particular CSS class. Even better than that, you can say that for every GridView control, the header will be blue, the row style will be gray, and the alternating row style will be white. When you drop a GridView on your page, it will just be formatted that way without you doing anything else. Furthermore, you can tell your application that in some situations it should make the GridViews all look as described above but, in other situations, it should make them look entirely different (based on profiles, browser specifications, and so on). You can also say to make some GridViews look this way and others look another way, based on a control ID. This is all done through the use of skins and themes, which will be discussed in Chapters 8 and 9.

Finally, developers need to make sure that their customers can easily get around their site and that the controls in place to navigate the site are consistent and intuitive. Historically, developers have tried to create Windows-style navigation controls by using JavaScript or third-party controls. The brave have even attempted to write their own navigation controls for their .NET projects. However, with the .NET 2.0 Framework, site navigation controls have been introduced to help developers create consistent and easy-to-use navigation elements on their sites. You want the drop-down navigation controls you see around the Internet (the kind that mimic Windows applications)? Those are now included in this control. You want to create a "breadcrumb" component to show site users where they are in the maze of pages that creates your site? That, too, is part of the default behavior now included in these controls. Developers can now create a `SiteMapDataSource` file that can be used throughout the entire site for navigation controls. Update the file, and all pages referencing it will be updated as well. Site navigation has come a long way with the 2.0 Framework, and you will learn how to use these features in Chapter 6.

Prerequisites

There really aren't a lot of prerequisites for learning good web design principles, whether in .NET or any other development platform. In fact, the mere fact that you have obtained this book and gotten this far into the first chapter shows a willingness to at least begin to think about design issues. Technically speaking, though, there will be a few assumptions about your ability level.

First and foremost, you should be at least fairly comfortable with HTML code. If the following code snippet looks completely foreign to you, the topics presented in this book will likely be confusing and hard to follow:

```
<strong>Hello world!</strong>
<br><br>
<p>This is my first paragraph for my first page!</p>
```

Obviously, if you have a familiarity with at least the elementary concepts of HTML, CSS, and good web design, you can breeze right through those sections. Similarly, if you have experience in developing .NET web applications (with any version), many of the new .NET concepts will be easier to understand. But there aren't any concepts that a dedicated reader can't grasp.

Another fairly crucial requirement is at least a cursory knowledge of .NET. It really doesn't matter if that knowledge is from .NET 1.0 or 1.1 for this level of discussion. A complete novice, though, will have trouble following some of the programming concepts presented. This book will not make attempts to explain in any great depth what a namespace or an object or a page class is. When pertinent, enough details about how those features interact with the topic at hand will be given. However, do not rely on the book to give a thorough breakdown of the .NET Framework. There are books that go into much broader explanations of the Framework; this book is specific to some exciting new features of the .NET 2.0

Framework. To get the most out of this book, the reader should be at a bare minimum familiar with object-oriented coding but really should have some level of experience in some level of .NET. Again, a lack of this experience will not be a total obstacle to getting something out of this text; but it will certainly be a hindrance (one only you can gauge).

To extend that thought, though, a familiarity with Visual Studio 2005 will really help your understanding of the concepts presented in the later chapters. Most of the code demonstrations are going to be performed in Visual Studio 2005. When introducing a new feature of Visual Studio, that feature will, of course, be explained in detail. However, if the concept is not new to Visual Studio 2005 and not necessarily pertinent to the discussion at hand, it will not be adequately explained to the person who has never seen the interface.

It should be noted that, for all of the demonstrations in Visual Studio 2005, you could recreate the functionality in Visual Studio Web Developer 2005 Express Edition. In fact, much of the learning done by the author was done through this free development tool. Obviously, if you have the wherewithal to purchase the full Visual Studio 2005 IDE, then you should. It has more features and is much more powerful. But if you are just getting started or are a hobbyist, there shouldn't be anything in this book that you can't do in the free version.

The biggest requirement, though, is a genuine interest in making the websites you develop more aesthetically pleasing. The desire to learn is something that shouldn't be downplayed and, if you have that desire, you can take advantage of the concepts in this book. The concepts presented here should be the foundation that every web developer builds on, not just the .NET folks. There are cool tricks that will be showcased that are specific to .NET, but the concepts are universal. If you develop on the web, you should get something out of this book.

Summary

The quintessential concept of aesthNETics is not really a new one. Web developers for years have struggled to make their sites look good while being powerful and useful. Thousands of books on the market talk about basic web design concepts. If you search for "web design concepts" in Google, you will get back more than 100,000,000 results (literally). There are hundreds of applications on the market that profess that they can turn the average Joe into a professional web designer. There are classes for elementary school students that teach the basics of web design. In short, there is no deficit of resources outlining the concepts of web design.

Where the deficit seems to come in is with the actual utilization of this information. Many developers, and, again, this is not specific to .NET developers, do not spend the time working on the aesthetics of the sites they develop. Throw a button control here, a couple of text boxes there, maybe try to implement a color scheme that was developed 10 years ago for the corporate intranet, and *bam*, you have a site.

What aesthNETics tries to push is using the powerful tools of the .NET 2.0 Framework to make your sites aesthetically pleasing. This book is focused on the .NET development community. Many of the concepts are universal, and other developers might find some good information in its content. But the primary audience is .NET developers. Most tools illustrated are ones that are specific to .NET 2.0 and Visual Studio 2005. While other platforms may have similar functionality, that is not really the point of discussion of this text. The point of this book is to make .NET developers better.

There are certainly many reasons to want to be better. The ever-evolving expectations of clients and managers is certainly one of the first and foremost reasons. Everyone expects today's developers to do it all. A typical job posting might include .NET experience, database experience, nUnit testing experience, project management experience, and even graphics experience. To stay competitive, developers need to keep learning. They need to broaden their horizons and challenge themselves to learn things that are potentially outside their comfort zone. And to the serious developer, *that* is the best reason to learn aesthNETics. The challenge should be the real appeal of learning new concepts. The difference between a good developer and a great developer is often simply the genuine desire to keep learning. As Steve McConnell stated in *Code Complete 2nd Edition*, "The characteristics of a superior programmer have almost nothing to do with talent and everything to do with a commitment to personal development."

So sit back, boot up your laptop, and begin your quest to be a better .NET developer.

2

Web Design 101

The quintessential element of any web design is, in fact, the web design itself. This may come off as a bit simplistic, but many people forget about that crucial component. The primary audience for this book is programmers who are already familiar with ASP.NET but who want to learn more about how to make the sites they develop more stunning and user-friendly. The core of this idea, though, is not exclusive to .NET programmers. In order to make dramatically dazzling user interfaces, programmers need to understand the basic concepts of web design. This would include areas of layout, color, and graphics.

But it should also include a fair understanding of the audiences that will be consuming the sites you produce. What kind of browsers should you target? What will your site look like if the user turns off stylesheets? How about JavaScript? What kind of bandwidth limitations are there? How likely is your clientele to print the pages you produce? What else?

This chapter will elaborate on some the basic concepts of web design. You will begin to understand style, color, and layout. You will hear some of the current topics and trends of web design, some of which may be completely new to you. You will begin to appreciate the work that goes into creating good web design.

This chapter will not, however, go into any topics necessarily limited to the ASP.NET arena. Concepts of good web design are universal and, as such, should never be thought of strictly in terms of a specific programming language. Obviously, since this book is about ASP.NET design, later chapters will focus on how the tools in Visual Studio 2005 can help developers incorporate these universal design concepts. However, for this chapter, the concepts are the same for any web designer/developer; not just .NET developers.

Design Basics

The very first consideration to web design is "Who is my audience and how will they consume the pages I create?" This seems simple enough, but these questions should be given due consideration before you hastily decide on your site standard. Simply saying "most of my users will probably be using Internet Explorer 7 with at least a screen resolution of 1280 by 768" is almost never going to lead to successful web design. Granted, if you are designing applications for a corporate intranet and there are policies and procedures (and a budget) in place to ensure that all employees have top-of-the-line computers with accelerated graphic cards and the most recent software packages, that philosophy might work for you. But if you are designing for the real world, there are more things to consider.

Screen Resolution

First and foremost is your target screen resolution. There is nothing more frustrating than going to a site and having to scroll right, then down and to the left, then right again, then down and to the left again, and so forth and so on. Most users are willing to scroll up and down to consume the page; that is a necessary evil in most web applications. However, they loathe having to scroll left and right to see everything.

For some time now, a generally accepted target screen resolution has been 800 pixels wide by 600 pixels high. However, this should not be confused with the amount of web real estate you have to work in. You have to take into account the scrollbar areas on most browsers and any padding that may be done by default. Most applications would be safe with a width of approximately 750 pixels. This generally allows the web application to fit into most browser windows.

But what about the height? That is a different monster altogether. First, you have to take into account different browsers. Pretty much all browsers have different size standard toolbars as their default. For example, think how big the browser toolbar for IE6 was as compared to the sleeker one provided with IE7 and compare both of those with the standard toolbars and buttons of FireFox. Each one is different and, as such, takes up a different amount of screen real estate. Add to that the fact that many users may add new toolbars or even third-party toolbars to their browser. You also have to take into consideration the taskbar of the Windows operating systems (or similar considerations in other operating systems). All of this steals from the available height of your web application — the available height without scrolling, that is. As mentioned earlier, most web users are comfortable with the fact that they may have to scroll down to get through all of the content of a given site. However, if you are really determined to try to fit all of the content in a single browser window without scrolling at all, you should probably try to use a height of approximately 400 pixels.

An alternative to this fixed-pixel discussion is the idea of *liquid design*. Essentially, this allows a page to grow or shrink to fit the browser window as necessary to accommodate for various browser and resolution settings. In simple terms, this means that rather than stating that the content of your site will be exactly 700 pixels wide, you state that it will be 85% of the available screen. Or maybe you would say that the page is divided into three sections, each constituting 30% of the screen's width. This means that, for the sake of easy math, if you have 1000 pixels available on one user's machine, the web design will take up 900 pixels, leaving 100 pixels of padding. If another user comes to the same site with an available screen resolution that is 700 pixels wide, the site will shrink to 630 pixels automatically.

Consider the following statistics:

Resolution	Number of Users
1024 × 768	39,840,084 (52%)
1280 × 1024	18,106,879 (24%)
800 × 600	9,366,914 (12%)

Resolution	Number of Users
Unknown	4,812,017 (6%)
1152 × 864	2,613,989 (3%)
1600 × 1200	487,669 (0%)
640 × 480	127,355 (0%)

These statistics come from `TheCounter.com` (`www.thecounter.com/stats`) and represent the breakdown of screen resolution settings for all users accessing sites using their counters for May 2007. As you can see, 1024 × 768 is the resolution used by the majority of users (at least according to these statistics). However, targeting solely that audience would negatively impact almost 10 million users (800 × 600 and 640 × 480 users). That is 10 million uses who would have to scroll to the right to see all of your content and, out of frustration, may look for their content elsewhere.

But this is just part of the picture. Designers should assume that the pages they will produce will be printed. Knowing this, failing to accommodate this is unacceptable. There should be some consideration of this need, either by coding the page to be printable or by having a printer-friendly version available. Like everything else relating to resolution, there really isn't a set standard for this. You have to take into consideration the dpi of the printers being used, the margins allowed on the page sizes printed, the orientation and size of the papers being printed on, and other factors that you just cannot predict. Generally speaking, though, a fixed-pixel width of approximately 700 pixels will fit on the page in most printing scenarios. This is in line with the optimal line length for readability standards available for printing on standard letter page size. Using this standard, you can fit between 50 and 80 characters across a single line of text on a printed document. This roughly translates to 500–800 pixels wide when talking about screen resolution. However, even with that being true, you have to also take into consideration the actual readability of the text. If you have a layout that spans the entire width of a user's window (liquid or fluid design) and a user accesses the page with a 1600 × 1200 resolution monitor with the browser maximized, that user will have trouble reading your text because, by the time they get to the end of a line of text, their eye will have trouble negotiating back to the next line of text. This is due to the ending point of one line of text being so far away from the starting point of the next line of text. So, even though you can fit roughly 700 pixels of web content on your printed document, you may want to try to limit the area that has textual content to something even smaller than 700 pixels, such as, maybe, 500 pixels, to ensure the readability of your text.

Screen resolution is probably in the top 10 items of controversial web design topics. Ask a group of web designers what resolution to target and you will get varied, and often very passionate, responses. Some believe 800 × 600 is the safest bet. Others believe that 800 × 600 is antiquated and that the new standard should be 1024 × 768. An increasing number of developers, though, tend to follow the liquid design concept of web design.

But it really boils down to the clients you serve. If you know your audience and you know their platform and surfing habits (e.g., whether or not they browse the Internet in a full browser), you might be able to get away with having a fixed screen resolution target of 1024 × 768. However, if you don't know, you should probably target a smaller resolution or consider fully migrating to a liquid design approach to web design.

Browsers

A consideration that many developers have when designing their projects is the type of browser that will be engaging their site. With many smaller browsers challenging the monopoly Microsoft Internet Explorer has in this arena, it is interesting to revisit the statistics from TheCounter.com (www.thecounter.com/stats); this time examining browser utilization:

Browser	Number of Users
MSIE 6.x	44,213,704 (56%)
MSIE 7.x	11,839,333 (15%)
FireFox	9,295,726 (12%)
Netscape comp.	9,076,448 (11%)
Safari	2,269,581 (3%)
Unknown	825,539 (1%)
MSIE 5.x	736342 (1%)
Opera x.x	495,033 (1%)
Netscape 7.x	196,201 (0%)
Netscape 5.x	128,764 (0%)
MSIE 4.x	83,775 (0%)
Netscape 4.x	42,532 (0%)
Konqueror	16,334 (0%)
Netscape 6.x	2,294 (0%)
MSIE 3.x	679 (0%)
Netscape 3.x	315 (0%)
Netscape 2.x	86 (0%)
Netscape 1.x	14 (0%)

These statistics are from May 2007 and show that Internet Explorer is still dominating in the browser wars that have been raging for years, and, maybe surprisingly, IE6 is still the number one provider by a large margin, even though IE7 was released in November 2006. If you add up all of the versions of Internet Explorer, you reach approximately 72% of the total browser hits accounted for by these statistics. However, if you analyze the statistics over a period of time, you will notice that FireFox, at least, is showing an upward trend. For example, in May 2006, FireFox users only accounted for 1.2 million hits, or 9% of the total. Over the course of a year, this rose to almost 9.3 million hits, constituting 12% of the total. Conversely, IE6 had 113 million hits, or 84% of the total, in May 2006 but by May 2007 only accounted for a little over 44 million hits, or 56% of the total.

The full statistics for May 2006 are not included here but are available online at TheCounter.com *(*www.thecounter.com/stats/2006/May/browser.php*). You might also be interested in seeing a* *different perspective of browser statistics by visiting the ones reported by W3 Schools (www.w3schools .com/browsers/browsers_stats.asp) that show that IE only accounts for approximately 59% of the total hits, as opposed to the 72% shown in the above example.*

What does that mean? Should you only target Internet Explorer when developing your applications? If you do, you will probably regret it. FireFox alone accounts for almost 6.5 million hits in this graph; Safari accounts for another near 1.5 million. There are a lot of people out on the web who do not and *will* not use Microsoft products, and often they seem the most vocal about compatibility. If the site you develop does not render properly for these users, you will likely lose their patronage. And in a highly competitive marketplace, it seems silly to lose users simply because of lack of foresight and testing.

Another consideration you need to include in your project planning is browser configuration. You have to understand that, just because a user has the latest and greatest browser installed and in use, that does not mean that they have all of the features turned on. In fact, you should have a fallback plan to allow for many of the popular settings to be turned off.

For example, consider the following additional information from TheCounter.com May 2007 statistics:

JavaScript	Number of Users
JavaScript 1.2+	75,354,907 (95%)
JavaScript <1.2	92,922 (0%)
JavaScript false	3,774,871 (4%)

What does this mean? Simply put, this means that almost 4 million people turned off JavaScript in their browser settings. So what does that mean to you? Well, if you use a lot of JavaScript, it could mean a lot of errors or, worse, broken pages. What happens if you have all of your form submission routines set on hyperlinks with a JavaScript submit() method? What happens to your form if the user has JavaScript turned off? What happens to those almost 4 million users? Can they now not use your shopping cart to buy your products because you failed to account for this? In your testing, you need to account for this and turn off JavaScript, for example, to see what happens. Even if you don't plan to fix it, you should know what the ramifications are so that you can make a more informed decision about how to handle this issue.

In the projects illustrated in this book, you will not be testing much with JavaScript turned off. The only exception to this is in Appendix B when you are working on a Silverlight project, you will see how Silverlight renders without JavaScript. However, for the rest of the book, JavaScript is not specifically tested. The only time that it might be a consideration is in Chapter 6 when JavaScript code is added for you by the CSS Friendly Control Adapters for IE6 users. As that is the only place JavaScript is used and it only affects one browser, testing was not specifically documented in this book. However, when you get to that Chapter 6, you may want to turn off JavaScript to see how the menu controls render in IE6 if you have that browser available for testing.

What these statistics do not show is accessibility issues. You will learn more about that later in the "Accessibility" section of this chapter, but you should realize that more and more people are using text readers for their browsing and/or turning off stylesheets. For a complete testing experience, you should run your application through a browser with CSS turned off and see how it renders. If one is available, you should also consider using some type of screen reader just to see what your site sounds like for those that can't see it.

Many of these browser considerations, like many of the other considerations in this chapter, are only relevant if you are targeting an unknown audience. If you are strictly doing intranet sites for your small company of 10 people and you know exactly the browsers and browser settings each of them uses, these considerations may not be that relevant to you. But if you are targeting any number of unknown users, you should give attention to these concepts in your project planning. Even if you think you know your audience, you have to think "Do I really?" If your corporate intranet is open to several offices spread out across the country, encompassing 20,000 employees and an unknown number of corporate partners who also have access, can you ensure that they will all have JavaScript enabled and CSS turned on? Even if you can determine that they are all using Internet Explorer 7, for example, do you know what settings they have in place within IE7? Do you have contingency code in place to accommodate those instances where the users don't have their browser configured the way you think they should? If not, you are opening yourself up to usability and compatibility issues that would have been easier resolved in planning than in a helpdesk situation.

Color Depth

When planning the look and feel of your project, consideration should also be given to the depth of color used in the pages produced. Essentially, this refers to the total number of colors a particular computer can render. Can the graphic card support 24-bit true color rendering? If so, that means it can display all 16,777,216 colors possible with RGB. But how universal is this? An analysis of the TheCounter.com May 2007 statistics may provide some insight:

Color Depth	Number of Users
(32bit)	64,847,496 (86%)
65K (16bit)	7,976,534 (10%)
16 M (24bit)	2,172,918 (2%)
256 (8bit)	335,044 (0%)
Unknown	19,770 (0%)
16 (4bit)	3,145 (0%)

This shows that basically 88% of users can display 24-bit or 32-bit colors. What is the difference between 32-bit and 24-bit? For this discussion, there isn't much difference. You do not have a broader range of colors you can display. Essentially, the extra 8 bits allows for the use of alpha channels in your image or just pads the image with an extra 8 bits of empty space. This was done in order to align with computers that process data in units of 32 bits. But, again, for these discussions, 24-bit and 32-bit graphic rendering is materially the same.

This still allows for 12% of potential users who are not capable of rendering the full RGB spectrum. Sixteen-bit color is fairly close, allowing 5 bits each for red and blue and 6 bits for green, since the human eye is more sensitive to green, which allows for 65,536 distinct colors. But even at that level, you are losing many of the color variations distinguishable by the human eye.

So what happens if you use a color not in the acceptable range for part of your project? Say, for example, that you use a background color that is within the 16.7 million colors of 24-bit rendering but is not available in 16-bit mode? What happens when a user with a 16-bit graphics card accesses your site? What will he or she see?

In this situation, the computer must "guess" at what color you are talking about in your site. The computer is accessing your site, seeing a color it doesn't know, and thinking "what the heck do I do with this?" The more formal name for guessing in this scenario is *dithering*. This is where the processor uses the colors that it has available in its palette to attempt to recreate the color that it does not have available. Figure 2-1 how dithering works.

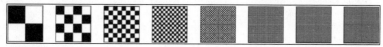

Figure 2-1

The first block (at the far left) shows rather large pixels of black and white. As you move to the right, the pixels are reduced to half of their size in the preceding image. With each decrease in the size of the pixels, the image approaches a shade of gray until the last image essentially looks gray and you cannot see that it is actually composed of tiny black and white pixels. This is what dithering attempts to do. In this example, you have chosen to use a shade of gray that is not available to the graphic card of the user accessing your page. The computer, in turn, is using black and white, which is available in its palette, to try to recreate the shade of gray that is not otherwise available in the current palette.

This can potentially cause a lot of problems, not the least of which is grainy pixilated images. You are essentially relying on a piece of equipment that only understands zeros and ones to apply some predefined algorithm to determine what combination of colors it can use to try to create the color that it doesn't understand in the first place.

To try to accommodate for these limitations, many developers use a subset of the 256-color palette called web-safe colors. Web-safe colors are 216 colors that were originally identified as colors that should be fairly universally applied across operating platforms and browsers that support at least 256-color rendering. This means that true black is true black on a Macintosh running Netscape Navigator 6.2 as well as on a new Windows Vista computer running Internet Explorer 7.

The advantage to web-safe colors, obviously, is their platform and browser independence. The disadvantage is that you are limited to 216 colors. When you consider that the human eye is capable of viewing at least the full 16.7 million colors in the RGB palette, you are giving up a considerable amount of color availability in your projects.

How important is that, though, really? How much are images affected by these limitations?

To illustrate, examine Figures 2-2 and 2-3.

Figure 2-2 uses 24-bit true color processing to render the image. You can see that the colors blend smoothly between various shades located in the picture. Notably, the changes in the shades on the dog are not noticeable to the human eye. The image that you see is materially the same as you would see in real life.

Contrast that with Figure 2-3, which uses only the web-safe color palette.

While some of the awkwardness of the color dithering may not be as evident on, say, the grass, you should be able to notice a distinct shift in the way the colors are processed on the dog. The colors do not blend into each other as smoothly, and the photo looks, for lack of a better word, bad. This effect might be considered "artistic" and desirable on some sites. But you should still realize the effects of web-safe colors so that you can plan accordingly in your projects.

Figure 2-2

Figure 2-3

What is the solution? Again, you must understand your audience. If you have a known set of users with a known set of graphic rendering capabilities, you can target that platform. If, for example, you know that all users of your application have 24-bit graphic capabilities, you can essentially use the entire spectrum of RGB in your color scheme and graphics. However, if there is any element of unknown user graphic capabilities, you must consider the consequences of using 24-bit colors on a 16-bit platform (or lower).

It has been true for a number of years that developers have started stepping away from web-safe colors and instead are focusing on 16-bit colors or higher. This is in large part due to the proliferation of higher-end graphics cards on today's computers and laptops. Most computers no longer even have a setting to drop the computer to 256 colors.

However, in recent years, there has been a slight resurgence of web-safe colors. Why? The explosion of handheld devices and PDAs, many of which have had significant restraints on color, have forced developers to rethink the color palettes they use in their projects. However, even this isn't as true as it used to be. The latest versions of Windows Mobile, BlackBerry, and Palm operating systems now support 16-bit colors. As time goes on, there will be less and less need to target web-safe colors.

Is that time now? Like everything else, it depends on your audience. It is certainly something that today's developer needs to be informed about in order to make educated decisions on what color palette to target. Referencing the May 2007 Color Depth table earlier in this section, using 16-bit colors would satisfy 98–99% of the users. The question becomes "How important is it to satisfy that other 1–2%?" For many, that 1–2% is critical. To others, it may not be that important. There is no universal answer to whether to target this 1–2% of users. But at least you now know about the 1–2%, and you can decide how critical these users are to the success of your projects, in your planning.

Similarly, it might be worth considering that between 5 and 10% of people are color-blind. That is a significant percentage of people who will visit your site. Although addressing color blindness is beyond the scope of this book, if you are interested, a good resource for useful information and helpful tools is the Society for Technical Communication's website (`www.stcsig.org/usability/topics/ colorblind.html`*).*

Images

Once you have a fair understanding of colors, you should be better able to understand the basics of images and how each handles color. With this understanding, you will be better able to appreciate the differences in file size, functionality, and utilization of different image types in web development and, hopefully, make more informed decisions about what types of images to use for each scenario that presents itself in your projects. While there are numerous types of image formats out there, this chapter will focus on the primary formats used in web application development.

The first real contender for web graphics was the Graphic Interchange Format, or GIF. This format was formally introduced in 1987 and was (and still is) limited to 256 colors. The original format was just an image format without any real customization options. However, in 1989 the image format was modified to allow for image transparency, animation, and interlacing. While transparency and animation are fairly intuitive, interlacing may not be. Interlacing allows an image to skip lines while loading the image, then go back and fill in the lines that were originally omitted. This allows the initial image to pop on the screen more quickly, although it will appear fuzzy. Non-interlaced images load fully one line at a time from the top to the bottom. So while the parts of the image that show are clear, they are just segmented line by line in the initial rendering (meaning you see one line, then the next, and then the next). It takes longer to fill up the image dimensions but, when you do, it is fully rendered.

GIF images are still used on the web for various purposes. For one thing, they are still the only format that allows animation. They also generate smaller file sizes, generally speaking. They are very good for displaying line art or cartoons and can serve well for displaying text objects. However, the color limitations make them less than ideal candidates for real-life images or any image that requires fine detail for that matter.

To try to make a better photographic-style image format for the web, the Joint Photographic Experts Group, or JPEG, format was introduced and adopted in the early 1990s. This format creates much more detailed images, since it allows up to 24-bit color processing. It also allows for compression, allowing the images to be compressed to smaller sizes for use on the web. Of course with this compression, there is a tradeoff. The compression is done through a lossy algorithm, meaning that quality is sacrificed for image size reduction. This essentially means that, if you save a JPEG image at 50% compression, you are only storing 50% of the image algorithm in the file. This creates a much smaller image footprint but also results in a significant reduction in image quality.

JPEG images also allow for the progressive rendering of the image, which is very similar to interlaced GIF images. Just as with interlacing, the image is loaded by skipping every other line and then going back to the top and filling in the lines that were skipped on the initial pass through. Again, the image dimensions are filled more quickly, but the initial result is fuzzy. Sequential JPEGs display the image line by line, which takes longer to fill the image dimensions but, when the dimensions are filled, the image is fully rendered.

One limitation of JPEG images, though, is that they do not support transparency. To help remedy this, the Portable Network Graphic, or PNG, format was introduced in the mid-1990s. This format allows for better graphic compression than GIF images, up to 48-bit colors, and transparency. The image quality is comparable or even superior to that of JPEG images and offers the transparency of GIF images. It also allows for transparency of an alpha channel, which offers greater flexibility than the single-color transparency color allowed in GIF images. Essentially, this means that you can set the opacity of the transparency instead of just saying that this whole color is invisible to the user. This seems like the perfect graphic format for the web.

So why has it been so slow to be adopted? One easy-to-identify reason is lack of consistent browser support. For example, versions of Internet Explorer previous to IE7 do not support alpha channel transparency natively. There are workarounds and fixes you can download, but that is hoping for a lot from your clients. IE7 has incorporated alpha channel transparency and, as that browser makes it into the hands of more users, the PNG image format may become more widely used.

However, it should also be noted that PNG graphics have a slightly different color output than JPEG or GIF images. It's not so significant that if you create a blue image and produce it as a PNG it will turn red, but it is noticeable none the less. This produces some hurdles that web designers must contend with in designing their web applications. For example, if you produce an image in Photoshop and select some colors within that image to set the background color and accent colors of the application and then produce the image as a logo for the site in PNG format, the images you chose in Photoshop will no longer match exactly to the logo used on the site. Again, this isn't something that you can't work around, but it is certainly a consideration.

Differences in these three image formats can be seen in Figure 2-4. Even represented in grayscale, some of the differences are fairly noticeable.

The graphics (logos), from left to right, are in the following formats: GIF, JPEG, and PNG. The GIF format allows the white background color of the original be set to a transparent color. However, if you look closely at the edges of the text, you can see that the transition is not very smooth; it is fairly pixilated and you can still see some of the white background that did not become transparent. The text on the image does not look crisp, but it is probably acceptable for most purposes. The compression yielded a file size of only 3KB, the smallest of the three versions.

Figure 2-4

The JPEG image did not allow for any transparency. However, the font looks very crisp and clear. Although not apparent in this example, the colors are exactly matched to RGB colors that we might want to use for our project. The compression for this image was set to 100% (no loss) with sequential rendering. The file size for this image was 23 KB, the largest of the three.

The final image looks the best in this scenario. The text on the image is crisp and clear and illustrates the effects of the alpha channel transparency in this image. (You can see the striped background through the text "Images.") There is no pixilation at the edge of the text either. The image looks great. However, this is because it was viewed in IE7. If we had used an earlier version of the browser, you would not be able to see this transparency.

So what format is the best to use? Well that depends on what you need it for. If you are producing any-thing with animation, GIF is the only way to go. It is also probably the best for making line art graphics or cartoon images. If you need a more photorealistic image, JPEG is probably still the standard. However, if you want to create some photorealistic images with alpha channel transparency, and you are comfortable with the color variance and limited browser support, you should use PNG.

Text

When considering the layout and design of your web application, thought should be given to the universal font that will be used throughout the pages. Failure to identify a font will result in the browser using whatever default it has set up (including font style and size). A browser can only use a font if it is installed on the computer it is running on (the client's computer). Developers should decide and enforce font size and types in their design in whatever manner seems best. For example, it is becoming standard practice to incorporate the fonts used in a web project in an attached CSS file. In that file, which will be covered in more detail in Chapter 4, you declare the name of the font in a prioritized list. This means that you state what your preference is, then what your first alternative is in the case that your preference isn't available, and so forth. For example, you might include the following stylesheet declaration in your CSS file:

```
body
{
    font-family: Arial, Helvetica, sans-serif;
}
```

In this example, you are setting the priority of the fonts for your project to be Arial, then Helvetica, and, finally, sans-serif. The final option, sans-serif, is a generic font name that will resolve on the operating system of the machine accessing your page. Generic font family names should always end your font family declarations to ensure that your pages do not just accept the default browser font.

The following generic font names are established for use in your web projects:

- ❑   serif (such as Times New Roman)
- ❑   sans-serif (such as Arial)
- ❑   cursive (such as Comic Sans)
- ❑   fantasy (such as Western)
- ❑   monospace (such as Courier)

When declaring your fonts, you should also ensure that you encapsulate any font names that contain spaces in their names (such as "Arial Black," "Courier New," "Times New Roman," and so on) with quotation marks. For example, the following code would add a serif style font as the main body font:

```
body
{
      font-family: "Times New Roman", Times, serif;
}
```

The following combinations are fairly safe when it comes to universal application across operating systems and browser platforms:

- ❑   Arial, Helvetica, sans-serif
- ❑   Geneva, Arial, Helvetica, sans-serif
- ❑   Verdana, Arial, Helvetica, sans-serif
- ❑   Georgia, Times New Roman, Times, serif
- ❑   Times New Roman, Times, serif
- ❑   Courier New, Courier, monospace

That being said, there probably is no true standard for acceptable fonts. As with everything else, it depends on your audience. If you can ensure that all users of your site have, for example, Microsoft Windows XP SP2 installed, then you might be able to get away with using a font like Algerian. However, if you can't ensure that, then you have to think "Will all of my users have Algerian font installed?" What about previous versions of Microsoft operating systems; did they have this font installed? What about Macintosh operating systems? Is it installed by default for them? If not, what is an acceptable alternative font to use instead?

Using the list provided above will provide assurance that users will experience your page in a fairly consistent way. But nothing can completely ensure that every user who accesses your page will be able to see the site exactly as you programmed it. This, of course, includes fonts but pretty much every other aspect of your site as well.

CSS vs. Tables

A discussion about web design standards and best practices wouldn't be complete without at least a cursory review of the debate on whether to use CSS or tables for design layout. People who have an opinion about this topic, generally speaking, have a very strong opinion about it. There aren't a lot of people who ride the fence on this particular issue. If you were to go on the Internet and do a search about this debate, you might find articles like "An objective analysis of CSS versus tables and why using Tables is stupid."

This all began back in the infancy of the Internet. When tables were introduced in HTML, developers finally had a tool they could use to layout their page. And many did exactly that. You could span the table across the entire browser window, lay out one row that spanned all columns to include the header, and then break up the other rows as necessary for content. Developers could nest tables inside tables in order to further control exactly how the layout was presented to the end user. Tables were fast, they were easy, and they were consistent across browsers.

But in the last few years, web standards have began picking up steam. Cascading Style Sheets, discussed in more detail in Chapter 4, are being used more and more to control most aspects of web pages. Accessibility has become an issue for a rising number of vocal users of the web. Tables are no longer the new cool thing and, maybe as expected, have begun to garner a fair amount of criticism.

However, for every person touting the advantages of CSS in web design, there are at least as many people screaming that tables are not only acceptable for web design but are also preferable. The following sections outline some of the arguments on both sides of this debate.

CSS Is the Way to Go!

One of the main arguments on the side of CSS is the need to address accessibility standards. Text-based browsers and screen readers have a tough time deciphering page layout when trying to interpret tables. If the site is laid out using CSS, the user can simply turn off CSS in the browser and the page should still provide the same experience. You should understand that most assistive technology reads in source code order. The use of accessibility features in CSS allows developers to lay out the content in a linear fashion that makes sense if read in source-code order. Developers are not forced to think in a matrix mentality, as they are when using tables. CSS allows developers to go down a logical path in their code while, at the time, allowing them to position content in whatever order they want for CSS-enabled browsers. Tables often render the page content so illogically in a text-based browser that it is materially inaccessible to many users.

Another primary point is that taking tables out of the structure takes a lot of the bloat out of web pages. To illustrate this point, consider the following page layout using tables:

```
<table width="100%" cellpadding="0" cellspacing="0" border="0">
    <tr>
        <td colspan="2" width="100%">
            <img src="/logo.jpg" border="0" alt="Corporate Logo">
        </td>
    </tr>
```

```
        <tr>
                <td width="200px" valign="top" align="center">
                        This is our navigation area to the left...
                </td>
                <td width="100%" valign="top" align="left">
                        <table border="0" cellpadding="5" cellspacing="0">
                                <tr>
                                        <td>
                                                This is our content area
                                        </td>
                                </tr>
                        </table>
                </td>
        </tr>
        <tr>
                <td colspan="2" width="100%">
                        &copy; Copyright 2006-07
                </td>
        </tr>
</table>
```

This is a fairly common way to lay out a page using tables. To compare this to CSS, the following codes shows how the same layout would be created using CSS:

```
<div class="headerArea"><img src="logo.jpg" border="0" alt="Corporate Logo"></div>
<div class="contentArea">
        <div class="navigationArea">This is our navigation area to the
        left...</div>
        <div class="textArea">This is our content area</div>
</div>
<div class="footerArea">&copy; Copyright 2006-07</div>
```

As you can see, there is a lot less code in the CSS example than in the tables version. Is this a completely fair comparison? No. You have to also set up the CSS classes for headerArea, contentArea, navigation-Area, textArea, and footerArea. When that is all created, will you really see a difference in file size? If you are strictly talking about lines of code, you will probably not notice much difference (if any). However, the consideration shouldn't be really the numbers of lines of code; the focus should be more on speed and maintainability. When you use a linked stylesheet, you will gain rendering speed in at least two regards. For one, browsers can render out CSS faster than nested tables. This is because a browser, when examining nested tables, must find the innermost nested table and then work its way out from there before it starts rendering. However, with CSS, the code is generally more linearly based and as such the browser can just start outputting the rendered code immediately. This can save some bandwidth, but the real savings occur when you take into account the fact that browsers cache CSS documents. This means if you have 100 pages that all reference the same CSS document, the CSS document will be loaded into memory the first time you load the first page. All subsequent page loads will use the cached version of the CSS document. If all of the structure of your site is stored in cached memory as opposed to a series of nested tables that has to be loaded for every page, your pages will load much faster.

There is also the point of maintainability. In six months when you have to go back to make some changes to the code, which approach would be easier to navigate through to make the changes? Most would probably agree that the CSS one is. And, if you don't see the difference, it is likely because this is such a small and simplistic example. Imagine dozens of nested tables spread out through your code.

What if you accidentally delete part of a closing TD tag while updating the text and it breaks everything? Maintainability is certainly a valid advantage of CSS over tables.

Another valid point made by CSS proponents is that you should keep your content and your layout separate. Using linked CSS files allows the designer to design in the CSS file and the developer to fill content in the HTML (or .NET) page. In the above example, if design specifications changed and required you to make sweeping changes to the layout of the page (colors, positioning of some items, width, and so on), you would only need to make changes in the CSS file and not touch the code pages at all. In the table example, you would likely need to design an entirely new page using tables to recreate the new design specifications and then extract all of the content and place it in the appropriate areas of the new site. To extend this idea, you could even have different stylesheets for different functions. For example, you might have one stylesheet that is for the structure/layout of your web project and then another CSS document that contains your colors, fonts, and other style rules. That way, you know that if you need to switch the header region to be 100 pixels high, you go into the structure document; if you need to change the font of the site to Arial, you go to the style document. This is certainly a consideration worth taking seriously.

It is worth noting that even CSS purists believe it is acceptable to use tables for tabular data. In fact, they believe that is what they were created for in the first place, not page layout, and they should be used for that (and only that). So nobody is really saying that tables should die a slow death (or a fast one). Most are just saying that, for page layout, they shouldn't be used.

No Way. Tables Are Where It's At!

It seems like the most often cited reason for sticking with tables is simply "If it ain't broken, don't fix it." Is that valid? In almost any argument, no, that is not valid. But then, neither is change for the sake of change. So what are the valid arguments?

The best argument for sticking with tables is that they work. For the most part, it doesn't matter what browser or version you are hitting the site with; it works and it looks the same. A table is a table is a table. If you lay it out with Internet Explorer 7 in mind, it will likely render exactly the same in Netscape or FireFox. This just isn't true with CSS. Laying out a page using pure CSS may potentially render a page differently in Internet Explorer than FireFox and more differently still than in Netscape. This is due to varying degrees of support for CSS standards. As web standards gain popularity, more of the browsers are jumping on the bandwagon and implementing CSS the same way. But it still isn't consistent, and if you use CSS you need to make sure that you test. And retest. And maybe test one more time.

Another argument that has some validity is that CSS, at least if you are coming from a tables mentality, has a fairly steep learning curve; tables are easier. Again, tables are tables are tables. Once you learn the basic rules of how a table operates, you can deploy them with limited effort or thought as to how they will function in the browser. Using CSS can potentially take a lot more time up front to implement. You have to think more about how positioning or screen widths or padding will work. And to get a good handle on how all of those pieces work together takes some time. However, the mere fact that you are reading this book shows that you are willing to spend at least some time increasing your knowledge and understanding, so maybe this isn't as big of a deal to you. Just realize that to become a CSS guru, assuming that there is such a thing, you will spend a lot of time reading and learning how it works. And if you are going to implement CSS over tables, you will probably spend more upfront time setting up the page layout than you did with tables.

It is also noteworthy that most of the staunch table supporters still believe that CSS has its place. There is sufficient cross-browser support for things like font and paragraph formatting to use CSS for these items. However, the quirks in the ways different browsers handle other formatting in CSS suggests that the world of web design is not quite ready to fully deprecate tables for page layout.

Who Wins?

This is mostly a judgment call. Certainly the overwhelming argument for tables is the limited cross-browser support of CSS at this time. That being said, CSS is probably a better way of coding. It allows you to separate design from code, it improves accessibility, and it makes maintenance easier. For every argument for CSS, there are probably hundreds of people out there with counterarguments. This would be the same for any argument made for tables.

There is no real clear winner. Neither approach has an absolute edge over the other. There are pros and cons for each. And the point of this book is not "to make converts" for either position.

However, for this book, CSS will be used for style layout. This seems to be the way the future of web design is heading. Certainly, if you are serious about web design, you at least need to understand how CSS is implemented for style. That way, even if you are a tables person, at least you will have an understanding of the CSS approach.

Accessibility

What does accessibility mean when used in conjunction with web design standards? You may have heard this referenced as 508 compliance. Or maybe you have heard it called ADA standards, in reference to the Americans with Disabilities Act. But what it really boils down to is making your site accessible to all people interested in viewing it. This seems like an elementary thing to do, but you might be surprised. Have you ever tested what it's like to navigate your site without a mouse? How about with all of your stylesheets turned off? You might be shocked at how difficult it is to get around your otherwise awe-inspiring web application. But these struggles are a daily occurrence for many Internet surfers. And, as a reasonable and responsible web developer, you should learn what you need to do to make sure these people are given the same experience as your other patrons.

Why Accessibility Matters

In a 2003 study commissioned by Microsoft and performed by Forrester Research, Inc, it was estimated that a whopping 100.4 million working-age adults, age 18 to 64, could benefit from the use of assistive technology and accessibility design. That is a full 60% of the population that is affected in some way by accessibility issues. Here is the breakdown from that report (www.microsoft.com/enable/research/workingage.aspx):

Type of Accessibility	Likely (millions)	Very Likely (millions)	Total
Visual	27.4	18.5	45.9
Dexterity	31.7	12.0	43.7
Hearing	32.0	4.3	36.3
Cognitive	29.7	3.8	33.5
Speech	4.3	1.9	6.2

So if someone tells you that nobody is really affected by the ramifications of not thinking of the visual accessibility in your design, for example, you know they are wrong. A full 45.9 million users are at least likely impacted; 18.5 million of those users are very likely impacted. In most circles, this wouldn't constitute "nobody."

It should also be noted that the people making up these numbers are not otherwise classified as "disabled" in other studies. These are not the legally blind or deaf. These are people whom you may work or live with. These are people that you might not consider disabled and, most likely, they would agree with you. However, when it comes to accessibility on the Internet, these are the forgotten millions.

And remember, these are just the working-age adults. What about the aging baby boomer generation? As those groups of people continue to age, they will face increasingly limiting handicaps that affect their use of computers. Thus these numbers are likely going to keep rising, which makes addressing accessibility now the smart thing to do.

And consider this: disabled persons have an increasing amount of disposable income. The Employer's Forum on Disabilities (www.employers-forum.co.uk), a UK-based organization focusing on disabilities that affect business, reports that the annual purchasing power of people with disabilities is £80 billion ($158 billion). And that is just in the UK. In the United States, the Department of Justice estimates that Americans with Disabilities have approximately $175 billion in discretionary income (www.usdoj.gov/crt/ada/busstat.htm). Are these hundreds of billions of dollars your business can afford to lose because of lack of planning or testing? Or worse, apathy?

And remember, these dollar estimates are for those people that are actually identified as disabled and do not include the income of the 101.4 million people in the Microsoft survey. That is a lot of money to discount.

The Cost of Noncompliance

So what happens to your site if it isn't ADA compliant? Besides losing out on potentially billions of dollars of income? Well, if that still isn't enough reason, there are also federal and state regulations that may impact your livelihood.

Section 508 compliance is a reference to Section 508 of the Rehabilitation Act of 1973 (29 U.S.C. 794 d). This is federal law. And that is just one of the regulations out there. There are also sections 501, 502, and 505 of the Rehabilitation Act. There is section 255 of the Telecommunications Act of 1996. There is the Assistive Technology Act of 1998. There is the Workforce Investment Act of 1998.

And these are just a few of the federal regulations. Many states have also implemented similar, and sometimes even more stringent, regulations.

State agencies are now required to ensure Section 508 compliance for projects created after July 1, 2006 or risk losing federal funds. If you are a contractor or employer of a state or federal agency, this can directly affect your livelihood.

One of the more interesting pieces of legislation is the Disability Discrimination Act (DDA) in the United Kingdom. This act states that all websites, regardless of whether they are private or public sector portals, must provide the same service to disabled persons as to any other person visiting the site. Failure to do so can result in the company actually being sued. Granted, this has not happened as of the publication of this manuscript, but it has come up on at least two occasions (companies were approached by the Royal National Institute for the Blind about their compliance, and both companies made changes to their sites rather than face legal action). This is likely the future of the web.

Accessibility proponents are getting louder and gaining a lot of support. And legislators are listening. There will likely be an increase in federal and state regulations over the upcoming years. So if losing the business of the impacted users isn't enough of an argument, maybe the threat of losing state and/or federal contract dollars will seal the deal.

If these numbers still don't convince you to jump on the ADA bandwagon, maybe you should think of the ever-increasing mobile device market. While such users not typically considered part of 508 compliance beneficiaries, they should be. The small screens and historically limited graphic abilities of mobile devices make them perfect recipients of the advantages of accessibility programming on the web. This group of users likely includes some of the most technically savvy users (and potentially affluent ones) on the web. If you fail to cater to them, you may lose their business to a competitor that will.

Don't forget the kids! Kids today are on computers as much, if not more often, than many adults. Yet this group of users often lacks the manual dexterity of its older counterparts and could significantly benefit from accessibly programming.

Just because a user group is not officially designated as "disabled" does not mean that they are not impacted by your failure to comply with ADA regulations. And, if they are inconvenienced, you or your clients may suffer right along with them.

Ensuring Accessibility

There are a number or recommendations out there, but the primary source for this manuscript is the World Wide Web Consortium (www.w3.org) and its Web Accessibility Initiative. A detailed explanation of this initiative can be located at www.w3.org/TR/WAI-WEBCONTENT-TECHS.

Here are some of the items you should take into consideration while programming your next website:

❑ You must include a text alternative to every non-text element on your page. This is generally done through the ALT and LONGDESC properties of media items like the <IMG> tag.

❑ Use color smartly. Ensure that nothing in your application will get lost if all color is removed or if the page is viewed in black and white. Make sure that the background and text provide adequate contrast to be viewable by persons who may be color-blind or suffer from other color deficit disorders.

❑ Ensure that you are using HTML standards, including the use of DOCTYPE declarations at the top of the page.

❑ Use CSS! This goes back to the tables vs. CSS discussion, but the WAI standard is to use CSS for structural layout, not tables, for most situations.

❑ Use relative positioning and sizes rather than absolutes to ensure that the pages are displayed appropriately across different monitors and with various assistive technologies.

- ❑ Provide clear navigation controls, even if CSS and JavaScript are disabled.

- ❑ Use JavaScript sparingly or not at all. If you do use it, make sure that the page works when JavaScript is disabled.

- ❑ Another thing to keep in mind is to have a label associated with each control on your site. If, for example, you have a TextBox control on your page, make sure that you have a label for that item and make sure it is associated that way in the code. For example:

```
<label for="inputBox">Search:
    <input type="text" id="inputBox" name="searchTerms" value="" maxlength="10">
</label>
```

These are, for the most part, the biggies that will tend to get you if you are not careful. This is not an exhaustive list, but it gives you a place to start. As with anything else, you should make sure you test for compliance.

Testing for ADA Compliance

Many people believe that the only way to test for ADA compliance is through the purchase of expensive technology, such as JAWS. However, this just isn't true. If funds are available and you can get management approval, that is probably a good way to go. But never let budget get in the way of accessible web design.

A web developer was once asked how one should test for ADA. He said "turn off graphics in your browser and throw your mouse over your monitor. Now try to navigate the page." This seems like a very rudimentary approach to testing, but it will make an impact if you have never tested for ADA before. Imagine all of your images are turned off, all of your colors are disabled, and you can't use your mouse. Can you still get around your site? Are you still sane afterwards?

Fortunately, there are a lot of really good (and free) validators available today.

First, there are the validators available through the W3C:

HTML Validator: http://validator.w3.org

CSS Validator: http://jigsaw.w3.org/css-validator

Running www.google.com through the HTML validator yielded results displayed in Figure 2-5.

As you can see, Google actually failed the HTML validation with a total of 48 errors. This seems especially interesting when you consider how simple the layout of Google really is.

A similar free tool for HTML validation is The Wave provided by WebAIM (Web Accessibility In Mind): http://wave.webaim.org/index.jsp. To see the results of this validator running against Google, examine Figure 2-6.

As you can see, the report is strikingly different. There is not nearly the verbose explanation for errors, and the page looks similar to the way it is presented normally. However, the tags are nice because they show you exactly where your errors are occurring in the interface and their severity (red obviously being the most severe).

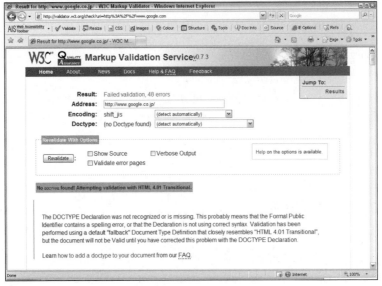

Figure 2-5

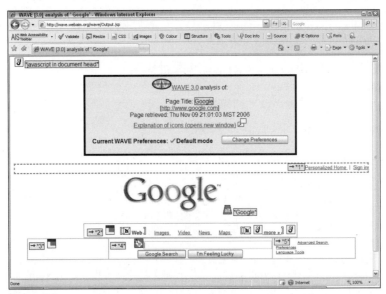

Figure 2-6

All of the tools from W3C and WebAIM will allow you to enter a URL, upload a file, or simply copy the relevant code directly into the page to access the reports.

Of course, the cooler way to do this is through a browser plug-in that is available at www.wat-c.org. The Web Accessibility Toolbar provided by this group, the Web Accessibility Tools Consortium, actually integrates the above tools in a toolbar you can download for Internet Explorer or Opera browsers. You can see what it looks like in Figure 2-7.

Figure 2-7

Clicking the Validate button brings up a drop-down menu that lets you validate your HTML or CSS directly with the WAI validators above. Under Tools you will find an option for "The Wave" that will let you validate directly against the validators from WebAIM.

> *While a few free resources and tools have been shown to this point, the examples are by no means exhaustive. For example, FireFox offers Firebug, which validates CSS and JavaScript on the fly (http://getfirebug.com). This tool is specific to FireFox browsers, but if you use FireFox, this can put a lot of free and powerful accessibility checks at your fingertips.*

Finally, you should also incorporate the tools that come with Visual Studio 2005. If you have a page open that is valid for checking (an ASPX or similar page; not any of the code-behind pages or classes), you will see the Check Accessibility option appear as the first item under your tools menu, as shown in Figure 2-8.

Figure 2-8

Clicking on this will allow you to validate your code against the Web Content Accessibility Guidelines (WCAG) Priority 1 and Priority 2 standards of W3C (www.w3.org/TR/WAI-WEBCONTENT) as well as the Access Board Section 508 standards, as shown in Figure 2-9.

Figure 2-9

If you were to copy the rendered output of the Google homepage into an HTML document in Visual Studio 2005 and run the report with the above options, you would get output similar to that in Figure 2-10.

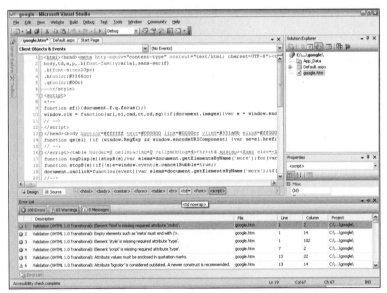

Figure 2-10

As you can see, this report generates 108 errors and 63 warnings in the document, far more than either of the other validation test results provided by the W3C or WebAIM products discussed previously. The nice thing about this is that you are actually at the source code level, and when you double-click on any of the findings, Visual Studio will take you directly to the offending line of code and highlight the segment of that line that is causing concern. This makes accessibility testing much easier during the development phase of a project.

This should be considered a good start but not necessarily a complete check. You should also run tests with the other free tools provided. While Microsoft has made great strides in accessibility compliance, they are not the authors of the standards. It is always a good idea, when available, to actually validate against the source of the standards. And websites dedicated to accessibility issues, and in particular the W3C, which actually authored the standards, are probably a better and more up-to-date source for validation. Use the tools of Visual Studio while developing your applications. But when they get moved into user or acceptance testing, make sure that you run them through some of the validators discussed earlier in this section just to be sure. When it comes to accessibility, you can never test too much.

AJAX 508 Compliance

Is AJAX 508 compliant? The short answer: No.

AJAX stands for Asynchronous JavaScript And XML and is a web development tool that allows you to post back small pieces of your page rather than the entire page, saving a lot of bandwidth and reducing the screen flicker of posting pages. It is undoubtedly one of the coolest development tools to come along in a while.

However, the second word in AJAX is JavaScript, and any time you see that, you need to be cautious. JavaScript is not completely disallowed, but it should be scrutinized. Do I need this to be in JavaScript? Can I put the functionality server-side? What will happen to my page if JavaScript is turned off?

AJAX provides a considerable headache to ADA enthusiasts. Besides the fact that it is JavaScript, you need to understand the basic functionality of AJAX. When you access a page, its entire contents are loaded into your browser. This probably includes a number of graphics and HTML that will not change from page to page. It may also include referenced CSS files and other server-side includes. If, for example, on the page you load you have a GridView control that has pagination turned on and you click on Page 2, what happens? In a normal situation, the page flickers with the postback because you are sending a request to the server, it is sending back the entire page, and your browser is then rendering that entire page again. With AJAX, when you click on the Page 2 link, you are only sending a small request to the server to essentially say Page 2 was clicked. The server then sends back just the data for the GridView, not all of the HTML headers or other related information. So instead of sending maybe 100 KB or more of data through the pipe, you might only be sending 4K. It is much less intensive on bandwidth and the server and provides a much smoother interface for the user.

However, what it also doesn't do is trigger a new header for the page. With much of the assistive technology on the market, when the AJAX transaction occurs, the browser doesn't know that anything changed. This is not good for accessibility standards.

And, since it has JavaScript in the title, guess what? You have to have JavaScript enabled for this technology to even work. So what happens to those 3.8 million users that have JavaScript disabled? Do you have a fallback plan in place for them?

AJAX is a very cool technology and, with enough thought and planning, you can probably find a way to make it ADA compliant. However, to do so, you may have to offer alternative pages that do not have AJAX installed on them, which requires a lot more development time (and is a potential maintenance nightmare). Weighing the cool factor of AJAX against the standards can be tough, but for many developers determined to comply with 508 standards, AJAX simply is not a solution worth pursuing.

The Importance of Accessibility

So what does all of this mean? Accessibility is a real issue that is not going away any time soon. Millions of people with hundreds of billions of dollars in disposable income are impacted by accessibility concerns. Failure to cater to these users could cost you business and, in some cases, open your business up to legal action. There is a lot of information on the web about accessibility, and there are plenty of free resources to use to validate your pages, so you really have no excuse not to make your pages more accessible.

So make your sites accessible because it makes good business sense to do so. Make your sites accessible because it is the law. Make your sites accessible because it is the right thing to do.

Summary

Many times, when programmers begin a new project, they immediately jump into the business logic and data access design concepts and implementation. Too often they immediately think "Okay, how will I meet this requirement? What is the best way to approach the customer's need for XYZ." As an afterthought, if they consider it at all, they might think "Okay, how should I display the final project to the client." Many programmers probably do not give much thought to the various aspects of the design elements that should go into a project or, more importantly, the demographics of the audience that will eventually consume the sites they produce.

Hopefully you will now have a fair understanding of some of the concepts you, as a developer, should incorporate in the design of new projects. You should have at least a basic understanding of graphics and color, browser use and settings, and some of the current debates in web design. You should also now have at least a cursory knowledge of accessible design and how to ensure that you are delivering your products to the widest global audience possible.

These concepts will be critical to much of your learning in future chapters. It was important to lay down the basics of web development before going further into ASP.NET design concepts. For example, it probably wouldn't be appropriate to talk about creating your own graphics in Photoshop, which you will see in Chapter 3, without at least ensuring that you know what a JPEG image is, what web-safe colors are, and what image formats support transparency. Many of the future topics will be based on the CSS discussions of this chapter. If you don't feel completely comfortable with the topics addressed, you may want to reread this chapter before proceeding. Without a good understanding of the topics addressed here, you may find it difficult to fully understand the meat of upcoming chapters.

And, more importantly, you may not be as well equipped to produce the best project possible when you close this book.

3

Photoshop: Cool Tips and Tricks for Developers

In a perfect world, perhaps, a developer is simply a person who crunches out code. No need to meet with clients and gather their requirements; that is the job of the project manager. No need to design or ensure the integrity and security of the database infrastructure; that is the job of the DBA. No need to worry about IIS configuration issues or the segregation of environment platforms (e.g., development, acceptance testing, production); that is the job of the network guys. And certainly no need to worry about color schemes, graphics, or logos used in the application; that is the job of the graphic designer.

But more and more, this is becoming less and less acceptable. In an interview, it is no longer uncommon to hear that the potential employer wants to know that the developer they hire can carry a project all the way from the requirements gathering to production and maintenance. For any of the steps involved in the Software Development Life Cycle, it is becoming increasingly hard to say "that isn't my job." Everything is your job. As a developer, you are expected to gather customer requirements, develop proof-of-concept designs, make decisions on application and database platforms, create and maintain databases for your projects, administer the IIS of the web servers (at least at the development region), and work with your clients through acceptance testing and eventually production moves and maintenance.

There are plenty of certification tracks out there to demonstrate that you have mastered many of these skills. For example, there is a Certified Project Management Professional (PMP) that teaches you about how to gather requirements and carry a project to its logical completion. There are plenty of Microsoft certifications that can prove to others that you understand Microsoft Technologies. Recently, a new branch of these certifications has been created, the Microsoft Certified Technology Specialist (MCTS), specializing in web applications. But take a look at the requirements (www.microsoft.com/learning/exams/70-528.mspx) for the web-based client development exam (70-528). Plenty of the requirements call for you to show that you know how to implement the tools in the .NET 2.0 Framework. Notice, however, there are no requirements on *when* you should implement these controls. There is also no discussion of web standards or style and design.

So why do so many developers fully accept the responsibilities of the Software Development Life Cycle but still say that design isn't part of their job? Is it the battle between the left side and the right side of the brain? Many developers seem to think in zeros and ones in a very linear and analytical manner, which actually comes in very handy in much of their programming. When creativity comes up, these developers shy away from this challenge and either offer up bland sites or rely on templates purchased or downloaded from third parties to fill the gap.

Why is this? Is it lack of motivation or interest? Is it truly a lack of ability or creativity? Or is it just a lack of exposure to the graphic arts? This chapter will operate under the assumption that it is the latter.

The wonderful thing about graphics is that you don't have to be overly creative to come up with some engaging designs if you know a couple of tricks. This chapter will show you the basic workings of a graphic design application, Photoshop CS2, and some tricks that you can use when creating your next web project. Will you be a certified graphic designer at the end of this chapter (whatever that is)? No. But hopefully you will have a sufficient exposure to something you have historically shied away from and a renewed interest in finding out more.

Prerequisites

This chapter uses Adobe Photoshop CS2 for all of its examples. However, many, if not all, of the examples could be pretty easily ported into similar applications, such as Macromedia Fireworks. You may even find the functionality comparable in the freely distributed GIMP, which is great if you are without the budget for the more commercial solutions.

It is also fair to say that most, if not all, of the examples provided would be materially the same in previous versions of Adobe Photoshop (Photoshop 6).

So if you have a previous version of Photoshop or an entirely different image manipulation program, you should still be fine. The concepts presented will be fairly universally true and, with a little playing around in whatever program you are using, you should be able to apply the concepts in your own application. However, if you do have Photoshop CS2, you will be able to use the examples line for line to create the graphics used for the rest of this book.

> *Please note that using a graphic application other than Adobe Photoshop CS2 to recreate the projects in this chapter may or may not result in the same functionality. While every attempt was made to keep the examples universal, there will be differences between different applications and different versions of the same application. Please keep this in mind as you read through this chapter.*

It should be noted that this chapter will not get overly intensely into graphic design tips and tricks. If this were a chapter on car maintenance, you would not be leaving, for example, with a complete understanding on how to rebuild an engine. You would, however, leave with a good understanding on how to change your oil, air filter, and spark plugs.

This chapter does not assume that you have any previous experience in creating graphics. It is perfectly fit for the complete novice.

The images used in this chapter were obtained from Photos To Go Unlimited (`http://unlimited.photostogo.com`) and licensed by the author of this manuscript. Photos To Go Unlimited is a subscription service that allows subscribers to download unlimited numbers of royalty-free images for use in their own projects at a reasonable price. Of course, there are a variety of image service companies (such as Corbis at www.corbis.com and Getty Images at www.GettyImages.com), and you may already have a favorite. It is possible to follow along and use images from another service or even your own photos. The primary purpose of this chapter is to help you get a feel for how Photoshop works and to have you get comfortable with some of its basic tools and processes. You don't really have to create the final products to accomplish this. However, to follow along in all the chapters of the book, it would be best to use these images. The identification number of the images from Photos To Go Unlimited will be provided so that if you choose to subscribe you can download the exact images used in these tutorials. You can search through their database before joining to get an idea of what kind of images are available.

Project Guidelines

The project you will be building for this book will be a personal website for a client. The project will be used to outline the publications and presentations of the client and will not be used to conduct any business. Therefore, there really isn't the need for any kind of corporate branding or other marketing considerations.

However, in creating this project, you will be working on smaller projects that will focus on specific components or aspects of the website. You will need to create different header graphics and color schemes that complement each other (this chapter). You will need to ensure the site is accessible and meets the accessibility guidelines presented in Chapter 4. You will need to create a navigation system, with certain links available only to the client (Chapter 6). You will need to create a template to carry through to all pages (Chapter 7) and ensure that the .NET controls of the project follow the color scheme you have set up (Chapter 8). Finally, you will need to guarantee that visitors to the site can easily access it through a mobile browser (Chapter 10).

The only design guideline is that the client goes by the moniker "surfer5", which is a play on the long-board surfing days of his youth and his Internet surfing he now does as an adult. You should plan to use this theme throughout the project. For example, the website will be hosted at www.surfer5.com, and the proposed name of the portal is "surfer5 Internet Solutions." In keeping with this idea, you should try to incorporate surfing images into the graphic headers you create for the site.

To that end, this chapter will take you through the steps of creating the graphics and color schemes. You will start with basic stock photos and manipulate them to meet the needs of this project. This will include cutting out sections of the image (silhouettes), drawing lines, filling in regions with different opacity fills, and adding text. You will learn how to dissect these graphics to meet the needs of the layout, and you will learn how to use these images to create a complementary color scheme that you will carry out through the remaining chapters of this book.

The intent is that if you see how to use some of these common tricks in Photoshop, you will be able to take that knowledge back to your own projects. Sure, this chapter has some very specific examples in it. However, once you know how to cut out the background from an image, you can use that knowledge for many different purposes. Once you know how to add text to the top of the graphic, you can use that skill in most of the graphics you create in the future. You won't learn how to use every function in Photoshop. There are entire series of books that probably can't touch every single piece of functionality of Photoshop. But through these examples, you will learn the basics of graphic design and, with that, be armed with the appropriate content should you want to further that knowledge.

Photoshop: An Overview

Obviously, before getting too far into how to make graphics in Photoshop, you should probably have a basic roadmap of how to navigate through some of the features of the application. This section will not go through all of the various panes and areas of the applications but will showcase the ones you will be using in this chapter.

First, Figure 3-1 shows you the application as it will probably appear when you first open it up.

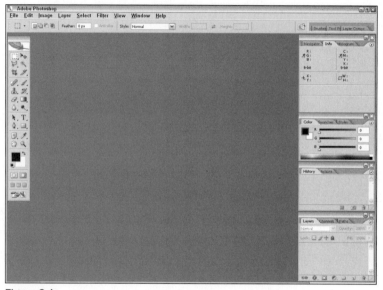

Figure 3-1

As you can see, there is a standard toolbar at the top. This looks like pretty much any other application you have used, with File, Edit, Window, and Help menus as well as a few that are specific to Photoshop, such as Image and Layer. These drop-down menus provide much of the functionality and power of Photoshop. However, much of this functionality is also available through the toolboxes (called palettes), some of which are shown on the screen.

Of the palettes shown, there are probably only three that are critical for these tutorials. The first of these is the Tools palette (also known as the toolbox), which is shown in Figure 3-2.

This will probably be the most widely used palette for these projects. If you want to select an area of the photo for cropping, you will go here. If you want to paint an area of the photo, you will go here. If you want to write text on top of your image, this is where you will go. You will get a fair understanding of some of the major components of this palette that will help you in a lot of your projects, but there are others here that will not be addressed in this book. You are encouraged to continue your research into Photoshop to get a better understanding of the tools available. A good place to start is at the Adobe Design Center at www.adobe.com/designcenter/tutorials.

Figure 3-2

The next critical palette, possibly the most important palette in Photoshop, is the Layers palette, which can be seen in Figure 3-3.

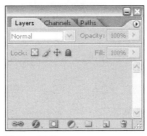

Figure 3-3

For these tutorials, you will only use the Layers tab of this palette but, as you advance your knowledge of Photoshop, you will find a lot of cool functionality you can use on the Channels and Paths tabs.

However, to understand what the Layers tab/palette does, you first have to understand what a Layer is, at least in terms of graphic design. Essentially, layers are levels of the graphic that are seen, one on top of the other. In other words, if you have four layers of graphics, one on top of the next, you will see them starting at the top layer looking down to the bottom layer. To illustrate, assume that you have three layers, as shown in Figure 3-4. The image first applies Layer 1, then Layer 2, and finally Layer 3 to get the end result.

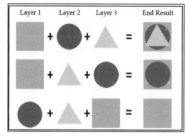

Figure 3-4

As you can see, the order in which the layers are applied significantly affects the outcome of the final image. For example, in the first line, you first lay down the square, then put the circle on top of it, and finally lay the triangle on top of that. In the resulting image, you can see all three components fairly well. However, in the second example, because the triangle is applied before the circle, you can only see the bottom tips of the triangle, with the rest of the triangle being covered up by the circle. Finally, in the last example, because the square is applied last and is bigger than all of the other objects in this example, you can only see the square; the circle and triangle are completely lost.

To illustrate using a more real-world example, examine the photo in Figure 3-5 (Image 904079).

> As mentioned earlier in the chapter, these images are from Photos To Go Unlimited (http://unlimited.photostogo.com). Image numbers are provided so that you can easily find, download, and work with the same images.

Figure 3-5

Assume that the family is on a layer by itself (you can do this on your own by cutting them out of the image, which will be demonstrated later in this chapter), which looks something like Figure 3-6.

Now you can drop this layer on top of another background to create a completely different image. For example, you might consider using a cityscape background. Using Image 820439 as the backdrop and then adding the new layer on top of that and then some text on top of that, we get the image in Figure 3-7.

40

Figure 3-6

Figure 3-7

The other thing that is illustrated above is the transparency of the red box that houses the text on the image. This, too, is controlled through the layers palette. In Photoshop, you can set the transparency of each layer, resulting in several different effects. In this example, there is a red box drawn on a layer that is above both the background (cityscape) and family layers but below the text layer. The red box is set to an opacity level of 41% (this was set arbitrarily — there was no reason to choose 41% as opposed to 40% or 42% — this is just where it looked right when playing with the slider that sets the opacity). All other layers, in this example, are set to 100% opacity.

The final palette that you need to understand, although it is not necessarily required for these tutorials, is the history palette, which is shown in Figure 3-8.

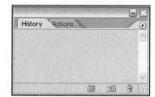

Figure 3-8

Even though this palette will not necessarily be illustrated throughout the tutorials, it is a good one to be familiar with. When thinking of the History palette, think of the Undo functionality of many applications. This palette is like a supercharged Undo tool. Essentially, while working on a project, the most recent actions you have performed are listed in the history with a small icon next to each action indicating what type of action had occurred (e.g., cropping, resizing, pasting, applying a filter, etc.).

By default, Photoshop CS2 saves 20 history states of your project. In other words, it saves the last 20 things you did to your Photoshop project. So, if you are working on something and you realize that five steps back you made a mistake, you simply click on the history state five steps back and your project is taken back to that version. You can fix your mistake and then move forward again. Note, though, that once you make a change, the history that happened after the history state you went back to is lost.

You should also know that when you shut down your project, you lose your history for that project. Say you think you are finished — you export your finished project to a JPG file and then close down the project. Afterward, you realize that you messed something up. If you open your project back up, there are no history states to return to. You have to fix the problem on its own without the assistance of returning to a particular state of the project. Saving your project periodically is good practice but realize that it has no effect on your history. In other words, saving does not immediately erase your history, but it does not preserve your history either; nothing can do that. So remember to save your project periodically because it is good practice, but don't let it lure you into a false sense of security regarding the state of your history.

Also remember that, as stated previously, the default is to have 20 history states for a given project. This can be modified if you deem it necessary. To change this setting, while in Photoshop, click on Edit ➪ Preferences ➪ General to access the General Preferences of Photoshop CS2 (you can also access this screen by pressing the Ctrl button along with the letter "K"). This brings up the screen shown in Figure 3-9.

You can see that the section called History States is set to 20 in this example. To allow for more states, simply increase the number; to allow for fewer states, reduce the number. The risk of increasing this number is that Photoshop saves the history states in your RAM or on your scratch disk. So increasing the number of history states may seriously impact the performance of Photoshop. If you continually create small files or have more RAM than you know what to do with, this may not be very noticeable to you. However, if you change this setting and you notice that your computer seems to crawl as you get up to 100 or so history states, you now have an idea of what may be going on.

Before you get your hopes up, you should understand that the section for History Log isn't what it sounds like. The name of that section at least implies that you can save your history with your files so that you can go through them again the next time you open them up. That isn't what that is for. Instead, if enabled, this feature saves the text of the history (as well as session and action information if you so choose) to the metadata of the file. This really won't impact you very much. If you open your file by using something like File ⇨ Open, you will not notice any difference. In fact, in your history palette, you will only see the opening of your file. The only way to see the text is by using something like Adobe Bridge, which is something like an advanced photo explorer that shows all of the files in a directory and their relevant information (e.g., file size, format, etc.). If you are using Adobe Bridge, there is a palette that has a metadata tab. Using that tab you can view the text of all changes made to a file. However, this isn't exactly the same thing as being able to just go back through your history and make changes as necessary.

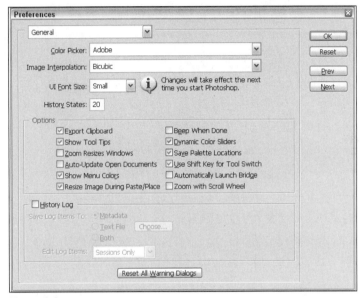

Figure 3-9

If you have a clear understanding of these concepts, you are ready to begin the project that will be used throughout this book.

Your First Graphics

In this section, you will begin to work on the graphics and color schemes of the book project. You will start with basic stock photos, which you will learn techniques to manipulate and tweak to fit the requirements of the book project. You want the entire width of the entire web content to fit in an 800 × 600 display. This means you will need to resize the images to fit this requirement. You will want to add text and some graphic styling to the stock photo to make it custom for this project. Finally, you will want to use the colors in the final image to select a color scheme that will be used throughout the remaining chapters of this book.

Later, you will learn how to create a second header graphic (learning more new techniques) that you can use in place of the one created in this section. You will also learn how to convert that image into one that is more compatible with mobile browsers. By the end of this chapter, you will have created two distinct header graphics for desktop/laptop browsers and one header graphic for mobile devices. You will also create complementary color schemes for these graphics that you can reuse as the project develops.

For this example, you will need to find a good surfing image. Using Photos To Go Unlimited, there are several potential images that would serve these purposes. For this tutorial, you can use Image 854489, which is shown unedited in Figure 3-10 (if you have saved the image to your hard drive, you can click File ⇨ Open to find the image and open it up in Photoshop).

As mentioned earlier in the chapter, these images are from Photos To Go Unlimited (`http://unlimited.photostogo.com`). *Image numbers are provided so that you can easily find, download, and work with the same images.*

Figure 3-10

Okay, this isn't a longboard, but it's still a pretty cool image. And it will be the basis for the first logo.

Image Size and Manipulation

The first step you will need to do is to evaluate the size and, potentially, resize this image to fit the dimensions of this project. The width is the most important consideration for this graphic, as you want to make sure it fits in the requirements of an 800 × 600 screen resolution. You can't make the image 800 pixels wide because you have to take into consideration the area that is consumed by the scrollbars and borders of the browser. While there are different opinions for what is a safe width to use, none of them go below 700 pixels. So, for this example, you want the header graphic to be, in its final form, approximately 700 pixels wide and 300 pixels high. The 300 pixels high is a fairly arbitrary setting. What you want is something that looks good and doesn't overwhelm the visitors to the site. In all honesty, 300 pixels may be too big. However, for this image, 300 pixels is at least a starting point. If you see that it is too much as the project matures, you can resize it later using the techniques learned in this chapter.

With the image open in Photoshop, you can easily determine the size of the photo by clicking Image ⇨ Image Size. This will produce the screen shown in Figure 3-11.

As you can see, this image has a dimension of 1105 pixels wide and 731 pixels high. The first step is to resize it to 700 pixels wide. This will automatically make the height 463 pixels, which is above our required 300 pixels, meaning we will need to crop the image later. For now, click the OK button to accept the resizing.

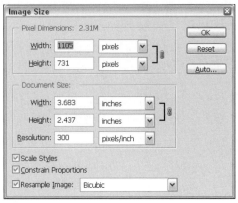

Figure 3-11

You should now have an image that is 700 pixels wide and 463 pixels high and looks identical to the previous version. You now need to crop the image to fit the 300 pixel height requirement. There are, as with most things in programming, several ways to do this. For this example, you can use the Canvas Size to automatically crop the photo for you. To do this, click on Image ⇨ Canvas Size to get the dialog box depicted in Figure 3-12.

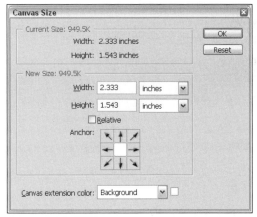

Figure 3-12

For web design, inches doesn't really mean very much. So, in the height section, select "pixels." This will update both the width and height to pixels, which are more easily used in this project. Change the textbox for Height to 300.

In the anchor section, you are telling the method how to chop off the extra parts of the image. For example, we are taking a 463 pixel high image and chopping off 163 pixels to reduce it to only 300 pixels high. The application needs to know where to chop the 163 pixels from. All from the top? All from the bottom? Half from each? The default is to split the difference and take half of the pixels from the top and half from the bottom. The little white box in the anchor area signifies which part of the current image will remain. So, in Figure 3-12, it shows that the part that will remain is in the center of the image. If you were to select the box immediately above the current location of the white box, you would get something looking like Figure 3-13.

Figure 3-13

Doing this would result in all 163 pixels coming off of the bottom of the image, meaning that the new image would only consist of the top 300 pixels of the image. However, in this case, you want to preserve the image of the surfer, which is near the middle of the image. So, for this particular image, you want to keep the part that is in the middle. So accept the defaults that are illustrated in Figure 3-12. Click OK to continue. You will receive a warning message informing you that the new image dimensions are smaller than the originals and, consequently, some clipping will occur. This is the desired behavior, so just click Proceed to clip the image. This should result in an image similar to the one depicted in Figure 3-14.

Figure 3-14

Translucent Boxes

The next step is to add a couple of semi-transparent boxes on the top and bottom of the image. The top box will be used in conjunction with text to set apart the label of the site ("surfer5 Internet Solutions"). Similarly, you will use the bottom box to distinguish the site navigation that you will create in Chapter 6. These areas are included strictly for aesthetic or stylistic reasons. However, using semi-transparent areas of an image is a good way to draw attention to whatever you are placing on top of those areas.

In order to make this a little easier, you may want to stretch out the box that encompasses your image. To do so, look for the little drag area on the lower-right side of the box (depicted in Figure 3-15).

Figure 3-15

If you drag the box a little bigger, you will have something that looks more like Figure 3-16.

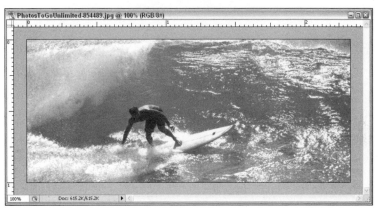

Figure 3-16

Doing this allows you to click on the gray area surrounding the actual image, which makes selecting the x- and y-coordinates of (0, 0) much easier to do, which is what you want to be able to do for the next step.

You need to first find the Rectangular Marquee Tool, shown in Figure 3-17.

Figure 3-17

This is located at the top-left corner of the Tools palette. If something shows up besides the Rectangular Marquee Tool, just click on whatever it is and hold your mouse button down. A list should come up with options that are available for this button, one of which should be the Rectangular Marquee Tool. When the options come up, navigate to the proper tool and release your mouse button. Once you have this tool selected, click somewhere in the gray area of the picture box above and to the left of the upper-left corner of the image. Hold your mouse button down as you drag a box that goes all the way over to the other side of the border and around 10–15% of the way down the image. This will produce a selected area that is designated by a moving dashed line, often referred to as the "marching ants," as shown in Figure 3-18.

Figure 3-18

Layers

You will now need to create a new layer (up to this point you should only have had one layer, the background layer comprising the above picture). If you take nothing else away from this chapter, learn to appreciate and love layers. Layers allow you to modify the look and feel of a particular image without damaging that image. For this example, you are going to put the semi-transparent boxes on their own layer. This way, the transparency of the boxes will allow the stock surfing photo to show through them, which affects the overall look and feel of the image. However, if you were to remove or hide the layer that contained the new boxes, the original image would look exactly as it did. Remember, layers are seen in a linear fashion from the top down. So each layer overlays the layers below it. If this isn't entirely clear, it will be as this chapter progresses.

To create a new layer, select Layer ⇨ New ⇨ Layer from the menu bar. This will give you the screen depicted in Figure 3-19.

Figure 3-19

In the name box, change the default to "top bar" or something else that will remind you what this layer is for (you will be glad of this when you have images with dozens of layers). Also, because this layer is going to be semi-transparent, set the opacity to 65%. Click OK to create your new layer. Your layer palette should now look something like Figure 3-20.

Figure 3-20

This indicates that you now have two layers; a background layer that is the surfing image and a new layer that will be used for the top bar. With the top bar layer active, you will now need to paint the selected area. To do this, you need to select the Paint Bucket Tool from the Tools palette, which is shown in Figure 3-21.

Figure 3-21

Like the Marquee Select Tool before, this button may be hidden behind another button (the Gradient Tool). If you do not see the Paint Bucket Tool but do see the Gradient Tool, click on the Gradient Tool and hold your mouse button. You should see options presented, one of which should be the Paint Bucket Tool. Navigate to the Paint Bucket Tool and release your mouse button. This should enable that tool.

You now need to pick the color you want to paint with. If you look at the bottom of your Tools palette, you will see tools for setting the foreground and background colors (see Figure 3-22).

Figure 3-22

The big boxes show the current selections, with the top-left one being the foreground and the lower-right one being the background color. So, by default, the foreground is Black and the background is White. If you ever have something else showing and you want to go back to the default black and white configuration, you can click the smaller boxes in the lower-left corner and this will bring you back to the default. However, what you want for this example is a white foreground, since the Paint Bucket Tool is going to paint with the foreground color. The easiest way to do this is to simply click on the bent double arrow. This reverses the two colors currently selected (sets the foreground color as the background color and vice versa). This will make the foreground white and the background black.

With this configuration, and with the "top bar" layer active, click anywhere in the selected area. This will paint that entire selection the foreground color, in this instance white, resulting in something that looks like Figure 3-23 (you can press Ctrl-D to remove the selection after painting the area).

Figure 3-23

You should be able to see that there is now a white box at the top of the image that allows for some of the details of the background image to come through. You want to create a similar bar at the bottom of the image so as to frame in the surfer. Rather than going through all of the steps you did before and risking having uneven boxes (if you reselect an area at the bottom you can't guarantee that it is the same dimensions as the top one), you can simply create a copy of the current layer. There are a couple of ways of doing this, but the simplest is to make sure the "top bar" layer is selected and press Ctrl-J on your keyboard. That will create an exact copy of the layer and name it "top bar copy." This layer should also now be the active layer. The problem is that, as an exact copy, it is sitting in the same location as the other layer. So you want to drag it to the bottom of the image. In order to do this, you need to select the Move Tool on the Tools palette, which is shown in Figure 3-24.

Figure 3-24

Once you do this, you will notice that handles come up around the boundaries of the layer. These handles will allow you to stretch the image or rotate it or do a number of other things. However, all you want to do at this point is drag the layer to the bottom of the image. So click anywhere in the layer (within the confines of the handles), and simply drag the layer to the bottom. Make sure that the layer gets all the way to the bottom of the image, resulting in the image shown in Figure 3-25.

You now have two identically sized semi-transparent bars at the top and bottom of the image. You may want to rename the bottom bar just so that it is named something more indicative of what it really is than "top bar copy." To do this, click on the layer and select Layer Properties. This will give you the options presented in Figure 3-26.

You can change the name to something like "bottom bar" that will make more sense in six months when you come back to edit this file. You will notice as you are typing in the Name field that the layer is automatically updated in Photoshop. Once you have the name you want, click OK.

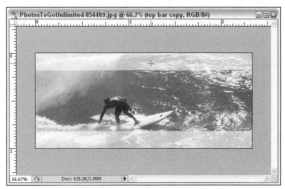

Figure 3-25

Figure 3-26

Next, you want to create a couple of solid bars around the semi-transparent ones to set them apart from the surfing image. To do this, you need to create a new layer. So, select Layer ⇨ New ⇨ Layer to get the New Layer options. Change the Name field to "solid lines" and keep the opacity at 100%. Click the OK button to create this layer. With the "solid lines" layer active, hold down the Ctrl button and click on the "top bar" layer thumbnail image (the small image to the left of the text "top bar" in the Layers palette). This will create a selection area around the entire top bar layer, while keeping the "solid lines" layer active. Once you have done this, select Edit ⇨ Stroke to get the Stroke properties (stroke is just drawing a line around a selection, whether that be text or an image or a drawn object), as shown in Figure 3-27.

Figure 3-27

You will want to set the width to 5 px (5 pixels). You can just type in **5** and Photoshop will use pixels; you don't have to specify "px." For this particular use, you want to make sure that the Location is set to Outside. This will draw the lines on the outside of the selection, so in this example, you will only see the effect on the bottom of the selection, since the outside of the selection area for the sides and top falls outside of the image itself.

Repeat these steps for the "bottom bar" selection. This will create the image shown in Figure 3-28.

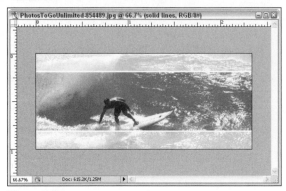

Figure 3-28

This probably is not easily noticeable in the context of this manuscript, but hopefully you will notice the effect in Photoshop.

Text

The final modification you need to make to this image before exporting it to a web graphic is to add some text. To do this, choose the Horizontal Type Tool on the Tools palette, as depicted in Figure 3-29.

Figure 3-29

With this tool selected, click somewhere around the center of the top of the image (to give you room to type). When you do this, the top of Photoshop will change to show the text-editing toolbar, as shown in Figure 3-30.

Figure 3-30

The first drop-down box allows you to set the font for the text you are typing. In the example for this chapter, Viner Hand ITC was used. If this is not available on your system, just choose a font that is appealing to you. You can also set the font size using the third drop-down box. One of the better settings in these options is the text color editor, which looks like the solid-colored box after the alignment options. Clicking anywhere in this box brings up the Color Picker Tool, as shown in Figure 3-31.

You can select anywhere in the big box to choose any color you want. If you are not in the right shade, you can click anywhere in the rainbow area to move to that hue (e.g., move to the orange and that will change the big box to shades of orange from which you can now choose). But the cooler way to choose your color is to pick it directly from the image itself.

With the Color Picker still up, move it over a bit so that you can see your image. Move your cursor over the image and you will notice that it turns into what looks like a little eyedropper. Click anywhere in the image, and the Color Picker will use that color. You can click several times in the image until you find a color that you like. When you are done, click OK.

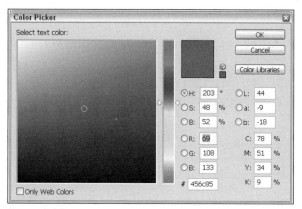

Figure 3-31

The cool thing about doing it this way is that you are sure that the color you pick will complement the colors of your image because you are using a color directly from the image. This is a good way to make sure that everything flows. You should take care, though, that the colors you pick do not blend too much into the background colors. For example, if you chose a really light color, the text of "surfer5 Internet Solutions" would be lost on its white background.

The other nice thing about the Color Picker is that it gives you the color properties in several useful formats, including RGB and hex. Many web development color schemes are based on Hex colors. So, when you need your color in hex, just use the Color Picker; pick your color, look at most lower-left textbox, and copy that value, and you now have the hex value for your CSS files or other ASP.NET controls. Pretty cool.

> *Note: CSS also provides for using the* RGB() *method to define colors (e.g.,* background-color: rgb(0,0,0);)*. However, it is easier to copy and paste one value (hex) than to copy and paste each of three RGB values into your CSS document. It is worth knowing, though, that if you should find it useful, RGB is supported in CSS.*

Once you have all of your options set, you can type the name of the site: **surfer5 Internet Solutions**. When you are done, make sure that you press the checkmark at the right-hand side of the text toolbar. Once you have finished, you will have something resembling Figure 3-32.

Figure 3-32

Saving the Image

That should be pretty much all you need to do for this image before saving it to an acceptable format for the web. However, before doing this, you need to save this image (if you haven't done so already). To save a Photoshop file, select File ⇨ Save As (or File ⇨ Save, if you have saved it previously), and then choose the location you want to save your file to. Make sure that you keep the resulting file in the proprietary PSD format. This will preserve your layers so that you can go back and make changes later as necessary.

The tricky part of this particular save is that you want to chop this image into two smaller images. Why? Because the bottom bar area will be used for the background for a navigation area that you will build in Chapter 6. So that means we need one image that is the bottom bar area and one image that is the rest of the image (everything except the bottom bar area). These will be seamlessly placed together later to make it look like one image, but, for now, you can save them separately.

To do this, it is not as hard as it may seem. With any layer active (it doesn't matter which one), hold the Ctrl button down on your keyboard and click in the layer thumbnail area of the "bottom bar" layer, thereby selecting all of the contents of that layer. Once you have just the bottom area selected, select Image ⇨ Crop, and Photoshop will crop your image to the new dimensions, only including the "bottom bar" layer dimensions (you will be very glad you saved your image at this point . . . just in case). Now, to export this image to a web format, you need to select File ⇨ Save For Web to get the Save For Web properties screen. If it is not already selected, choose the 4-up tab at the top of the screen to give you a view of four different options for saving your image (see Figure 3-33).

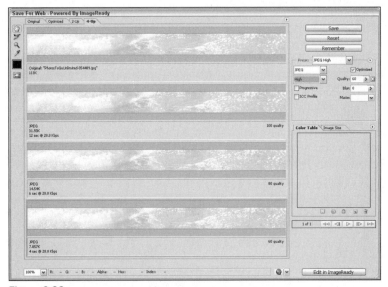

Figure 3-33

The nice thing about the 4-up tab is that you can change the settings for your exported image in four different ways and compare the quality and file size of each. In this example, there is the original file, which weighs in at 111KB all the way down to the High quality JPG (60%) at only 7.857KB. To change the settings for one of the four views, click on it and then change the parameters to the right. You can select

PNG, GIF, JPEG, or BMP formats. You can set the compression ratio. You can set the transparency. You can compare the quality and file size of each change to find the one that best meets your needs.

For this project, you can use JPG at the High setting, which should yield acceptable quality and a small file size.

Click the Save button to save the image to your hard drive. This will close the Save For Web tool and take you back into your project in Photoshop.

Now the History palette will come in handy. You should see a long list of history states in the History palette; the last two were probably something like Crop and Load Selection. If you click on the Load Selection history state, you will have your full image back and it should still have the "bottom bar" layer content selected. Now choose Select ➪ Inverse to invert the selection (i.e., you will now have everything besides the "bottom bar" layer content selected). You should now crop your image (choose Image ➪ Crop) and then save the image using the same settings as before (JPEG High). When you come back to your image in Photoshop, you might want to use the History palette to return to the full image and then save again just to be sure that you didn't mess anything up.

The end result should be that you have two new images, resembling Figures 3-34 and 3-35, which will be pushed together in your web project to look like one image. This means that you will have a header graphic region that is simply there for stylistic reasons and then the navigation area seamlessly attached below it. The header graphic area will be Figure 3-34, and the navigation area will have a background of Figure 3-35. These images will be defined in your CSS code generated in Chapter 4, modified to include the site navigation in Chapter 6, and then, finally, included in your site template in Chapter 7.

Figure 3-34

Figure 3-35

Picking a Color Scheme

Once you have your image, it is a good idea to go ahead and choose some colors to make up your web page. Generally speaking, you are going to want a dark and light color to use in the content of your pages (e.g., alternating row colors on GridView controls, content header colors, etc.) as well as a background color that will show outside of the content of the website you design.

First, you want to create a new image that will hold your color scheme data (call it something like `color_scheme.PSD`). It doesn't really matter the dimensions but, for the purposes of this tutorial, you can use a width of 600 pixels and a height of 150 pixels.

You can do this fairly easily using the tools that you have already seen. First, while you still have your image open, you want to select the Eyedropper Tool shown in Figure 3-36.

Figure 3-36

As you drag your cursor over your image, you will see that the color in the Color Foreground box (lower portion of the toolbox) changes to reflect the color you are currently hovering over. Move your cursor around the image to see if you can find a good color for the dark, light, and background colors of your website.

While in your color scheme image, draw a box using the Rectangular Marquee Tool demonstrated earlier. Now, in the logo image, find a color that you like for your dark color. This will be the color used for headings and maybe even the font colors. You can now paint the rectangle selection area in the `color_scheme` file with this color. Before you go looking for a different color, double-click on the Color Foreground area of your toolbox. This will bring up the Color Picker Tool discussed earlier in this chapter. From that screen, copy the hexadecimal color and save it for later use in your CSS and HTML documents.

Repeat the process to find a lighter accent color and a background color. You don't need to be particularly careful about the placement of the rectangles because you are probably the only one who will see the file; you only need it as a reference for when you are selecting colors later in the web design process. Make sure that you record the hexadecimal colors for use in the subsequent chapters of this book.

The hexadecimal colors identified through this process are:

Color Name	Hexadecimal Color
Dark Color	477897
Light Color	bcdbfa
Background Color	4d6267

At this point, you should have the logo for your web project as well as a color scheme that complements the logo. You should also have a fair understanding of some of the elementary functions of Adobe Photoshop CS2. In the next lesson, though, you will learn a few more tips and tricks to add to your arsenal of graphic design tools.

A Second Graphic

To expand the concepts learned with your first header graphic, this section will show you a different set of tips and techniques for creating a different header graphic. It should be noted that the graphic created in this section will not be used in the remaining chapters of this book. Rather, it is provided to show additional techniques that you should be familiar with as you begin working with the graphic arts. However, you should also be aware of the fact that the mobile graphics created later in this chapter are dependent on the graphics created in this section.

If you like the graphics in this section better, feel free to use them as a substitute for the graphics created earlier in this chapter as the book project matures through the subsequent chapters. This may help you think of what you are actually doing when you are creating the project rather than simply copying and pasting code verbatim from the manuscript.

If there is one universal trick that most people seem to use in Photoshop at some time or another it is selecting a piece of one image and moving it into another. For example, earlier in this chapter you saw how a family was cut out of a photo from a beach scene and dropped into a cityscape backdrop. There are a lot of interesting uses for this idea and at least as many ways in Photoshop to accomplish it, each with its pros and cons. For example, some methods are quick but leave very pixilated images that look grainy and unprofessional. Other ways are time-consuming but yield excellent results. In this lesson, you will learn one of the easier (and more reliable) ways of doing this trick. There are approaches that will yield better results, but they are more complicated and time-consuming. This approach will teach you a solid approach to cutting out the silhouette from an image with acceptable accuracy and is fairly easy to use.

The first step is to pick out an image that you want to extract something out of. Since the theme for this project is surfing, it would be nice to have something surf related. To this end, you might use Image 495856, which can be seen in Figure 3-37.

As mentioned earlier in the chapter, these images are from Photos To Go Unlimited (`http://unlimited.photostogo.com`). Image numbers are provided so that you can easily find, download, and work with the same images.

Figure 3-37

Because this will be going on the logo that is only going to be 300 pixels high, you need to resize the image to that dimension. So select Image ➪ Image Size, set the height to 300 pixels, and click OK. This should produce a file that is 462 pixels wide and 300 pixels high.

Selecting and Extracting Images

You want to extract only the surfer and surfboard, completely cutting out all of the background stuff. There are many ways to do this but, what often seems the best and easiest is to use a tool called the Magnetic Lasso Tool, which can be seen in Figure 3-38.

Figure 3-38

Like some of the other tools previously discussed, the Magnetic Lasso Tool may not be immediately visible on the Tools palette. In fact, by default, the Lasso Tool is displayed. If this is the case, click the button and hold your mouse button down until options are presented, one of which should be the Magnetic Lasso Tool. Navigate over to the Magnetic Lasso Tool and then release your mouse button. The Magnetic Lasso Tool should now be active. After you do this, your toolbar at the top of Photoshop should change to look more like Figure 3-39.

Figure 3-39

The feather value allows you to soften the edges of your selection. For this demonstration, you don't want that, so you can leave the value at 0px. The other values you may want to play with would be:

❑   **Width** — For this demonstration, this is how big the selection tool gets. When using this tool, you will have a crosshair icon that you run over the part of the image you are trying to select. The analysis of contrast is done within this crosshair section. The tool automatically detects the change in contrast and makes the selection based on this difference. So the bigger the number in this field, the bigger the crosshair tool is. For a highly contrasted image with not a lot of nooks and crannies, you can use a higher number; otherwise you should stick to a lower number. The image you will be using has a pretty distinct contrast between what you will be selecting and what you will not be, and much of the selection is very smooth, so it is fairly safe to use a bigger number. However, you shouldn't need anything above 10 pixels.

❑   **Edge Contrast** — As stated above, this tool works by detecting the contrast between the object you are selecting and the background, which you do not want to select. So, if you have a bright white background and a very colorful object to select, there is a high contrast (so you can use a high number in this field). If, however, the contrast is not nearly as evident, as is the case with a black object on a dark gray background, you would need to use a much smaller number. This is something you can play around with when you start using the tool. If you find that you aren't grabbing the edges of what you want to grab as effectively as you would like, then you may need to adjust this number.

❑   **Frequency** — This represents the rate at which the tool will drop anchors around your selection. As you are making your selection, you will see little boxes appear (they look like the handles around images). These are the anchors, or fastening points, for the selection. If you are selecting a relatively smooth image, you may not need them to be dropped as frequently. If you are using an image with a lot of nooks and crannies, you may need to drop them more frequently. Again, this is a number you will have to play around with to see what best meets your needs.

Once you have your settings similar to those in Figure 3-39, you are ready to begin. As you hover your mouse over the image, you will see the cursor looks much like the icon for the tool. To make it look like the crosshairs mentioned previously, press the Caps Lock on your keyboard. Within the crosshair section you want to have pieces of both what you are selecting and what you aren't. You need to have both so that the tool can determine the contrast shift and make the selection. Figure 3-40 shows you what a decent placement might look like.

Figure 3-40

You can see that the tool is basically centered between the surfboard and the background. The actual cross is directly on the line you want to select on. You don't have to be this precise (having the cross on the line you are selecting), but you do need to make sure that you have both the area you want to select and the area you want to omit within the circle of the tool.

Now you are set to make your selection. Hover over part of the image that you want to start your selection (maybe somewhere on the surfboard) and click your mouse. You do not need to hold the mouse button down. You can now start following the edges of the image you are trying to cut out. As you do so, you will notice the fastening points adhering to the edges of the image. Hopefully, your image selection will begin to look something like Figure 3-41.

Figure 3-41

When you get back to your original position, double-click on your mouse button and the selection will connect to the starting point. You should now have your entire selected area within a selection boundary (the marching ants), similar to Figure 3-42.

Figure 3-42

Background

Now you are going to want to drop the selection onto a different background (at least in this instance). So you need to decide what type of background you want to use. For this example, you want to use a dramatic sunset as the backdrop. The image used, Image 603896, can be seen in Figure 3-43.

As mentioned earlier in the chapter, these images are from Photos To Go Unlimited (`http://unlimited.photostogo.com`). *Image numbers are provided so that you can easily find, download, and work with the same images.*

Figure 3-43

You will need to resize this image and crop it again. So select Image ⇨ Image Size, set the width to 700 pixels, and then click OK. This will reduce the image to 700 pixels wide by 468 pixels high. You now need to reduce the image to 300 pixels high. Select Image ➪ Canvas Size, and set the height to 300 pixels, leaving the Anchor area alone (it is fine to have the pixels deleted from both the top and the bottom evenly). Click OK. You should now have an image that is 700 pixels wide by 300 pixels high and looks similar to Figure 3-44.

Figure 3-44

With your surfer still selected, you can copy that selection to the clipboard by selecting Edit ➪ Copy. Now go back to the background image and paste the surfer into it by selecting Edit ➪ Paste. This will likely paste the surfer to the center of the image. You should be able to drag him over to the lower left-hand corner so that your image now resembles Figure 3-45.

Figure 3-45

Silhouettes

This isn't exactly the desired effect, so you need to do one more thing to the surfer image: make it a silhouette. The first step is to make sure that the background color is set to black, as shown in Figure 3-46.

Figure 3-46

Remembering the earlier discussion, you may have to set this if you have modified the properties previously. To get it to this state, first click on the small black and white boxes in the lower-left corner. This will return the colors to their default (black foreground and white background colors). To reverse this, click on the bent double arrow. You should now have a white foreground and a black background color.

Once you have done this, make sure that your surfer layer is active and then press Shift-Ctrl-Backspace at the same time. This will fill the entire contents of that layer with the background color (black in this case), resulting in an image similar to Figure 3-47.

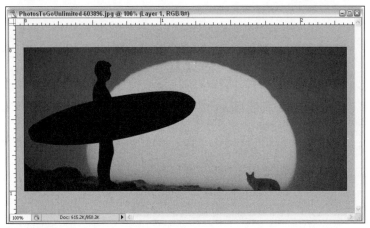

Figure 3-47

Obviously, the wolf looks a little out of place. It also might be nice to just make everything that isn't the sunset be a silhouette (or at least appear to be one). The easiest way to do this is just to draw over all of that with a black brush using the Brush Tool, which is shown in Figure 3-48.

Figure 3-48

You may need to adjust the parameters of the brush using the toolbar at the top of Photoshop, shown in Figure 3-49.

To get the drop-down menu items, simply press the down arrow next to the Brush icons. You want to set the Hardness to 100%. A softer brush will produce an airbrush or graffiti effect. With the hardness set to 100%, the edges of the brush will be solid. The master diameter is set to 24 pixels for this example, but that is fairly arbitrary. Pick a size that works for you and looks good.

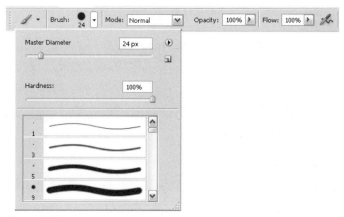

Figure 3-49

You will also need to set your foreground color back to black (you can just reset the colors back to their defaults as shown a few steps back).

The layer you paint on really isn't that important. You may want to just paint on top of the background layer. Or maybe you want to paint on the surfer layer, keeping the background layer intact while covering up the parts you want to hide. Or maybe you want to create an entire new layer (Layer ➪ New ➪ Layer) just for the paint brush stuff. This is really up to you. Regardless of which approach you take, you should paint the bottom of the image by holding down your mouse button and moving the cursor across the area you want to cover up. The end result should look something like Figure 3-50.

Figure 3-50

Text

You now need to add the same text as the other logo, "surfer5 Internet Solutions," in the upper-right corner of the image. For this logo, use a 7-point Pristina font for the text. For now, it really doesn't matter what color you use because you are going to back it out in the next step. At this point, your image should resemble Figure 3-51 (which uses black for the font).

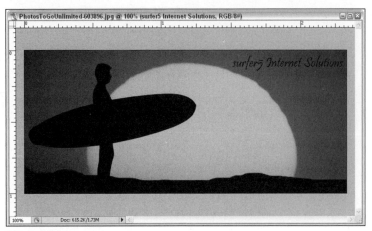

Figure 3-51

Now you need to add some formatting to the font. So, while the text layer is active, right-click on the layer and, from the options presented, select Blending Options and then click on Outer Glow. You should now see the screen displayed in Figure 3-52.

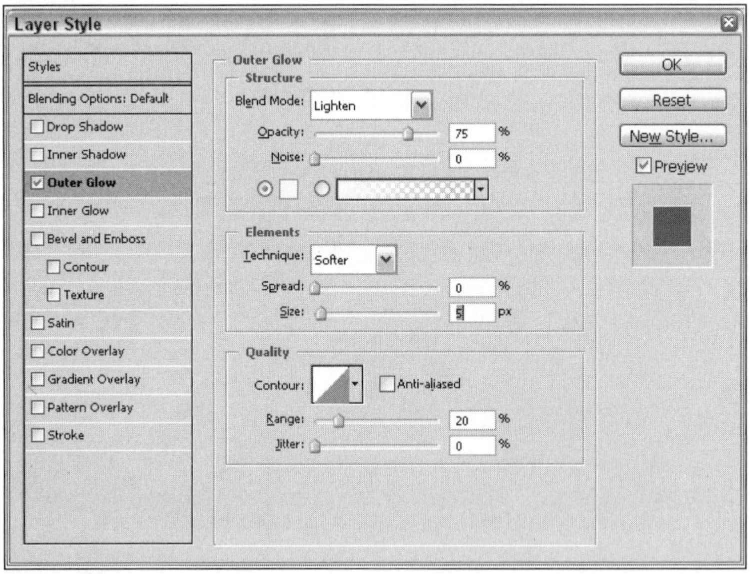

Figure 3-52

You will need to tweak the properties on this screen a bit to get the effect you are going after. For this example, try setting the Spread to 0, the Size to 5, and the Range to 20. You should be able to see the effect being applied to the text behind the Layer Style window. Once you are happy with the effect, click OK to apply it. You should now have an image that looks like Figure 3-53.

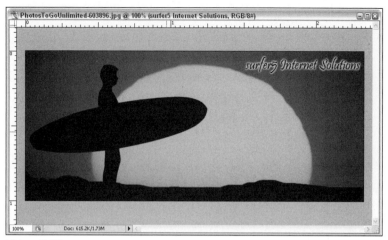

Figure 3-53

This is a good point to talk about the difference between opacity and fill with regard to layers. If you look at your layer palette, you will see that there is a setting for Opacity and one for Fill. In many regards, they seem like they do the same thing. In the very first example with the family dropped on a cityscape, if you set the Opacity of the red box to 50% or the Fill to 50%, you will accomplish essentially the same thing. However, with this type of text layer, where layer styles are applied, these two take on entirely different effects. What happens when you drop the opacity down to 10%, for example, is that the entire layer's opacity goes down to 10%, as illustrated in Figure 3-54.

Figure 3-54

However, if you keep the opacity at 100% and drop the fill to 10% instead, the text's opacity drops to 10%, but the opacity of the layer style (the outer glow in this instance) stays at 100%, resulting in something like Figure 3-55.

Figure 3-55

You can see that the glow is still at 100% but that the text inside of it is faded to almost nothing. Instead, you can see the gradient of the background through the text. This can provide some pretty cool effects.

For this logo, though, drop the Fill all the way to 0 and leave the opacity at 100%. This should give you an image similar to Figure 3-56.

Figure 3-56

Optional Modification

Although the image could probably stand alone, it might be kind of cool to put some binary code coming up in the sky, since this will be the personal site of a computer geek. And geeks love binary code.

To do this, you will need to do a couple of things. First and foremost, you will notice that your background layer is different from all of your other layers, as shown in Figure 3-57.

Figure 3-57

The easy thing to spot, perhaps, is that there is an image of a lock on the layer. You will also see that the font is in italics for the Background layer, which isn't true of any of the other layers. This is a locked background layer, which limits what you can do to it. First, you can't put any layers below it. You also cannot have any transparency on this layer. What you really need to do is convert this layer to a standard layer. To do this, double-click anywhere on the layer in the layer palette. Doing so will bring up the property pane shown in Figure 3-58.

Figure 3-58

As shown in Figure 3-58, you should name the layer something you will remember (in this case, "sunset") and set the mode to Darken. This is because you are going to overlay this layer on top of a layer of binary code text. Click OK to continue.

You should now see that your background layer is a standard layer. The lock image is gone, and the name of the layer is no longer in italics. You are ready to proceed.

You will need to add your binary code as text. You can just type a bunch of zeros and ones; nobody can tell what it means anyway. Or, if you are so inclined, you can use a binary code translator and hide some cool phrase in binary. Even if you are the only one that knows it is there, it's still kind of cool.

Either way, you should end up with a layer that looks similar to Figure 3-59 (this uses a 7-point Agency FB font).

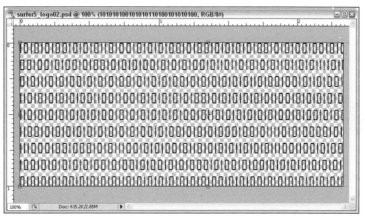

Figure 3-59

This layer needs to be at the bottom of the image so, if it is anywhere above the bottom, you need to click on it in the Layer palette and drag it to the bottom position (below the sunset layer). This will create an image similar to Figure 3-60.

The next thing you might want to do is change the color of the font. There are a couple of ways of doing this, but probably the easiest is to add a layer style to the font layer. So you will need to right-click on the layer and choose Blending Options and then, when the Layer Style screen appears, click on the Color Overlay section, as depicted in Figure 3-61.

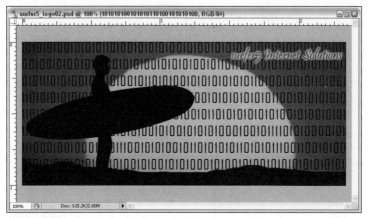

Figure 3-60

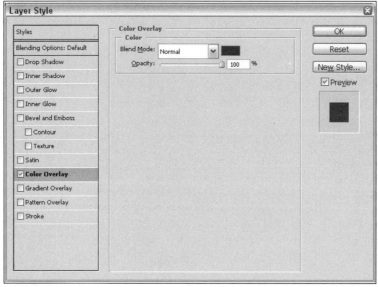

Figure 3-61

If you click on the solid color in the Color section (next to the drop-down box), you will get the Color Picker again. What you want to do is pick a color that is the darker shade of the red in the image. This means that, as the shade of reds approach that darker color, the binary code will fade away. Once you find a color you like, click OK. Hopefully, you ended up with something like Figure 3-62.

As you can see, the binary code fades out as it approaches the sides of the graphic. The only thing left to do is to delete the binary code from the sun so that it is just in the sky. This isn't as simple as it sounds, though. You can't just delete part of a text layer. You have to first convert it to a standard layer. The downside to that is that you lose the ability to modify the type. So, if in a couple of months somebody figures out that your binary code translates to something embarrassing, you have to redo the entire layer instead of just adding a zero or a one in a few strategic places (and hope that it doesn't now say something even worse).

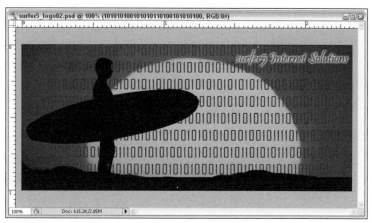

Figure 3-62

So what you may want to do first is make a copy of the layer and then make it invisible. That is one nice feature about layers; you don't have to display them in the final result. This is a good way to store a history state. In other words, if you want to preserve the history state of this binary code layer immediately before converting it to a layer for which you can no longer edit the type, you can make a copy of it at that particular state and then turn it off so that it doesn't impact the rest of the image. That way, when someone tells you that you really need to think about adjusting what your binary message says, you can do it fairly easily.

So, while on the binary code text layer, simply press Ctrl-J to make an exact copy of that layer. Then, on the layer that you want to use to maintain your history state, click on the little eye next to the layer (to the left), as shown in Figure 3-63. This will make that layer invisible.

Figure 3-63

Now you need to convert this text layer to a graphic layer. In Photoshop, this is called rasterizing the layer. To do this, right-click on the layer you want to convert and select Rasterize Type. Your layer is now a graphic layer that you can treat much like any other graphic layer you have been working with up to this point. You will notice that the layer itself, in the layer palette, has changed to look like a graphic layer rather than a text layer, as shown in Figure 3-64.

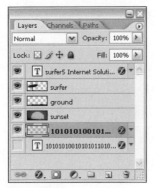

Figure 3-64

At this point, you want to erase the part of the image that is in the sun. There are several ways to do this. However, for this example, you will see how to use one of the more controversial tools in the Photoshop arsenal of tricks: the Magic Wand.

In some circles, this is referred to as the "Tragic Wand" because the results are so unpredictable and often not what you are looking for. It is nothing to see very pixilated rough edges around your images after using the Magic Wand to select your area. However, in some circumstances, it is the perfect tool. And for this one, it is the best fit. Just be warned; it is not the perfect tool for all of your selection needs. It serves its purpose, but just be careful that you don't expect it to exceed its limitations.

The Magic Wand tool has its own button, so you won't have to worry about it being hidden behind another icon. You can see it in Figure 3-65.

Figure 3-65

When selected, the Magic Wand has several options appear on the toolbar at the top of Photoshop, as shown in Figure 3-66.

Figure 3-66

The most important setting for this purpose is the tolerance. If you have it set at 1, the Magic Wand will only capture contingent pixels that are the exact same color as the pixel you selected. As you increase the number in the tolerance field, the farther away from the original pixel color the acceptable color in the selection of contingent pixels will be. In other words, your selection area will probably get larger. So if you have an image of a summer sky and you have a tolerance set to 1, you may only grab five or six pixels of, say, blue where all of the colors are exactly the same. If you set the tolerance to 100, you may end up grabbing the entire sky, even if there are very wispy light clouds in the scene because they are similar enough in color as to be caught in the selection. This just takes practice to get used to.

In this project, though, you just want to delete the area of the text where the sun is. The good thing about this image is that the sun is a bright yellow and is immediately met by a strong contrasting red. So the Magic Wand Tool will be excellent for this use. Simply jack up the tolerance to 100 and then click anywhere in the sun area (making sure the sunset layer is the active layer). This should give you a selection similar to the one in Figure 3-67.

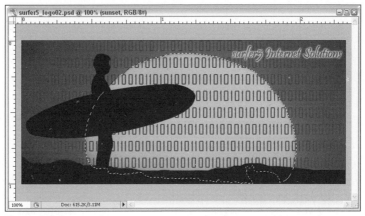

Figure 3-67

Now, in the layers palette, click on the binary text layer (the rasterized one) and press Delete on your keyboard. You should have now deleted all of the binary code text that was on top of the sun, resulting in an image similar to Figure 3-68.

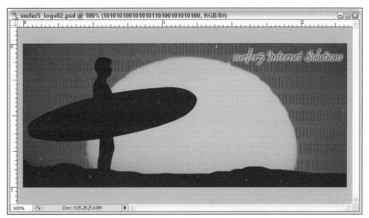

Figure 3-68

You now have a finished logo that is pretty cool and very professional. So you are ready to proceed to the next steps.

Saving the Image

Just as before, you need to save the image (export it) in a format that is consumable by a web browser. Just like in the previous example, you should save to a High JPEG format for a good compromise between quality and file size.

There is one issue, though. In the previous example, there was an area at the bottom designated for a menu that will be added in Chapter 6. If you look at that image, it had a height of 54 pixels. If you use the bottom 54 pixels of this image, you will run into the sun and sky, at some places by a pretty good margin. So it really is not a good idea to match that design of the previous graphics example exactly. Besides, the bottom of the image is a solid black color, which can be easily reproduced in HTML code and using an image for that would be overkill (and increase the site's bandwidth issue).

What you should probably do is just trim off as much of the black area on the bottom of the image as you can without taking away from the rest of the scene. The easiest way to do this is to just adjust the canvas size and move the anchor so that all of the deleted pixels come from the bottom. For this image, that means that you will need to change the canvas size to 275 pixels high. This will result in an image similar to that shown in Figure 3-69.

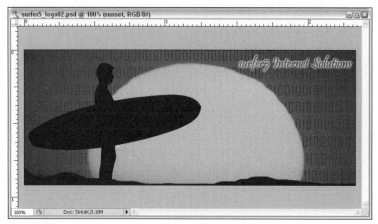

Figure 3-69

When you use this in your web project, you will just need to create an area for the navigation that is solid black and push it up against this image. This will result in a seamless integration between the logo graphic and the navigation area.

Once you have done this, you should export your image (File ➪ Save For Web) to the same High JPEG format used earlier. This will result in the final image shown in Figure 3-70.

Figure 3-70

Color Scheme

Using the same techniques as previously discussed, you can get the color scheme hexadecimal colors shown in the table below.

Color Name	Hexadecimal Color
Dark Color	a20000
Light Color	fb7171
Background Color	520114

At this point, you have finished this second set of graphics, which accomplished several things. First and foremost, it provided you with exposure to additional tools and approaches you can use in your exploration of the graphic arts. But it also provided you with an alternative set of graphics and colors you can use as the book progresses. This will make some of the examples a bit more challenging to follow, since you won't be able to use the code provided verbatim, but that might help solidify some of the concepts for you. Finally, this graphic will be used for the foundation of the mobile graphic, which you will see in the next section.

A Mobile Browser Graphic

If someone tried to visit a site on their mobile browser and there was a 700 pixel wide and 300 pixel high logo greeting them, that is practically all they would see in their browser. So you need to create a much smaller graphic that can be used when the site is accessed by a mobile visitor. To this end, you should choose one of the graphics already created and make it fit more demure dimensions, say 75 pixels high and 300 pixels wide.

Before getting too far into this section, it is important to sit back and consider the obstacles that catering to mobile browsers can create. As just mentioned, there is a reduced screen size (120 pixels wide by 400 pixels high), so having a graphic of 700 pixels wide by 300 pixels high will monopolize the entire screen. But you also need to be aware of things like font size, color depth, and bandwidth issues. For example, a standard font on a desktop browser set to a resolution of 1024 × 768 will look much different in the mobile browser. While color depth isn't quite as relevant with the current mobile browsers, it is still something you should think about. Many of the older mobile browsers had very limited colors, and you should at least take that into consideration when designing your mobile interface. There are readily available mobile device emulators (Visual Studio 2005 has a series installed by default, and you can download more with the Compact Framework SDK). It is a good idea to test your mobile web pages in at least a few emulators (like desktop browsers, the more the better). You will see more on these considerations and emulator testing in Chapter 10.

For this example, you will use the second logo created (the binary skyline surfer silhouette design). The first step, obviously, is to shrink it down. Start with taking it to 75 pixels high using Image ➪ Image Size. This will produce an image that is 75 pixels high and 191 pixels wide. You want to add an extra 109 pixels to the right-hand side of the image using Image ➪ Canvas Size to increase the width to 300 pixels, and modify the anchor to look like Figure 3-71.

Figure 3-71

This will create an image with the necessary dimensions but will have a large transparency area on the right side of the image (designated by the gray and white checkerboard pattern), as shown in Figure 3-72.

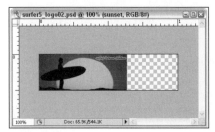

Figure 3-72

As you can see, the binary code is illegible and indecipherable, so there is no real reason to keep it. It just looks like wavy lines and adds confusion to the image. So, in your sunset layer, set the mode to Normal by using the drop-down box at the top of the layers palette (with the sunset layer being the currently active layer). This will make the layer palette look like Figure 3-73.

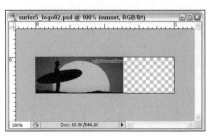

Figure 3-73

Since you are not using the binary code layer, you can either delete them or set them to invisible by clicking on the little eye next to that particular layer in the layer palette.

You now need to create a new layer that will be the bottommost layer (Layer ➪ New ➪ Layer). This should create a completely transparent layer (nothing is on this layer yet). Drag this layer to the bottom of the layer palette, and fill the layer with black using the Paint Bucket Tool (make sure that you set your foreground color to black first). This will create an image that looks like Figure 3-74.

You need a way of fading the original graphic into the black background behind it. This is done fairly easily through the use of a layer mask. A layer mask is a way of modifying an image to show or reveal parts of it without actually destroying the image. For example, with the surfer you cut out for this image, you cut out the entire background. This means that, if in the future you ever wanted the background for some reason, too bad; it's just gone. However, with a mask, you could have achieved the same effect of having the surfer alone in the layer with the background seemingly removed. But instead of having the layer actually deleted, it is just hidden by a layer mask. That way, if you ever did need the background, you could either delete or hide the mask and you would see the background again. This is a preferred method because of its nondestructive nature.

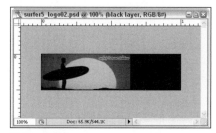

Figure 3-74

In order to apply a layer mask on the sunset layer (make sure that the sunset layer is the active layer), you simply select Layer ⇨ Layer Mask ⇨ Reveal All. This will create a mask on the sunset layer, as shown in Figure 3-75.

Figure 3-75

You will also notice that the layer mask is the active layer right now (it has the bars around its thumbnail image). So any work you do on the image, affects the layer mask and not the graphic in that layer.

The way you fade the image to the layer below it is by painting a gradient fill on the layer mask using the Gradient Tool (located under the Paint Bucket Tool on the Tools palette), as depicted in Figure 3-76.

Figure 3-76

For the best effect, you want to have your colors set to a foreground color of white and a background color of black (the defaults for the layer mask). To fade the image, you are essentially hiding part of the sunset layer. When it is hidden, the black layer shows through. So, to hide part of the layer through a layer mask, you paint that part of the layer black. The part of the layer mask that is still white shows through, the parts that are black are hidden, and the area of the fade is gradually faded away.

To see how this works, click your mouse on the head of the surfer and hold your mouse button. Then drag your mouse down to the lower-right side of the sunset logo. Do not go past the border of the sunset logo (e.g., do not go into the black area). If you go too far, you will be able to see the line between the sunset layer and the black layer when the gradient fill is applied. Your drag area should look similar to Figure 3-77.

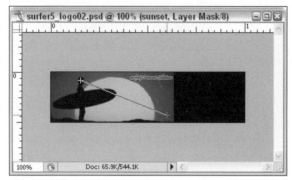

Figure 3-77

When you release your mouse button, the gradient will fill the layer mask and the fade effect will be noticeable, as shown in Figure 3-78.

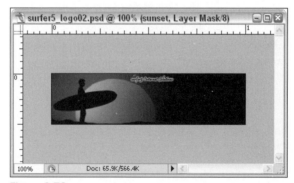

Figure 3-78

The last step for this image is to make the text legible. Like everything else, there are various ways of doing this. Below you will find out about the way that is probably the easiest and most precise way of achieving this.

First, you need to make sure the text layer that you want to modify is the currently active layer. Next, you will need to click on the Move Tool on the Tools palette, shown in Figure 3-79.

When you do this, you will notice little handles will pop up all around the text in the image. At this point, you can drag the handles to resize the image. For example, if you drag one of the corner handles diagonally, the text will increase in height and in width. If you drag one of the handles on the sides, the text will get wider but not taller. And, if you drag one of the handles on the top or bottom of the image, the text will grow taller but not wider.

Figure 3-79

However, if you drag one of the corner handles diagonally while holding down the Shift key, the image will grow proportionately to its original size. This means that you won't have to worry about making the new image too skinny or too fat; it will be the same proportion it was originally.

Once you are happy with the new size, click the checkmark icon in to toolbar at the top of the screen or simply press the Enter key on your keyboard.

If, after resizing, you need to move the image, simply click inside of the text (within the handles) and drag the text anywhere within the image.

By playing around with these tools, you might produce an image similar to the one in Figure 3-80.

Figure 3-80

All that is left to do at this point is save the image using File ⇨ Save For Web and saving the image as a JPEG. However, for this instance, when you look at the 4-up, you will see that, because the image is so small perhaps that there is some quality degradation on the High setting. Moving the format up to the Very High or even Maximum is much better and still renders a file size that is manageable. Using the Very High setting, the final image is shown in Figure 3-81.

Figure 3-81

Since this image started off from the second logo you created earlier, there is no need to create a new color scheme; you can use the same one since the colors are identical.

As this section closes, you have started to think about some of the basic considerations of mobile web development. You will see this in greater detail in Chapter 10, but at least you are thinking about it at this early stage of the development process. You have seen how to take a graphic intended for a much larger screen and modify it to fit the limited screen resolution of a mobile browser. Hopefully, you have gotten a bit more familiar with some of the tools you have used earlier in this chapter and even seen a couple of new ones. You are now ready to move onto website layout and design, which are covered in Chapter 4.

Extending Your Photoshop Skills

Hopefully, if you are at this point in this chapter, you have learned a lot of new and interesting techniques and tools to get you started with graphic arts. You have created three distinct header graphics (two standard ones and one for a mobile browser) and the complementary color schemes for each. You have learned about the Magnetic Lasso, color and gradient fills, opacity, the Eyedropper and Color Picker Tools, selecting and deselecting regions of an image, and, most importantly, layers. You have also seen how to export images to different formats for the web and how to resize images to meet your design needs.

You will use these skills again in Chapter 4 when you create a sidebar graphic for your design and again in Chapter 10 when you begin manipulating the mobile graphic you just created.

But beyond that, hopefully you will use these skills again and again as you continue in your web design career or hobby.

With all of that being said, it is important to realize that this chapter has only scratched the surface of what you can do with Photoshop. There are amazing tools such as filters, masks, and actions that you will really want to start getting familiar with. Just as in any coding project, there are probably better ways, or at least different ways, to accomplish some of the tasks outlined in this book. But the only way you will know that is to keep going with your efforts in the graphic arts. This is only one chapter of a book; there are volumes of material out there to help you go to the next level.

To that end, there are a lot of resources out on the web. As mentioned earlier, Adobe's page www.adobe.com/designcenter/tutorials has some really useful tips and tutorials. Beyond that, you should start looking at the National Association of Photoshop Professionals (NAPP) and its related website, (www.photoshopuser.com). This organization is a members-only site but offers a periodic magazine, free tutorials, and relevant links and articles for its members.

There are also a lot of really good books out there. Some fun books are the *Down & Dirty Tricks* series by Scott Kelby (president of the NAPP). These books are all tips and tricks and not much filler. The tips are fairly short and easy to follow.

The point is, don't let this chapter be the end of your graphic arts pursuit. Rather, let it serve as the beginning of your pursuit. There are so many resources out there that this book should serve only as a starting point of your knowledge of Photoshop.

Summary

In the world of web design, you only have a limited window to get people to stay at your site. In an ideal world, that might mean that all of your patrons will be running their browser maximized to their 1280 × 1024 monitors. However, as alluded to in Chapter 2, this will almost never be the case. Many people have smaller resolutions, and many Internet surfers, especially those with large monitors, do not surf with maximized browser windows. So, within those confines, you have to provide the information they need in a way they can find it. Your site has to be visually appealing and not obtrusive or annoying. Graphics and colors are vital to a successful website. And as a web programmer, regardless of whether or not this has historically been your job, they may be one day. And even if design isn't in your job description, knowing how to navigate around Photoshop is always a good thing.

In this chapter, you learned the basics of Photoshop. You learned how to get around a lot of the buttons on the Tools palette. You saw the importance and utilization of layers in a Photoshop environment. You found out how to use layer masks and how to use fonts in your image. You even learned the difference between opacity and fill and how to use both to make stunning graphics.

Hopefully, you learned a lot of tricks to at least make it appear that you know what you are doing (which is all anyone can ever do). But more importantly, hopefully you learned that you *can* use Photoshop and, maybe even more important than that, that you actually want to learn more. If so, there are millions of books and websites waiting for you to find them. This chapter can get you started. It's up to you to take the next step.

It is also important to remember that, regardless of whether you use Photoshop or some other graphics tool, you should keep true to sound design principles. Hopefully, this chapter helped you start to understand how to put those principles into practice.

Cascading Style Sheets (CSS)

Depending on whom you ask, Cascading Style Sheets (CSS) are either a godsend or an overhyped glorified HTML formatter with very little purpose in today's web design culture. There are a large number of people that are probably somewhere in the middle, but they are neither as vocal nor as fun to listen to debate on this hot topic.

The concepts of Cascading Style Sheets were officially announced to the world with 1994's *Cascading HTML Style Sheets* by Hakon Wium Lie (`www.w3.org/People/howcome/p/cascade.html`). The code structure of the proposal looks a bit foreign compared to today's CSS formatting, but this document was the first to specifically call for a linked document for style definitions that enabled a true separation of code and design in websites. While it was originally targeted to HTML, its scope has been expanded to include XML, XHTML, SVG, XUL, and most derivations of SGML. Now, if you ever have to answer a trivia question about the origins of CSS, you are ready.

> *Most current generation browsers support the CSS Level 2(CSS2) specification. You can find out more about what this entails by visiting the W3C documentation located at* `www.w3.org/TR/REC-CSS2`.

The purpose of this chapter is not to force you into believing that CSS should be used in one way or another. As already stated in Chapter 2, there are as many reasons to go to a completely CSS-based web design platform as there are to staying away from it all together. The point of this chapter is not to debate this issue any more than was already done in Chapter 2. In this chapter, you will learn how to start taking the steps towards a CSS-based web design platform. You will learn how to create structural layouts of your sites that resemble a table-based design but are done using only CSS. You will learn how to place elements on the page and stretch them according to your needs. You will learn how to create a sidebar that will stretch with the content area (or at least appear to).

You will also learn about some of the tools in Visual Studio 2005 that can help you create your CSS files and how to apply those files to your web projects. At the end of the chapter, you should have the basic layout of the surfer5 design completed and be ready to put that design into an ASP.NET Master Page in Chapter 7.

But, again, you will not be preached to about the merits, or perils, of CSS in web design. That is more of a judgment call each developer must make. The major arguments are laid out in Chapter 2, and there are plenty of supporting websites and other manuscripts for each side of the debate. This chapter is not meant to force you to one side or another; its purpose is to give you the tools you need in order to proceed with a CSS design if that is the path you choose. All subsequent chapters, though, will use the designs created in this chapter so, if for no other reason than to understand better what is going on in those chapters, it is a good idea to understand what is being said in this one. But, again, whether or not you use the concepts presented in the chapter in your future projects is a decision only you can make.

Prerequisites

You should have at least a basic familiarity with Cascading Style Sheets to fully understand the concepts presented in this chapter. It is not necessary that you be an expert in CSS (or else why would you even read this chapter?), but you should at least have a cursory understanding of what CSS is and how it might be used in your projects.

If you are a complete novice, you may want to read further about CSS in other manuscripts. *Beginning CSS Cascading Style Sheets for Web Design* by Richard York (Wrox Publishing) is an excellent source to help get you started. It goes into much more detail about CSS than this chapter will get into. If you find that you want to learn more about CSS, this book would be a great place to start.

There are also a lot of really good resources on the web, such as the following:

- ❑ **Cascading Style Sheets home page** — www.w3.org/Style/CSS
- ❑ **W3 C Schools** — CSS Tutorial: www.w3schools.com/css/default.asp
- ❑ **Quirksmode** — CSS contents and browser compatibility; www.quirksmode.org/css/contents.html
- ❑ **A List Apart** — www.alistapart.com
- ❑ **CSS Zen Garden** — www.csszengarden.com

For the most part, it is assumed that you have a basic familiarity with CSS, particularly with regard to text formatting (such as setting the color, style, or size of fonts). For this reason, this chapter will not address these topics at all. Rather, this chapter will help you with your understanding of basic web page layout using only CSS rules. If you need to have a better understanding of CSS text formatting and styling, you may need to consult a different reference, such as the ones above, to continue your learning.

That Looks Like Table-Based Design

In this chapter, you will learn how to structure your site to look much like a design you would have created using tables. You will have the typical header and footer with a side panel area and then a content area. The final result will look something like Figure 4-1.

Figure 4-1

You will be using the graphics and color schemes you created in Chapter 3. If you did not create these files, you may substitute with whichever graphics you do have available.

In addition to these files, you will need to create one additional file that will be used for the sidebar graphic. For this demonstration, the sidebar will be exactly 150 pixels wide. However, as with sidebar graphics you might use in a table-based layout, this graphic will be a repeating graphic. Therefore, it only needs to be, say, 1 pixel high so as to minimize file size and yet give a consistent look to the sidebar area.

In PhotoShop CS2, open your color scheme file for this project if you do not already have it open. Use the Color Picker tool on your tools palette to set the foreground color to the color you want to use for the sidebar. In the example illustrated in Figure 4-1, you would have used the medium color, which is represented by the hexadecimal value # 477897. Flip the colors in the tools palette to now set that color to the background color. If you have the default colors set up, this would mean you have a black foreground and a dark blue background.

Once you have this set up, select File ➪ New to bring up the screen in Figure 4-2.

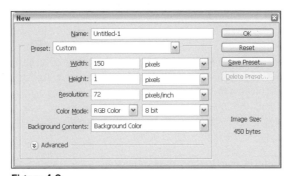

Figure 4-2

Set your values to reflect those shown in Figure 4-2, making the Width 150 pixels and the Height 1 pixel, and setting the Background Contents to Background Color. Click the OK button. This will create a file that is all you will need for you background graphic. Simply select File ➪ Save for Web, and then save the graphic to your hard drive. The file is so small, it would be fine to use the Maximum setting.

At this point, you should have the following three files prepared:

❑ The top part of the logo graphic from Chapter 3, called `logo01_top.jpg` in this example, shown in Figure 4-3

❑ The bottom part of the logo graphic from Chapter 3, called `logo01_bottom.jpg`, shown in Figure 4-4

❑ The sidebar graphic you just created, called `sidebarGraphic.jpg`, shown in Figure 4-5

Figure 4-3

Figure 4-4

Figure 4-5

You will need to copy all of these files into a subdirectory of the project folder you want to use. For example, if you are going to create your project in the `c:\surfer5` folder, you will want to create a subdirectory `c:\surfer5\images` to hold your images.

While you can choose whatever directory structure makes sense to you, `c:\surfer5` will be used as the book project directory for the remainder of the book.

Once you have your directory structure set up, create a new website in that folder. Open up Visual Studio 2005 and select File ➪ New ➪ Web Site to get the screen displayed in Figure 4-6.

84

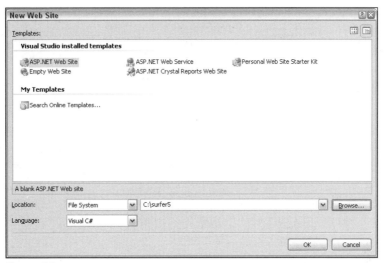

Figure 4-6

Make the selections shown in Figure 4-6, selecting ASP.NET Web Site as the template and the directory structure you set up previously as the location of our project. Language is not so important for the examples in this book. Most of the examples in this book will not even use programming in terms of C# or VB. However, in those instances where they are used, code samples will be provided in C# but should be fairly easily translated to VB if you are more comfortable with that language. For your tests, use whichever language you feel most comfortable. Realize, though, that the project screenshots in the book will mostly have C# so, if you see a page declaration in code, it will include a reference to the C# language. This is not indicative of the way you *should* code; it is simply the language that was set up to create the project for the screenshots of the book.

Press OK to create your project. If you are using a folder that already exists (e.g., you are using the same folder you used when creating the graphics from Chapter 3), you will likely encounter the screen depicted in Figure 4-7.

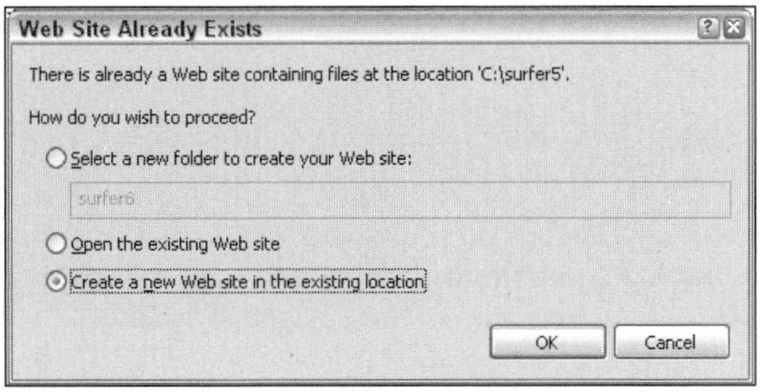

Figure 4-7

If you encounter this screen, you should just select the third option, "Create a new Web site in the existing location," in order to create a standard web project in your directory. Click the OK button to finalize the project setup.

You should, at this point, have an initial project similar to the screenshot shown in Figure 4-8.

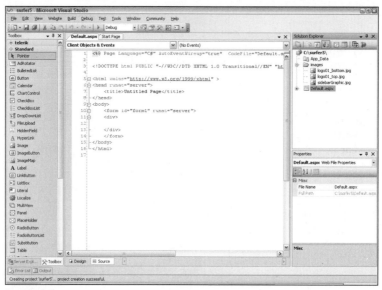

Figure 4-8

You now have your project set up that will carry you through the rest of this book. For the remainder of this chapter, you will add your stylesheet and begin storing the project style definitions in that document.

CSS Basics

The first thing that you probably need to understand before getting too deep into CSS is how CSS gets applied to your page. Generally speaking, there are three ways in which you can bring CSS formatting into your web page:

❑ **Inline** — This means that you are adding style directly within the parameters of a particular element (e.g., `<p style="color: Olive">Hello, World</p>`).

❑ **Internal stylesheet** — This sets up your style definitions in a `<style>` block of your `<head>` region of your web document.

❑ **External stylesheet** — This sets up your style definitions in a stylesheet document that is linked to a page (or multiple pages) through the `<link>` tag in the `<head>` region of your web document.

These styles are applied in linear order. This just means that they will get applied to a particular element in the order they appear in code. With that being true, the Inline definition will always win out because it is declared in the `<body>` region of your web document and the other two methods are brought into the document within the `<head>` region of your web document.

The more interesting question comes up with the Internal and External stylesheets. Which one wins? Well, it depends. In this instance, what makes the difference is the order in which the reference is made in the <head> region. If you declare your link to your external stylesheet first and then add a <style> block after that with a conflicting style definition, the <style> block will win. If, however, you create your <style> block first and then, subsequently in code, you add a link to an external stylesheet that has a conflicting style definition, the style will be applied from the external stylesheet.

For the rest of this book, the book project will use external stylesheets to bring in its style definitions.

So what goes into the style definitions? Well, there are three fundamental building blocks in any CSS file: the element, class, and ID. In order to have a clear understanding of how CSS works, you need to have a clear understanding of what each of these are and how they are represented in your CSS code.

An element is, essentially, a reference to all of a particular HTML element in your website. For example, if you wanted to represent all paragraphs in your HTML document with the <p> tag in code and have a text alignment of justified, you could write the following in your CSS code:

```
p
{
    text-align: justify;
}
```

When applied to your website, the CSS formatting will apply a justified alignment to all <p> tags in your HTML code.

But what if you want some paragraphs to have a center-alignment, for example? You will want most paragraphs to have a justified alignment but, in certain circumstances, you want the paragraph to have a center-alignment. This is where classes come in.

With classes, you can set one "class" of an element to have different formatting than other classes of the same element (or the default class). So, say you want to set up a class called "centerAlign" for paragraphs. It would look something like this:

```
p.centerAlign
{
    text-align: center;
}
```

The way this is coded, the centerAlign class would only apply to <p> tags (by the way, this is not case-sensitive; it would also apply to all <p> tags). If you wanted to have this attribute available to any element that called the class, you would simply leave off the "p" at the front of the declaration. For example, you might have the code look more like the following:

```
.centerAlign
{
    text-align: center;
}
```

This would allow any element in your code to pull in the formatting set up in your CSS code. The following code shows what a full page might look like using this code:

```
<%@ Page Language="C#" %>

<!DOCTYPE html PUBLIC "-//W3C//DTD XHTML 1.0 Transitional//EN"
    "http://www.w3.org/TR/xhtml1/DTD/xhtml1-transitional.dtd">

<script runat="server">

</script>

<html xmlns="http://www.w3.org/1999/xhtml" >
<head runat="server">
    <title>Untitled Page</title>
    <style>
    p
    {
        text-align: justify;
    }
    .centerAlign
    {
        text-align: center;
    }
    </style>
</head>
<body>
    <form id="form1" runat="server">
    <div>

    <p>This paragraph does not call the centerAlign class.</p>

    <p class="centerAlign">This paragraph <b><i>DOES</i></b> call the
    centerAlign class.</p>

    <div class="centerAlign">This div tag also calls the centerAlign Class.</div>

    </div>
    </form>
</body>
</html>
```

If you ran this code in your browser, it would resemble Figure 4-9.

The final division of CSS coding you will need to understand is the ID. The ID is similar to a class in CSS in that it references a special case of an element. However, the main difference is that an ID can only be used once in your HTML code whereas a class can be used as many times as necessary. IDs are primarily used for things like headers or footers where there should only be one ID necessary per page. For example, you wouldn't need multiple header or footer areas, right? Although you could certainly accomplish the same effect by using classes, IDs are generally preferred to Classes for maintainability of single occurrence formatted elements ("preferred" because this is not enforced). This means that, while you will not receive any errors and your page will be rendered if you use the same ID name multiple times in a single web document, you will fail if you do any sort of markup validation. So, in order to maintain valid markup, it is a good practice to use IDs only once within a single web document. This will also help when other developers need to either assist in developing or maintaining the page down the road.

Figure 4-9

For example, if you modified the earlier sample code to use IDs rather than classes, you would have the following:

```
<%@ Page Language="C#" AutoEventWireup="true"
    CodeFile="Default.aspx.cs" Inherits="_Default" %>

<!DOCTYPE html PUBLIC "-//W3C//DTD XHTML 1.0 Transitional//EN"
    "http://www.w3.org/TR/xhtml1/DTD/xhtml1-transitional.dtd">

<html xmlns="http://www.w3.org/1999/xhtml" >
<head runat="server">
    <title>Untitled Page</title>
    <style type="text/css">
    p
    {
        text-align: justify;
    }
    #centerAlign
    {
        text-align: center;
    }
    </style>
</head>
<body>
    <form id="form1" runat="server">
    <div>
    <p>This paragraph does not call the centerAlign class.</p>

    <p id="centerAlign">This paragraph <b><i>DOES</i></b> call the
    centerAlign class.</p>

    <div id="centerAlign">This div tag also calls the centerAlign Class.</div>

    </div>
    </form>
</body>
</html>
```

Notice that the "." of the classes in your style block are now changed to "#". IDs are identified by a "#" symbol in your CSS code. They are then referenced by "id=" in your HTML code rather than "class=".

If you look at this project in Visual Studio, you will see errors in the error list, similar to that in Figure 4-10.

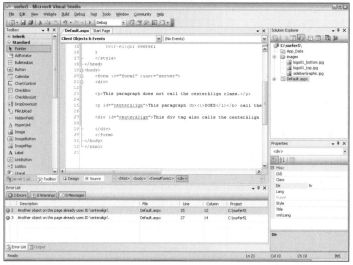

Figure 4-10

You will notice a couple of things. First, both of the ID declarations in your HTML code have the red squiggly line under them, indicating that there is an error. You will also see two errors in the error list, both stating "Another object on this page already uses ID 'centeralign.'" They even have the official looking red x's next to them. But if you run the project, it compiles and loads and renders the output shown in Figure 4-11.

Figure 4-11

As you can see, Figure 4-11 looks exactly like Figure 4-9, which used classes rather than IDs to format the text. The code showed errors inline in your source code, generated errors in your error list, yet still compiled and rendered the same HTML styling that you saw when using classes.

90

Does this mean that it is okay to use either? Technically, perhaps. But to fully embrace CSS design, you should not use IDs to signify more than one item on a page. If you need to make several references to the same CSS block, use classes. If not for the reasons of maintaining a standardized approach or markup validation, you should still really follow the one-ID-per-page rule to assist with debugging and troubleshooting your pages as your project matures.

DOCTYPEs

The DOCTYPE is the first thing in your HTML code, coming before your HTML tag (but after your page declarations for .NET). This basically tells your browser how strictly to interpret the code you have provided. For example, XHTML 1.0 Transitional, which is what comes up by default in your Visual Studio projects, implies that your code is not perfect in regard to W3C standards. It allows some level of deprecated code, such as <center> and <u>. It does not fully comply with W3C standards. In order to do that, you must modify your DOCTYPE to use either HTML 4.01 Strict or XHTML 1.0 Strict. XHTML 1.0 Strict, which will be used for the examples in this book, means that the document complies with the stricter (as opposed to HTML) syntax rules and disallows deprecated HTML tags and attributes.

So, following this thought, the earlier code examples, in order to be compliant, should look more like this:

```
<%@ Page Language="C#" AutoEventWireup="true"
    CodeFile="Default.aspx.cs" Inherits="_Default" %>

<!DOCTYPE html PUBLIC "-//W3C//DTD XHTML 1.0 Strict//EN"
    "http://www.w3.org/TR/xhtml1/DTD/xhtml1-strict.dtd">

<html xmlns="http://www.w3.org/1999/xhtml" >
<head runat="server">
    <title>Untitled Page</title>
    <style type="text/css">
    p
    {
        text-align: justify;
    }
    .centerAlign
    {
        text-align: center;
    }
    </style>
</head>
<body>
    <form id="form1" runat="server">
    <div>

    <p>This paragraph does not call the centerAlign class.</p>

    <p class="centerAlign">This paragraph <b><i>DOES</i></b> call the
    centerAlign class.</p>
    <div class="centerAlign">This div tag also calls the centerAlign Class.</div>

    </div>
    </form>
</body>
</html>
```

This uses the more rigid XHTML 1.0 Strict guidelines and uses classes rather than IDs for the multiple instances of the centerAlign formatting.

> *You can read more on the differences between Strict and Transitional DTDs at* wikipedia.org: http://en.wikipedia.org/wiki/HTML#Transitional_versus_Strict.

Creating a Stylesheet

In Visual Studio 2005, there are a couple of tools that can help you in generating your CSS code. However, the first step is to actually create a CSS file that will be referenced from within your code. In order to do this, with your project open, select Website ⇨ Add New Item to get the screen shown in Figure 4-12.

Figure 4-12

You will select Style Sheet and then name the file something that makes sense. Since this project is for the surfer5 project, and thinking ahead that there may be more than one version of this CSS file, surfer5_v1.css is used for this example. Realistically, this could be any name but, for the purposes of these demos, this will be the name used.

This should create a blank CSS file for you in your project with simply a "body" block set up and no properties attached to it yet. You will also notice a new tabbed palette has appeared to the left of your screen (where your toolbox generally resides) called CSS Outline. This can help you keep grip on the many formatting blocks you add to your CSS file.

While in your CSS file, click on the word "body" to make sure that is the currently selected block. You could also select "body" in the CSS Outline tab. When you are in the right region, you will notice that the Build Style button is enabled, as seen in Figure 4-13.

Figure 4-13

Click on this button to bring up the interface shown in Figure 4-14.

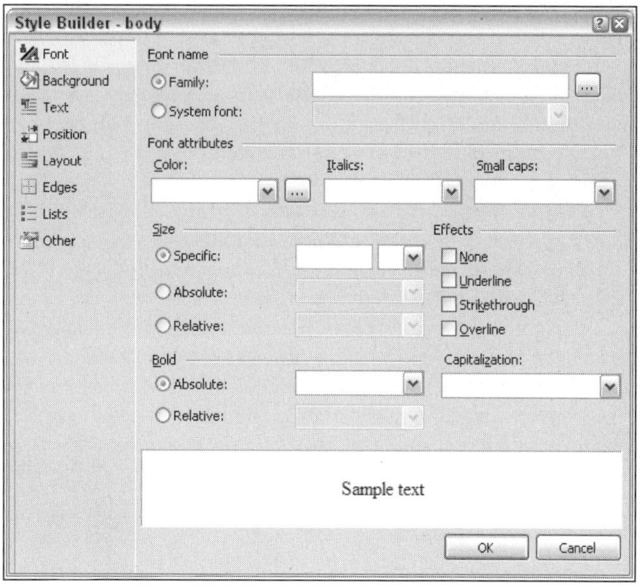

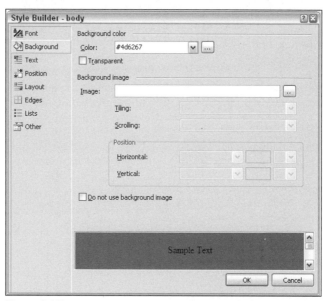

Figure 4-14

As you can see, this provides a GUI-like look and feel to your CSS files. You can fairly easily navigate through fonts and colors using this interface. For example, go to the Background tab by clicking on Background on the left side of the screen. In the `Background Color` section, type in the hexadecimal value "#4d6267" in the Color field. This was the background color that was picked from the logo in Chapter 3. Your screen should now look like Figure 4-15.

Figure 4-15

Next, go to the Text tab and choose Centered in the Horizontal field of the Alignment section. Go to the Position tab, and type in "98" in the Height field and change the drop-down to reflect percentages (%) rather than pixels (px). Finally click on the Edges tab, and enter in zeros for all of the margin values and ones for all of the padding values, and change all margins and padding parameters to percentages rather than pixels. When you have completed these steps, press OK. You will be taken back to your CSS file, and the body block should be modified to look like the following:

The settings made in the preceding paragraph are fairly arbitrary. What you are trying to accomplish in these steps is to have a fairly consistent look and feel in all browser windows. Each browser has a default stylesheet that it applies to pages and, unless you override those settings, you will have variations in the way your pages are displayed. So, with the margins, you are setting everything back to the corners of the browser window. You are next adding a 1% padding on all sides of the browser window. In this example, you are using 1% because you don't know what the width or height of the available window is. With percentages, you can more align the padding with the actual dimensions of the browser window. With the height setting, you are trying to consume the remainder of the browser window. Since there is a 1% padding at the top and a 1% padding at the bottom, you want to take up the remaining 98% of the screen with you web project. Again, these settings are fairly arbitrary and could be easily modified in other situations.

```
body
{
    padding-right: 1%;
    padding-left: 1%;
    padding-bottom: 1%;
    margin: 0%;
    padding-top: 1%;
    height: 98%;
    background-color: #4d6267;
    text-align: center;
}
```

Without knowing CSS and only looking at this file, you probably would not be able to tell exactly what is going on. But with the help of the Build Style Wizard, you have a much easier interface in which to deal with while making style choices.

However, if you look back at your ASPX page, there has been no change at this point. In order for these changes to take effect, you have to reference the CSS file within the ASPX (or HTML or whatever you are using) file.

The end result of this, no matter which way you go about it, should be that there is an external stylesheet referenced in the header section of your HTML code that looks something like the following:

```
<%@ Page Language="C#" AutoEventWireup="true"
    CodeFile="Default.aspx.cs" Inherits="_Default" %>

<!DOCTYPE html PUBLIC "-//W3C//DTD XHTML 1.0 Strict//EN"
    "http://www.w3.org/TR/xhtml1/DTD/xhtml1-strict.dtd">

<html xmlns="http://www.w3.org/1999/xhtml" >
<head runat="server">
    <title>Untitled Page</title>
    <link href="surfer5_v1.css" rel="stylesheet" type="text/css" />
</head>
```

```
<body>
    <form id="form1" runat="server">
    <div>

    </div>
    </form>
</body>
</html>
```

You can see that just under the title section there is a section for the reference to the CSS file. You could merely type that in and it would work.

However, the simplest and most reliable way to add this link is to just drag the stylesheet into your web page. In order to do this, you must have the Design view open for your page in Visual Studio 2005 and, from the Solution Explorer, you simply drag the CSS file onto the page and it is applied. If you go back to the Source view, you will notice that the code above is typed for you in exactly the right place. Doing it this way is simple because all you are doing is dragging the stylesheet into your web page. More importantly, it is the most reliable way because it automatically places your link in the correct location and adds all of the mandatory properties for you without your having to give it any thought.

You can also drag the CSS file from your solution explorer into the Source view. However, when doing this, the CSS reference will be typed at whatever point the cursor is at when the mouse button is released. So, if you are floating near the form tag in your code, that is where the CSS reference will be typed out. So you need to take special care if you are going to do it this way.

But, again, the easiest way (and most reliable) is to just drag the CSS file directly into the Design view of your document. You won't have to worry about whether you got the syntax right or the placement correct; Visual Studio will take care of that for you. And don't you have more important things to do than worrying about such things?

Laying Out Your Page for CSS

Before you get too far into creating your CSS file, you should probably go ahead and modify your HTML (ASPX) document to get it ready for formatting. You need to create the areas of the page in the logical units you will need for presentation. It is probably easier to do this in the HTML code first and then create the formatting in the CSS.

In this project, you know that you will need a header section, a navigation section, a body section (which will contain a sidebar area and a content area), and a footer section. So, for each of these "divisions," you will want to create an associated `<div>` tag in your HTML code. This should resemble the following:

```
<%@ Page Language="C#" AutoEventWireup="true"
    CodeFile="Default.aspx.cs" Inherits="_Default" %>

<!DOCTYPE html PUBLIC "-//W3C//DTD XHTML 1.0 Strict//EN"
    "http://www.w3.org/TR/xhtml1/DTD/xhtml1-strict.dtd">

<html xmlns="http://www.w3.org/1999/xhtml" >
<head runat="server">
    <title>Untitled Page</title>
    <link href="surfer5_v1.css" rel="stylesheet" type="text/css" />
</head>
```

```
<body>
    <form id="form1" runat="server">
    <div>

    <div id="headerGraphic"></div>
    <div id="navigationArea">| link1 | link2 | link3 |</div>
    <div id="bodyArea">
        <div id="bodyLeft">left text</div>
        <div id="bodyRight">right text</div>
    </div>
    <div id="footerArea">© 2006 - 2007: surfer5 Internet Solutions</div>

    </div>
    </form>
</body>
</html>
```

You will notice that all of the new divisions use ID tags rather than classes. That is because each division will be strictly unique and used only once. For example, you should not need a second `headerGraphic` section on the page, (Why would you want to have the logo spread out in a different area of the page as well?)

This, however, will not make your site look any different than it did previously. The code above adds some filler text so that you can see where things fall, but there is no formatting applied. You can see the result of this rendered in a browser in Figure 4-16.

Figure 4-16

Again, you can see all of the text in the browser, but no formatting. Now it is time to add formatting to these new divisions.

Back in your CSS file, you will see a small icon next to the Build Style Wizard used before. If you hover over the icon, you will see that this is the Add Style Rule button, as shown in Figure 4-17.

Figure 4-17

Clicking on this button brings up the Add Style Rule dialog box shown in Figure 4-18.

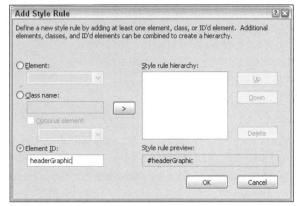

Figure 4-18

This merely gives you the option to add a formatting block for an element, a class, or an ID. Since the formatting set up for this project has been all IDs, click on that radio button and type in "headerGraphic". You will see that the Style rule preview is updated to show "#headerGraphic" as well. Click the OK button. You CSS file should now look similar to the following:

```
body
{
    padding-right: 1%;
    padding-left: 1%;
    padding-bottom: 1%;
    margin: 0%;
    padding-top: 1%;
    height: 98%;
    background-color: #4d6267;
    text-align: center;
}
#headerGraphic
{
}
```

In essence, all this did was add a new section called "#headerGraphic" to your CSS file. Did this save you any time? Probably not. Did it make it any easier? Doubtful. As long as you can remember to type in a "#" symbol before your IDs and a "." before your classes, it would probably be just as quick to copy the class name from your HTML code and paste it into your CSS file.

Now, however, while in your style block for the headerGraphic ID, you want to go back into the Build Style Wizard and click first the Background tab. In the Background Image section, click the button next to the Image field in order to look up the logo image you will use for the background of this division. The screen that appears should look like Figure 4-19.

97

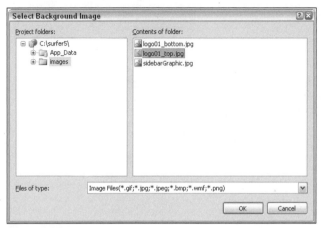

Figure 4-19

This screen brings up all of the subdirectories and files in those directories for this project. You want to select the `logo01_top.jpg` file (or whatever you named the top portion of the logo file you created in Chapter 3), and select OK. Navigate back to the Position tab and make the height 246 pixels and the width 700 pixels. Finally, on the Layout tab, find the Flow Control section at the top. There, set the drop-down option "Allow Text To Flow" to "Don't Allow Text On Sides" and the drop-down option "Allow Floating Objects" to "Do Not Allow." These two settings will ensure that the header graphic is sitting in its own space and that other floating `<div>`'s do not nudge themselves up next to this `<div>`. If you are still thinking in terms of a tables mentality, this essentially ensures that the header graphic will be its own row, colspanning all other columns. When done, click the OK button. Your modified CSS file should resemble the following:

Remember earlier in this chapter you set the padding rules for the body element using fairly arbitrary percentage amounts. In this section, you are, instead, using very specific pixel dimensions for the height and width of this region. This is because you are trying to exactly match the dimensions of the image that you are using for the area. For `logo01_top.jpg`, the dimensions are 700 pixels wide and 246 pixels high. If you are unsure of your image's dimensions, you can open it in PhotoShop and click Image in the toolbar and select Image Size.

It is also important to realize that setting the dimensions as fixed pixel width will not conflict with the percentage amounts set earlier for the body element. When the page is rendered, the percentages will be translated to pixel amounts. So if, say, your browser window has 1000 pixels available width, there will be 10 pixels padding on both sides (1% of 1000 pixels) and your web content stays fixed at 700 pixels wide. This leaves 280 pixels that will be split on both sides of the web content (since you are centering the content in the body).

```
body
{
    padding-right: 1%;
    padding-left: 1%;
    padding-bottom: 1%;
    margin: 0%;
    padding-top: 1%;
    height: 98%;
```

```
        background-color: #4d6267;
        text-align: center;
}
#headerGraphic
{
        background-image: url(images/logo01_top.jpg);
        width: 700px;
        height: 246px;
        clear: both;
        float: none;
}
```

At this point, your design should look something like Figure 4-20.

Figure 4-20

You will notice that the header appears as though it were dropped into code using an `<img>` tag. However, the advantage to the way you have done it is that the image is set through CSS and, if an accessibility browser accesses your site with CSS turned off, the user won't see the image or a placeholder saying something arbitrary like `[logo of surfer5 Internet Solutions]`. You wouldn't want to always do this. There are some graphics that you would want to persist in an accessibility browser. For example, you may have a chart or some other pertinent business graphic that you need to either be shown or represented through text in the `ALT` property of your image tag. But for the logo at the top of the page? It is probably just fine that you lose it entirely for your accessibility visitors that would more than likely have CSS and Images turned off anyway. You are removing the graphic for them without fundamentally changing the content or experience of the site and without adding text to their browser that just gets in the way. After all, does `[logo for surfer5]` materially add anything to users' experience?

You now need to define an area for your navigation area. This will use the bottom half of the logo graphic, `logo01_bottom.jpg`, as the background, span the width of your site, have the navigation links pushed to the right of the area, and have a dark blue font. To do this, create the block #navigationArea in your CSS file and then launch the Style Builder Wizard and make the following changes:

❑ **Font tab** — In the Font name area, set Family to Arial; in the Font attributes area, set Color to the hexadecimal value #477897; in the Size area, select Specific and set the size to .8 em; and in the Bold area, select Absolute and select Bold.

❑ **Background tab** — In the Background image section, set the Image to images/logo01_bottom.jpg (or whatever name and location is appropriate for your project), and set Tiling to Do not tile.

❑ **Text tab** — In the Alignment section, set Horizontal to Right and Vertical to middle. In the Spacing between section, set Letters to Custom and then set it to .04 em.

❑ **Position tab** — Set the Position mode to Position in normal flow and the Height to 26 pixels and the Width to 690 pixels. Both of these may seem counterintuitive to you because the graphic itself is actually 700 pixels wide by 54 pixels high. So why the different dimensions in this block? The easiest element to address is the width. In the next steps, you will set the padding on the right side to 10 pixels. You do this in order to not have the navigation links kissing the side of the graphic. But this doesn't do *exactly* what you think it will do. If you set the width of the division to 700 pixels and then add a padding of 10 pixels, you might think that the entire division would stay at 700 pixels; you would just have 690 to work with inside of that area, since you have 10 pixels on the side. This is not how CSS works. If you have a 700 pixel wide division and a 10-pixel padding to that division, you will need 710 pixels. So, in this case, you set the block to 690 pixels wide, add a 10-pixel padding to the right. Thus, the entire division, in the browser, is now 700 pixels wide. So you have to do a little thinking when setting padding and margins in this way. As far as the width, there really isn't a good reason for it other than, when the image was first loaded, 54 pixels just seemed too big. So the div was reduced to 26 for aesthetic reasons. Since the image is a background, the extraneous area of the image is just chopped off. This acts much in the same way it would in a table cell. If you have a table cell that is 100 pixels wide with a background set to a graphic that is 400 pixels wide, you will only see the first 100, and the rest is hidden. This shouldn't be a new concept to you.

❑ **Layout tab** — In the Flow control, set "Allow text to flow" to "Don't allow text on sides" and "Allow floating objects" to "Do not allow." As before, this just ensures that this row sits by itself.

❑ **Edges tab** — In the Margins section, set all values to 0%. In the Padding section, set the Top to .3 em, the left and bottom to 0%, and the right to 10 pixels.

After you have made all of these settings, Click the OK button, your CSS file should now look something like this:

```
body
{
    padding-right: 1%;
    padding-left: 1%;
    padding-bottom: 1%;
    margin: 0%;
    padding-top: 1%;
    height: 98%;
    background-color: #4d6267;
    text-align: center;
}
```

```
#headerGraphic
{
    background-image: url(images/logo01_top.jpg);
    width: 700px;
    height: 246px;
    clear: both;
    float: none;
}
#navigationArea
{
    clear: both;
    padding-right: 10px;
    padding-left: 0%;
    font-weight: bold;
    font-size: 0.8em;
    float: none;
    background-image: url(images/logo01_bottom.jpg);
    padding-bottom: 0%;
    margin: 0%;
    vertical-align: middle;
    width: 690px;
    color: #477897;
    padding-top: 0.3em;
    background-repeat: no-repeat;
    font-family: Arial;
    letter-spacing: 0.04em;
    position: static;
    height: 26px;
    text-align: right;
}
```

And your project should look similar to Figure 4-21.

Figure 4-21

You will notice that the two divisions are now touching with no space between them, which was the unspoken intention. If you do not add code to put space between them, there will not be any. You will also notice that the code that disallowed text from outside of the division had no affect on the text *inside* the division; the text "link1," "link2," and "link3" were not affected.

The Holy Grail of CSS

The next section gets into one of the hotly discussed topics in CSS design: expandable columns. What this is referring to is having two columns of presentation side by side that grow at the same rate. To put that in more web-geek language, you have a sidebar area that expands with the content area of web page. The problem is that there really isn't any way for one division to yell over to another division "hey, I'm growing, and you better, too!" In a table, if you have two cells in the same row and one grows to 1000 pixels high, the other one will as well. This is just a fact of tables. And a quest for CSS.

Many of the tables enthusiasts point at this one critical issue as a glaring flaw to going to an entirely CSS design. And, in all honesty, their argument has merit. At this point, there is no way for the side-by-side columns to grow in tandem. Using the example above, if your content division grows to 1000 pixels but your sidebar division requires only 100 pixels of space to contain its data, the content area will grow to accommodate all 1000 pixels of space required to host its data and the sidebar will grow to accommodate all 100 pixels of space required to host its data. So, if you have a sidebar color background, you will see your sidebar is 100 pixels high and your content is 1000 pixels high. This is a problem.

There are a lot of articles on the web and in print on best practices for handling this. There are two primary and popular ways of accomplishing this, though: the faux column and negative margins. Both techniques will be discussed here but, for the remainder of the chapter, the faux column methodology will be used. This is because it has been around longer and seems to be cleaner code for maintainability. But the negative margin technique is cool, so you should probably understand it as well, just so if you are ever at a hyper-elitist CSS party you will not look stupid. And, in the real world, you may very well want to implement this methodology.

Option 1: The Negative Margin Approach

The basic principle of this approach to making two columns the same height, regardless of the content they contain, is to add a bunch of padding to the bottom of each division, then add an equally large but negative margin, and then crop off the overlap. This means, in essence, you are pushing the height of the division way off the end of the page and then chopping off the extra. So, as long as your divisions never approach that actual height, they will appear to grow at the same rate because the same number of pixels is shown on the y-axis of your screen. With this way, it really doesn't matter how many pixels your height must be to contain your content; what will show is based on the padding you have added. So, to use the earlier example, if the sidebar area only needs to grow to 100 pixels in length to accommodate the content of that area, and the content area needs to grow to 1000 pixels to contain its material, they will both show 1000 pixels. This is because both columns will have a potentially arbitrarily huge amount of padding at the bottom that is only visible to the point of the largest division (for example, the one with the content requiring the greater height).

So how much padding should you add? This depends on your own project speculations. For example, Apple's current Safari browser has a constraint of 32,767 pixels. Since, hopefully, your content will never reach that many pixels high (or you should seriously consider splitting the content between different pages), this is a good figure to use. This setting is, after all, fairly arbitrary; you could easily pick 20,000 pixels or even 2000 pixels for this setting. You are just trying to set a reasonable maximum height of your web page. However, for the remainder of this discussion, you will be using a setting of 32,757 pixels. (To accommodate a 10-pixel padding, you will adjust the 32,767 limitation by 10 pixels.)

The first step in this process is to define the rules for the `bodyArea` division of the page. Remember that you set up an encompassing division, calling it `bodyArea` in your design, that encompasses both the `bodyLeft` division (for the sidebar) and `bodyRight` area (for the main content of the site). Regardless of which method you use, you will need to define the `bodyArea` rules first. The rules you need for this approach, though, are fairly limited. All you really need is to set the width of the section at 700 pixels, matching the other parameters of this project, and the overflow method. The overflow method basically tells the browser what to do with content that potentially falls out of the realm of the controlling block or division. In this case, you want to tell the `bodyArea` block what to do with any content that goes outside of it. In essence, you are telling it how to handle the 32,757 pixels that will be bleeding off of your design.

In order to set up these rules, create a new block in your CSS file for `#bodyArea` and then start the Style Builder Wizard. On the Position tab, set the Width to 700 pixels. Go to the Layout tab, and look for Overflow in the Content section; this should be around the middle of the screen. Set this drop-down option to "Content is clipped." Click the OK button. This should result in a new section of your CSS file that resembles the following:

```
bodyArea
{
    overflow: hidden;
    width: 700px;
}
```

Rerunning the code at this point will not show any changes in your browser. This is more of a preparation step for the next few steps.

Now you need to create a new definition in your CSS document for your `bodyLeft` division by creating a `#bodyLeft` area in your CSS file and launching the Style Builder Wizard. Once it is launched, make the following changes:

❑ **Font tab** — Set Family to Arial in the Font name section. In Font attributes, set the Color to White. In the Size section, select Absolute, and type in ".7 em."

❑ **Background tab** — In the Background color section, set the Color to the hexadecimal value "#477897".

❑ **Text tab** — In the Alignment section, set Horizontal to Centered and Vertical to "top."

❑ **Position tab** — Set the Position mode to "Position in normal flow." You will also need to set the Width to 130 pixels. The actual width of this division will be 150 pixels, but you will be adding 10 pixels padding all around it, meaning that 10 pixels will be on both the left and right side of the content. In order to set the end result to 150 pixels, you need to back out the 10 pixels from both sides, yielding a division width of 130 pixels.

❑ **Layout tab** — In the Flow control section, set "Allow text to flow" to "To the right." In the Content area, set Overflow to "Content is clipped."

❑ **Edges tab** — Here is where the fun starts. In the Margins section, try to set the Bottom value to −32757 pixels (to accommodate a 10-pixel padding, you need to adjust the 32,767 limitation by 10 pixels). It will drop the value down to only −1024 pixels. This is a setting in Visual Studio

2005 (apparently anything over 1024, positive or negative, is disallowed). For now, leave it as −1024. In the Padding section, set all of the values to 10 pixels with the exception of the Bottom section. Again, try to set it to 32767 pixels and it will revert to 1024 pixels. Accept the 1024 setting for now; you will be changing this, as well as the −1024 margin, in the CSS document later in this section.

Click the OK button to finalize your set of rules for this division, and you should end up with a new section in your CSS file that resembles the following:

```
bodyLeft
{
    padding-right: 10px;
    padding-left: 10px;
    font-size: 0.7em;
    float: left;
    margin-bottom: -1024px;
    padding-bottom: 1024px;
    vertical-align: top;
    overflow: hidden;
    width: 130px;
    color: white;
    padding-top: 10px;
    font-family: Arial;

    position: static;
    background-color: #477897;
    text-align: center;
}
```

At this point, you will notice that, as expected, the padding-bottom rule is set to 1024 pixels and the margin-bottom rule is set to an offset of −1024 pixels. You will need to decide if this is enough for your applications. Certainly, for many, 1000 + pixels below the header and navigation area will suffice. If this is the case for your project, you can leave these numbers alone. If, however, you want to hedge against growth beyond 1000 pixels, you need to adjust these numbers to a higher pixel count. As explained earlier, the remainder of this example will use 32,767 pixels for the maximum height. Keeping this in mind, you need to modify your CSS definition for #bodyLeft to set the padding-bottom to "32767px" and the margin-bottom to "32757px." This will make your browser pad the bottom of your content by 32,767 pixels and then bring back the margin 32,757 pixels, leaving a 10-pixel padding at the bottom of the content. Your modified #bodyLeft definition should resemble the following:

```
bodyLeft
{
    padding-right: 10px;
    padding-left: 10px;
    font-size: 0.7em;
    float: left;
    margin-bottom: -32757px;
    padding-bottom: 32767px;
    vertical-align: top;
    overflow: hidden;
    width: 130px;
    color: white;
    padding-top: 10px;
```

```
    font-family: Arial;
    position: static;
    background-color: #477897;
    text-align: center;
}
```

If you decide to not make this change, you need to remember that, using the1024 amounts, you are not leaving any padding at the bottom of your content. In other words, you are pushing down 1024 and then back up 1024, which leaves no padding at the bottom. This is significant because you have 10-pixel padding on all three of the other sides of your content. So, if you are in the larger region (the one that is forcing the growth of the columns), your content will be flush with the bottom of the area. So, if you are not going to adjust the margins as suggested in this example, you will probably at least want to modify the margin-bottom definition so that it is ''−1014px'' to allow a 10-pixel margin at the bottom of your content.

You will now repeat a very similar process for the `bodyRight` division of your HTML layout. So, create a new block in your CSS file for `#bodyRight`, launch the Style Builder Wizard, and make the following selections:

❑ **Font tab** — In the Font name section, set Family to Arial. In the Font attributes section, set Color to the hexadecimal value ''#477897.'' In the Size section, select Specific, and type in 0.8 em.

❑ **Background tab** — In the Background color section, set Color to White.

❑ **Text tab** — In the Alignment section, set Horizontal to Justified and Vertical to top.

❑ **Position tab** — Set Position mode to Position in normal flow. Set the Width to 530 pixels.

❑ **Layout tab** — In the Flow control section, set ''Allow text to flow'' to ''To the right'' and ''Allow floating objects'' to ''Only on the left.'' In the Content area, set Overflow to ''Content is clipped.''

❑ **Edges tab** — In the Margins section, set the Bottom to −1024 pixels (for now). In the Padding section, set the Bottom to 1024 pixels (again, for now), and set all other values in that section to 10 pixels.

Click the OK button to finalize your selections. You should now have a new section of your CSS file that resembles the following:

```
bodyRight
{
    clear: right;
    padding-right: 10px;
    padding-left: 10px;
    font-size: 0.8em;
    float: left;
    margin-bottom: -1024px;
    padding-bottom: 1024px;
    vertical-align: top;
    overflow: hidden;
    width: 530px;
    color: #477897;
    padding-top: 10px;
    font-family: Arial;
```

```
        position: static;
        background-color: white;
        text-align: justify;
    }
```

As you did with the #bodyLeft definition earlier, you will need to adjust the padding-bottom rule to "32767px" and the margin-bottom rule to "−32757px" to allow for your 10-pixel bottom margin. Your modified CSS definition should resemble the following:

```
bodyRight
{
    clear: right;
    padding-right: 10px;
    padding-left: 10px;
    font-size: 0.8em;
    float: left;
    margin-bottom: -32757px;
    padding-bottom: 32767px;
    vertical-align: top;
    overflow: hidden;
    width: 530px;
    color: #477897;
    padding-top: 10px;
    font-family: Arial;
    position: static;
    background-color: white;
    text-align: justify;
}
```

At this point, when you run your application, your page should look similar to Figure 4-22.

Figure 4-22

This screenshot, and others in this section, are using Internet Explorer version 7. If you are using a different browser, you may, and probably will, see different results. This will be addressed more completely at the end of this chapter in the section "Browser Check."

At first glance, this may not seem that impressive. The two areas are just side by side and the same height. But in CSS, this is an accomplishment. If you have ever tried to get two columns to grow together in CSS, you will appreciate how the two columns will now grow together, or at least appear to, as your content expands. To show that this really works, you might want to add some extra dummy text to each of the content areas to see what the results are.

Many times, you need to fill up your site prototype with text, and you either do not have any content or you do not want the content you make up to take away from the design itself. After all, if you just make up a lot of silly text, the reviewers of the project might get stuck on reading your humor rather than the hours you spent making the layout. It is always a good idea, then, to use some sort of almost nonsensical text that will fill up your page to show how a page would look with text without actually providing distracting made-up content.

One way to do this is to provide what is referred to as "Lorem Ipsum" text, which is commonly used by web designers, graphic artists, and other media content providers as the standard for dummy text. It looks very much like Latin and, some speculate, may actually have its roots in some ancient form of Latin. The important things to know about Lorem Ipsum are: (1) it is a standard in media content, and (2) there are numerous online generators that will provide you with dummy text for free. One such site is www.lipsum.com. This site has additional history, if you care to read more about it, but, more importantly for this discussion, it has a Lorem Ipsum generator. You can specify the length of the content you want provided (number of words, paragraphs, bytes, or lists), and it will spout out the text for you. You can then just copy the text into your web project to fill it up.

So, to use this, either come up with some dummy text on your own or simply generate one paragraph of Lorem Ipsum from the resources provided and fill the leftArea division with this text. Your HTML code should look something like the following:

```
<%@ Page Language="C#" AutoEventWireup="true"
   CodeFile="Default.aspx.cs" Inherits="_Default" %>

<!DOCTYPE html PUBLIC "-//W3C//DTD XHTML 1.0 Strict//EN"
   "http://www.w3.org/TR/xhtml1/DTD/xhtml1-strict.dtd">

<html xmlns="http://www.w3.org/1999/xhtml" >
<head runat="server">
   <title>Untitled Page</title>
   <link href="surfer5_v1.css" rel="stylesheet" type="text/css" />
</head>
<body>
   <form id="form1" runat="server">
   <div>

   <div id="headerGraphic"></div>
   <div id="navigationArea">| link1 | link2 | link3 |</div>
   <div id="bodyArea">
      <div id="bodyLeft">Lorem ipsum dolor sit amet, consectetuer
adipiscing elit. Vivamus felis. Nulla facilisi. Nulla eleifend est at lacus.
Sed vitae pede. Etiam rutrum massa vel nulla. Praesent tempus, nisl ac auctor
```

```
convallis, leo turpis ornare ipsum, ut porttitor felis elit eu turpis. Curabitur quam
turpis, placerat ac, elementum quis, sollicitudin non, turpis. Ut tincidunt
sollicitudin risus. Sed dapibus risus et leo. Praesent interdum, velit id volutpat
convallis, nunc diam vehicula risus, in feugiat quam libero vitae justo.</div>
        <div id="bodyRight">right text</div>
    </div>
    <div id="footerArea">© 2006 - 2007: surfer5 Internet Solutions</div>

    </div>
    </form>
</body>
</html>
```

Save your ASPX file with this new content in it (do not fill the bodyRight section yet). When you refresh your browser, it should look similar to Figure 4-23.

If you are not using IE7, you may not see the same results in your browser. This will be addressed at the end of this chapter in the "Browser Check" section.

Figure 4-23

You can see that the sidebar area grew, as expected, to fill up with the dummy text. More impressively (at least in the world of CSS) is that the content area grew at the same rate, making it look like they grew together.

Again, realize that they didn't actually "grow." What happened is that more of the monumentally padded content area is now visible, because the dummy text pushed the boundaries of visibility.

Now, to test that the expansion of the site content area will have a similar effect on the sidebar area, add more dummy text to the bodyRight division. If you are using the Lorem Ipsum generator, generate, say, six paragraphs of content, copy that into the bodyRight division of your HTML code, and save the file. The bottom of the rendered page should look similar to Figure 4-24.

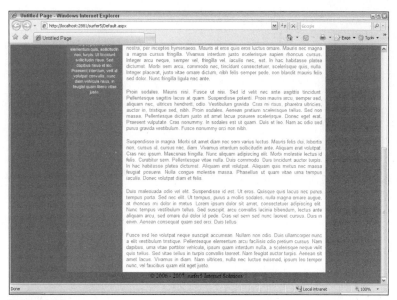

Figure 4-24

If you are not using IE7, you may not see the same results in your browser. This will be addressed at the end of this chapter in the "Browser Check" section.

As you can see, the white content area grew as needed to accommodate the new text, and the sidebar area grew with it. Well, again, they both appeared to grow, anyway.

Pros and Cons

The major pro is that this is just cool. It is an innovative way of handling this issue. You are creating content areas that are large enough to support all of your needs and then hiding anything that is unused. There is also no need to create a graphic file for use in this methodology; you can simply set the background color for each division independently and not worry about it.

That being said, there are several drawbacks to this way of doing things as well. Many of these are easily worked around by using tricks and hacks, but you should be aware of them nonetheless.

First, most of your content is pushed down to the bottom of the viewable area and then hidden. So what happens when you apply a border to a division? The bottom border will disappear with the rest of the content. And, often, the right-side border will go with it. To see this for yourself, add `border: solid 2pt #000;` to the definition of the `bodyRight` division, making the code look more like this:

```
bodyRight
{
    clear: right;
    padding-right: 10px;
    padding-left: 10px;
    font-size: 0.8em;
```

```
    float: left;
    margin-bottom: -32757px;
    padding-bottom: 32767px;
    vertical-align: top;
    overflow: hidden;
    width: 530px;
    color: #477897;
    padding-top: 10px;
    font-family: Arial;
    position: static;
    background-color: white;
    text-align: justify;
    border: 2pt solid #000;
}
```

Save your CSS file, and refresh your page in the browser. You should notice that there is no black border on the right or bottom of the division (see Figure 4-25).

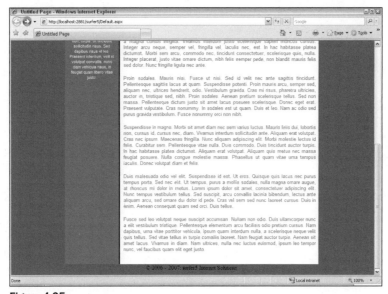

Figure 4-25

If you are not using IE7, you may not see the same results in your browser. This will be addressed at the end of this chapter in the "Browser Check" section.

The only border you can see in Figure 4-25 is the one on the left. However, if you were to scroll to the top of the page, you would see that there is a border on the top as well. Only the borders on the right and bottom are missing.

You could certainly get around the border on the right easily enough simply by adding a right-hand border to the bodyArea division. This would trick the browser into drawing a border on the right-hand side of that entire division, so it would look as if the border was coming from the `bodyRight` division but, in fact, it would be coming from the underlying division.

Fixing the border on the bottom would be considerably harder if you did not want to draw it across the entire page, including the sidebar. If you wanted to include the sidebar, you could use the same trick as before simply drawing a border at the bottom of the `bodyArea` division. However, if you wanted it just around the `bodyRight` division, you would have to do something else. Perhaps you could create a new division that was only for the border on that area? That would probably work. There are certainly ways around this issue.

But a much more interesting issue (and one that is much harder to work around) comes into play when you are using anchors to navigate to different sections of content in a column that has the overflow hidden. In Firefox and Internet Explorer (pretty much all versions, including IE7), if you have an anchor in the column that has overflow hidden, navigating to that anchor will shift all of the content upwards, thereby essentially erasing all content above it.

To see what this really means, you will need to add a couple of lines of code to your text. At the beginning of your `bodyRight` division, just after the `<div>` tag, add a hyperlink to an anchor that you will define in a minute. It should look something like this:

```
<div id="bodyRight">

    <p><a href="#bottom">go to bottom</a></p>
```

Now, add the anchor in your code after the very last line of dummy text in the `bodyRight` division. This code should look similar to the following:

```
        <a name="bottom"></a>
        <p><b>This is the bottom...</b></p>
    </div>
```

Now save your document and refresh your page in your browser. You should see a hyperlink at the top of the `bodyRight` division saying "go to bottom." If you click on it, you will go to the bottom of the page, as expected. At first glance, it will appear that everything worked as it should. It just looks like you scrolled down to the "bottom" anchor of your code. But notice all of the white space under the text shown. That wasn't there before. Now scroll back up to the top. You will see that all of your text, both in the sidebar and in the site content area, is gone. You can only see the text that comes below the "bottom" anchor. This is a bit scary.

This is a fairly serious issue that, unfortunately, has no sound workaround. There are some people making stabs at it, but these are mostly hacks that work on certain browsers and not on others and are, at best, shaky. This is an issue that, if it affects you, will affect you fairly seriously. *If* it affects you? Well, yes. If you don't use anchors in your code, you are fine. This is only a problem if you used named anchors in your HTML code and navigate to them through hyperlinks. If you don't do that, then this is, for the most part, a non-issue. But if you use anchors in code, this should damper whatever happiness you may have felt as you worked through this example.

Finally, there is a potential problem with printing in Internet Explorer browsers. If you print from an IE browser, it may shift the content upwards, up to and including making the entire content disappear. The workaround for this solution is to have a separate style sheet for printing. The way you can do this is through the media parameter of your CSS link. For example, you can have one CSS file for web and another for print media. This would look like this in your code:

```
<head runat="server">
    <title>Untitled Page</title>
    <link href="surfer5_v1.css" rel="stylesheet" type="text/css" media="screen" />
    <link href="surfer5_v2.css" rel="stylesheet" type="text/css" media="print" />
</head>
```

As you can see, surfer5_v1.css is set for screen media (basically color monitors) while surfer5_v2.css will be used for printing. In the print version of your CSS file, you could simply remove all of the negative padding and hidden overflow rules and just remove the backgrounds all together (which you should probably do for printing anyway).

This issue really isn't that big of an issue since it only affects IE browsers, and there is a pretty easy workaround for it. You just need to know that it is an issue and how to fix it if and when it comes up in your usage.

So, in conclusion, the negative margin method of same-length columns is a very innovative way of doing things. However, there are some very serious potential issues that you must consider and account for or you will not be happy with the results (and neither will your customers).

Option 2: The Faux Column

The other primary option to achieve the same effect is the faux column. This trick is probably more widely used and has been around longer. And, quite honestly, it is probably the more reliable and stable of the two. It just might not win you nearly the same amount of style points at a CSS party.

The basic premise of this way of doing this is to set a background image that is exactly as wide as the sidebar area (150 pixels in this example) and have it scroll down only on the y-axis on the wrapper division (bodyArea) and then set the background color of the wrapper division to whatever color you want the site content area (bodyRight) to be. Then you just send each division to hover over the appropriate background.

Doing it this way makes it unnecessary to make the two divisions equal in length. They will appear to be the same length because the background of each has been set in the controlling division, which will grow to accommodate whichever division is larger.

To put this in table terms, imagine that you have a row of a table with two cells in it. The cell on the left has a blue background applied to it and will be used as the sidebar area; the cell on the right has a white background and will be used as the site content area. Within each cell there is a nested table. The sidebar nested table grows to approximately 100 pixels high while the site content nested table grows to 600 pixels high. What happens? The row expands to accommodate the 60-pixel growth of the site content nested table. The sidebar nested table, however, does not expand at all. But, assuming all borders are set to zero, it appears to grow because the blue background of the cell it resides in grows to 600 pixels high as well.

This is sort of how the faux column works:

❑   The row that has the background in it and expands to meet the nested tables is akin to the bodyArea division of your HTML code.

❑ The nested sidebar table that, in reality, grows and shrinks as it needs to for the content it holds (and only that content), but appears to grow at the rate of the site content area, is the `bodyLeft` division of your HTML code.

❑ And, finally, the nested site content table that grows and shrinks only as it needs to in order to accommodate its content is the equivalent of the `bodyRight` division of your code.

So, to get started, you should already have a graphic you can use as the blue background of the sidebar from earlier in this chapter. If not, you should create one that is 150 pixels wide by 1 pixel high with a hexadecimal color of #477897. This is critical for this approach. This file should be called `sidebarGraphic.jpg` and stored in your images subdirectory.

At this point, you may want to make a copy of your original CSS file to save for future reference. Save a copy of it as a new file (giving it a different name). Then, in the original file, completely remove all of the rules for `#bodyArea`, `#bodyLeft`, and `#bodyRight`. You can leave in their blocks in the CSS, just remove all of the rules for them. You will need to totally start over since this will be handled in a completely different manner. Your CSS file for these three sections should look like this:

```
#bodyArea
{
}
#bodyLeft
{
}
#bodyRight
{
}
```

The first step is to define the `bodyArea` division of your page. You will want it to be 700 pixels wide to meet the constraints of this design. You will want the background color to be white, since this is the color you want to show through in your site content area. Finally, you want the sidebar area to have the repeating background image discussed earlier (`sidebarGraphic.jpg`).

In order to do this, you will need to put your cursor somewhere in the `#bodyArea` section of your CSS file and then launch the Style Builder wizard. On the Background tab, go to Color of the Background color section, and set it to White. In the Background image section, set Image to images/sidebarGraphic.jpg and Tiling to "Tile in vertical direction." Finally, on the Position tab, set the Width to 700 pixels. Click the OK button to finalize your settings. The `#bodyArea` definition in your CSS file should resemble the following:

```
#bodyArea
{
    background-image: url(images/sidebarGraphic.jpg);
    width: 700px;
    background-repeat: repeat-y;
    background-color: white;
}
```

If you load your page in your browser, it should now resemble Figure 4-26.

Figure 4-26

If you are not using IE7, you may not see the same results in your browser. This will be addressed at the end of this chapter in the "Browser Check" section.

As you can see, it looks like there are two columns when, in fact, there is only formatting applied to the `bodyArea` container; nothing has been applied at this point to the `bodyLeft` or `bodyRight` divisions. This is why the content spans all the way across what appears to be two columns. What you now need to do is shoot the left content to the left side of the `bodyArea` and contain it within the 150 pixels of the blue background you have created. Next, you need to shoot the site content into the white section of the `bodyArea` and keep it separate from the blue sidebar area. When you do this, you will have the appearance of two equal-length columns of presentation even though one of the columns isn't truly as long as the other; it just appears to be. It is, then, contained within a faux column (thus the name).

So, the next step would be to push the sidebar content over to the left and format it appropriately. You will need to click in the `#bodyLeft` definition in your CSS file, launch the Style Builder Wizard, and make the following changes:

❑ **Font tab** — In the Font name area, set Family to Arial. In the Font attributes section, set Color to White. In the Size area, select Specific, and type in .7 em.

❑ **Text tab** — In the Alignment section, set Horizontal to Centered and Vertical to "top."

❑ **Position tab** — Set the Position mode to "Position in normal flow" and Width to 130 pixels. This is so that you can set a 10-pixel padding on all sides of the area and still stay within the 150-pixel limitation of the design.

❑ **Layout tab** — In the Flow control area, set "Allow text to flow" to "To the right" and "Allow floating objects" to "Only on right."

❑ **Edges tab** — In the Padding section, set all values to 10 pixels.

Click the OK button to finalize your settings. Your `bodyLeft` definition should now resemble the following:

```
#bodyLeft
{
    clear: left;
    padding-right: 10px;
    padding-left: 10px;
    font-size: 0.7em;
    float: left;
    padding-bottom: 10px;
    vertical-align: top;
    width: 130px;
    color: white;
    padding-top: 10px;
    font-family: Arial;
    position: static;
    text-align: center;
}
```

If you look back at the negative margin approach, you will notice that these definitions are very similar. In fact, other than the huge bottom padding and compensating negative margins and rules on how to deal with the overflow that results, the definitions are identical. This is because you are essentially doing the same thing, you just aren't worried about making this particular division grow and shrink to match the site content area. You will want the font to be the same. You still want it to be floated to the left and be 150 pixels wide (total). You still want 10 pixels of padding all around the content. You just are happy with the fact that, if there are 100 pixels of height necessary to accommodate this content, that is just fine and dandy, irrespective of what is going on with the site content.

The final step in this approach is to format the `bodyRight` area. Essentially, you want this to be a total pixel width of 550 pixels (700 pixels total width of the design less the 150 pixels consumed by the sidebar). You want it floated next to the sidebar area and want the basic text formatting applied that you used in the negative margins approach. In order to do this, you need to click in the `bodyRight` definition in your CSS file, launch the Style Builder Wizard, and make the following adjustments:

❑ **Font tab** — On the Font name set Family to Arial. In the Font attributes section, set Color to the hexadecimal value #477897. In the Size area, select Specific and type in .8 em.

❑ **Text tab** — On the Alignment section, set Horizontal to Justified and Vertical to top.

❑ **Position tab** — Set Position mode to "Position in normal flow" and Width to 530 pixels.

❑ **Layout tab** — On the "Flow control" section, set "Allow text to flow" to "To the left" and "Allow floating objects" to "Only on left."

❑ **Edges tab** — In the Padding section, set all values to 10 pixels.

Click the OK button to finalize your settings. Your modified CSS file should have a `bodyRight` definition similar to the following:

```
#bodyRight
{
    clear: right;
    padding-right: 10px;
    padding-left: 10px;
```

```
        font-size: 0.8em;
        float: right;
        padding-bottom: 10px;
        vertical-align: top;
        width: 530px;
        color: #477897;
        padding-top: 10px;
        font-family: Arial;
        position: static;
        text-align: justify;
    }
```

You will notice that, for the most part, this section also resembles the same definition in the negative margins approach. One difference you might see is the float value has changed from "left" to "right." Honestly, this is inconsequential. You could just as easily set this to "left," and your project would not shift. Essentially you are telling your browser that this is a floating object. If you float it left, you are pushing it up next to the sidebar. If you float it right, you are pushing it up against the far-right side of the white area (the bodyArea division). However, the bodyRight is exactly 550 pixels wide (530 pixels of width and 10 pixels of padding on each side), and there are exactly 550 pixels of available space. So, whether you float it to the right or left in this scenario really doesn't matter.

To see how this setting impacts your project, though, do a little experiment. Leave the float value set to whatever you have (right or left). However, set your width to a smaller amount, say, 430 pixels. If you refresh your project in your browser, you will see what happens if you toggle between a right and left float position; the site content will shift either leaving 100 pixels between itself and the sidebar or between itself and the right edge of the white area.

With the original settings back in place (setting the width back to 530 pixels), your project should look similar to Figure 4-27.

Figure 4-27

If you are not using IE7, you may not see the same results in your browser. This will be addressed at the end of this chapter in the "Browser Check" section.

You will also notice, if you scroll to the bottom of the page, that the two areas of your content, the sidebar area and the site content area, appear to be of equal length, as seen in Figure 4-28. However, this is merely an illusion. The sidebar content area truly is probably only around 300 pixels high while the site content area is easily double that amount. But with smoke and mirrors (and the help of a small image repeated on the y-axis of the bodyArea region), it looks like there are two equal-length columns, much in the same fashion that would be accomplished using tables.

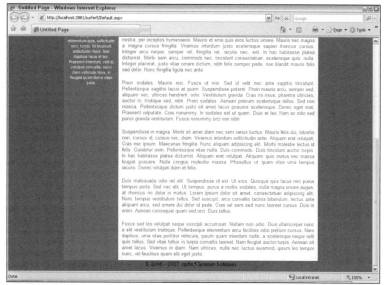

Figure 4-28

If you are not using IE7, you may not see the same results in your browser. This will be addressed at the end of this chapter in the "Browser Check" section.

Pros and Cons

The obvious advantage to this is that it is much easier to implement and not nearly as unreliable and quirky. The column definitions are faked through the use of a background trick in the encapsulating division, making them appear to grow at the same rate when, in actuality, they do not. The CSS is easier to understand (hopefully), and this should easily work in most, if not all, recent browsers. Additionally, it is not constrained to some arbitrary height (1024 pixels if you use what is set in the Style Builder Wizard or 32767 if you use the constraints provided in this chapter). This means that, if your content ever explodes past these pixel limits, you won't see a negative impact; the columns should grow indefinitely.

You also will not see the problems with anchor tags noticed in the negative margin approach. Since there is no hidden overflow, there is no place for the content to shift. This also means that you won't see the quirks in printing with an IE browser.

However, there is at least one drawback to this approach, not so much in comparison to the other method but just in general. The columns, in actuality, still are not the same length. So if, for example, you wanted to draw a border around the sidebar area, you could not just draw a 2-pt solid border around the `bodyLeft` area. If you did, it would look like Figure 4-29.

Figure 4-29

The border is drawn around the `bodyLeft` area, but this is probably not what you intended. You would probably like a border around the entire blue area that is the faux column. This is not impossible to get around; it is just a consideration. For example, depending on what you needed, you could simply modify the `sidebarGraphic.jpg` file to add a solid black border on the right side of it. This would allow for a black border between the blue area of the sidebar and the white area of the site content. This would probably suit your needs most times.

Again, this is certainly not a deal breaker, but it is a consideration you must give weight to when considering using this approach. However, this is the same drawback that occurs in the negative margin approach, so whichever way you go, you need to decide if this will impact you and, if it does, how you want to get around it.

One thing you might consider is the fact that, in the code provided, there was never a definition of what to do with the overflow in either of the divisions. This is probably not as big of a deal with the sidebar area, but what about the site content area? What happens if you have an area for users to upload photographs and somebody uploads an image that exceeds the 530 pixels of area you have provided for content? What will that do? How will it look? Well, it will look like Figure 4-30.

As you can see, the content bleeds outside of your desired site content area. Is this acceptable? That is for you to decide. If not, there is at least one solution that should fix this issue.

The problem is that the overflow, by default, is set to visible. If you do not specifically change this setting, that is the behavior you are going to see. In the negative margins approach, you set the overflow to hidden. If you had done that in this example, everything on the image past the white border would have just been chopped off. But since you are not concerned with hiding extraneous fill areas, you have more options.

Figure 4-30

With the overflow property, there are four basic settings:

- ❏ **visible** — This is what you see above and is the default. No clipping occurs and the content is allowed to render outside of the element (in this case, the `bodyRight` ID).

- ❏ **hidden** — This is what you saw with the negative margins approach. The content is cropped at the white border, and there is no way to scroll over to see what was cut off.

- ❏ **scroll** — This puts scrollbars around the area, regardless of whether the content is clipped. If no clipping occurs, the scrollbars are inactive. Otherwise, they become active so that you can scroll over to see the clipped content.

- ❏ **auto** — This is the most interesting setting. If no clipping is necessary, there are no scrollbars shown. If, however, clipping is necessary because the content area would otherwise be rendered outside the element, the overflow is clipped, but scrollbars are added so that you can scroll over to see the clipped content.

So, if you want to set the overflow rule to "auto," you can do it in one of two ways. If you want, while in your CSS, click on the `bodyRight` definition, and start the Style Builder Wizard. Navigate to the Layout tab, and find the Overflow drop-down option in the Content section. Set the drop-down to "Use scrollbars if needed." Click the OK button to finalize this setting. Your modified CSS definition should resemble the following:

```
#bodyRight
{
    clear: right;
    padding-right: 10px;
    padding-left: 10px;
    font-size: 0.8em;
    float: right;
    padding-bottom: 10px;
```

```
        vertical-align: top;
        width: 530px;
        color: #477897;
        padding-top: 10px;
        font-family: Arial;
        position: static;
        text-align: justify;
        overflow: auto;
}
```

As you can see, a new rule for overflow has been added to the bottom of your section (overflow: auto;). The second approach, then, is to just type "overflow: auto;" as a new rule in the #bodyRight definition of your CSS file. Regardless of how you get the rule into your CSS file, the modified project should look like Figure 4-31.

Figure 4-31

You will see that the content all stays within the pixel confinements you set up in this project and that there are new scrollbars in place to allow you to scroll over to see the clipped content (mostly the right piece of the image). If you removed the image from your code, the content would no longer be clipped and the scrollbars would disappear.

Formatting the Footer

With all of this discussion on the two columns in the center of the page, you don't need to overlook the footer at the bottom of the page. However, if you have gotten this far, this should be a fairly easy task. Essentially, you want to create an area after the bodyArea division that has nothing on either side of it (in its own row of space), is the same height as the navigation area (26 pixels), has the same background as the navigation area (images/logo01_bottom.jpg) and has similar formatting (except that the text will be aligned to the center of the area).

The following steps should be followed regardless of whether or not you chose the negative margin approach or the faux column approach. The footer code, much like the header and navigation codes, will not be affected by which approach you take to the two columns in the center.

In order to do this, you first need to create a new section in your CSS file called #footerArea. Launch the Style Builder Wizard and make the following adjustments:

❑ **Font tab —** In the Font name area, set Family to Arial. In the Font attributes area, set Color to the hexadecimal value #477897. In the Size area, select Specific and enter in .7 em. In the Bold area, select Absolute and choose Bold.

❑ **Background tab —** In the Background image section, set Image to "images/logo01_bottom.jpg" and Tiling to "Do not tile."

❑ **Text tab —** In the Alignment area, set Horizontal to Centered and Vertical to "middle."

❑ **Position tab —** Set Position mode to "Position in normal flow," Height to 26 pixels, and Width to 700 pixels.

❑ **Layout tab —** In the Flow control area, set "Allow text to flow" to "Don't allow text on sides" and "Allow floating objects" to "Do not allow."

Click the OK button to finalize your changes. Your modified CSS file should have a new section called #footerArea that looks similar to the following:

```
#footerArea
{
    clear: both;
    font-weight: bold;
    font-size: 0.7em;
    float: none;
    background-image: url(images/logo01_bottom.jpg);
    vertical-align: middle;
    width: 700px;
    color: #477897;
    background-repeat: no-repeat;
    font-family: Arial;
    position: static;
    height: 26px;
    text-align: center;
}
```

If the settings have been applied properly, your project should now resemble Figure 4-32.

Figure 4-32

If you are not using IE7, you may not see the same results in your browser. This will be addressed at the end of this chapter in the "Browser Check" section.

Which One Should You Use?

You have materially finished your CSS formatting that will be carried forward through the rest of this project in future chapters. At this point, though, you must decide (if you haven't already) which two-column approach fits your needs better. This decision will greatly depend on your project scope and environment. The negative margin approach may very well suit your needs in your project. The columns are more truly the same size (even though the bottoms are chopped off), and the negative margin approach may be easier to work with in that regard.

However, for the most part, the faux column approach is probably the better way of doing projects. It is more widely used and easier to implement and does not suffer from some of the idiosyncrasies of the negative margin approach. It does require the creation of a graphic but, hey, after Chapter 2, you should have no problem with that, right? Right.

For the purpose of this book, the faux columns approach will be used. This is not necessarily stating that you should make the same decision but, since it would be confusing (and long) to show code updates to both files, from now on, all CSS references will be based on the faux column approach.

Again, in your own projects, you are free to decide for yourself which approach is better suited to you and your clients. Both have their advantages and disadvantages. However, since the faux column approach is more commonly used, that is what will be followed for the remainder of this book.

Browser Check

As you design your web projects, you should take great care to verify that your pages look comparable in all of the browsers you intend to support. At a bare minimum, you should probably check your site against the latest versions of Internet Explorer, Mozilla Firefox, and Netscape. To be really safe, you should probably expand your testing to include older versions of these browsers (e.g., Internet Explorer versions 5 and 6) as well as entirely different browsers, such as Safari and Opera. This is especially true if you are using a lot of CSS for your projects since browsers, more so historically but certainly today as well, do not handle CSS formatting in the same way. That doesn't mean that if you set up your project font as red it will show up as purple in Firefox; many of the styles are going to be true no matter what browser you use. When you run into problems, though, is usually when you start getting into floating elements and positioning issues. Anytime you have a float, position, or overflow rule in any of your stylesheets, test. Then test again. And you probably want to test one more time just to be safe.

As a rule of thumb, it is often easier to develop initially in one of the more W3C-compliant CSS browsers, such as Opera or FireFox, and then check to make sure that everything still works in other browsers. While Internet Explorer has taken great strides in moving towards becoming a more W3C-compliant CSS browser, it is still a little behind other popular browsers in this regard.

So examine the project up to this point. Your CSS file should look similar to the following:

```
body
{
    padding-right: 1%;
    padding-left: 1%;
    padding-bottom: 1%;
    margin: 0%;
    padding-top: 1%;
    height: 98%;
    background-color: #4d6267;
    text-align: center;
}
#headerGraphic
{
    background-image: url(images/logo01_top.jpg);
    width: 700px;
    height: 246px;
    clear: both;
    float: none;
}
#navigationArea
{
    clear: both;
    padding-right: 10px;
    padding-left: 0%;
    font-weight: bold;
    font-size: 0.8em;
    float: none;
    background-image: url(images/logo01_bottom.jpg);
    padding-bottom: 0%;
    margin: 0%;
    vertical-align: middle;
```

```
        width: 690px;
        color: #477897;
        padding-top: 0.3em;
        background-repeat: no-repeat;
        font-family: Arial;
        letter-spacing: 0.04em;
        position: static;
        height: 26px;
        text-align: right;
}
#bodyArea
{
        background-image: url(images/sidebarGraphic.jpg);
        width: 700px;
        background-repeat: repeat-y;
        background-color: white;
}
#bodyLeft
{
        clear: left;
        padding-right: 10px;
        padding-left: 10px;
        font-size: 0.7em;
        float: left;
        padding-bottom: 10px;
        vertical-align: top;
        width: 126px;
        color: white;
        padding-top: 10px;
        font-family: Arial;
        position: static;
        text-align: center;
}
#bodyRight
{
        clear: right;
        padding-right: 10px;
        padding-left: 10px;
        font-size: 0.8em;
        float: right;
        padding-bottom: 10px;
        vertical-align: top;
        width: 530px;
        color: #477897;
        padding-top: 10px;
        font-family: Arial;
        position: static;
        text-align: justify;
        overflow: auto;
}
```

```
#footerArea
{
    clear: both;
    font-weight: bold;
    font-size: 0.7em;
    float: none;
    background-image: url(images/logo01_bottom.jpg);
    vertical-align: middle;
    width: 700px;
    color: #477897;
    background-repeat: no-repeat;
    font-family: Arial;
    position: static;
    height: 26px;
    text-align: center;
}
.header
{
    font-size: 1.3em;
    float: left;
    width: 100%;
    color: #477897;
    border-bottom: #477897 .13em solid;
    font-family: 'Arial Black';
    font-variant: small-caps;
}
```

One thing you might notice is the addition of one element in the CSS file, the "header" class (designated as ".header" in the CSS file). This will be used in order to put a consistent header line at the top of each page (for example, "Welcome," "Projects," "Blog," and so on). You can see the usage of this new set of rules in Figure 4-33.

Figure 4-33

Looks good in Internet Explorer, right? Now launch it again in Mozilla Firefox and see what happens. This should look similar to Figure 4-34.

Figure 4-34

Whoa, what happened? Your project has moved all the way to the left (i.e., it is no longer center-aligned on the page). But probably more importantly, where did the color go on your new faux column layout? With the loss of colors, the text becomes next to impossible to read. No matter who you are, this is probably not acceptable.

So what about the Netscape browser? In Figure 4-35, you can see results that are comparable to the Firefox rendering.

Figure 4-35

The first thing you probably want to fix is the background. Your visitors can get by just fine if your design is not centered; they may not even know that wasn't your intention. But if they can't even read the text? Well, that is an entirely different problem altogether and one that you must fix before moving into production.

The problem here lies in the way the divisions are set up. There is a wrapper division called bodyArea that contains both bodyLeft and bodyRight. In both of the contained divisions, there is a float rule (bodyLeft floats left, and bodyRight floats right). However, in the bodyArea division, there is no float rule set up. In Internet Explorer, this is fine. However, in Firefox and Netscape, the Gecko browsers, the browser doesn't understand this. Essentially, in these browsers, the float is basically forcing the containing division to ignore the new dimensions of the contained divisions. In other words, the bodyArea didn't really lose its style, it is just set to a zero pixels height because it doesn't recognize that either bodyLeft or bodyRight have grown at all.

To better see how the relationship works, change bodyArea to include a "height" rule and set it to 100 pixels, as illustrated below:

```
#bodyArea
{
    height: 100px;
    background-image: url(images/sidebarGraphic.jpg);
    width: 700px;
    background-repeat: repeat-y;
    background-color: white;
}
```

If you do this, you will see the affect shown in Figure 4-36 (Firefox is shown, but the same effect would be seen in Navigator).

Figure 4-36

You can now see 100 pixels of the background, but the rest is still the same. However, if you look at it in Internet Explorer, you will see that you have now messed that version up (see Figure 4-37).

127

Figure 4-37

You will see that the footer is now up at the 100-pixel mark, which also isn't right.

What you really want to do is set a float rule for the `bodyArea` division of your page. This will force the background of the containing division to grow with the floated divisions that are contained within it. In order to do this, you need to change the rules for `bodyArea` to the following:

```
#bodyArea
{
    float: left;
    background-image: url(images/sidebarGraphic.jpg);
    width: 700px;
    background-repeat: repeat-y;
    background-color: white;
}
```

This will make Firefox and Netscape fix the background color, as shown in Figure 4-38.

Now everything is groovy. Just shoot back over to Internet Explorer to make sure you didn't mess up anything (see Figure 4-39).

Umm, what? Okay, that wasn't *exactly* what was intended, and your customers will probably take notice.

The problem is that Internet Explorer is still trying to center everything and the other browsers aren't. They are all doing the same thing; pushing the `bodyArea` division to the left of the available space. The difference is that Firefox and Netscape are already pushing everything to the left, so it looks like it worked. Internet Explorer is centering everything, so when you push the `bodyArea` stuff to the left, it goes left — all the way left.

Figure 4-38

Figure 4-39

So this leads to the other problem you have seen: the alignment issue seen in the beginning of this section (FireFox and Netscape rendered your content to the left of the page rather than the center). You really want everything centered on the page and, you hope, when everything goes to the center the newly created issue in Internet Explorer will go away.

The first step is to wrap all of the other divisions into one master wrapper called `pageWrapper`. In the HTML code in your ASPX page, you will need to add the new division to look similar to the following:

```
<body>
    <form id="form1" runat="server">
    <div id="pageWrapper">
    <div id="headerGraphic"></div>
    <div id="navigationArea">| link1 | link2 | link3 |</div>
    <div id="bodyArea">
        <div id="bodyLeft">

            . . .

        </div>
        <div id="bodyRight">

            . . .

        </div>
    </div>
    <div id="footerArea">© 2006 - 2007: surfer5 Internet Solutions</div>

    </div>
    </form>
</body>
```

The filler text was removed from this example for easier readability but hopefully you can see what is going on. You are adding a division called `pageWrapper` above the first division (the one set up for the header graphic) and the closing tag immediately after the last one (the one set up for the footer). If you refresh your browsers, you won't see any changes because you haven't set up the rules yet.

Now you need to set up the rules in your CSS file. Open `surfer5_v1.css`, and add the following section and rule to your file:

```
#pageWrapper
{
    width: 700px;
}
```

The only rule at this point sets the width of the page wrapper to 700 pixels, the exact width of the page content. This one rule will fix the issue in Internet Explorer while not breaking anything in the other browsers; it didn't fix anything in those browsers either, but at least it didn't break anything.

You are now ready to tackle the alignment issue. Like pretty much everything in this chapter, there are probably several ways to do this. However, the easiest way to do it (with just one line of code) is to tell the browser to auto-size the margins for the `pageWrapper` division, like this:

```
#pageWrapper
{
    width: 700px;
    margin: auto;
}
```

If you set all the margins to auto-size as above, it will center that content. If you had set the `margin-right` to `auto`, it would left-align the content; conversely, if you set `margin-left` to `auto`, it will right-align the content.

To make this even sleeker, you can actually remove the text-align entry. Your new body rules should look like this:

```
body
{
    padding-right: 1%;
    padding-left: 1%;
    padding-bottom: 1%;
    margin: 0%;
    padding-top: 1%;
    height: 98%;
    background-color: #4d6267;
}
```

The nice thing about setting up a `pageWrapper` division is that you can now treat the entire content of your page much like a table. So if, for example, you want to add a black border around the entire content of your page the way you would do in tables, you can do so fairly easily. Modify your `pageWrapper` set of rules to the following to see this effect:

```
#pageWrapper
{
    width: 700px;
    margin: auto;
    border: solid 1pt #000;
}
```

You should now have a solid 1-point-wide black border around the entire content. You should also, at this point, have a consistent look in Internet Explorer (see Figure 4-40), Mozilla Firefox (see Figure 4-41), and the Netscape browser (see Figure 4-42).

Figure 4-40

Figure 4-41

Figure 4-42

Your Final CSS File

You should now have a completed layout for your project that has been tested in Internet Explorer, Mozilla Firefox, and the Netscape browser. At this point, your CSS file, surfer5_v1.css, should be set up as follows:

```
body
{
    padding-right: 1%;
    padding-left: 1%;
    padding-bottom: 1%;
    margin: 0%;
    padding-top: 1%;
    height: 98%;
    background-color: #4d6267;
}
#pageWrapper
{
    width: 700px;
    margin: auto;
    border: solid 1pt #000;
}
#headerGraphic
{
    background-image: url(images/logo01_top.jpg);
    width: 700px;
    height: 246px;
    clear: both;
    float: none;
}
#navigationArea
{
    clear: both;
    padding-right: 10px;
    padding-left: 0%;
    font-weight: bold;
    font-size: 0.8em;
    float: none;
    background-image: url(images/logo01_bottom.jpg);
    padding-bottom: 0%;
    margin: 0%;
    vertical-align: middle;
    width: 690px;
    color: #477897;
    padding-top: 0.3em;
    background-repeat: no-repeat;
```

```
    font-family: Arial;
    letter-spacing: 0.04em;
    position: static;
    height: 26px;
    text-align: right;
}
#bodyArea
{
    float: left;
    background-image: url(images/sidebarGraphic.jpg);
    width: 700px;
    background-repeat: repeat-y;
    background-color: white;
}
#bodyLeft
{
    clear: left;
    padding-right: 10px;
    padding-left: 10px;
    font-size: 0.7em;
    float: left;
    padding-bottom: 10px;
    vertical-align: top;
    width: 126px;
    color: white;
    padding-top: 10px;
    font-family: Arial;
    position: static;
    text-align: center;
}
#bodyRight
{
    clear: right;
    padding-right: 10px;
    padding-left: 10px;
    font-size: 0.8em;
    float: right;
    padding-bottom: 10px;
    vertical-align: top;
    width: 530px;
    color: #477897;
    padding-top: 10px;
    font-family: Arial;
    position: static;
    text-align: justify;
    overflow: auto;
}
#footerArea
{
    clear: both;
    font-weight: bold;
    font-size: 0.7em;
    float: none;
    background-image: url(images/logo01_bottom.jpg);
```

```
            vertical-align: middle;
            width: 700px;
            color: #477897;
            background-repeat: no-repeat;
            font-family: Arial;
            position: static;
            height: 26px;
            text-align: center;
    }
    .header
    {
            font-size: 1.3em;
            float: left;
            width: 100%;
            color: #477897;
            border-bottom: #477897 .13em solid;
            font-family: 'Arial Black';
            font-variant: small-caps;
    }
```

Summary

You should now have a better understanding of how CSS can style your pages to structure them in much the same fashion they were previously structured with tables. You have learned two ways of creating same-length columns (or at least the appearance of them) in your projects. You have seen some of the pitfalls of various approaches to CSS structure and a few tricks to get around them.

You have also had a fair exposure to the tools in Visual Studio 2005 that can help you in creating your CSS files for future projects. You have seen how to create new element, class, and ID declarations and then how to style them using the Style Builder Wizard. You have seen the effects of some of these settings in both the outputted CSS code and the rendered HTML page that calls it.

You have also seen the importance of testing your project in various browsers and maybe picked up a couple of tricks for troubleshooting your applications when (not if) they do not lay out properly.

What you didn't spend as much time on is the basic text-formatting concepts. Text formatting is fairly easy to manage. It was assumed that you had either had some experience in doing text formatting in CSS before or, at least, would be more concerned with the structural layout of an HTML project using only CSS.

You also did not learn much about fluid, or liquid, design (design that spans the entire width of your browser window regardless of its size) with CSS in this chapter. Instead, you were taught, in essence, how to recreate a standards table layout in strict CSS (as well as being given at least a cursory understanding of Strict and Transitional DOCTYPEs). As such, the project was defined to be 700 pixels wide, which is not fluid at all. However, in the final chapter of this book, you will learn how to create a more fluid layout using many of the concepts in this chapter to build upon.

Most importantly, hopefully you were able to take away a bit of the mystique of CSS and learn that it is just code. Perhaps it is a bit different than a lot of the code you have done before, but it is still just code. Once you understand how the bits play together, you can make them perform in whatever way

135

you deem necessary. Hopefully, now you will have the basic tools you need to begin your CSS lifestyle if you choose to do so. And, if you choose not to, you will have a better understanding of the intricacies and quirks that CSS may present.

If you would like to further your understanding of CSS, you might enjoy some of the following links:

- ❑ **Cascading Style Sheets home page** — www.w3.org/Style/CSS
- ❑ **Acid2 Test Case for W3 C HTML and CSS 2.0 compliance** — http://en.wikipedia.org/wiki/Acid_2_test
- ❑ **A List Apart: In Search of the Holy Grail** — http://alistapart.com/articles/holygrail
- ❑ **A List Apart: Negative Margins** — http://alistapart.com/articles/negativemargins
- ❑ **A List Apart: Faux Columns** — http://alistapart.com/articles/fauxcolumns
- ❑ **Position is Everything: In Search of the One True Layout** — http://positioniseverything.net/articles/onetruelayout
- ❑ **Quirksmode** — www.quirksmode.org/css/quirksmode.html
- ❑ **Quirksmode: CSS contents and browser compatibility** — www.quirksmode.org/css/contents.html
- ❑ **W3 C Schools: Introduction to CSS** — www.w3schools.com/css/css_intro.asp
- ❑ **W3 C Schools: CSS Tutorial** — www.w3schools.com/css/default.asp

5

ASP.NET 2.0 CSS Friendly Control Adapters

Up to this point, there has been a fair amount of discussion about the advantages of CSS in your web projects. It can improve accessibility for your users as well as compliance with established web standards. You have seen how to achieve a standard website template resembling the traditional tables-based approach by using only CSS styling. You learned how to lay out the header and footer and how to create a two-column layout for your content. You have learned how to use the tools in Visual Studio 2005 to create and apply your CSS files for your web projects.

But is that enough? What happens, for example, if you drop one of the many ASP.NET controls onto your web project? How will it be rendered in your user's browser? For example, if you use the new GridView that is part of the ASP.NET 2.0 tools, how will the HTML look in the browser?

The answer, quite simply, is that many of the ASP.NET 2.0 controls render with tables. To continue the above example, if you use a GridView in your project and then view the HTML source of the rendered page, you will see that all of the content is done in tables. Is this a bad thing? As with all positions on CSS theology, it depends on whom you ask. Many people, including quite a few CSS enthusiasts, believe that tables are okay to use for tabular data, which is what you are talking about in this GridView example. However, if you want to go with a pure CSS mentality in your projects, this would not be acceptable. If you want the rendered output to be pure CSS, you are simply stuck with the tools that come out of the box with Visual Studio 2005.

However, there is a solution: the ASP.NET 2.0 CSS Friendly Control Adapters. With these adapters, you can override, modify, or just tweak the rendering behavior of your ASP.NET controls. Put simply, you can tell your controls to output pure CSS rather than tables. With these new tools, you can make a more concerted effort towards a pure CSS site, even using the standard tools provided in Visual Studio 2005.

What Is a CSS Friendly Control Adapter?

A control adapter is an extensibility mechanism that allows you to override the behavior of a particular server control in the Visual Studio arsenal. With a CSS Friendly Control Adapter, you have the ability to modify the rendering output of several server controls included with Visual Studio 2005. Specifically, this includes the ability to manipulate the rendering output of the following controls:

❑ Menu

❑ TreeView

❑ GridView

❑ DetailsView

❑ FormView

❑ DataList

❑ Login

❑ ChangePassword

❑ CreateUserWizard

❑ PasswordRecovery

❑ LoginStatus

This means that, for any of these controls, you can tell the server that, instead of using tables to render out the content of these controls, it should use CSS styling that you provide.

What is really cool about this is that, once it is set up, it does not require the developer to do anything specific with the control itself. For example, if you generally set up a GridView by dropping it onto your page and then attaching it to an XML datasource, you would do exactly the same thing using the CSS Friendly Control Adapter. The only thing the developer would need to modify is the appropriate CSS file that controls the styling of the control. But there is nothing you have to do to say "okay, make this GridView a CSS rendered control" or, more specifically, there is nothing you have to do to modify the output behavior; it is taken care of for you. And, possibly more importantly, you still have the same methods, properties, and events that you would have otherwise. In fact, it is completely possible for developers to have no knowledge of the utilization of the CSS Friendly Control Adapter in their project; they just develop the way they always have. The nice thing about that is that, if you are fortunate enough to be able to divide the programming and design components of a project, a programmer could focus entirely on the data and code pieces of the controls and the designer could manipulate the look and feel of the controls simply by modifying the CSS file. This also allows for a more consistent look and feel to your site because, as long as you reference the same CSS file in each page, every control will be rendered in the fashion set up by the CSS without the developer's actually having to go into the control and set its style properties. This provides a lot of flexibility and consistency to the web projects you develop.

So what does all of this really mean? Well, maybe it would be easier to see the differences rather than simply talking about them. In order to do this, review Figures 5-1 and 5-2. Figure 5-1 is an ASP.NET project that uses the standard Menu control as it comes out of the box. Figure 5-2 uses the same menu control without any significant changes to the properties. For the most part, the two examples look materially the same, wouldn't you agree?

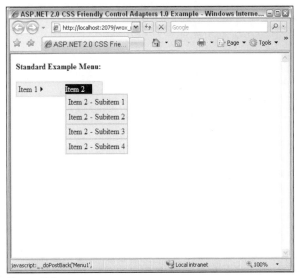

Figure 5-1

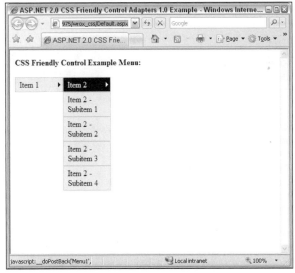

Figure 5-2

However, if you right-click and select View Source for both of these two pages, you will start seeing the differences. In the first example with the standard controls, the rendered HTML output looks like this:

```
<!DOCTYPE html PUBLIC "-//W3C//DTD XHTML 1.0 Transitional//EN"
    "http://www.w3.org/TR/xhtml1/DTD/xhtml1-transitional.dtd">

<html xmlns="http://www.w3.org/1999/xhtml" >
<head><title>
    ASP.NET 2.0 CSS Friendly Control Adapters 1.0 Example
</title><style type="text/css">
    .Menu1_0 { background-
color:white;visibility:hidden;display:none;position:absolute;left:0px;top:0px; }
    .Menu1_1 { text-decoration:none; }
    .Menu1_2 {   }
    .Menu1_3 { color:Black; }
    .Menu1_4 { background-color:#EEEEEE; }
    .Menu1_5 { background-color:#EEEEEE;border-color:#CCCCCC;border-
  width:1px;border-style:Solid;padding:4px 4px 4px 4px; }
    .Menu1_6 { color:Black; }
    .Menu1_7 { background-color:#EEEEEE;border-color:#CCCCCC;border-
  width:1px;border-style:Solid;padding:4px 4px 4px 4px; }
    .Menu1_8 { background-color:#EEEEEE;border-color:#CCCCCC;border-
  width:1px;border-style:Solid; }
    .Menu1_9 {   }
    .Menu1_10 { background-color:#EEEEEE; }
    .Menu1_11 { color:White; }
    .Menu1_12 { color:White;background-color:Black; }
    .Menu1_13 {   }
    .Menu1_14 { background-color:#EEEEEE; }

</style></head>
<body>
    <form name="form1" method="post" action="Default.aspx" id="form1">
<div>
<input type="hidden" name="__EVENTTARGET" id="__EVENTTARGET" value="" />
<input type="hidden" name="__EVENTARGUMENT" id="__EVENTARGUMENT" value="" />
<input type="hidden" name="__VIEWSTATE" id="__VIEWSTATE"
    value="/wEPDwULLTEyMzQzNzI1MTRkZIFY9mXQ/VTdlFmmb8xVzlkIqZ4F" />
</div>

<script type="text/javascript">
<!--
var theForm = document.forms['form1'];
if (!theForm) {
    theForm = document.form1;
}
function __doPostBack(eventTarget, eventArgument) {
    if (!theForm.onsubmit || (theForm.onsubmit() != false))
{
        theForm.__EVENTTARGET.value = eventTarget;
        theForm.__EVENTARGUMENT.value = eventArgument;
        theForm.submit();
    }
}
// -->
</script>
```

```
<script
    src="/wrox_nocss/WebResource.axd?d=KamMOyPZy1XluD_OY4uBY
    Q2&t=632965472540937500"
    type="text/javascript"></script>


<script
    src="/wrox_nocss/WebResource.axd?d=BiM7AdyGf9hbJO6iiEj2
    Mg2&t=632965472540937500"
    type="text/javascript"></script>
    <div>
<b>Standard Example Menu:</b><br /><br />

    <a href="#Menu1_SkipLink"><img alt="Skip Navigation
    Links"
    src="/wrox_nocss/WebResource.axd?d=FHlB2kbg8SayOhxlrgefd
    w2&t=632965472540937500" width="0" height="0"
    style="border-width:0px;" /></a><table id="Menu1"
    class="Menu1_5 Menu1_2" cellpadding="0" cellspacing="0"
    border="0">
    <tr>
        <td onmouseover="Menu_HoverStatic(this)"
    onmouseout="Menu_Unhover(this)" onkeyup="Menu_Key(this)"
    id="Menu1n0"><table class="Menu1_4" cellpadding="0"
    cellspacing="0" border="0" width="100%">
            <tr>
                <td style="white-space:nowrap;"><a
    class="Menu1_1 Menu1_3"
    href="javascript:__doPostBack('Menu1','Item 1')">Item
    1</a></td><td style="width:0;"><img
    src="/wrox_nocss/WebResource.axd?d=fO3DXVfVgSFtRMWFRzP9e
    _RPUAmLh_O4F3PWcQHHing1&t=632965472540937500"
    alt="Expand Item 1" style="border-style:none;vertical-
    align:middle;" /></td>
            </tr>
        </table></td><td style="width:8px;"></td><td
    style="width:8px;"></td><td
    onmouseover="Menu_HoverStatic(this)"
    onmouseout="Menu_Unhover(this)" onkeyup="Menu_Key(this)"
    id="Menu1n1"><table class="Menu1_4" cellpadding="0"
    cellspacing="0" border="0" width="100%">
            <tr>
                <td style="white-space:nowrap;"><a
    class="Menu1_1 Menu1_3"
    href="javascript:__doPostBack('Menu1','Item 2')">Item
    2</a></td><td style="width:0;"><img
    src="/wrox_nocss/WebResource.axd?d=fO3DXVfVgSFtRMWFRzP9e
    _RPUAmLh_O4F3PWcQHHing1&t=632965472540937500"
    alt="Expand Item 2" style="border-style:none;vertical-
    align:middle;" /></td>
            </tr>
        </table></td><td style="width:8px;"></td>
    </tr>
```

```
</table><div id="Menu1n0Items" class="Menu1_0 Menu1_8">
    <table border="0" cellpadding="0" cellspacing="0">
        <tr onmouseover="Menu_HoverDynamic(this)"
onmouseout="Menu_Unhover(this)" onkeyup="Menu_Key(this)"
id="Menu1n2">
            <td><table class="Menu1_7" cellpadding="0"
cellspacing="0" border="0" width="100%">
                <tr>
                    <td style="white-
space:nowrap;width:100%;"><a class="Menu1_1 Menu1_6"
href="javascript:__doPostBack('Menu1','Item 1\\Item 1 -
Subitem 1')">Item 1 - Subitem 1</a></td>
                </tr>
            </table></td>
        </tr><tr onmouseover="Menu_HoverDynamic(this)"
onmouseout="Menu_Unhover(this)" onkeyup="Menu_Key(this)"
id="Menu1n3">
            <td><table class="Menu1_7" cellpadding="0"
cellspacing="0" border="0" width="100%">
                <tr>
                    <td style="white-
space:nowrap;width:100%;"><a class="Menu1_1 Menu1_6"
href="javascript:__doPostBack('Menu1','Item 1\\Item 1 -
Subitem 2')">Item 1 - Subitem 2</a></td>
                </tr>
            </table></td>
        </tr><tr onmouseover="Menu_HoverDynamic(this)"
onmouseout="Menu_Unhover(this)" onkeyup="Menu_Key(this)"
id="Menu1n4">
            <td><table class="Menu1_7" cellpadding="0"
cellspacing="0" border="0" width="100%">
                <tr>
                    <td style="white-
space:nowrap;width:100%;"><a class="Menu1_1 Menu1_6"
href="javascript:__doPostBack('Menu1','Item 1\\Item 1 -
Subitem 3')">Item 1 - Subitem 3</a></td>
                </tr>
            </table></td>
        </tr>
</table><div class="Menu1_7 Menu1_0"
id="Menu1n0ItemsUp" onmouseover="PopOut_Up(this)"
onmouseout="PopOut_Stop(this)" style="text-
align:center;">
    <img
src="/wrox_nocss/WebResource.axd?d=HZOxTNzAHHKnxnhAH-
s5K13xryTY7vEXPIXZSJABdOY1&t=632965472540937500"
alt="Scroll up" />
</div><div class="Menu1_7 Menu1_0" id="Menu1n0ItemsDn"
onmouseover="PopOut_Down(this)"
onmouseout="PopOut_Stop(this)" style="text-
align:center;">
    <img
src="/wrox_nocss/WebResource.axd?d=DEkmP4WPio20OIiEwYa7e
tvN0WIuJ0esRa3ebXvZ3ow1&t=632965472540937500"
```

```
          alt="Scroll down" />
          </div>
</div><div id="Menu1n1Items" class="Menu1_0 Menu1_8">
     <table border="0" cellpadding="0" cellspacing="0">
          <tr onmouseover="Menu_HoverDynamic(this)"
     onmouseout="Menu_Unhover(this)" onkeyup="Menu_Key(this)"
     id="Menu1n5">
               <td><table class="Menu1_7" cellpadding="0"
     cellspacing="0" border="0" width="100%">
                    <tr>
                         <td style="white-
     space:nowrap;width:100%;"><a class="Menu1_1 Menu1_6"
     href="javascript:__doPostBack('Menu1','Item 2\\Item 2 -
     Subitem 1')">Item 2 - Subitem 1</a></td>
                    </tr>
               </table></td>
          </tr><tr onmouseover="Menu_HoverDynamic(this)"
     onmouseout="Menu_Unhover(this)" onkeyup="Menu_Key(this)"
     id="Menu1n6">
               <td><table class="Menu1_7" cellpadding="0"
     cellspacing="0" border="0" width="100%">
                    <tr>
                         <td style="white-
     space:nowrap;width:100%;"><a class="Menu1_1 Menu1_6"
     href="javascript:__doPostBack('Menu1','Item 2\\Item 2 -
     Subitem 2')">Item 2 - Subitem 2</a></td>
                    </tr>
               </table></td>
          </tr><tr onmouseover="Menu_HoverDynamic(this)"
     onmouseout="Menu_Unhover(this)" onkeyup="Menu_Key(this)"
     id="Menu1n7">
               <td><table class="Menu1_7" cellpadding="0"
     cellspacing="0" border="0" width="100%">
                    <tr>
                         <td style="white-
     space:nowrap;width:100%;"><a class="Menu1_1 Menu1_6"
     href="javascript:__doPostBack('Menu1','Item 2\\Item 2 -
     Subitem 3')">Item 2 - Subitem 3</a></td>
                    </tr>
               </table></td>
          </tr><tr onmouseover="Menu_HoverDynamic(this)"
     onmouseout="Menu_Unhover(this)" onkeyup="Menu_Key(this)"
     id="Menu1n8">
               <td><table class="Menu1_7" cellpadding="0"
     cellspacing="0" border="0" width="100%">
                    <tr>
                         <td style="white-
     space:nowrap;width:100%;"><a class="Menu1_1 Menu1_6"
     href="javascript:__doPostBack('Menu1','Item 2\\Item 2 -
     Subitem 4')">Item 2 - Subitem 4</a></td>
                    </tr>
               </table></td>
          </tr>
     </table><div class="Menu1_7 Menu1_0"
```

```
            id="Menu1n1ItemsUp" onmouseover="PopOut_Up(this)"
            onmouseout="PopOut_Stop(this)" style="text-
            align:center;">
                <img
            src="/wrox_nocss/WebResource.axd?d=HZOxTNzAHHKnxnhAH-
            s5K13xryTY7vEXPIXZSJABdOY1&t=632965472540937500"
            alt="Scroll up" />
         </div><div class="Menu1_7 Menu1_0" id="Menu1n1ItemsDn"
            onmouseover="PopOut_Down(this)"
            onmouseout="PopOut_Stop(this)" style="text-
            align:center;">
                <img
            src="/wrox_nocss/WebResource.axd?d=DEkmP4WPio20OIiEwYa7e
            tvNOWIuJ0esRa3ebXvZ3ow1&t=632965472540937500"
            alt="Scroll down" />
         </div>
    </div><a id="Menu1_SkipLink"></a>

        </div>

    <div>

        <input type="hidden" name="__EVENTVALIDATION"
        id="__EVENTVALIDATION"
        value="/wEWCgKO7KC8BgLQ4sjeAwLQ4tTeAwL9upirAwL+upirAwL/
        upirAwK93cLIDwK+3cLIDwK/3cLIDwK43cLIDws3WjxekaPvS6M3MtikupL9f5u+" />
    </div>

    <script type="text/javascript">
    <!--
    var Menu1_Data = new Object();
    Menu1_Data.disappearAfter = 500;
    Menu1_Data.horizontalOffset = 0;
    Menu1_Data.verticalOffset = 0;
    Menu1_Data.hoverClass = 'Menu1_14';
    Menu1_Data.hoverHyperLinkClass = 'Menu1_13';
    Menu1_Data.staticHoverClass = 'Menu1_12';
    Menu1_Data.staticHoverHyperLinkClass = 'Menu1_11';
    // -->
    </script>
    </form>
    </body>
    </html>
```

Do you see all of the nested tables being rendered? What about all of that Java Script?

Now, take a look at the code for the page using the CSS Friendly Control Adapters:

```
<!DOCTYPE html PUBLIC "-//W3C//DTD XHTML 1.1//EN"
    "http://www.w3.org/TR/xhtml11/DTD/xhtml11.dtd">

<html xmlns="http://www.w3.org/1999/xhtml" >
<head><title>
```

```
    ASP.NET 2.0 CSS Friendly Control Adapters 1.0 Example
</title><link href="CSS/Import.css" rel="stylesheet"
  type="text/css" /><link href="SimpleMenu.css"
  rel="stylesheet" type="text/css" /><style
  type="text/css">
  .Menu1_0 { background-
  color:white;visibility:hidden;display:none;position:abso
  lute;left:0px;top:0px; }
  .Menu1_1 { text-decoration:none; }
  .Menu1_2 {  }

</style></head>
<body>

<b>CSS Friendly Control Example Menu:</b><br /><br />

<div class="SimpleMenu" id="Menu1">
    <div class="AspNet-Menu-Horizontal">
          <ul class="AspNet-Menu">
              <li class="AspNet-Menu-WithChildren">
                  <a
  href="javascript:__doPostBack('Menu1','bItem 1')"
  class="AspNet-Menu-Link">
                        Item 1</a>
                  <ul>
                      <li class="AspNet-Menu-Leaf">

                                          <a
  href="javascript:__doPostBack('Menu1','bItem 1\\Item 1 -
  Subitem 1')" class="AspNet-Menu-Link">
                                Item 1 - Subitem 1</a>
                      </li>
                      <li class="AspNet-Menu-Leaf">
                          <a
  href="javascript:__doPostBack('Menu1','bItem 1\\Item 1 -
  Subitem 2')" class="AspNet-Menu-Link">
                                Item 1 - Subitem 2</a>
                      </li>
                      <li class="AspNet-Menu-Leaf">
                          <a
  href="javascript:__doPostBack('Menu1','bItem 1\\Item 1 -
  Subitem 3')" class="AspNet-Menu-Link">
                                Item 1 - Subitem 3</a>
                      </li>
                  </ul>
              </li>
              <li class="AspNet-Menu-WithChildren">
                  <a
  href="javascript:__doPostBack('Menu1','bItem 2')"
  class="AspNet-Menu-Link">
                        Item 2</a>
                  <ul>
                      <li class="AspNet-Menu-Leaf">
```

```
                                    <a
    href="javascript:__doPostBack('Menu1','bItem 2\\Item 2 -
    Subitem 1')" class="AspNet-Menu-Link">
                                        Item 2 - Subitem 1</a>
                        </li>
                        <li class="AspNet-Menu-Leaf">
                                    <a
    href="javascript:__doPostBack('Menu1','bItem 2\\Item 2 -
    Subitem 2')" class="AspNet-Menu-Link">
                                        Item 2 - Subitem 2</a>
                        </li>
                        <li class="AspNet-Menu-Leaf">
                                    <a
    href="javascript:__doPostBack('Menu1','bItem 2\\Item 2 -
    Subitem 3')" class="AspNet-Menu-Link">
                                        Item 2 - Subitem 3</a>
                        </li>
                        <li class="AspNet-Menu-Leaf">
                                    <a
    href="javascript:__doPostBack('Menu1','bItem 2\\Item 2 -
    Subitem 4')" class="AspNet-Menu-Link">
                                        Item 2 - Subitem 4</a>
                        </li>
                    </ul>
                </li>
            </ul>

    </div>
</div>

</body>
</html>
```

You can see that there are no tables at all in the code; the rendering is all being performed with pure CSS styling. Potentially more interesting is that there is significantly less code being rendered to the browser. You don't necessarily need to be able to troubleshoot the HTML code presented here, but it should still make you realize the differences that the CSS Friendly Control Adapters produce in code.

At least as important, though, is how each of these pages reacts to accessibility browsers. Specifically, look again at the pages with CSS turned off. Figure 5-3 is the standard control version, and Figure 5-4 is the version incorporating the CSS Friendly Control Adapters. The only difference between these figures and the ones previously presented is that CSS is turned off in the browser.

In Figure 5-3, look at the order in which the links appear. First you see Item 1 and Item 2 on the top line. Next you see all of the subitems for Item 1, followed by a couple of arrow images, and finally by the subitems for Item 2. Is this intuitive? If you were navigating your own site and these were the links that you were forced to follow, would they make sense? Assuming that the text for each link was more "real world," would you understand that "Item 2 – Subitem 1" was a subitem of Item 2? Or would it look like all of the subitems were actually subitems of Item 1 because they all fall under that particular heading?

146

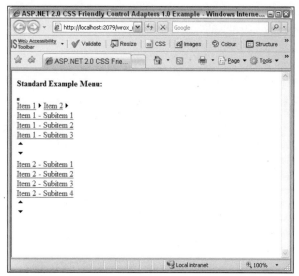

Figure 5-3

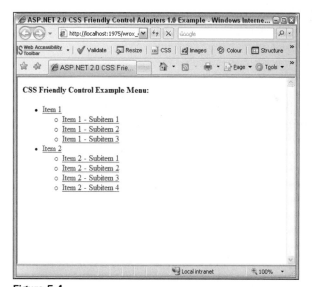

Figure 5-4

Contrast that with Figure 5-4. The menu items are put in an unordered list (UL) so the subitems are actually listed under the appropriate heading. This should provide a much easier to understand navigation system for visitors using accessibility browsers (or any browsers that do not support CSS or have it turned off for whatever reason).

Hopefully, this will illustrate that the CSS Friendly Control Adapters, simply put, give you much more control over the projects you create, allowing for more accessible sites and more flexibility in the output of the controls you use.

Installing the Control Adapters

Actually installing the control adapters is almost as simple as using them. To get the free download, simply go to the following URL: www.asp.net/cssadapters.

You will be downloading a Visual Studio Installer (VSI) file (e.g., ASPNETCssFriendlyAdapters.vsi) to your local computer. It is not important where you put this file, as long as you remember where it is so that you can launch it once the download is complete.

The only prerequisite for this install is the previous installation of either Visual Studio 2005 or Visual Web Developer 2005 Express Edition. If you have one or both of these installed, you are ready to install the control adapter.

Once the file is completely downloaded to your hard drive, run the file. The file acts as an executable and, as such, launches in the same fashion as any other EXE file. For example, if you downloaded the file to your C drive root, you could go Start ➪ Run and enter C:\ASPNETCssFriendlyAdapters.vsi and then press the OK button. You could also simply double-click the file in Windows Explorer. Regardless of how you launch the installation application, you should be presented with the screen shown in Figure 5-5.

Figure 5-5

Obviously, you can make whatever selections suit your needs but, as a recommendation, you might want to consider leaving all of the checked options selected. If you are only going to install one thing, install the language-specific (VB or C#) version of the ASP.NET CSS Friendly Web Site. This will give you all that you need for your projects. However, again, it is recommended you install all four components so that you are prepared for anything that may come up in the future.

Press the Next button and then press the Finish button on the next screen to install the adapters.

At this point, you have installed the control adapters and are ready to use them in your web projects!

Integrating the Control Adapters

Now that you have the CSS Friendly Control Adapters installed, it is time to integrate them into your web projects. There are really two scenarios where this will come up: a completely new project or an integration with an existing project. Both situations are fairly easy to work with. However, that being said, a new project is almost shamefully simple and, as such, will be discussed first.

A New Project

Once you have the CSS Friendly Control Adapters installed, it literally takes only one small click to create a new project using the adapters. To start, create the project just as you always do (File ➪ New ➪ Web Site. . .) to get the screen shown in Figure 5-6.

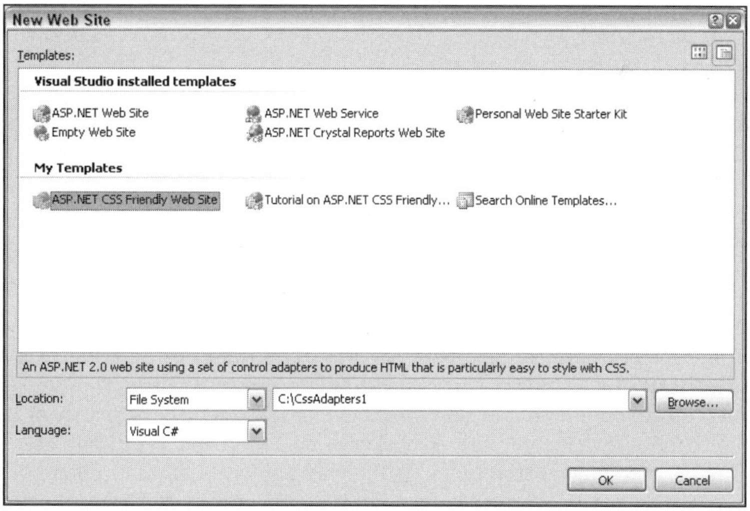

Figure 5-6

As you can see, there should now be an option for ASP.NET CSS Friendly Web Site in the My Templates section. So, just click on that option and fill out the other fields just as you always do, and press the OK button.

And that's it; you have just created a web project that is set up to use your recently installed CSS Friendly Control Adapters. Wasn't that easy?

You will notice, when the project is created, that the project loads slightly different content than that normally seen in the default website, as shown in Figure 5-7.

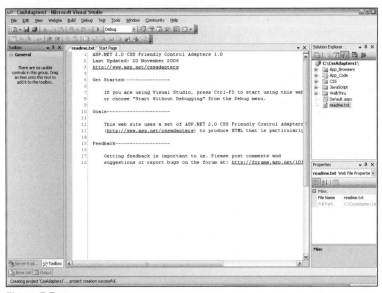

Figure 5-7

The first thing you will probably notice is that there is a new readme.txt file that opens up instead of Default.aspx. In this file, you will see a couple of notes about the CSS Friendly Control Adapters. The most interesting part is that pressing Ctrl-F5 will launch the site and give you examples of the control adapters in place. Specifically, launching the application will give you links to a Menu control example and several variations of the TreeView control. It might be worth it to launch the application and run the samples just to see how things work.

Back in Visual Studio 2005, you will notice that there are also several new items in the Solution Explorer. Many of the new directories are not necessary for typical projects. For example, there is no need to keep the WalkThru directory; it is strictly to hold the example projects of this application. However, until you get comfortable with shaping your controls, you may want to keep the directory at least for a reference. There are CSS files in there that show the exact classes you will need to put into effect in your application to make your control adapters look the way you want them to. Many of the classes, such as .SimpleEntertainmentMenu ul.AspNet-Menu, may not be intuitive. There are plenty of comments in these CSS files that can help you understand what is actually being formatted by the class rules. Again, until you get comfortable with creating your own style rules, the CSS files in this directory are a really good starting point.

You will also notice that there is a JavaScript and a CSS directory. Both of these directories contain files that may be necessary, depending on which control you are using. For example, if you are using a Menu control, you will need to have the `MenuAdapter.js` file in place. You don't need to worry about coding your page to reference the JavaScript file; the control adapter does that for you. But you do need to make sure that the files are still there. Similarly, there are CSS files that will need to be in place for various controls. To continue with the Menu example, you will need to ensure that `Import.css` and `BrowserSpecific/IEMenu6.css` are in the CSS directory. However, unlike with the JavaScript files, you will need to reference these files directly. You will also probably need to have either a CSS file strictly for your control or class rules integrated in with another CSS file. For both of these, the examples in the `WalkThru` directory are invaluable.

There are also two ASP.NET folders created in your project that you should never delete: `App_Browsers` and `App_Code`. You are probably familiar with `App_Code` if you ever use any `Class` files, since this is where they are stored as well. And, as such, the contents probably will not be that surprising: a slew of language-specific class files. As an example, for the Menu control, you will notice a class file in this directory called `MenuAdapter.cs` or `MenuAdapter.vb`. As you might suspect, this is where all of the new rendering logic of the control is housed. Going into this code, you can actually see where the CSS divisions are being written out. If you want to change something in the rendering logic, you can actually do it here. This is one of the nice things about the control adapters: they are completely customizable. Granted, as written, they will probably do what you need them to do. They will certainly write out a pure CSS counterpart to the standard controls. However, if you find that you need to tweak something, you can go directly into the class file and make whatever changes you need to make. Just be careful that you don't corrupt the control adapter. Making changes can seriously impact the results of the rendering logic. So, if you are going to make changes in this class file, you probably want to make a backup copy of the file so that you can revert to the original if you need to.

The other directory, `App_Browsers`, may be new to you. Essentially, this is for setting up browser-specific information of your web applications, doing so in `.browser` files. However, with this functionality, you are now allowed to specify control adapters. For example, using the Menu example, you will find the following code in the `CSSFriendlyAdapters.browser` file:

```
<adapter controlType="System.Web.UI.WebControls.Menu"
    adapterType="CSSFriendly.MenuAdapter" />
```

This is telling your application to override the standard Menu control with the CSS Friendly version of the control, which is defined in the `MenuAdapter` class file mentioned previously. It is also important to understand that this is not language-specific. In other words, the code would look exactly the same in a C# project as it would in a VB one.

In essence, your web project has completed a custom browser file with the default CSS Friendly Control Adapter definitions in it. You could just as easily add new control adapters (assuming that you knew how to code them) in this file to override other controls in the ASP.NET toolkit.

To understand this relationship better, change the above code in the `CSSFriendlyAdapters.browser` file to the following:

```
<adapter controlType="System.Web.UI.WebControls.Menu"
    adapterType="CSSFriendly.MenuAdapterMod" />
```

If you try to compile the project, you will get errors. The last error in your Error List should say something like "Could not load type 'CSSFriendly.MenuAdapterMod.'" This simply means that it cannot find the class `MenuAdapterMod` in the current project. To make it work again, open the `MenuAdapter.cs` file and change the class declaration at the top of the file to the following:

```
public class MenuAdapterMod :
    System.Web.UI.WebControls.Adapters.MenuAdapter
```

If you were using VB rather than C#, you would need to modify the class declaration in the `MenuAdapter.vb` file to read as follows:

```
Public Class MenuAdapterMod
    Inherits System.Web.UI.WebControls.Adapters.MenuAdapter
```

Basically, you are just changing the class name from `MenuAdapter` to `MenuAdapterMod`. Once you do this, you should be able to compile your project, and the Menu control example should still work as it originally did.

There is no need to change the name of the class file itself; keeping it named `MenuAdapter.cs` (or `MenuAdapter.vb`) is completely fine. The reference is to the class name itself, not the file name.

Adding the Control Adapters to an Existing Project

Setting up an existing project to incorporate the CSS Friendly Control Adapters isn't that much more difficult than creating a new project, as detailed above. That being said, though, the steps may not be completely intuitive. The steps below will help you add the CSS Friendly Control Adapters to your existing surfer5 application started in Chapter 4.

Step 1: Installing the CSS Friendly Control Adapters

If you haven't done so already, you will need to install the adapters as discussed earlier in this chapter. This will create the ASP.NET projects that can be used for new projects and will also set up the files necessary for subsequent steps in this process.

Step 2: Creating a Reference Directory

Unfortunately, there isn't anything set up that you can pull files into directly. In other words, you can't simply navigate to some directory and import all of the necessary files into your project. There also isn't any sort of import wizard that will update your project for you. So, in order to pull the necessary files into your project, you need to put them somewhere you can pull from (i.e., somewhere on your hard drive). There are basically two ways of doing this: create a new CSS Friendly Control Adapter project as a dummy project you can pull from or unzip the files from the project zip file to a location on your hard drive. Both options will be outlined below.

Option 1: Installing a Dummy Project

This is probably the easiest solution. You need only follow the steps outlined previously for creating a new CSS Friendly Control Adapter project. Basically, you just need to open Visual Studio 2005, and select File ⇨ New ⇨ Web Site to get the screen shown in Figure 5-8.

As shown in Figure 5-8, you should create the project using the "ASP.NET CSS Friendly Web Site" template and the appropriate language (C# or VB), and create a new folder that you can find easily when you need to import the necessary files; future references to this directory will use "C:\CSSFriendlyTemplate." Press the OK button. You have now created a dummy directory that you can use to import the requisite files for your existing projects.

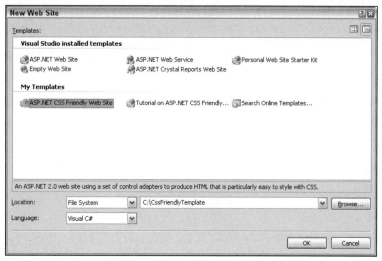

Figure 5-8

Option 2: Unzipping the Project Files

The other option is to unzip the files from the zip files that were copied to your system when you installed the CSS Friendly Control Adapters earlier. Template files are simply zip files copied to your system that Visual Studio locates and uses to create new projects. So you need to locate the zip file and extract the contents to your hard drive.

Your project templates should be located in your user-specific My Documents folder of your computer. For example, if your login is Doe-John, you might find the zip files in one of the following directories (depending on which language you want to use):

❑ C:\Documents and Settings\Doe-John\My Documents\Visual Studio 2005\Templates\ProjectTemplates\Visual Web Developer\CSharp

❑ C:\Documents and Settings\Doe-John\My Documents\Visual Studio 2005\Templates\ProjectTemplates\Visual Web Developer\VisualBasic

In either of these directories, you should find a file titled either ASPNETCssFriendlyAdaptersSlimCS.zip or ASPNETCssFriendlyAdaptersSlimVB.zip. There will probably be at least one other CSS Friendly Control Adapter template zip file in each directory, but these contain a lot more files than you will probably need for your project. However, that being said, if you want the additional files that come with this project, feel free to use this file instead. It contains two themes that can adjust how the project appears to your users. Themes will be discussed in Chapters 8, 9, and 10. Just know that this other zip file, named either ASPNETCssFriendlyAdaptersCS.zip or ASPNETCssFriendlyAdaptersVB.zip, will contain much more information and examples, if that better suits your needs. For the examples in this book, the slimmed down version will be used for the dummy directory.

If you cannot locate the files in the directories mentioned, do a search of your computer for the file names to find their location. It is possible that the files were copied to another location. If you still cannot find the files, it is possible that your installation was corrupt, and you may need to try the install routine again.

Once you have located the zip file, open it up using whatever zip application you prefer and then extract all of the contents to the C:\CSSFriendlyTemplate directory (you may need to create this directory first). This should create a very similar directory to the one created by generating a new project in Visual Studio (outlined previously).

The Final Template Folder

Regardless of which method you use to create your dummy directory, the directory structure should resemble Figure 5-9.

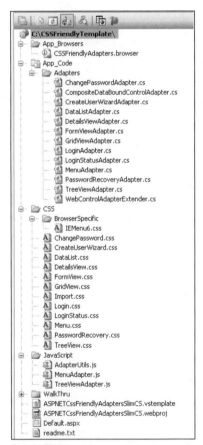

Figure 5-9

You will notice that there are the folders discussed earlier in this chapter: App_Browsers, App_Code (with an Adapters subdirectory), CSS (with a BrowserSpecific subdirectory), a JavaScript directory, and a WalkThru directory. These directories contain all of the files you will need for importing files into your existing project.

Step 3: Importing the Directories and Files

You now need to open up the project you started in Chapter 4. This project should be located in C:\surfer5 and should contain the basic layout and CSS files you created in that chapter. You should be able to open this project by launching Visual Studio 2005 and clicking File ⇨ Open ⇨ Web Site. Once you have the project open, your Solution Explorer window should resemble Figure 5-10.

Figure 5-10

The first step is to create the ASP.NET folder(s) necessary for the adapters to work. If you do not already have an App_Browsers folder in your project, which is probably true, you will need to add this specific folder in a different manner than some of the other folders. While in the Solution Explorer, right-click on the project name (C:\surfer5\ in Figure 5-10) and, when the drop-down menu is presented, select Add ASP.NET Folder and then App_Browsers. Additionally, if you do not already have an App_Code directory in your project, you will need to add this folder in the same fashion (Add ASP.NET Folder ⇨ App_Code).

For maintainability, and to mimic the manner in which the project is set up when you use the templates, you may want to create a subdirectory in the App_Code system folder to hold the CSS Friendly Control Adapter classes. However, this is not necessary. You can copy the files directly into the root of this folder, and they should work fine. However, in order to make it seem more like the way the templates are set up, the remainder of the book will use the subdirectory created as part of the standard template. In order to set this up, click on the system folder in the Solution Explorer and, when the drop-down menu is presented, select New Folder. This will create a folder within your system folder and allow you to type in a new name for the folder. Using this approach, create the folder "Adapters" in your App_Code directory.

Similarly, you will want to create folders for your CSS and JavaScript files. So, while in the Solution Explorer, right-click on the project and, when the drop-down menu appears, select New Folder, and then type in the name of the folder. You will need to create a folder called "CSS" and one called "JavaScript" using this approach. You will also need to create a folder in your CSS folder entitled "BrowserSpecific."

At this point, your project should now look something like Figure 5-11.

Figure 5-11

Now you need to import the actual files into these newly created folders. Specifically, you will need to follow these steps:

❑ Right-click on the App_Browsers folder and, when the drop-down menu appears, select Add Existing Item... from the options presented. This will bring up a fairly typical windows file locator screen so that you can find the resource you want to import. Navigate to the App_Browsers folder of your dummy directory (e.g., C:\CSSFriendlyTemplate\App_Browsers), and select CSSFriendlyAdapters.browser. Click the Add button to add this resource to your project.

❑ Right-click on the Adapters folder in the App_Code directory and, when the drop-down menu appears, select Add Existing Item... from the options presented. Navigate to the App_Code/ Adapters folder in your dummy directory (e.g., C:\CSSFriendlyTemplate\App_Code\ Adapters), and select all files (Tip: press CTRL-A when you have the appropriate folder open to select all of the files), and then press the Add button.

❑ Right-click on the CSS folder, and select Add Existing Item.... Navigate to the CSS folder of your dummy directory, press CTRL-A to select all of the files, and press the Add button. While in the CSS folder, right-click on the BrowserSpecific folder, and select Add Existing Item.... Navigate to the BrowserSpecific subdirectory of your CSS folder, select the only file in that folder, and press the Add button.

❑ Right-click on the JavaScript folder and select Add Existing Item.... Navigate to the JavaScript folder of your dummy directory, press CTRL-A to select all of the files, and click the Add button.

You should now have all of the files in place and, as a result, your site should be creating CSS Friendly controls for the controls that are included in this release. Your project, at this point, should resemble Figure 5-12.

As you get comfortable with what goes where, you might just want to copy the selected directories and files directly from your C:\CSSFriendlyTemplate *directory and paste them into your project. However, you need to have a solid understanding of what directories you need, what files go in what directory, and how they all work together. For that reason, you should probably follow the preceding directions the first few times you set up a CSS Friendly project but, once you feel comfortable with the process, it might be easier to just copy and paste the files and folders directly to your project through something like Windows Explorer.*

For the CSS to display properly in your project, however, you need to add the following code to the <HEAD> section of the page(s) that will be using the adapters:

```
<link runat="server" rel="stylesheet"
    href="~/CSS/Import.css"
     type="text/css"/>
<!--[if lt IE 7]>
    <link runat="server" rel="stylesheet"
        href="~/CSS/BrowserSpecific/IEMenu6.css" type="text/css">
<![endif]-->
```

This will bring in the master CSS files that control the basic operations of the controls. The first file, Import.CSS, is actually only a reference to all of the other CSS files in the project. It essentially serves as a way to import 11 CSS files by only making one reference. To understand what this means, examine the contents of this file and you will see the following:

```
@import "ChangePassword.css";
@import "CreateUserWizard.css";
@import "DataList.css";
@import "DetailsView.css";
@import "FormView.css";
@import "GridView.css";
@import "Login.css";
@import "LoginStatus.css";
@import "Menu.css";
@import "PasswordRecovery.css";
@import "TreeView.css";
```

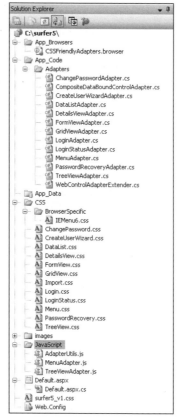

Figure 5-12

You can learn more about the `@import` *rule in CSS by reading the W3 C's CSS Specification at* www.w3.org/TR/CSS21/cascade.html#at-import.

So, instead of making 11 different CSS links on your web page, you make one reference to a master CSS file and that one file imports all of the other CSS files. This is done to make your code cleaner in the web page itself. However, if you wanted to, you could just as easily reference each one of these 11 files into your web page directly and ignore the `Import.CSS` reference. Or, even more specifically, you could import only the ones that you needed for your project and ignore the others. For example, if you are only using the Menu controls for the adapters, there is no real reason to import the `LoginStatus.CSS` file, for example. So, in this case, remove the link to the `Import.CSS` file in your web page and add a reference to `Menu.CSS` instead. As you get more comfortable with the adapters and how they work, this very possibly will be a scenario you see played out in the projects you design.

The second file, `IEMenu6.CSS`, is only used by Internet Explorer version 6 to handle some of the functionality of the Menu control. This file is meant to supplement, not supplant, other CSS files used for this control. This just means that you need to have another CSS file that contains the same elements and classes somewhere in your project; the rules in this file are meant to add functionality to those classes and elements, not replace them. The commented section of the code (`<!--[if lt IE 7]>`), called Conditional Comments, ensures that the stylesheet is only used by versions of Internet Explorer prior to version 7.

> *Conditional Comments are currently only supported by versions of Internet Explorer and, within IE, only since version 5.*

Step 4: Using the Adapters!

Once you have these steps completed, you are ready to start using the control adapters in your projects. This example probably leaned heavily towards overkill. You started with a project that had, basically, three or four files in it. You had your default page, your CSS file, and some images in a subdirectory. You took that project and imported at least 30 files in at least 6 folders and subdirectories you had to create. It probably, in this case, would have been much simpler to start a new project with the ASP.NET CSS Friendly Web Site template and then just import your three or four files from your existing project. However, if you had a much more real-world project with potentially hundreds (or even thousands) of files, you would probably appreciate just importing the 30 or so files and, honestly, many of the folders would already be set up for you. In that scenario, it would be a great relief to understand exactly what you have to import and what changes you need to make to an existing project to make it work.

Once you have your project modified to use the adapters, you simply have to style the controls that you want to affect by using CSS styling.

Using the Control Adapters in Your Project

Once you have your project up and the adapters installed, you probably would like to actually use them, right? The good thing about the adapters is that they are styled via CSS styling. This means that you can literally control the look and feel of all GridView controls, for example, through CSS coding and one property setting in each GridView (you have to tell the GridView, or whatever control you are playing with, which CSS classes to use for styling). This may not sound impressive, but it is a huge step forward in creating a consistent look and feel to your site. In the past, you may have used CSS to format certain text in your page. Maybe you have certain styling applied to your H1 tag to make it bold and in the Arial Black font, for example. Or maybe you have coding in your Body element so that it makes your page bleed all the way to the browser window's edge.

However, what you have not been able to do is to say "Okay, for the first row in a GridView, I want the color to be gray and the second row to be white. And there should be a black border around the whole thing. And the header row should be black with a white font." You could have achieved this effect by applying an individual style to each component of the GridView by setting the colors and the like in the properties of the GridView itself. You might even have used the `CssClass` property of each of those pieces to style them. Doing so would look something like this:

```
<asp:GridView ID="GridView1" runat="server"
    GridLines="None" BorderColor="Black" BorderStyle="Solid"
    BorderWidth="1pt">

    <HeaderStyle BackColor="Black" ForeColor="White" Font-
    Names="Arial Black" Font-Size="Medium" />

    <RowStyle BackColor="Gray" Font-Size="Small" />

    <AlternatingRowStyle BackColor="White" Font-
    Size="Small" />

</asp:GridView>
```

Of course, you could replace a lot of that code by using the `CssClass` property in each of the components, similarly to this:

```
<asp:GridView ID="GridView1" runat="server"
    GridLines="None" CssClass="GridViewMain">

    <HeaderStyle CssClass="GridViewHeader" />

    <RowStyle CssClass="GridViewRow" />

    <AlternatingRowStyle CssClass="GridViewAlternatingRow" />

</asp:GridView>
```

But wouldn't it be simpler to simply use the following?

```
<asp:GridView ID="GridView1" runat="server"
    CssSelectorClass="MyGridView" />
```

Using adapters, this is exactly what you can do. Granted, you still need to add the elements of the GridView (the data that will come in), but you are finished with the styling. You can simply drop in a GridView control, hook it into your datasource, set the `CssSelectorClass` to your GridView styling, and you are done. No need to worry about styling the control; it is taken care of. No need to worry whether this GridView looks the same as the one you programmed last month. If you use the same `CssSelectorClass`, they will look identical. And if you need to change the look of your GridViews at some point, you simply change the coding in the CSS page, and it will carry through to all of your controls that reference it.

A couple of points before getting into the styling. First, you will get a nasty little green squiggly line under your `CssSelectorClass` property in your control and, if you hover over it, you will see the message "Validation (ASP.NET): Attribute 'CssSelectorClass' is not a valid attribute of element 'GridView'." Don't let this make you nervous. This just means that Visual Studio doesn't know about this property yet. Since the CSS Friendly Control Adapters aren't inherently a part of the Visual Studio installation, the application simply doesn't know about this property. That being said, you shouldn't sweat it too much. The application will compile with a warning, but it will compile. Your application will not have any runtime or compilation errors. This just means that you will always see a warning message in your error list when you compile (at least until Visual Studio integrates the adapters at some point, assuming that they will). But hey, who has code without at least one warning in it anyway?

Another thing to realize is that, once you use the control adapters, you can't set the style of the control in the properties of the control anymore. So, if you use the first or second example of the GridView code above but don't set the `CssSelectorClass` property and/or don't set up the CSS rules, the GridView just won't be styled. So don't think of the CSS rules as a supplement to your control properties. It's not as if the adapters will look first at your control properties and then go into your CSS and reconcile them and display what they think you want. The adapters completely ignore the styling properties of your controls. Now, does this mean that they ignore all of the properties? Certainly not. If you set the `AllowPaging` property to true, that will still work. The same will be true for something like `AllowSorting`. Basically any nonstyling property of the control will still work and should still be set on the control itself. Just don't spend time trying to style the control because it will be for naught.

The final thing to realize is that, once you set up your adapters to run in your project, there is no real way to turn them off. It's not as if you can say "okay, GridView 1, you use the adapters. But GridView 2? No way; I want to style you myself." If they are on, they are on. If they are off, they are off. There really isn't much gray area to play in. The quasi-exception to that is the use of another nonstandard property: `AdapterEnabled`. This will also present a green squiggly line under it, since it isn't a known property in Visual Studio. The worse (actually, worst) news is that this is only there for experimentation. Will it work? Don't know. The author of the controls, Russ Helfand, states the following in the CSS Friendly Control Adapters white papers:

> Beware: this is not supported and often does not work well. Fundamentally, the framework does not support disabling adapters on a per control basis. The `AdapterEnabled` attribute is only intended to be used experimentally.

What happens when you set the `AdapterEnabled` property to false is that the application will attempt to use the standard rendering methodology of the control. This just means that, if typically a GridView renders out HTML tables, setting `AdapterEnabled` to false will try to force the application to render out tables and ignore the CSS rendering you have set up. Again, this is not reliable, and you should exercise extreme caution in going down this path. The results will be unpredictable and may cause you heartache that just isn't worth it. So, for the most part, you really should ask yourself before applying a CSS rendering override to your control, "is this okay for every instance of this control I drop into this project?" If the answer is yes, then you should feel free to proceed. However, if the answer is "maybe" or, even worse, "no," then you may need to weigh out the pros and cons of using the adapters before you make the switch.

That being said, remember that the CSS Friendly Control Adapters are not an all or nothing proposition. They are set up in the .browser file(s) you have in your `App_Browsers` folder. So if you wanted to use most of the adapters but specifically wanted to avoid using the GridView override, you could open your .browser file and look for the following line of code and remove it:

```
<adapter controlType="System.Web.UI.WebControls.GridView"
    adapterType="CSSFriendly.GridViewAdapter" />
```

Without this line of code in your .browser file, the application will treat the control (and every instance of that control) the same way it always has.

Is It Working?

Now that you have made the decision to use the adapters, have successfully installed them and set up your project to use them, it is time to test your controls. To illustrate this, you will be using a GridView with an XML datasource attached to it, just to get the idea. So the first thing you need is an XML file. For this illustration, create an XML file in your project called GridViewSource.xml, and set it up as follows:

```
<?xml version="1.0" encoding="utf-8" ?>
<Links>
    <Resource Name="Wrox Press" URL="http://www.wrox.com" />
    <Resource Name="CSS Friendly Control Adapters"
   URL="http://www.asp.net/cssadapters/" />
    <Resource Name="Control Adapters Forum"
   URL="http://forums.asp.net/1018/ShowForum.aspx" />
    <Resource Name="Google" URL="http://www.google.com" />
    <Resource Name="CNN" URL="http://www.cnn.com" />
</Links>
```

Now, in your project, create a new file called GridView.aspx, and drop an XMLDataSource control onto your page. You can do this simply by dragging the control from your toolbox in Visual Studio into either the Source or Design view or simply by double-clicking the control in the toolbox. You will need to add the property DataFile to the control, and set its value to GridViewSource.xml. Your datasource should look similar to the following:

```
<asp:XmlDataSource DataFile="GridViewSource.xml"
    ID="XmlDataSource1" runat="server" />
```

Now add a GridView to your project. You can do so in the same way that you added the XMLDataSource control to your project (dragging or double-clicking the control in the toolbox). You will need to add your XMLDataSource as the datasource for the GridView. The easiest way to do this is to go into the Design view of Visual Studio and click on the small hover arrow on the upper-right side of the GridView. This should present options similar to those shown in Figure 5-13.

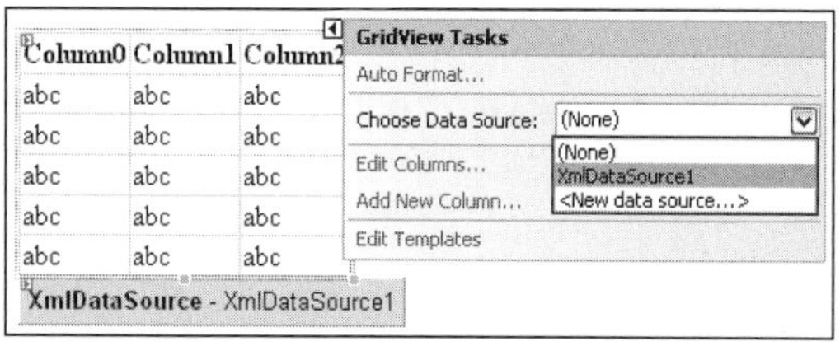

Figure 5-13

You can select your XMLDataSource control from the drop-down options presented in the Choose Data Source property. Once you do so, the GridView should be populated with the items from your XML document. If you run the page at this point, the GridView should look pretty boring but, if it runs, this means you are ready to start styling it. Press either F5 (Start Debugging) or CTRL-F5 (Start Without Debugging) to launch your GridView example in your browser. It should look like Figure 5-14.

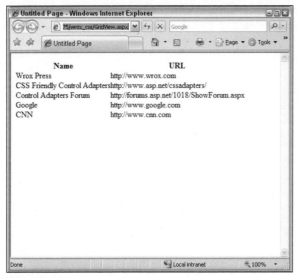

Figure 5-14

Again, this is a pretty boring example. You are mostly verifying that you set up the CSS Friendly Control Adapters properly. If you want to check the HTML that was rendered, while your page is still being displayed in your browser, right-click in the page and choose View Source. Do this and verify that all of the contents of your GridView are now rendered in CSS and that you do not see any HTML table code. If you are surprised at what you see, there is a reason.

The GridView is a good example of a quasi-exception to the CSS Friendly Control Adapters. This control adapter is one of two that actually still render tables (the other is the DataList). Does this mean that the control adapter isn't working? Well, yes and no. It is not generating pure CSS as you might have expected. It is, instead, generating a *better* table design for the control than is natively produced by the .NET Framework. But understand: it is still tables.

So what does better mean? This means that the tables are well structured, including defined regions of the tables (header, footer, and body regions). The styling of these regions is done through CSS rather than inline styling. The result is a much cleaner and accessible version of the control.

To see the difference, examine the code for your GridView example. It should look similar to the following:

```
<div class="AspNet-GridView" id="GridView1">
    <table cellpadding="0" cellspacing="0" summary="">
        <thead>
            <tr>
                <th scope="col">Name</th>
                <th scope="col">URL</th>
            </tr>
        </thead>
        <tbody>
            <tr>
                <td>Wrox Press</td>
```

```
            <td>http://www.wrox.com</td>
        </tr>
        <tr class="AspNet-GridView-Alternate">
            <td>CSS Friendly Control Adapters</td>
            <td>http://www.asp.net/cssadapters/</td>
        </tr>
        <tr>
            <td>Control Adapters Forum</td>
            <td>http://forums.asp.net/1018/ShowForum.aspx</td>
        </tr>
        <tr class="AspNet-GridView-Alternate">
            <td>Google</td>
            <td>http://www.google.com</td>
        </tr>
        <tr>
            <td>CNN</td>
            <td>http://www.cnn.com</td>
        </tr>
    </tbody>
</table>

</div>
```

As you can see, there is a header region (`<thead>`) that contains the table output for the column headers and a body region (`<tbody>`) for the actual contents of the GridView. You can also see that the alternating rows in the body region have a special class set up and that the other rows do not. This just further streamlines your code; the application assumes that the rows that do not have the special class will be formatted by the default setting for rows in the table class associated with this control (AspNet-GridView). For the particular example used in this book, there is no footer row. Had you set up a FooterRow, however, there would have been a distinct footer region of your code as well.

Now compare that to the natively rendered output of the exact same control:

```
<table cellspacing="0" rules="all" border="1"
    id="GridView1" style="border-collapse:collapse;">
        <tr>
            <th scope="col">Name</th><th
scope="col">URL</th>
        </tr><tr>
            <td>Wrox Press</td><td>http://www.wrox.com</td>
        </tr><tr>
            <td>CSS Friendly Control
Adapters</td><td>http://www.asp.net/cssadapters/</td>
        </tr><tr>
            <td>Control Adapters
Forum</td><td>http://forums.asp.net/1018/ShowForum.aspx</td>
        </tr><tr>
            <td>Google</td><td>http://www.google.com</td>
        </tr><tr>
            <td>CNN</td><td>http://www.cnn.com</td>
        </tr>
    </table>
```

The easiest thing to notice is that there are no defined regions of the table; every table row is just set in the table. There are no header or body regions as shown in the CSS Friendly version. It would also probably be fair to say that this code is a little harder to muddle through.

One thing that isn't as obvious in this particular example is where the styling comes from. If you had set up your rows to alternate gray and white and set up your header row to be black, you would see all of this code would come through in style commands in the individual rows of data; it would not be set apart in a detached CSS file. Of course, if you had set up CssClass properties, that would still reference an external CSS file. But you are not forced to do so.

The nice thing about the CSS Friendly Control Adapter for the GridView is that it forces you to put your styling in a detached CSS file. And a lot of designers will agree, this is where it belongs.

You should also remember that the many hardcore CSS zealots touting the total abolishment of tables will still concede that tables can, and probably should, be used to represent tabular data, which is the only thing that comes through in a GridView.

So is it worth it? Most assuredly so. The control adapter cleans up the code and forces it into a layered design, which facilitates code reuse. It keeps tabular data in the format that most would agree it belongs: tables. It is a compromise of ideals, but the perfect give and take on both. You still use your tables but you use better tables and you style them in CSS.

One last thought while on this topic: if you aren't happy with the controls...change them. The CSS Friendly Control Adapters are provided as a starting point, not necessarily a finished product. This doesn't mean that they are buggy or incomplete by any stretch of the imagination. You can certainly use the adapters exactly as provided and get all of the benefits advertised. However, what about for the controls that don't have adapters yet? Or what if you want to modify the rendering output of the adapters that *are* included? The beautiful thing about these adapters is that they are, well, adaptable. The ones provided are meant to be examples of what you can do. The classes come intentionally uncompiled so that you can sift through the code and see how they did it. The creators hoped that you would go in there and think "hey, I can do this" and go off and write your own (or modify the ones you want tweaked).

For example, go into your project and find the control adapter for the GridView; it should be in the Adapters subfolder in the App_Code directory of your project and called GridViewAdapter.cs (or GridViewAdapter.vb). If you start looking through the code, what is really going on will start to become apparent. For example, look at the RenderContents() method, which looks similar to the following:

```
protected override void RenderContents(HtmlTextWriter writer)
    {
        if (Extender.AdapterEnabled)
        {
            GridView gridView = Control as GridView;
            if (gridView != null)
            {
                writer.Indent++;
                WritePagerSection(writer, PagerPosition.Top);

                writer.WriteLine();
                writer.WriteBeginTag("table");
                writer.WriteAttribute("cellpadding", "0");
```

```
            writer.WriteAttribute("cellspacing", "0");
            writer.WriteAttribute("summary", Control.ToolTip);

            if (!String.IsNullOrEmpty(gridView.CssClass))
            {
                writer.WriteAttribute("class", gridView.CssClass);
            }

            writer.Write(HtmlTextWriter.TagRightChar);
            writer.Indent++;

            ArrayList rows = new ArrayList();
            GridViewRowCollection gvrc = null;

            /////////////////////// HEAD ///////////////////////////////

            rows.Clear();
            if (gridView.ShowHeader && (gridView.HeaderRow != null))
            {
                rows.Add(gridView.HeaderRow);
            }
            gvrc = new GridViewRowCollection(rows);
            WriteRows(writer, gridView, gvrc, "thead");

            /////////////////////// FOOT ///////////////////////////////

            rows.Clear();
            if (gridView.ShowFooter && (gridView.FooterRow != null))
            {
                rows.Add(gridView.FooterRow);
            }
            gvrc = new GridViewRowCollection(rows);
            WriteRows(writer, gridView, gvrc, "tfoot");

            /////////////////////// BODY ///////////////////////////////

            WriteRows(writer, gridView, gridView.Rows, "tbody");

///////////////////////////////////////////////////////////

            writer.Indent--;
            writer.WriteLine();
            writer.WriteEndTag("table");

            WritePagerSection(writer, PagerPosition.Bottom);

            writer.Indent--;
            writer.WriteLine();
        }
    }
    else
    {
        base.RenderContents(writer);
    }
}
```

To better illustrate what is going on, focus on the top of the code that renders the beginning of the control:

```
writer.WriteBeginTag("table");
writer.WriteAttribute("cellpadding", "0");
writer.WriteAttribute("cellspacing", "0");
writer.WriteAttribute("summary", Control.ToolTip);
```

If you focus on just this section, you will understand more fully how to modify the adapters for your own purposes. For example, look at the first line, `writer.WriteBeginTag("table");`. What do you suppose this will do? As you can probably guess, it renders the HTML tag `<table>`. Immediately following that line are lines setting properties for the table tag. If you know tables, cellpadding and cellspacing are nothing new to you and, as you can see by the code, you are setting both to zero. So, by the third line of code, you have a rendered HTML tag that looks something like this:

```
<table cellpadding="0" cellspacing="0">
```

The fourth line is really interesting. In particular, the last attribute of the method, `Control.ToolTip`, shows you how cool the adapters can really be. At this point, you are going to the GridView control on your ASPX page and getting the property called `ToolTip`. If you do not set the `ToolTip` property in your control itself, the way the code is written, it will generate an empty string for the summary property of the HTML table, similar to the following:

```
<table cellpadding="0" cellspacing="0" summary="">
```

But what if you wanted to only generate the summary property if the `ToolTip` property was set in the control? You can actually get into the class code and change the functionality. For example, to make the summary property conditional on the `ToolTip` property's being set, you might change that line of code in the control adapter to something like this:

```
if (Control.ToolTip.Trim() != "") {
   writer.WriteAttribute("summary", Control.ToolTip); }
```

This just says that if the string value returned by looking at the `ToolTip` property of your GridView control is empty (putting the `Trim` in is not necessary, but it does hedge against someone accidentally putting a space in there), then don't render out the property. So with this modification in place, refresh your page in your browser. Assuming that you have not set the `ToolTip` property on your GridView control at this point, your rendered HTML table tag should look like this:

```
<table cellpadding="0" cellspacing="0">
```

Now go back into `GridView.aspx`, and add a `ToolTip` property and set it to "example." Refresh your rendered page and look at the code. It should now resemble the following:

```
<table cellpadding="0" cellspacing="0" summary="example">
```

So you have just modified the rendering output logic of your CSS Friendly Control Adapter.

This is a pretty minor change, but it should show you how easy it is to get into the code and actually make changes. So if, for example, you wanted to go into the GridView control and modify it to generate pure CSS code (a very daunting, but not impossible, task), you could certainly do so. Your first block of code would probably look more like this than the previous example:

```
writer.WriteBeginTag("div");
writer.WriteAttribute("class", "GridViewContainer");
```

This would set up your base CSS division that you would style in a class called `GridViewContainer` in your CSS file. You would probably then set up divisions for each row that would control the alternating background colors of that "row" of data and then more nested divisions to encapsulate the actual data. You would have to play around with it a lot to make it work, but it certainly could be done.

Again, if you are happy with CSS Friendly Control Adapters the way they are, you never need to get into the code and change them. If, however, you want to make them work a little differently, then you have the full power to do so. And you are certainly able to use the existing ones as models to create future ones. Just remember to add them to your `.browser` file so that your application knows it should use them.

And remember, most people will agree that tables are acceptable for tabular data, so there really is no need to try to create a fully CSS version of the GridView. However, if you are bored one night and you want an interesting challenge, give it a shot. And make sure that you post your final code on the CSS Friendly Control Adapter forum on ASP.NET:

http://forums.asp.net/1018/ShowForum.aspx

Stylin' and Profilin'

Now that you have everything set up for your control adapters and, if you are truly courageous, have rewritten them all to suit your needs, you are ready to start styling them, which basically means setting up your CSS stylesheet and creating the appropriate rules.

A good rule of thumb would be to create separate CSS files for each of your controls. This will allow you to focus only on the control in your CSS file and, when you need to make a change, it is easier to find the area you need to change if you have them broken down by control. So if, for example, you need to change the style of the alternating row for your GridView control, you just go to the GridView stylesheet and make the changes there rather than wading through thousands of lines of CSS rules to find where you need to make the change.

Of course, as with any other rule of thumb, you are completely free to ignore this one. You can certainly put all of your CSS rules in one file; there is nothing programmatically stopping you. It is just a recommended best practice to break them up. However, if that doesn't suit your needs (or personal style), do it the way you feel most comfortable with.

Remember that once you have your control adapters set up, you will no longer need to set any style properties in the control itself. In fact, to take it a step further, you will no longer *be able* to make style changes in the properties of your control. Once the control adapters are working, they completely ignore any style type properties of your control. So if you set the `ForeColor` to red, it will not show up in your rendered control. To illustrate this, modify the GridView code in your `GridView.aspx` file as follows:

```
<asp:GridView ToolTip="example" ID="GridView1"
   runat="server" AutoGenerateColumns="False"
   DataSourceID="XmlDataSource1">
   <Columns>
       <asp:BoundField DataField="Name" HeaderText="Name"
   SortExpression="Name" />
       <asp:BoundField DataField="URL" HeaderText="URL"
   SortExpression="URL" />
   </Columns>
   <RowStyle ForeColor="Red" />
</asp:GridView>
```

Now rerun your application and see what happens. It should look exactly the same; the `ForeColor` property is ignored. In order to make changes to the style of the rendered output, you will need to make the changes in CSS.

First, for the GridView control, you should know the CSS classes you need to set up and what they do. In order to properly do that, you should see what an example of the CSS file looks like (from the examples on the CSS Friendly Control Adapters homepage at `www.asp.net/CSSAdapters/GridView.aspx`):

```css
.foo {} /* W3C CSS validator likes CSS files to start with
   a class rather than a comment. Soooooo.... */

/* This style sheet is intended to contain OFTEN CHANGED
   rules used when the GridView control adapter is enabled.
   */
/* Empty rules are provided merely as a convenience for
   your future use or experimentation. */

.PrettyGridView .AspNet-GridView
{
    width: 100%;
}

.PrettyGridView .AspNet-GridView div.AspNet-GridView-
   Pagination,
.PrettyGridView .AspNet-GridView div.AspNet-GridView-
   Pagination a,
.PrettyGridView .AspNet-GridView div.AspNet-GridView-
   Pagination span
{
    color: #00FFFF;
    background: #284775;
    font-weight: normal;
    padding: 2px;
}

.PrettyGridView .AspNet-GridView table
{
    border: solid 1px #CCCCCC;
    width: 100%;
}

.PrettyGridView .AspNet-GridView table thead tr th
```

```css
{
    color: #F7F6F3;
    background: #5D7B9D;
    font-weight: bold;
    border-bottom: solid 1px #CCCCCC;
    border-right: solid 1px #CCCCCC;
    padding: 2px;
}

.PrettyGridView .AspNet-GridView table thead tr th a
{
    color: #F7F6F3;
}

.PrettyGridView .AspNet-GridView table tbody tr td
{
    color: #333333;
    background: White;
    padding: 2px 20px 2px 2px;
    border-bottom: solid 1px #CCCCCC;
    border-right: solid 1px #CCCCCC;
    text-align: right;
}

.PrettyGridView .AspNet-GridView table tbody tr.AspNet-
    GridView-Alternate td
{
    background: #F7F6F3;
}

.PrettyGridView .AspNet-GridView table tbody tr.AspNet-
    GridView-Selected td
{
}

.PrettyGridView .AspNet-GridView table tfoot tr td
{
}
```

Before explaining what each block does, you should see how this affects the rendered output of your GridView. In order to apply these styles, follow these steps:

1. Make sure that your reference the `Import.CSS` file, as shown earlier in this chapter.

2. Create a new stylesheet in your project (right-click on your project, select Add New Item..., and choose Style Sheet from the options presented). Name this file `myStyleSheet.css`.

3. Fill `myStyleSheet.css` with the above code by either copying it from the source provided in the URL or just type it out. Save the file.

4. Reference this stylesheet in your `GridView.aspx` page. The easiest way to do this is to go into your Design view and just drag `myStyleSheet.css` from the Solution Explorer to your page. You could also type out the reference. If you do that, it should look something like this:

```html
<link href="myGridView.css" rel="stylesheet" type="text/css" />
```

5. Add a new property to your GridView control for `CssSelectorClass` and set it equal to "`PrettyGridView`", which should make it resemble the following:

```
<asp:GridView CssSelectorClass="PrettyGridView"
    ToolTip="example" ID="GridView1" runat="server"
    AutoGenerateColumns="False"
     DataSourceID="XmlDataSource1">
```

If you look in the Design view of your project, it will look like nothing happened but relaunch your page in your browser and check out the results. You should see something similar to Figure 5-15.

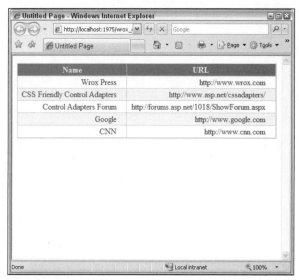

Figure 5-15

You will see that your GridView has totally changed. You now have a distinct header and alternating row colors (although they are probably not very apparent in black and white figures in this manuscript). You probably also noticed the green squiggly lines indicating errors in your `GridView.aspx` file when you added the `CssSelectorClass` property to your GridView control. Remember that this is just part of these particular control adapters. The CSS Friendly Control Adapters need special CSS classes set up to work. This is how the adapters are coded. So, in order for it to work as coded, you have to add a property to your control that isn't there.

If you are unhappy with the way this works, you can simply go into the control adapter code and change this approach. Perhaps pull in this class name through an existing (and valid) property, like the CssClass property? Or maybe just have it hard-coded in your control adapter what name it should use, which just means that all of your controls of this type will use the same styling because, remember, if you are able to set this dynamically, you could have one set of rules for a certain class of controls and another set of rules for a distinctly different control. So maybe you want some GridViews to look one way and others to look another. If that is true, you need to have a way of passing which one to use. As coded, the nonexistent `CssSelectorClass` property is used for this purpose. But, again, you could certainly modify the code to accept the value of another property to use in this capacity; it is really up to you.

For this demonstration, though, the control adapters will be used as-is.

The first thing to notice when looking through the files is the use of the class `PrettyGridView`. You first use this in your control itself in the `CssSelectorClass` property. You should also notice that every line in the CSS file starts off with this class. This is no accident. If you changed `CssSelectorClass` to something else, the control adapters would stop working. You would have to modify each line of the CSS file to use the new name. This is not hard to do, though. If `PrettyGridView` is just not cool enough for you and you want to use something like `myKickButtGridView`, then you can do that. You simply need to modify the GridView control to use the new `CssSelectorClass` property `myKickButtGridView`, as follows:

```
<asp:GridView CssSelectorClass="myKickButtGridView"
    ToolTip="example" ID="GridView1" runat="server"
    AutoGenerateColumns="False"
    DataSourceID="XmlDataSource1">
```

Before going any further, reload your page in a browser. You will notice that this doesn't cause it to crash. All that happens is that the GridView goes back to looking pretty plain; all style is removed. What has happened is that you have told the control adapters to find a class called `myKickButtGridView` in a referenced CSS file, and it couldn't find it, so it didn't apply any style rules. You won't get a compilation error or runtime error; you just won't get any style.

Now, go back to your CSS file, and do a find and replace to make all instances of `PrettyGridView` say `myKickButtGridView`. Save the file and reload your page in the browser. You should now see the Grid-View styled as before. This shows that you aren't limited to using `PrettyGridView` as the class you are styling. You can change this name without changing any code in the control adapters if you so choose.

> *Before proceeding, you should change your CSS* Class *and* CssSelectorClass *property back to* PrettyGridView. myKickButtGridView *was only used here to illustrate that you aren't locked into any particular class name. However, all examples from this point forward will be using* PrettyGridView.

Next, you should understand what each of the sections are and what they do. The only section that won't be elaborated on is the first section for `.foo` since that section is adequately explained in the code itself.

The first set of rules are as follows:

```
.PrettyGridView .AspNet-GridView
{
    width: 100%;
}
```

This is pretty simple. This rule is being applied to the master class of the GridView. If you look back at your rendered HTML for your page, you will remember that one of the first lines of code output for the GridView was as follows:

```
<div class="AspNet-GridView">
```

This is just a wrapper around the table. All you are saying here is that it should be set to 100%. You can play with this if you want (e.g., set up a border, set a defined width, etc.), but it really isn't necessary to do so.

The next section is much more interesting:

```
.PrettyGridView .AspNet-GridView div.AspNet-GridView-Pagination,
.PrettyGridView .AspNet-GridView div.AspNet-GridView-Pagination a,
.PrettyGridView .AspNet-GridView div.AspNet-GridView-Pagination span
{
    color: #00FFFF;
    background: #284775;
    font-weight: normal;
    padding: 2px;
}
```

This section controls the way that the pagination area looks in your rendered output. So far, the example has not included pagination, so you won't be able to see what is affected. However, if you wanted to see it, you could set `AllowPaging` to `True` and `PageSize` to 3 for your GridView control, as follows:

```
<asp:GridView CssSelectorClass="myKickButtGridView"
    AllowPaging="True" PageSize="3" ToolTip="example"
    ID="GridView1" runat="server"
    AutoGenerateColumns="False"
    DataSourceID="XmlDataSource1">
```

Doing so will render out your GridView similar to Figure 5-16.

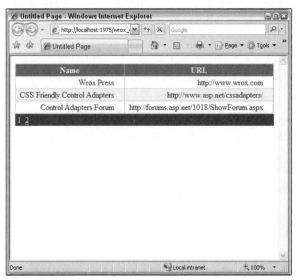

Figure 5-16

In your CSS rules, you are essentially setting up the font color (`color: #00FFFF;`), the background color of the pagination area (`background: #284775;`), and the font weight (`font-weight: normal;` — as opposed to "bold" or some other weight). You are also adding a 2-pixel padding around the entire area. If you change any of these rules for this class, you will notice the affect immediately. For example, change the background rule to `background: #FF0000;` and see what happens.

The next section should resemble the following:

```
.PrettyGridView .AspNet-GridView table
{
    border: solid 1px #CCCCCC;
    width: 100%;
}
```

Like the first section, this one should be fairly easy to understand. The only things you are doing is saying that the width of the rendered output should be 100% and that the table should have a 1-pixel solid border with a color of #CCCCCC. You should note that this only affects the outer border of the rendered table and not the individual gridlines within the table; that is done later on. It also only affects the table. This is important to realize because this means that the pagination area, since it is not a part of the table itself but, rather, in a separate CSS div by itself, will not be included in this border. This may have been apparent in your examples before if you have sharp eyes but, if not, change the border rule to border: solid 1px #000000; to see the affect this has. You will see the border go all the way around the content of the table, but it will not include the pagination area.

The next two sections should be taken together, since they both apply to the header region of your GridView control:

```
.PrettyGridView .AspNet-GridView table thead tr th
{
    color: #F7F6F3;
    background: #5D7B9D;
    font-weight: bold;
    border-bottom: solid 1px #CCCCCC;
    border-right: solid 1px #CCCCCC;
    padding: 2px;
}

.PrettyGridView .AspNet-GridView table thead tr th a
{
    color: #F7F6F3;
}
```

The first set of rules is setting up the row style. These rules set the color and border and the bold attributes of this row; the second set of rules sets the font color for any hyperlinks in the header row. This means that, if your rows are sortable and, therefore, have hyperlinks, they will be styled with the color set up in the second set of rules. If they are not clickable links, then they will be styled with the color set up in the first set of rules. In this case, both sets of rules set the font to the same color. The intent of this, obviously, is to make the font look the same whether or not it is a link.

The next two sets of rules can be looked at together as well:

```
.PrettyGridView .AspNet-GridView table tbody tr td
{
    color: #333333;
    background: White;
    padding: 2px 20px 2px 2px;
    border-bottom: solid 1px #CCCCCC;
    border-right: solid 1px #CCCCCC;
```

```
            text-align: right;
    }

    .PrettyGridView .AspNet-GridView table tbody tr.AspNet-GridView-Alternate td
    {
        background: #F7F6F3;
    }
```

This is the style that will be applied to your rows of data. The first set of rules is the default rules for rows in your GridView. You can see that you are setting the color and background properties. You will also notice that you have `text-align` set to right (if you were wondering why all of your contents shifted to the right of your table cell when you applied the CSS Friendly Control Adapters to your GridView, this is why). The second set of rules tells the browser how to handle the alternating rows or data. The only thing you have to set here is the background color because this is the only thing that is different than the default row styling of your rows of data. If, for example, you also wanted the font color to be red in your alternating rows, you could add `color: #FF0000;` to this second set of rules and that would take care of it. In the absence of rules in this second set, the row takes on the rules of the default definition set in the first set.

The last sections, as the comments in the CSS file explain, are just placeholders for now:

```
    .PrettyGridView .AspNet-GridView table tbody tr.AspNet-GridView-Selected td
    {
    }

    .PrettyGridView .AspNet-GridView table tfoot tr td
    {
    }
```

The first set would be used if you allow for selected rows in your GridView; the second set of rules would apply if you had a footer region defined. Neither one of these areas apply to this particular example, so no extra rules are required for these sections. However, if you wanted to play around in these sections, you could certainly use the tools in Visual Studio shown in Chapter 4 to set up rules and see how they appear. Just remember that you need to set up the GridView itself to work properly with these sections. For example, to allow row selection, you will need to modify your GridView as follows:

```
<asp:GridView CssSelectorClass="PrettyGridView"
    AllowPaging="True" PageSize="3" ToolTip="example"
    ID="GridView1" runat="server"
    AutoGenerateColumns="False"
    DataSourceID="XmlDataSource1">
    <Columns>
        <asp:CommandField ShowSelectButton="True" />
        <asp:BoundField DataField="Name" HeaderText="Name"
    SortExpression="Name" />
        <asp:BoundField DataField="URL" HeaderText="URL"
    SortExpression="URL" />
    </Columns>
</asp:GridView>
```

The change, in case it isn't apparent, is that you added a new column in the `<Columns>` section of the GridView for `Selection`. To do this another way, go into your Design view, click on the hovering arrow button on the GridView, and check the Enable Selection option, as shown in Figure 5-17.

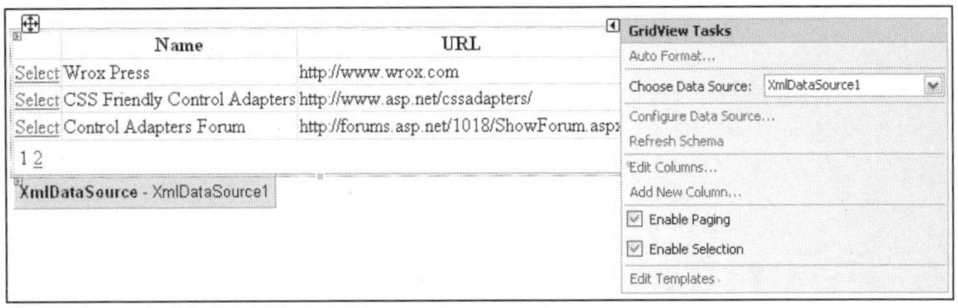

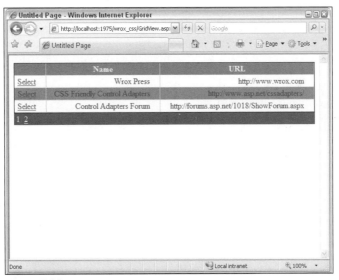

Figure 5-17

Now go back into your CSS file and make the following changes:

```
.PrettyGridView .AspNet-GridView table tbody tr.AspNet-GridView-Selected td
{
    background: #FF0000;
}
```

If you rerun your application, you will see the new Select buttons for each row. If you click on one of them, you will notice that row turns red, as shown in Figure 5-18.

Figure 5-18

One thing to keep in mind when you are playing with the stylesheets is that you do not have to use the Build Style Wizard to make changes. In fact, once you start getting increasingly more comfortable with CSS language, it is probably easier and more efficient to just type in the stylesheet page rather than use the tool. You will find that IntelliSense is included for your CSS documents and makes it very easy to make small changes quickly. Use the included CSS files as a starting point, and then play around with them to make them work the way you want them to. It will take a little while to get used to all of the different rules you can set up for each control but, once you do, this will go very quickly.

In the next chapter, you will learn more about navigation controls in general and, as part of that discussion, you will see how to style the menu control as part of your project. If you get a good understanding of these two controls, you will be well on your way to mastering this cool enhancement to the .NET 2.0 Framework.

For More Information

This book gives you a good foundation for the ASP.NET 2.0 CSS Friendly Control Adapters 1.0. However, you will probably want to further your understanding as you get more into utilizing these adapters in your project. The first place to look for information, especially if you are just talking about formatting the outputted HTML, is the home page of the adapters: www.asp.net/cssadapters.

This site has working examples of all of the controls included in the current release with notes on how to style them. There are also tutorials and a white paper that gives additional information on the controls themselves. This is also the first place to look for enhancements and future releases.

If you have a question that wasn't covered on that site (or in this book), you might want to go to the support forums, located on ASP.NET: http://forums.asp.net/1018/ShowForum.aspx.

As a general rule, forums are a great place to learn about new technologies or just things you might be unfamiliar with. The really great forums, like the ones at ASP.NET, are monitored and patrolled by industry experts who routinely respond to questions posed on the forums. The CSS Friendly Control Adapters section of the ASP.NET forums is continuously monitored by the creator of the adapters, Russ Helfand, and he makes it a point to answer questions that come up in those forums personally. If you have a question, it has likely been asked and answered in those forums. If not, post a new question and he will probably answer it. And if he doesn't, someone else knowledgeable in these adapters almost surely will. This is a great resource for finding the answers to questions that you may have about .NET in general, not just the control adapters. But it is certainly the premiere location to find the answers to questions on the CSS Friendly Control Adapters.

Summary

You wanted to find out how to begin your journey towards a fully CSS world of design, didn't you? You began your trip in Chapter 2 learning about accessibility and web standards. In Chapter 4, you learned how to format your page to mimic the old tables way of doing things using only CSS rules and definitions. You continued down the path in this chapter, learning how to override the rendering habits of several ASP.NET controls to spit out CSS code rather than the tables in the HTML it serves your patrons.

Hopefully, you learned what the CSS Friendly Control Adapters are. You learned how they work under the hood and how you can make changes to them, or even create new ones, if you should so choose. You learned how they work with CSS files to style the controls you use in your projects. You learned how they interact with the controls, even ignoring some of their properties, in the rendering of HTML output. You learned how to install, integrate, and implement the adapters for your projects.

Hopefully, you also learned what the CSS Friendly Control Adapters are not. They are not fully CSS, since two of the controls in the package still render tables (but hopefully you are okay with that).

You learned that they are not a closed source enhancement and that you are not only allowed but encouraged to make code changes to meet your needs. And, on that same note, you learned that the CSS Friendly Control Adapters are not shipped as a final product, but more as a template to show you what you can do and probably should do in your own projects.

But most importantly, hopefully you learned how cool these adapters are, how easy they are to implement, and how powerful they can be. Hopefully, you learned these are tools that you don't know how you got by without and can't see going forward without them.

6

Consistent Navigation

Historically, web page developers have struggled with the art of mastering a consistent site navigation system that was easy to maintain and worked in all browsers. Although not unique in this regard, ASP and ASP.NET seemed almost impossible to get a menu to work right and act the way you wanted. Most people resorted to purchasing third-party controls or relying on straight text hyperlinks or possibly images to create their navigation. The brave would attempt to write their own hovering drop-down menus, probably in JavaScript or something similar.

But that was then. Today's .NET developers have an easily maintainable site navigation system and a variety of tools at their disposal for presentation to their customers. These developers no longer have to look any further than the standard toolbox of Visual Studio to have a powerfully simple and simply powerful set of navigation tools for their next project.

Overview: ASP.NET Navigation Controls

With the introduction of the .NET 2.0 Framework, Visual Studio integrated several controls to help developers create a consistent navigation system into the projects they develop. Specifically, these controls include a TreeView control, a Menu control, and a SiteMapPath control. These new controls literally allow developers to drag and drop complex navigation systems right onto their page, which remain very flexible and easily modifiable. And, maybe most importantly, these controls have CSS Friendly Control Adapter overrides available to make them render out much more accessible HTML code and further expand your control over the way they look and feel.

Possibly one of the most notable features of these new controls is that they can, and should, tie directly into a controlling datasource. Generally speaking, this is an XML-based backend file called a sitemap. This sitemap file, called `web.sitemap` by default, creates the hierarchal infrastructure of your site in a format that is probably at least familiar to most web developers.

Although all of the navigation tools are useful and cool, this chapter will primarily focus on the drop-down navigation tools and the `web.sitemap` integration, since these are going to be the primary sources of site navigation used by most developers. Additionally, if you learn how to wire these up together, you will have the basic knowledge to go forward with the other tools as well.

First, you will learn the basics of the menu control, how to set it up, how to format its default installation, and how to create your first menu control items. Next, you will learn about the sitemap file and how to connect it to your menu control. Finally, you will learn how to format your menu control with the CSS Friendly Control Adapters discussed in Chapter 5. If you master all of these ideas, you will not only have a good understanding of the navigation features of ASP.NET 2.0 but also a better understanding of how to use the CSS Friendly Control Adapters in a real-world scenario.

Getting Started

If you do not already have a new project open or started, do so now.

If you try to continue using the book project, you will encounter problems that will be resolved later in this chapter. So for now, it is a good idea to create a temporary project to illustrate the finer points of the Navigation controls. At the end of the chapter, you will open back up the book project and update it with the new concepts you have learned throughout the chapter.

While you are looking at one of the ASPX pages (`Default.aspx` for example), you should see a section of the toolbox entitled "Navigation" as shown in Figure 6-1.

Figure 6-1

You can add a Menu control item by dragging it into either the Design or Source view of Visual Studio or, alternatively, simply double-click on the control in the toolbox. Doing so should produce similar code to be generated in your .NET page:

```
<asp:Menu ID="Menu1" runat="server">
</asp:Menu>
```

To see how the menu will function, add a couple of menu items directly into the code. For this example, you want to create a hierarchal layout similar to the following:

❏   Page 1

❏   Page 2

 ❏   Page 2 Subitem 1

 ❏   Page 2 Subitem 2

❏   Page 3

 ❏   Page 3 Subitem 1

 ❏   Page 3 Subitem 2

❏   Page 4

❏   Page 5

In order to do this, you should modify your control code to look more like this:

```
<asp:Menu ID="Menu1" runat="server">
<Items>
    <asp:MenuItem NavigateUrl="p1.aspx" Text="Page 1" />
    <asp:MenuItem NavigateUrl="p2.aspx" Text="Page 2">
        <asp:MenuItem NavigateUrl="p2s1.aspx" Text="Page 2 Subitem 1" />
        <asp:MenuItem NavigateUrl="p2s2.aspx" Text="Page 2 Subitem 2" />
    </asp:MenuItem>
    <asp:MenuItem NavigateUrl="p3.aspx" Text="Page 3">
        <asp:MenuItem NavigateUrl="p3s1.aspx" Text="Page 3 Subitem 1" />
        <asp:MenuItem NavigateUrl="p3s2.aspx" Text="Page 3 Subitem 2" />
    </asp:MenuItem>
    <asp:MenuItem NavigateUrl="p4.aspx" Text="Page 4" />
    <asp:MenuItem NavigateUrl="p5.aspx" Text="Page 5" />
</Items>
</asp:Menu>
```

You can see that, within the Menu control code, you have added a new section entitled Items. This will essentially define the items that are a part of your control. Within this section, you have created a total of five items, two of which have two subitems associated with them. If an item has no subitem, you can close the declaration with "/> ". However, if you want to include subitems, you need to make sure that you do not close the command in this manner; instead you close the declaration with "></asp:MenuItem>" with any related subitems in between the tags.

Doing it this way, there are several properties for each item in the Menu control, as shown in the table below. These properties will be visible through IntelliSense as you are typing the control. You can also find the list in the Properties window of Visual Studio.

Property	Description
Enabled	Sets whether or not the item is clickable/expandable. Setting the Enabled property to false makes the menu item display like a typically disabled control (grayed out). If the item is disabled, it will not expand to show its child items if you hover over it.
ImageUrl	Sets the image that is displayed next to the item when it is displayed. For example, if you wanted a little floppy disk icon next to a menu item that was for saving your page, you would set the path to this icon with this property.
NavigateUrl	Sets the URL the user will be directed to if he clicks on the menu item. If you do not want the menu item to be a clickable link (e.g., for an item that is only there to encompass several child items), you can leave this property off.
PopOutImageUrl	Sets the image that will be displayed to indicate the menu item has child items. For example, if you want to display a small arrow icon next to your menu item to indicate it has child items, this is where you would dictate the URL to that icon graphic.

Continued

Property	Description
Selectable	Sets whether the menu item is selectable/clickable. This is different than the Enabled property in that the item is still enabled, it is just not clickable. When the item is displayed, it will show in plain text (e.g., Black font if that is your default) rather than a disabled text. The end result, however, is the same (you have the text of your link displayed but with no functionality associated with it).
Selected	Although this can be used to set the selected status of a menu item, it is more commonly used to determine which menu item has been selected in your code behind. However, even that use is not that common, since it is a more common practice to use the SelectedItem property in the code behind to determine the same thing.
SeparatorImageUrl	Sets the URL to the image file that you want to use as a visual separator between menu items. This image can be pretty much any image format (e.g., JPG, GIF, PNG, etc.) as long as the client's browser can support it.
Target	Sets the target of the NavigateURL property. This is akin to the target property of a standard HTML hyperlink tag. For example, you can set this to _blank to open a new window or to _top to break out of any frame it may be contained in currently. You can also set the frame or window you want the URL to redirect into with this property. The default value is "", which means that the URL will go into the currently focused window or frame.
Text	Sets the display text for the menu item (i.e., the text that is displayed in the rendered menu item).
ToolTip	Sets the ToolTip that is displayed when a user hovers over the menu item. This is akin to setting the ALT property of a typical HTML hyperlink tag.
Value	Sets the value of the menu item. This is actually one of the more interesting properties. This setting allows you to display additional information about the menu item that is not displayed in code. This information can be used in your postback code. So maybe store an integer value that you will use to determine which view in a MultiView control you will display when the item is clicked. The value will not be rendered out but it will still be handled by your postback through code like e.Item.Value. That can be pretty handy.

You can play with these settings in order to get a better idea of how they will be rendered in your projects. However, for this example, you do not need to set any of them; the default values for each are fine.

That being said, you may want to play with a few of the properties of the menu control itself. Probably the most critical one, at least in this example, is the "Orientation" property, which can be set to "Horizontal" or "Vertical", depending on which type of menu orientation you want. Obviously, setting it to Horizontal will put the menu items side by side on the top level; setting it to Vertical will put the menu items below the previous one for the top-level items. The default setting is "Vertical". Change this to "Horizontal" to get a menu item that looks similar to Figure 6-2.

Figure 6-2

This menu is, to say the least, pretty boring at this point. In order to remedy this, you will probably want to set some of the style properties of the control. Note, though, that these properties will not hold if you override the menu control's functionality with the CSS Friendly Control Adapters, which you will do later in this chapter. However, if you are not planning on doing that, you will want to format the style either directly with the properties of the control or through CSS styles referenced from the control (not the same thing as the CSS Friendly Control Adapters — in which case, you reference CSS classes to control the look of the rendered menu item; the actual rendering methodology is not affected).

The first thing you will probably want to do is format the top-level items. In the menu control, these items are referred to as the "static" items. You can add style to these items in a couple of ways. The first is to set the properties directly in the menu control declaration. For example, you could set the background of the static menu items to beige by using the following code:

```
<asp:Menu ID="Menu1" StaticMenuStyle-BackColor="Beige" runat="server"
    Orientation="Horizontal">
```

The problem with this approach is that you may have many properties to set for all levels of your menu control. How confusing would it be to have, say, 100 properties set at the menu control level? Even if you think it might not be that bad, imagine going back in six months and trying to find the background color setting for the static menu items if there are literally over 100 items to parse through.

The better approach to handling this type of formatting, particularly from a maintainability standpoint, is to set up each class of properties in its own section of the menu object. This way, if you want to set the static menu properties, you just look for the static menu section of the control. For example, copy the following code into your project to set the properties of your menu control:

```
<asp:Menu ID="Menu1" runat="server" Orientation="Horizontal">
<StaticMenuStyle BackColor="Beige" BorderStyle="Solid" BorderColor="Tan"
    BorderWidth="2pt" HorizontalPadding="5px" VerticalPadding="5px" />
<StaticHoverStyle BackColor="BurlyWood" />
<StaticMenuItemStyle ForeColor="Brown" />
//the remainder of the menu control code is omitted for brevity but will be shown in
    its entirety later in this section
```

You can see that you now have a section for the general top-level menu style (StaticMenuStyle), the item style for the top-level menu (StaticMenuItemStyle), and for the hover effect of the top-level menu (StaticHoverStyle). In this example, you are declaring all of the properties within the menu object properties. However, for each section, you could just as easily set the property "CssClass" to a CSS class name in an included CSS file. That way you are totally removing styling from the page structure code and putting it in the CSS file where it probably belongs anyway. However, for illustrative purposes, the style properties will be set declaratively in the object itself.

Using the code above, you should now have a menu that looks something like Figure 6-3.

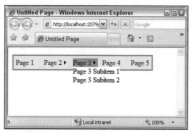

Figure 6-3

You can see that the width of the control is not set in this example. However, in the real world, you may have a very defined region that the navigation should fit within. In that scenario, you would set the width in the `StaticMenuStyle` properties to your width, say 700 pixels, to make sure the menu spans the entire width you have defined for it. You may also want to tweak the padding some to make sure it fits in the height of the region you have set up for the controls in your project. Once you get fairly comfortable with these properties, though, integrating this navigation system into any web project should be a snap.

The next thing you will probably want to work on are the drop-down items, which are called the dynamic menu items. Again, you could set these up declaratively in the menu object or separate them out like before as follows:

```
<DynamicMenuStyle BackColor="Beige" BorderStyle="Solid" BorderColor="Tan"
    BorderWidth="1pt" HorizontalPadding="2px" VerticalPadding="2px" />
<DynamicMenuItemStyle HorizontalPadding="3px" VerticalPadding="3px"
    ForeColor="Brown" />
<DynamicHoverStyle BackColor="BurlyWood" />
//the remainder of the menu control code is omitted for brevity but will be shown in
    its entirety later in this section
```

You can see that, for the most part, these properties look very similar to the ones set up for the static menu. The same colors are used and approximately the same padding (there are 2 pixels at the menu level and then 3 pixels at the item level for a total of 5 pixels, instead of just 5 pixels set at the menu level as in the static menu properties). If you run this code, your page should look similar to Figure 6-4.

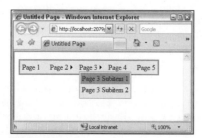

Figure 6-4

As you can see, you have a site navigation system set up that uses complementary colors and looks nice. With these basic properties, you should be able to set up a navigation system that looks professional and integrates seamlessly with your existing or future projects.

Your code, as it stands at this point, should look like this:

```
<asp:Menu ID="Menu1" runat="server" Orientation="Horizontal">
<StaticMenuStyle BackColor="Beige" BorderStyle="Solid" BorderColor="Tan"
    BorderWidth="2pt" HorizontalPadding="5px" VerticalPadding="5px" />
<StaticHoverStyle BackColor="BurlyWood" />
<StaticMenuItemStyle ForeColor="Brown" />
<DynamicMenuStyle BackColor="Beige" BorderStyle="Solid" BorderColor="Tan"
    BorderWidth="1pt" HorizontalPadding="2px" VerticalPadding="2px" />
<DynamicMenuItemStyle HorizontalPadding="3px" VerticalPadding="3px"
    ForeColor="Brown" />
<DynamicHoverStyle BackColor="BurlyWood" />
<Items>
    <asp:MenuItem  NavigateUrl="p1.aspx" Text="Page 1" />
    <asp:MenuItem NavigateUrl="p2.aspx" Text="Page 2">
        <asp:MenuItem NavigateUrl="p2s1.aspx" Text="Page 2 Subitem 1" />
        <asp:MenuItem NavigateUrl="p2s2.aspx" Text="Page 2 Subitem 2" />
    </asp:MenuItem>
    <asp:MenuItem NavigateUrl="p3.aspx" Text="Page 3">
        <asp:MenuItem NavigateUrl="p3s1.aspx" Text="Page 3 Subitem 1" />
        <asp:MenuItem NavigateUrl="p3s2.aspx" Text="Page 3 Subitem 2" />
    </asp:MenuItem>
    <asp:MenuItem NavigateUrl="p4.aspx" Text="Page 4" />
    <asp:MenuItem NavigateUrl="p5.aspx" Text="Page 5" />
</Items>
</asp:Menu>
```

The SiteMapDataSource Control

If you are only going to have one menu control on your entire site, possibly hosted in a Master Page (discussed in Chapter 7), the previous example might be fine. But what happens if you want to leave a breadcrumb trail at the top of your page to let your users know where they are currently in the hierarchal schema of your site (the SiteMapPath control)? Or what if you wanted to create a TreeView control that also had the site hierarchy represented in it? How would you do that? With the current setup, the simple answer is: you wouldn't.

The way the menu control is set up, it is selfish with its knowledge of your site's hierarchy. Sure, it knows the relationships between all of your pages and how to link through them. But it isn't sharing that knowledge with any other control.

So how do you make the controls play nicely together? The answer, as you may have guessed by the title of this section, is the use of the SiteMapDataSource control.

The purpose of this control is to link to an XML-based sitemap file that contains the hierarchal schema for the pages of your site. This is just a fancy way of saying that it stores what pages you want shown in your navigation controls and maintains the relationship between each page.

The web.sitemap File

By default, the SiteMapDataSource control links to a sitemap file called web.sitemap. The default setting is that the file must be `web.sitemap`. This can be modified, as will be shown later in this chapter but, for now, assume that you must call the file `web.sitemap`.

The first step in setting up your SiteMapDataSource control is to add a `web.sitemap` file to your project. So, with your project open, click Website on the toolbar and select Add New Item to get the screen shown in Figure 6-5.

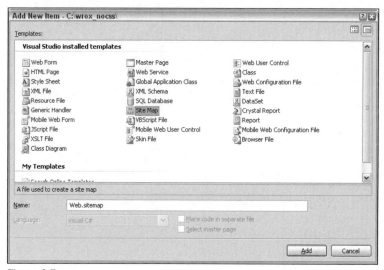

Figure 6-5

You will see that basically all of the options (language, code-behind, and master page) are disabled. The only option you can modify is the name of the file, which is set by default to `"web.sitemap"`. For now, leave the name as is and click the Add button to add a new sitemap file to your project. This will create a file that looks like this:

```xml
<?xml version="1.0" encoding="utf-8" ?>
<siteMap xmlns="http://schemas.microsoft.com/AspNet/SiteMap-File-1.0" >
    <siteMapNode url="" title=""  description="">
        <siteMapNode url="" title=""  description="" />
        <siteMapNode url="" title=""  description="" />
    </siteMapNode>
</siteMap>
```

You can see that the file is just basic XML structure. You have a single siteMapNode with two subnodes attached to it. This, however, is where some confusion can kick in. *You can only have one siteMapNode in your sitemap file.* Many developers, when first getting into working with this file, believe that they need to set up a new node for each page. While that is technically true, you need to make all of your pages subnodes of the master/controlling node. In other words, using multiple siteMap nodes will *not* work and will cause a server error when you try to use it as your SiteMapDataSource:

```
<?xml version="1.0" encoding="utf-8" ?>
<siteMap xmlns="http://schemas.microsoft.com/AspNet/SiteMap-File-1.0" >
    <siteMapNode url="p1.aspx" title="Page 1"  description=""/>
    <siteMapNode url="p2.aspx" title="Page 2"  description="">
        <siteMapNode url="p2s1.aspx" title="Page 2 Subitem 1"
    description="" />
        <siteMapNode url="p2s2.aspx" title="Page 2 Subitem 2"
    description="" />
    </siteMapNode>
    <siteMapNode url="p3.aspx" title="Page 3"  description="">
        <siteMapNode url="p3s1.aspx" title="Page 3 Subitem 1"
    description="" />
        <siteMapNode url="p3s2.aspx" title="Page 3 Subitem 2"
    description="" />
    </siteMapNode>
    <siteMapNode url="p4.aspx" title="Page 4"  description=""/>
    <siteMapNode url="p5.aspx" title="Page 5"  description=""/>
</siteMap>
```

Intuitively, this seems like it should work. You have individual nodes set up for each page with subnodes set up for the subitems. This may seem like it should work, but it won't.

In order to make it work, you need to wrap the entire contents in a single node, like this:

```
<?xml version="1.0" encoding="utf-8" ?>
<siteMap xmlns="http://schemas.microsoft.com/AspNet/SiteMap-File-1.0" >
    <siteMapNode url="" title="" description="">
        <siteMapNode url="p1.aspx" title="Page 1"  description=""/>
        <siteMapNode url="p2.aspx" title="Page 2"  description="">
            <siteMapNode url="p2s1.aspx" title="Page 2 Subitem 1"
            description="" />
            <siteMapNode url="p2s2.aspx" title="Page 2 Subitem 2"
            description="" />
        </siteMapNode>
        <siteMapNode url="p3.aspx" title="Page 3"  description="">
            <siteMapNode url="p3s1.aspx" title="Page 3 Subitem 1"
            description="" />
            <siteMapNode url="p3s2.aspx" title="Page 3 Subitem 2"
            description="" />
        </siteMapNode>
        <siteMapNode url="p4.aspx" title="Page 4"  description=""/>
        <siteMapNode url="p5.aspx" title="Page 5"  description=""/>
    </siteMapNode>
</siteMap>
```

The standard properties of the siteMapNode are as follows:

❑   **url:** This is the page that you want to redirect to when the menu item is clicked.

❑   **title:** This is the text that is displayed in the menu item.

❑   **description:** This is the ToolTip text that will be displayed when you hover over the menu item.

None of these are required (you can leave them all blank), but you should probably try to fill in all three if possible. Additionally, the properties in the following table are available.

Property	Description
provider	This property allows you to import a second sitemap into your current navigation architecture. For example, say you have standard.sitemap and extra.sitemap and you want standard.sitemap to import extra.sitemap into it. You would go into standard.sitemap and create a new siteMapNode at the location in standard.sitemap you want to add a reference to the name of the extra.sitemap file created in your web.config file (discussed later). It would look something like: <siteMapNode provider = "extra"/> Again, you would have to have "extra" set up in your web.config file to reference extra.sitemap, which you will learn how to do later in this chapter.
resourceKey	This allows you to localize your menu for your customers by entering the name in the global resource file (RESX) to match against. This way, you can have the displayed text of your properties show one thing for an English visitor and another for a Spanish one, for example.
roles	This allows you to define which roles (membership API) are allowed to view the menu items. For example, maybe you have a node that is only accessible to administrators. You simply set the roles to Administrators and then nobody else will even see the links. This will be discussed in more detail later in this chapter.
securityTrimmingEnabled	This property basically tells your applications whether or not to honor the roles property. You have to set this to true to be able to use roles in your menu.
siteMapFile	This is similar to provider in that it allows you to import a child sitemap into a parent sitemap without the hassle of going through the web.config file. To use the example shown in the provider discussion above, you would simply create the following node at the location you want to import the child menu: <siteMapNode siteMapFile = "extra.sitemap"/>

Resource files and roles will be discussed a little later in this chapter, but this should give you a good overview of the settings you can use when creating your nodes. As stated before, you should always include url, title, and description if they are available. These other settings are more advanced and not necessarily relevant to every project (but they are certainly cool).

SiteMapDataSource

Now that you have your web.sitemap file set up appropriately, you have to tie it into your menu control. The first step is drop a SiteMapDataSource onto the page that is hosting your menu control.

First, you will need to find the control in the Data group of your toolbox, as shown in Figure 6-6.

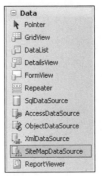

Figure 6-6

Either drag the SiteMapDataSource control directly onto your page or just double-click on the control in the toolbox. This will generate the following code on your page:

```
<asp:SiteMapDataSource ID="SiteMapDataSource1" runat="server" />
```

In order to make the menu control hook into the SiteMapDataSource, you need to set one property in the menu control object: `DataSourceID`. This should look something like this:

```
<asp:Menu DataSourceID="SiteMapDataSource1" ID="Menu1" runat="server"
    Orientation="Horizontal">
```

At this point, you should have the two wired together and can delete all of the Items you have hard-coded in for the menu control. Your code, to this point, should look like the following:

```
<asp:Menu DataSourceID="SiteMapDataSource1" ID="Menu1" runat="server"
    Orientation="Horizontal">
<StaticMenuStyle BackColor="Beige" BorderStyle="Solid" BorderColor="Tan"
    BorderWidth="2pt" HorizontalPadding="5px" VerticalPadding="5px" />
<StaticHoverStyle BackColor="BurlyWood" />
<StaticMenuItemStyle ForeColor="Brown" />
<DynamicMenuStyle BackColor="Beige" BorderStyle="Solid" BorderColor="Tan"
    BorderWidth="1pt" HorizontalPadding="2px" VerticalPadding="2px" />
<DynamicMenuItemStyle HorizontalPadding="3px" VerticalPadding="3px"
    ForeColor="Brown" />
<DynamicHoverStyle BackColor="BurlyWood" />
</asp:Menu>
<asp:SiteMapDataSource ID="SiteMapDataSource1" runat="server" />
```

If you launch your application in the browser, it should now look like Figure 6-7.

As you can see, this has slightly modified the look and feel of your original menu. What has happened is that it has created your container node (the one that holds all of your real nodes) as the top-level menu and then put all of the other nodes under that. This is a consequence of having to declare the one top-level node in the `web.sitemap` file.

189

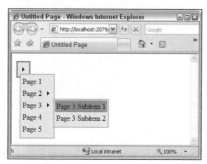

Figure 6-7

The good news is that there is a way around this. There is a Boolean property for the SiteMapDataSource object called ShowStartingNode; setting this to false will alter the SiteMapDataSource code as follows:

```
<asp:SiteMapDataSource ShowStartingNode="false" ID="SiteMapDataSource1"
    runat="server" />
```

Now if you rerun your application, it will look like Figure 6-8.

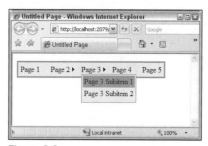

Figure 6-8

You can see that by setting this property to false, you now have a menu control that looks very similar to the one you initially created by hard-coding in the menu items in the menu control object.

A Different Sitemap File

Now suppose that you want to call your sitemap file something besides web.sitemap. Basically, this will make your menu control stop working. This could be a problem if you want to have multiple sitemap files for your site. Or you could just not like the name. Regardless of your reasoning, it is likely that at some point you will be faced with a project where you need to add a differently named sitemap file to your project. Here is how you wire that up.

First, you will just modify the existing project. So, in order to simulate a scenario that may present itself in the future, rename the web.sitemap file to menu.sitemap. If you were to run the project at this point, you would immediately be presented with an error stating that it cannot find the web.sitemap file. Now you need to tell your project how to find the newly named sitemap file.

You will need to go into your `web.config` file, which will probably look similar to this:

```xml
<?xml version="1.0"?>
<configuration>
    <system.web>
        <compilation debug="true"/>
    </system.web>
</configuration>
```

If you do not have a `web.config` *as part of your project at this point, you can add one by clicking Website or Project on your toolbar and selecting Add New Item. When the Add New Item dialog box appears, look for Web Configuration File on the third column of available templates. Select this item, and click the OK button. You should then see the file in your solution explorer in the root directory of your project.*

In the `system.web` section, you will need to add a new section entitled `sitemap` that should resemble the following:

```xml
<?xml version="1.0"?>
<configuration>
    <system.web>
        <compilation debug="true"/>
        <siteMap enabled="true">
            <providers>
                <add name="myMenu"
                    type="System.Web.XmlSiteMapProvider"
                    siteMapFile="menu.sitemap"/>
            </providers>
        </siteMap>
    </system.web>
</configuration>
```

You can see that you are adding a `providers` section in the `sitemap` section. In that section, you are adding a reference to `menu.sitemap` and calling it `"myMenu"`. Once you have this code in your `web.config` file, you can reference the `menu.sitemap` file by calling `"myMenu"`. So, back to the ASPX page that contains the `SiteMapDataSource` object. You will need to add a property to the object called `"SiteMapProvider"` and reference `"myMenu"`, as follows:

```
<asp:SiteMapDataSource SiteMapProvider="myMenu" ShowStartingNode="false"
    ID="SiteMapDataSource1" runat="server" />
```

At this point, your menu control should be wired to your custom-named sitemap file called `menu.sitemap`. If you run your application, you should now see that the menu once again works as originally coded.

You can do this same trick to add several other sitemap files to use as necessary in your projects.

Lock Down!

One of the coolest features of the navigation controls is that they can be integrated with the Membership API provided with .NET 2.0. A full discussion of memberships and roles is a bit out of the scope of this manuscript. However, enough detail will be given to show you how to implement roles into your site navigation if you have a fair understanding of the Membership API.

The basic principle of membership and roles in .NET is that you can define users based on some form of authentication. This might mean that you have one class of visitors that would be essentially anonymous and then one or more roles that would have to be logged in. For example, maybe there is one class of logged-in users that have basic rights to your site and then another class of users that would be administrators of the site that basically have rights to anything.

In the navigation controls, the process of restricting access to some links in your menu based on user roles is called Security Trimming, so to enable this functionality, you need to modify the sitemap section of your `web.config` file, as follows:

```
<siteMap enabled="true">
    <providers>
        <add name="myMenu"
            type="System.Web.XmlSiteMapProvider"
            siteMapFile="menu.sitemap"
            securityTrimmingEnabled="true"/>
    </providers>
</siteMap>
```

As you can see, you are just adding `securityTrimmingEnabled = "true"` to tell your application to honor your roles management you have set up for this project.

You will also want to set up your application to use Role Management, which you can do with the following section immediately after the providers section:

```
<roleManager enabled="true"/>
```

Next, you will want to set up a new link in your `menu.sitemap` file for a page called `Admin.aspx`. However, before doing this, you need to actually create this page as part of your project. To do this, click on Website or Project on your toolbar in Visual Studio and select Add New Item. When the Add New Item dialog box appears, select Web Form from the available templates (it should be the first one in the first column). In the Name field, type in Admin.aspx. For this project, accept Visual C# as the Language and make sure that ''Place code in separate file'' is checked. Click the Add button to add this page to your project.

Within `Admin.aspx`, you should add some text to the body of the page just as a placeholder so that you will know that you have reached it successfully. To this end, add `Welcome to Admin.aspx!` to the body, as shown here:

```
<%@ Page Language="C#" AutoEventWireup="true"
    CodeFile="Admin.aspx.cs" Inherits="Admin" %>

<!DOCTYPE html PUBLIC "-//W3C//DTD XHTML 1.0 Transitional//EN"
    "http://www.w3.org/TR/xhtml1/DTD/xhtml1-transitional.dtd">

<html xmlns="http://www.w3.org/1999/xhtml" >
<head runat="server">
    <title>Untitled Page</title>
</head>
```

```
<body>
    <form id="form1" runat="server">
    <div>
    Welcome to Admin.aspx!
    </div>
    </form>
</body>
</html>
```

For `Admin.aspx`, you will want to restrict access to only a certain role, `"Admin"` for example. This will look similar to the following:

```
<siteMapNode roles="Admin" url="Admin.aspx" title="Admin Link"
    description="Admin Stuff" />
```

You can see the use of the property `roles` to restrict this particular link to the `"Admin"` role. However, this isn't quite enough. You will also need to go to the main node (the one that contains all of the other nodes) and allow all roles. This will allow all users, anonymous or otherwise, to access all of your links. However, when it gets to the Admin link, the roles declaration will override this setting. In other words, unless otherwise declared on the individual node, all users are allowed to see this link. Your `menu.sitemap` file should now look like this:

```
<?xml version="1.0" encoding="utf-8" ?>
<siteMap xmlns="http://schemas.microsoft.com/AspNet/SiteMap-File-1.0" >
    <siteMapNode roles="*"  url="" title="" description="">
        <siteMapNode url="p1.aspx" title="Page 1"  description=""/>
        <siteMapNode url="p2.aspx" title="Page 2"  description="">
            <siteMapNode url="p2s1.aspx" title="Page 2 Subitem 1"
                description="" />
            <siteMapNode url="p2s2.aspx" title="Page 2 Subitem 2"
                description="" />
        </siteMapNode>
        <siteMapNode url="p3.aspx" title="Page 3"  description="">
            <siteMapNode url="p3s1.aspx" title="Page 3 Subitem 1"
                description="" />
            <siteMapNode url="p3s2.aspx" title="Page 3 Subitem 2"
                description="" />
        </siteMapNode>
        <siteMapNode url="p4.aspx" title="Page 4"  description=""/>
        <siteMapNode url="p5.aspx" title="Page 5"  description=""/>
        <siteMapNode roles="Admin" url="Admin.aspx" title="Admin Link"
                description="Admin Stuff" />
    </siteMapNode>
</siteMap>
```

Finally, back in the `web.config` file, you need to set up permissions for the file `Admin.aspx`. Essentially, you are telling the application to handle all of the other files one way but to handle this one file slightly differently. If you have more than one page, you can create multiple entries similar to the following:

```
<location path="Admin.aspx">
    <system.web>
        <authorization>
            <allow roles="Admin"/>
```

```
            <deny users="*"/>
        </authorization>
    </system.web>
</location>
```

This section should come outside of the typical `system.web` section of your `web.config` file. In other words, it would be appropriate to place it after `</system.web>` but before `</configuration>`. Again, this is setting up rules for this one page that essentially says deny everyone except for the role of Admin.

Your complete `web.config` file should resemble the following:

```
<?xml version="1.0"?>
<configuration>
    <system.web>
        <compilation debug="true"/>
        <siteMap enabled="true">
            <providers>
                <add name="myMenu"
                    type="System.Web.XmlSiteMapProvider"
                    siteMapFile="menu.sitemap"
                    securityTrimmingEnabled="true"/>
            </providers>
        </siteMap>
        <roleManager enabled="true"/>
    </system.web>
    <location path="Admin.aspx">
        <system.web>
            <authorization>
                <allow roles="Admin"/>
                <deny users="*"/>
            </authorization>
        </system.web>
    </location>
</configuration>
```

If you now run your application, assuming that you have not set up an Admin role on your own and you are not logged into that account, you should get a menu similar to the one shown in Figure 6-9.

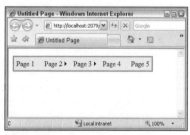

Figure 6-9

This may seem anticlimactic since you have, at least by appearance, created a page that looks exactly like the one you had before. But you have to think, you have completely hidden your new link to `Admin.aspx`.

Furthermore, if you were to navigate to Admin.aspx, you would see an error message similar to that in Figure 6-10.

Figure 6-10

You are completely locked out of the page. Not only can you not see it in the menu, but if you happen to stumble across it, you get an error message telling you that you are denied access to this page.

To test how this will work, you could add functionality to your Page_Load event to add all users to the Admin role. This might look similar to the following:

```
protected void Page_Load(object sender, EventArgs e)
{
    //create the "Admin" account if it does not already exist:
    if (!Roles.RoleExists("Admin")) { Roles.CreateRole("Admin"); }

    //add all users to the Admin account:
    if (!User.IsInRole("Admin")) { Roles.AddUserToRole(User.Identity.Name,
    "Admin"); }
}
```

Up to this point in this book you have not seen the Page_Load event, which is a part of the code-behind file for a particular page. To access this file in Visual Studio 2005, you should be able to click on the (+) sign next to a page to expand it to see its children. For example, if you click on the (+) next to Default.aspx, you should see its code-behind file, entitled something like Default.aspx.cs. Double-click on that file to get access to the Page_Load method (and the rest of the code-behind functionality).

Again, without going too far into the Membership API, you are creating a new role called "Admin" if it does not exist. This needs to match, verbatim, the name of the role you have allowed access to your secure pages in your web.config file. Next, you are adding all users to this new role. In the real world, you would never do this (obviously), but this should help you see what happens when you are now logged in as an administrator (see Figure 6-11).

As you can see, you now have the Admin Link added to your menu. If you click on it, you will be taken to Admin.aspx, which you can see in Figure 6-12.

You have effectively shut down Admin.aspx to all users that are not in the Admin role with the settings you have implemented in your menu.sitemap and web.config files. If you are not logged in as a user with an Admin role, you cannot see the page or the link to it but you can see and access all other pages. As soon as you log in as a user with the Admin role, you still see all other links, but you also see the new `Admin.aspx` link and are able to access that page.

Figure 6-11

Figure 6-12

It's worth noting that you can use this same technique to lock down entire directories. Instead of placing the name of a file in the location declaration in your `web.config` file, you simply put in the name of a directory. That way, you can set up a subdirectory on your website as an admin directory and lock that entire directory down to the Admin role.

This section's primary focus was on how to integrate the navigation controls with that Membership API. As such, the emphasis of this discussion was on the navigation controls and not the Membership functionality as much. If you would like to read more about ASP.NET 2.0 Membership, you might want to read the following articles:

❑ **How To: Use Membership in ASP.NET 2.0** — `http://msdn2.microsoft.com/en-us/library/ms998347.aspx`

❑ **Membership and Role Providers in ASP.NET 2.0** — `http://www.odetocode.com/Articles/427.aspx`

Hello = Hola

One other nice feature of the standard menu control is the ability to localize your menu based on the settings of your visitors. This means that, if an English-speaking visitor stops by, your menu shows English text. However, if a Spanish-speaking visitor accesses your site, he or she will see your menu with Spanish text instead.

Like the Security Trimmings already discussed, globalization and resource files are not necessarily in the scope of this manuscript. If you are wanting to localize your menu, it is assumed that you already know how to localize your site. This section is mostly here to show you how to incorporate this control with the technology you are already familiar with. A cursory overview of ASP.NET globalization will be provided so that, if you are totally new to this concept, you can at least get an idea of how this all works. But, again, the point of this section isn't to go deep under the hood of globalization in general; it is only to show you how to use globalization to localize your menu control.

Step 1: Setting Up the Sitemap File

The first thing you will need to do is prepare the sitemap file to allow for localization. This involves two distinct operations. The first thing you will need to do is to allow localization on the sitemap. This is done on the `sitemap` declaration (as opposed to the `sitemapnode` declarations). You do this through the property `enableLocalization`, as follows:

```
<siteMap enableLocalization="true" xmlns="http://schemas.microsoft.com/AspNet/
SiteMap-File-1.0" >
```

The next step is to tell the nodes which resource file they should use. There are actually a couple of ways to do this. The first thing is that you can set the resource declaration for each property. This is done using the following format: `$resources:RESOURCEFILE,CLASSNAME,DEFAULTTEXT`

For example, to map the `Title` property to p1Title and the `Description` property to p1Desc in a resource file called `menu.sitemap`, you would have something like the following:

```
<siteMapNode url="p1.aspx" title=" $resources:menu.sitemap,
    p1Title, Page 1" description=" $resources:menu.sitemap,
    p1Desc,Go to Page 1"/>
```

You would need to set up the appropriate resource keys (which will be shown in the next section), but there is a better way to handle this functionality: the `resourceKey` property.

Setting the `resourceKey` property causes the code to look for that key in the relevant resource file and returns the value. So, if you wanted to perform the preceding task using the `resourceKey`, the code would look like this:

```
<siteMapNode url="p1.aspx" resourceKey="p1" title="" description=""/>
```

Notice that both title and description are empty. Honestly, you could leave these properties out all together, making your `sitemapnode` reference even slimmer:

```
<siteMapNode url="p1.aspx" resourceKey="p1"/>
```

For brevity, only the `"p1.aspx"` menu item will be modified to use the resource files. Thus, your `menu.sitemap` file should now resemble the following (still including the security settings from the previous step):

```
<?xml version="1.0" encoding="utf-8" ?>
<siteMap enableLocalization="true" xmlns="http://schemas.microsoft.com/
    AspNet/SiteMap-File-1.0" >
    <siteMapNode roles="*"  url="" title="" description="">
```

```
            <siteMapNode url="p1.aspx" resourceKey="p1"/>
            <siteMapNode url="p2.aspx" title="Page 2"  description="">
                <siteMapNode url="p2s1.aspx" title="Page 2 Subitem 1"
            description="" />
                <siteMapNode url="p2s2.aspx" title="Page 2 Subitem 2"
            description="" />
            </siteMapNode>
            <siteMapNode url="p3.aspx" title="Page 3"  description="">
                <siteMapNode url="p3s1.aspx" title="Page 3 Subitem 1"
            description="" />
                <siteMapNode url="p3s2.aspx" title="Page 3 Subitem 2"
            description="" />
            </siteMapNode>
            <siteMapNode url="p4.aspx" title="Page 4"  description=""/>
            <siteMapNode url="p5.aspx" title="Page 5"  description=""/>
            <siteMapNode roles="Admin" url="Admin.aspx" title="Admin Link"
        description="Admin Stuff" />
        </siteMapNode>
    </siteMap>
```

Step 2: Adding Your Resources

Now you need to set up your resource files for this project. First, create the default resource file.
You have to name the file with the same filename as the file that will be using it and then add an
.resx file extension.

*This file extension is in addition to the file extension already associated with the file. This means that, for
"menu.sitemap", you need to create an associated resource file called "menu.sitemap.resx".*

To add the resource, click Website on the toolbar and select Add New Item to get the screen shown
in Figure 6-13.

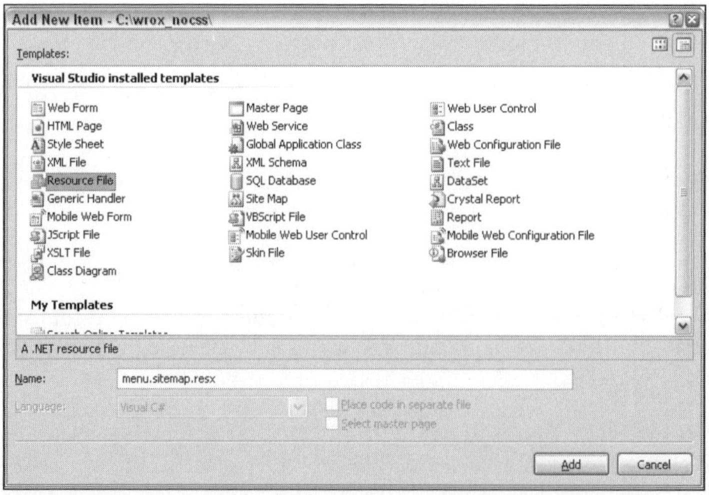

Figure 6-13

You will need to select "Resource File" and name the file "menu.sitemap.resx" as shown in Figure 6-13 and then click the Add button. If you have not added any resource files up to this point, you will probably get the message shown in Figure 6-14.

Figure 6-14

If you get this message, click Yes in order to create the ASP.NET folder App_GlobalResources, and then add your new file to that directory.

Once you have the new resource file created, you will be presented with a grid that allows you to set up key names, values, and comments. For this file, you want to create settings similar to those shown in Figure 6-15.

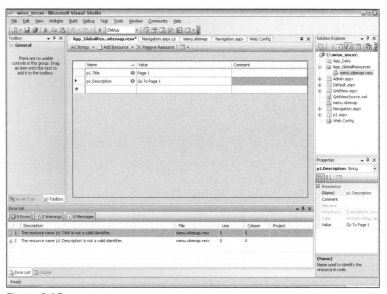

Figure 6-15

You will notice that naming the keys "p1.Title" and "p1.Description" causes errors. However, this is a known issue and will not cause any errors at runtime. In an MSDN article (http://msdn2.microsoft.com/en-us/library/ms178427.aspx), Microsoft states:

> *Key names in global resource files should not include periods (.). However, periods are necessary in global resources that are referenced in site-map files when using implicit expressions. This is because of the resourceKey syntax. In some editing environments, such as Visual Web Developer, you might get a design-time error if you use a period in the key name. However, this shouldn't affect the ability to edit or save the file and can be ignored.*

So, once you have added your resource keys, save the file. This file will serve as your default settings pulled into your sitemap file.

For illustrative purposes, create a second resource file called `menu.sitemap.es.resx` ("es" for "español"). This will be the Spanish equivalent of the default resource keys so that if Spanish visitors access your site, they will see Spanish text rather than the English one set up in the default file.

So, once you have your file created, add the key names, values, and comments shown in Figure 6-16.

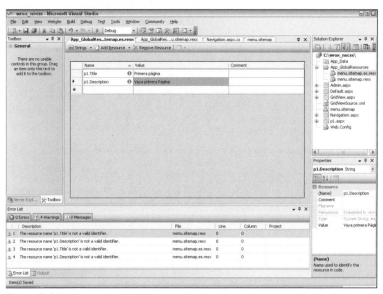

Figure 6-16

You have now set up two resource files, a default one (English) and a Spanish equivalent.

Step 3: Telling the Page to Look for the Language

The last step you will need to make is to modify your `Page` declaration for the page that is referencing your menu control to automatically detect the `UICulture`. This just means that the page will look for the language preference of the visitor and tell the menu control what language it should use. Your `Page` declaration, in order to do this, should look similar to the following:

```
<%@ Page UICulture="auto" Language="C#" AutoEventWireup="true"
    CodeFile="Default.aspx.cs" Inherits="_Default" %>
```

Step 4: Test!

At this point, you should be all set. Launch your application and, assuming that your default language is English, your application should look like Figure 6-17.

You can see that the title has been set to "Page 1" and the description is displaying "Go To Page 1". This is evidence that the application is pulling in the keys from your default resource file.

Figure 6-17

Now to verify that you have it set properly, you can change your language settings in Internet Explorer to a Spanish language (e.g., es-MX for Mexico). If you don't know where this is, go into Internet Options under Tools (in IE7) and click on the Languages button. You can add a new language and then move it to the top of the list to make it your default. Select "Spanish (Mexico) [es-MX]" and move it to the top of the list and click the OK button twice. Now refresh your page. You should see that the menu has changed so that it is similar to Figure 6-18.

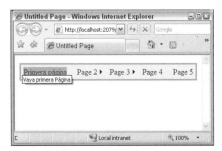

Figure 6-18

The menu for the first item (the only one set in this example) is now pulling in its values from the Spanish resource file you created.

Of course, you will need to set up all of your resource keys to handle all of the menu items for your own project, but this should show you how you need to do it so that you can make your applications accessible to an international audience.

Using the CSS Friendly Control Adapters

Now that you have an understanding of the Menu navigation control and how to better customize it to fit your needs, it is time to wire it up to the CSS Friendly Control Adapters.

As seen in Chapter 5, the default behavior of the Menu control is to render out HTML tables. This is in stark contrast to web standard guidelines and may provide accessibility issues for your visitors. For this reason, you really should consider using the CSS Friendly Control Adapters that not only solve these problems but also put the entire style declarations in a separate CSS file, keeping style and code in distinctly different files.

So, you will need to open up your project that was created in Chapter 4 (originally created in C:\surfer5\). This project was set up to use the CSS Friendly Control Adapters in Chapter 5 and should now be ready for you to add the menu navigation control to the project.

Before getting too far into the project, ensure that your main page, Default.aspx, has the following set up in the <head> area of the page:

```
<link href="surfer5_v1.css" rel="stylesheet" type="text/css" />
<link runat="server" rel="stylesheet" href="~/CSS/Import.css"
    type="text/css" id="AdaptersInvariantImportCSS" />
<!--[if lt IE 7]>
    <link runat="server" rel="stylesheet"
        href="~/CSS/BrowserSpecific/IEMenu6.css" type="text/css">
<![endif]-->
```

Basically, you have a main reference to the stylesheet created in Chapter 4 (surfer5_v1.css) and then links to the default CSS Friendly Control Adapter CSS files (Import.css and IEMenu6.css). You will need to make sure that these files are in place in the directory structure of your project. You need to make sure that you take special care to include the Conditional Comments to provide the IEMenu6.css stylesheet to Internet Explorer browsers less than Version 7. (Conditional Comments were discussed in Chapter 5.)

Adding a New web.sitemap File

This project will utilize the web.sitemap file and the SiteMapDataSource to maintain the following hierarchal schema of this site:

- ❑ Home (Default.aspx)
- ❑ Blog (Blog.aspx)
- ❑ Publications ()
    - ❑ Books (Books.aspx)
    - ❑ Magazines (Magazines.aspx)
    - ❑ Online (Online.aspx)
- ❑ Presentations ()
    - ❑ Upcoming Presentations (FutureEvents.aspx)
    - ❑ Past Events (PastEvents.aspx)
- ❑ Downloads (Downloads.aspx)
- ❑ Contact Me (ContactMe.aspx)
- ❑ Admin (Admin.aspx) [SECURE]

For this particular project, language-specific resource files will *not* be used. With this in mind, you should create a new web.sitemap file that looks similar to the following (if you don't remember how to add a `web.sitemap` file, please refer to "The web.sitemap File" section of "The SiteMapDataSource Control" earlier in this chapter):

```xml
<?xml version="1.0" encoding="utf-8" ?>
<siteMap xmlns="http://schemas.microsoft.com/AspNet/SiteMap-File-1.0" >
    <siteMapNode roles="*" url="" title="surfer5.com"  description="">
        <siteMapNode url="Default.aspx" title="Home"
    description="Main Page" />
        <siteMapNode url="Blog.aspx" title="Blog"
    description="Current Blog" />
        <siteMapNode url="" title="Publications" description="Current and
    Former Publications">
            <siteMapNode url="Books.aspx" title="Books" description="Books"/>
            <siteMapNode url="Magazines.aspx" title="Magazines"
        description="Magazines"/>
            <siteMapNode url="Online.aspx" title="Online Broadcasts"
            description="Online Broadcasts"/>
        </siteMapNode>
        <siteMapNode url="" title="Presentations" description="Presentations">
            <siteMapNode url="FutureEvents.aspx" title="Upcoming
            Presentations" description="Upcoming Presentations"/>
            <siteMapNode url="PastEvents.aspx" title="Past Events"
            description="Past Events"/>
        </siteMapNode>
        <siteMapNode url="Downloads.aspx" title="Downloads"
    description="Available Downloads" />
        <siteMapNode url="ContactMe.aspx" title="Contact Me"
    description="Contact Me"/>
        <siteMapNode roles="Admin" url="Admin.aspx" title="Admin"
    description="Administrative Tools"/>
    </siteMapNode>
</siteMap>
```

You will notice that all users (logged in or otherwise) have access to all pages except for the Admin one, which is restricted to the Admin role. This is of course dependent on `securityTrimmingEnabled` being turned on, which you must do in the web.config file.

Setting Up the web.config File

The next thing you will need to do is make some adjustments to the `web.config` file. You will need to add the sitemap and roles information for this project. Your `web.config` file should resemble the following:

```xml
<?xml version="1.0"?>
<configuration>
    <system.web>
        <compilation debug="true"/>
        <siteMap enabled="true">
            <providers>
                <add name="myMenu"
```

```
                    type="System.Web.XmlSiteMapProvider"
                siteMapFile="web.sitemap"
                securityTrimmingEnabled="true">
        </providers>
    </siteMap>
    <roleManager enabled="true"/>
</system.web>
<location path="Admin.aspx">
    <system.web>
        <authorization>
            <allow roles="Admin"/>
            <deny users="*"/>
        </authorization>
    </system.web>
</location>
</configuration>
```

The providers section includes a reference to the web.sitemap file (as opposed to menu.sitemap used earlier in this chapter) and the properties for the roleManager and the Admin role.

Adding the Menu Control and the SiteMapDataSource

You are now ready to add the Menu control and SiteMapDataSource object to your main page (Default.aspx). You will want to put these within the navigationArea <div> tags. Remember, you just need to drag the controls from the toolbox over to your page (you may need to delete any dummy text that is currently there). When you first drag both of these controls over to your page, it will create a section that looks similar to the following:

```
<div id="navigationArea">
    <asp:Menu ID="Menu1" runat="server" />
    <asp:SiteMapDataSource ID="SiteMapDataSource1" runat="server" />
</div>
```

For the SiteMapDataSource, you will need to make two adjustments. First, you need to set the SiteMapProvider property to "myMenu", which should correspond to the name you have set up for the web.sitemap file in your web.config. You will also need to set the ShowStartingNode to false so that the menu doesn't show the container node. Your SiteMapDataSource declaration should now look like this:

```
<asp:SiteMapDataSource SiteMapProvider="myMenu" ShowStartingNode="false"
    ID="SiteMapDataSource1" runat="server" />
```

You will also need to make two adjustments to the menu control declaration. First, you will want to wire it to the SiteMapDataSource through the DataSourceID property (setting it to "SiteMapDataSource1"). You will also want to set the orientation to "Horizontal" so that the menu spans sideways rather than up and down. The menu control declaration should now look like this:

```
<asp:Menu DataSourceID="SiteMapDataSource1" Orientation="Horizontal"
    ID="Menu1" runat="server" />
```

You should now have the basic wiring set up to run your project with the new menu controls added and formatted with the CSS Friendly Control Adapters.

Testing and Tweaking

At this point, you should probably run the project just to make sure that everything essentially looks right. Granted, there won't be any style, but you can at least make sure that it is placed basically where you want it and the buttons you want to see are there and the ones you don't aren't.

So, if you launch your project at this point, you should have a project that looks similar to Figure 6-19.

> *If your screenshot does not exactly look like the one shown, you may want to adjust the CSS properties in the #navigationArea rules in surfer5_v1.css of your current project. For example, you may need to modify "text-align" to "left" and "height" to "30px". However, these settings should persist throughout this chapter. If you make these changes to match the screenshot, you will want to change them back before proceeding.*

Figure 6-19

The good news is that the Administrative link is hidden as you had hoped. However, the bad news is that so are both of the sections that have drop-down menus (Publications and Presentations). This is because when you have nodes that have no URL associated with them, your application cannot determine if you have rights to this link or not. In fact, if you used an external URL (e.g., http://www.wrox.com) the same would be true; your application would have no way of knowing whether or not the visitor has access to that resource.

In both of these scenarios, you will need to specifically tell the application (in the web.sitemap file) what roles have access to these resources. So, since both of these drop-down menus only contain items you want shared by all, you can set the roles equal to "*". Your modified web.sitemap file should look like this:

```
<?xml version="1.0" encoding="utf-8" ?>
<siteMap xmlns="http://schemas.microsoft.com/AspNet/SiteMap-File-1.0" >
    <siteMapNode roles="*" url="" title="surfer5.com"  description="">
```

```
          <siteMapNode url="Default.aspx" title="Home"
description="Main Page" />
          <siteMapNode url="Blog.aspx" title="Blog"
description="Current Blog" />
          <siteMapNode roles="*" url="" title="Publications"
description="Current and Former Publications">
              <siteMapNode url="Books.aspx" title="Books" description="Books"/>
              <siteMapNode url="Magazines.aspx" title="Magazines"
     description="Magazines"/>
              <siteMapNode url="Online.aspx" title="Online Broadcasts"
     description="Online Broadcasts"/>
          </siteMapNode>
          <siteMapNode roles="*" title="Presentations"
description="Presentations">
              <siteMapNode url="FutureEvents.aspx" title="Upcoming
     Presentations" description="Upcoming
     Presentations"/>
              <siteMapNode url="PastEvents.aspx" title="Past Events"
     description="Past Events"/>
          </siteMapNode>
          <siteMapNode url="Downloads.aspx" title="Downloads"
description="Available Downloads" />
          <siteMapNode url="ContactMe.aspx" title="Contact Me"
description="Contact Me"/>
          <siteMapNode roles="Admin" url="Admin.aspx" title="Admin"
description="Administrative Tools"/>
      </siteMapNode>
</siteMap>
```

If you re-launch your application, it should now resemble Figure 6-20.

Figure 6-20

As you can see, all of your nodes that are open to all users are coming through and the one link you have locked down to only Admin role users is not shown. Granted, at this point, it isn't pretty. But that is what you will be working on in the next section.

Making It Pretty

As you might suspect, you will need to format your new menu control with CSS rules. For maintainability, it is advisable to create a new CSS file that contains merely the rules that define the style of the control. To this end, create a new stylesheet in your project, and call it `surfer5menu.css`.

You will also need to modify your menu control to reference the new class you will be defining in this file. To do this, you need to add the nonstandard (i.e., you will get the red squiggly line under it) property `CssSelectorClass` to your menu control and set it equal to the name of the class you will be setting. For this example, you can call it `surfer5menu`, but it is not necessary to match the name of the CSS file; you could name the class whatever you wanted. Anyway, your new menu control declaration should resemble the following:

```
<asp:Menu CssSelectorClass="surfer5menu" DataSourceID="SiteMapDataSource1"
    Orientation="Horizontal" ID="Menu1" runat="server" />
```

You will also need to add a reference to the new CSS file in the `<head>` region of `Default.aspx` that looks similar to the following:

```
<link href="surfer5Menu.css" rel="stylesheet" type="text/css" />
```

Now, in `surfer5menu.CSS`, set up your first two sets of rules:

```css
.surfer5menu .AspNet-Menu-Horizontal
{
    position:relative;
    z-index: 300;
}
.surfer5menu ul.AspNet-Menu /* Tier 1 */
{
    float: right;
}
```

These rules define the first level of the menu control. Basically all you are telling the browser is to render the menu inline with the other text and float it to the right in the container that holds it. You are also setting the z-index to 300 to try to make the menu float on top of other floating divisions.

The next section of rules defines the second tier of your menu:

> As it pertains to this example, tiers would be defined as the different levels of the menu. Tier 1 is the topmost level of your menu control; these are the items that you see when the page loads. Tier 2 items are the items that expand under each of the Tier 1 items. Tier 3 items expand out from Tier 2 and so forth and so on.

```
.surfer5menu ul.AspNet-Menu ul  /* Tier 2 */
{
    width: 9em;
    left: 0%;
    background: #eeeeee;
    z-index: 400;
}
.surfer5menu ul.AspNet-Menu ul li  /* Tier 2 list items */
{
    width: 8.9em;
    border:1px solid #cccccc;
    float: left;
    clear: left;
    height: 100%;
}
```

The first set of rules sets up the `<ul>` tag that is rendered for the list that is generated for the second tier. In these rules, you are setting the width to 9em and the background color to #eeeeee (a light gray). In the next set of rules you are defining the actual list items in the rendered unordered list. For this, you are setting the width to 0.1em smaller than the `<ul>` definition and setting the color to #cccccc, a slightly darker shade of gray.

The next two sets of rules define the basic formatting for any tiers beyond the second level and then formatting to all tier list items that are consistent (not necessary to alter between tiers):

```
.surfer5menu ul.AspNet-Menu ul ul  /* Tier 3+ */
{
    top: -0.5em;
    left: 6em;
}
.surfer5menu li /* all list items */
{
    font-size: x-small;
}
```

In the first set of rules you are telling the rendering to output the list slightly overlapping the originating list (i.e., Tier 3 will slightly overlap Tier 2). The last section is defining the font for all of the list items to x-small.

The next three sections finally start making the menu control look like it should:

```
.surfer5menu li:hover, /* list items being hovered over */
.surfer5menu li.AspNet-Menu-Hover
{
    background: #477897;
}
.surfer5menu a, /* all anchors and spans (nodes with no link) */
.surfer5menu span
{
    color: #477897;
```

```
        padding: 4px 12px 4px 8px;
        background: transparent url(arrowRight.gif) right center no-repeat;
}
.surfer5menu li.AspNet-Menu-Leaf a, /* leaves */
.surfer5menu li.AspNet-Menu-Leaf span
{
        background-image: none !important;

}
```

You may have noticed "!important" added after the background-image rule in the third section. This command is recognized by all major browsers and it states that this rule takes precedence regardless of what comes later. For example, if in the next line you added `background-image: url(someimage.jpg);`, *all browsers would retain the* `"none"` *rule and ignore the conflicting* `"someimage.jpg"` *background rule. It should be noted that support for the !important command is limited in Internet Explorer versions prior to IE7. Specifically, it would be ignored if a contradicting rule was in the same selector. Therefore, you should be careful and make sure you test often if you are going to attempt to use this handy command.*

The first section sets up the behavior of list items being hovered over. The background color is set to the dark blue color in the color palette you established in Chapter 3. You are using the same color in the next set of rules to define the text color of all list items in your menu control. You are also at this point creating the padding and background rules for these items. The last set of rules backs off the arrow image used to indicate a particular node has child nodes (i.e., it overrides the arrowright.gif rule stating that no image should be used for the nodes that have no children). If not already copied there, you will need to copy `arrowRight.gif` and `activeArrowRight.gif` into the root directory (they are part of the CSS Friendly Control Adapter walk-thru files).

The last two sections look really long but they aren't, and they are performing a simple function: defining the text color and arrow image of hovered text:

```
.surfer5menu li:hover a, /* hovered text */
.surfer5menu li:hover span,
.surfer5menu li.AspNet-Menu-Hover a,
.surfer5menu li.AspNet-Menu-Hover span,
.surfer5menu li:hover li:hover a,
.surfer5menu li:hover li:hover span,
.surfer5menu li.AspNet-Menu-Hover li.AspNet-Menu-Hover a,
.surfer5menu li.AspNet-Menu-Hover li.AspNet-Menu-Hover span,
.surfer5menu li:hover li:hover li:hover a,
.surfer5menu li:hover li:hover li:hover span,
.surfer5menu li.AspNet-Menu-Hover li.AspNet-Menu-Hover li.AspNet-Menu-Hover a,
.surfer5menu li.AspNet-Menu-Hover li.AspNet-Menu-Hover li.AspNet-Menu-Hover span
{
        color: White;
        background: transparent url(activeArrowRight.gif) right center no-repeat;
}
.surfer5menu li:hover li a, /* the tier above this one is hovered */
.surfer5menu li:hover li span,
.surfer5menu li.AspNet-Menu-Hover li a,
.surfer5menu li.AspNet-Menu-Hover li span,
.surfer5menu li:hover li:hover li a,
```

```
.surfer5menu li:hover li:hover li span,
.surfer5menu li.AspNet-Menu-Hover li.AspNet-Menu-Hover li a,
.surfer5menu li.AspNet-Menu-Hover li.AspNet-Menu-Hover li span
{
    color: #477897;
    background: transparent url(arrowRight.gif) right center no-repeat;
}
```

The first set of rules sets the hover text color to white and adds an arrow graphic to all menu items. However, the override from before eliminates this image for those nodes that don't have children. The last set of rules creates the text color of the initial (top-level) node and sets its arrow image. As before, the previously defined override removes the arrow for those nodes that don't have children.

At this point, your final CSS file should look like this:

```
.surfer5menu .AspNet-Menu-Horizontal
{
    position:relative;
    z-index: 300;
}
.surfer5menu ul.AspNet-Menu /* Tier 1 */
{
    float: right;
}
.surfer5menu ul.AspNet-Menu ul  /* Tier 2 */
{
    width: 9em;
    left: 0%;
    background: #eeeeee;
    z-index: 400;
}
.surfer5menu ul.AspNet-Menu ul li  /* Tier 2 list items */
{
    width: 8.9em;
    border:1px solid #cccccc;
    float: left;
    clear: left;
    height: 100%;
}
.surfer5menu ul.AspNet-Menu ul ul  /* Tier 3+ */
{
    top: -0.5em;
    left: 6em;
}
.surfer5menu li /* all list items */
{
    font-size: x-small;
}
.surfer5menu li:hover, /* list items being hovered over */
.surfer5menu li.AspNet-Menu-Hover
```

```
{
    background: #477897;
}
.surfer5menu a, /* all anchors and spans (nodes with no link) */
.surfer5menu span
{
    color: #477897;
    padding: 4px 12px 4px 8px;
    background: transparent url(arrowRight.gif) right center no-repeat;
}
.surfer5menu li.AspNet-Menu-Leaf a, /* leaves */
.surfer5menu li.AspNet-Menu-Leaf span
{
    background-image: none !important;
}
.surfer5menu li:hover a, /* hovered text */
.surfer5menu li:hover span,
.surfer5menu li.AspNet-Menu-Hover a,
.surfer5menu li.AspNet-Menu-Hover span,
.surfer5menu li:hover li:hover a,
.surfer5menu li:hover li:hover span,
.surfer5menu li.AspNet-Menu-Hover li.AspNet-Menu-Hover a,
.surfer5menu li.AspNet-Menu-Hover li.AspNet-Menu-Hover span,
.surfer5menu li:hover li:hover li:hover a,
.surfer5menu li:hover li:hover li:hover span,
.surfer5menu li.AspNet-Menu-Hover li.AspNet-Menu-Hover li.AspNet-Menu-Hover a,
.surfer5menu li.AspNet-Menu-Hover li.AspNet-Menu-Hover li.AspNet-Menu-Hover span
{
    color: White;
    background: transparent url(activeArrowRight.gif) right center no-repeat;
}
.surfer5menu li:hover li a, /* the tier above this one is hovered */
.surfer5menu li:hover li span,
.surfer5menu li.AspNet-Menu-Hover li a,
.surfer5menu li.AspNet-Menu-Hover li span,
.surfer5menu li:hover li:hover li a,
.surfer5menu li:hover li:hover li span,
.surfer5menu li.AspNet-Menu-Hover li.AspNet-Menu-Hover li a,
.surfer5menu li.AspNet-Menu-Hover li.AspNet-Menu-Hover li span
{
    color: #477897;
    background: transparent url(arrowRight.gif) right center no-repeat;
}
```

If you now launch your application in Internet Explorer; you should see something similar to the image shown in Figure 6-21.

You now have your menu control wired to a `web.sitemap` file, you have security settings in place, and you have the entire control formatted with the CSS Friendly Control Adapters for better accessibility and maintainability.

Figure 6-21

Browser Check

At this point, you are essentially done with the navigation system. However, as before, you should run it through all relevant browsers. For this discussion, you should run the site through, at a minimum, the latest versions of Internet Explorer, Mozilla Firefox, and Netscape Navigator.

The first test, running it through Internet Explorer, obviously works as seen at the end of the last section. You might want to run it through Internet Explorer 6, though, just to be sure that it looks okay there as well.

The second test, running it through Mozilla Firefox, also seems to be okay. Everything is formatted pretty close to the way it looks in IE; there are slight differences but nothing to cause any concern. The menu works as expected and looks good.

The last test, however, causes some concern. If you run the application in the Netscape browser, you will notice that the hover menus appear to work — at least at first. However, when you start going down them, they disappear. At first, they might seem to be arbitrarily doing this because, if you go fast enough perhaps, they work as expected. Or maybe sometimes they seem to work and other times they don't.

The problem is with the way you have the bodyRight division defined in the CSS file you created in Chapter 4. The offending command is the overlay rule set up to handle content that went outside the confines of the region. The rule was set up as "auto" meaning that it will create scrollbars if necessary and hide them if not appropriate.

However, it doesn't know how to handle the overflow coming in from outside. When the Menu control invades its turf, the overflow rule is chopping off the overlying menu.

So, in order to remedy this in the Netscape browser, you have to modify the overlay rule for the bodyRight declaration in surfer5_v1.css as follows:

```
#bodyRight
{
    clear: right;
    padding-right: 10px;
    padding-left: 10px;
    font-size: 0.8em;
    float: right;
    padding-bottom: 10px;
    vertical-align: top;
    width: 530px;
    color: #477897;
    padding-top: 10px;
    font-family: Arial;
    position: static;
    text-align: justify;
    overflow: visible;
}
```

Doing this should not affect the overall functionality of the menu in any of the other browsers but will fix the hover effect of the menu in the Netscape browser. However, that being said, you have changed the way the application will handle content that is larger than the 530 pixels defined for this region. So, if you put in an image that is, say, 600 pixels, it will just span outside of the white area.

At this point, that is probably the best alternative. You could tweak the application by adding functionality to point the Netscape browser users to a separate CSS file that would override this rule just for these visitors. But, for such a minimal impact, this is probably overkill. For now, it is fine to leave the overflow rule as visible and control the width of any content put in this region.

But Is This Enough?

As with anything else, you need to know your audience. If you feel that this covers your potential site visitors, then yes, this is enough. But if you aren't sure, maybe you need to plunge a little deeper into the browsers comparison. For example, in Figure 6-22 you can see how the site looks to someone accessing it using Internet Explorer 6.

As you can see, the menu is completely hidden. You might think that Internet Explorer would handle the CSS rules the same way in versions 6 and 7, but you would be wrong. This further illustrates the inherent risk of using CSS: lack of browser compatibility, even between versions of the same browser. It might be expected that things would shift around or be handled differently in Internet Explorer, Netscape, and Firefox. On the other hand, it is quasi-intuitive that the browsers would act materially the same between one version and the next. But that just isn't so.

The problem here is the way IE6 handles the width of the LI elements of the menu. Since you have not specifically set a width, the browser is hiding all of the content. If, for example, the browser only made the links shift in their appearance (e.g., tile vertically rather than horizontally), this might be acceptable. But, as shown in Figure 6-22, the links are completely missing. And, as shown in Chapter 2, in May 2007, IE6 users accounted for more than 44 million users, or 56% of the total hits measured. Obviously, as IE7 gets further and further in the market, it may be less important to focus on this version. However, at least for now, you should probably think of a way to make IE6 users happy.

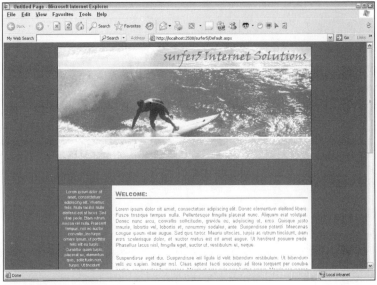

Figure 6-22

The fix is actually quite simple. All you really need to do is add the first row of links (the Tier 1 links) to a specified width. The nice thing is that, if you set the width too small, it will expand to hold its content. However, if it isn't specified, it just hides everything from the browser.

Since you are going to be playing with the specific rendering in IE6, you will probably want to set up a new CSS file that just holds the override rules for that particular browser. With this in mind, create a new CSS file called `surfer5menuIE6.css`. The only rules you need in this file are those that you want to override the existing rules in the original CSS menu file (`surfer5menu.css`). Again, all you want to do is override the width of the LI elements in the menu control for the first row. To do this you only need to add the following rule:

```
.surfer5menu ul.AspNet-Menu li /* Tier 1 */
{
    width: 1em;
}
```

As you can see, you are just setting the width to an arbitrarily small amount (1em in this case). None of the content is that small, so with each link on the top level, the width will grow to hold the text content of the link.

However, this presents a small problem (potentially). The content will grow but it will wrap to the next line if there is a space in the text. So, in the menu for this project, "Contact Me" will be truncated so that "Contact" is on one line and "Me" is on the next line. In order to fix this (assuming that you want to), you will need to create a rule for the text that basically says "don't wrap the content of this element." This can be done through the white-space property for that rule, as you can see below:

```
.surfer5menu ul.AspNet-Menu li /* Tier 1 */
{
    width: 1em;
    white-space: nowrap;
}
.surfer5menu ul.AspNet-Menu ul li  /* Tier 2 list items */
{
    white-space: normal;
}
```

In this example, you are telling the browser to not allow wrapping on the first row of links but to allow it on the second level. If you don't allow it on the second level, the menus will appear strange because some of the links will expand past the original definition of the menu and others will not. To remedy this, you just need to turn wrapping back on for the next series of links. For this project, you are not going beyond two tiers, but if you were, you would need to modify the further levels as well.

Finally, to bring these rules into your project, you need to modify the CSS references in your ASPX page. Specifically, you need to modify the area of the HEAD section of your project that deals with IE browser prior to IE7 to look something like this:

```
<!--[if lt IE 7]>
    <link runat="server" rel="stylesheet"
        href="~/CSS/BrowserSpecific/IEMenu6.css" type="text/css">
    <link href="surfer5menuIE6.css" rel="stylesheet" type="text/css" />
<![endif]-->
```

This will bring in the override rules you just set up only when a visitor is using a version of Internet Explorer prior to IE7 to access your site. Thus, you will not see any impact from these rules on any other browser or version of Internet Explorer. Your project, when viewed in Internet Explorer version 6, should now resemble Figure 6-23. For all other previous versions tested, no change should be evident.

Extra Credit: Breadcrumbs

One increasingly popular feature of websites is the breadcrumb. If you don't immediately know what that is, picture a site that shows what page you are on and how far into the site you are. For example, it might show something like: Home :: Publications :: Books.

One of the cool things about the new menu controls is just how easy it is to add this functionality to your site. In ASP.NET, this is called the SiteMapPath, which is located in the same Navigation tool group as the Menu control. In order to use it, simply drag it onto your page to create code similar to the following (drop it in the bodyRight <div> area of your page):

```
<asp:SiteMapPath ID="SiteMapPath1" runat="server" />
```

With just this amount of code, you now have a breadcrumb trail in your site similar to the one shown in Figure 6-24.

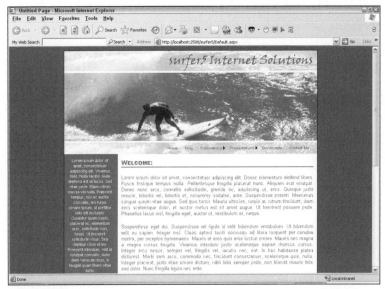

Figure 6-23

Figure 6-24

And that's it! The interesting thing about this control is that you don't manually wire it to your `web.sitemap` file; it is just directly wired there for you. As such, you can't turn off the initial node rendering out. If you wanted, you could modify the style through CSS or through properties of the control. You might also want to modify the separator between nodes. For example, you might want to change it to something like "::". To do so, modify your SiteMapPath control declaration as follows:

```
<asp:SiteMapPath ID="SiteMapPath1" runat="server" PathSeparator=" :: "/>
```

When looking at the way it is displaying, you may decide to tweak the header class in your CSS file to make it flow better with the breadcrumb trail. For example, you might change the class rules to the following:

```
.header
{
    font-size: 1.3em;
    float: left;
    width: 99%;
    color: #FFFFFF;
    font-family: 'Arial Black';
    font-variant: small-caps;
    background-color: #477897;
    padding-left: 1%;
}
```

Doing this will create a website that resembles Figure 6-25.

Figure 6-25

You should now have a completed look and feel to your site and are ready to move to the next level: Master Pages.

Summary

Any web project that has more than one view or data or page associated with it needs some sort of navigation system. The system should be easy to maintain, easy to understand and use by your visitors, and accessible to the largest population of users possible. Historically, this provided a considerable challenge to ASP developers (among others) that was not remedied with the first round of .NET (1.0 and 1.1).

However, with the new .NET 2.0 Framework, developers were given a series of tools that made creating and maintaining powerful navigation systems almost simple. In this chapter, you learned how to implement two of these controls: the Menu control and the SiteMapPath control. For the Menu control, you learned how to wire it to an XML-based datasource called the `web.sitemap` file. You also learned how to wire the menu control to your membership API and to globalize the content for an international audience. Finally, you learned how to integrate the control with the CSS Friendly Control Adapters in order to make the rendered output more accessible to more people.

You also got a peak at the SiteMapPath control that provides a breadcrumb trail to show your visitors where they are in the hierarchal schema of your site. You looked at browser compatibility issues and worked through them.

At this point, you should have a fair understanding of how to integrate a comprehensive navigation system that provides the maintainability that you will appreciate and an easy to use interface that your visitors will appreciate. You should have a project that has a clean look that is ready to be templated to all of your pages. You are ready for Master Pages.

7

Master Pages

No matter how good of a design you have for your site, it can be completely for naught if it isn't carried forward consistently throughout your site. Up to this point you have learned the basics of creating a site that is aesthetically pleasing and, hopefully, easy for your visitors to use. You have received an overview of the different considerations you should take into account when planning your web projects, such as browser variations, the potential audience, and accessibility. You have learned the basics of image creation and design. You have received an introduction and overview of Cascading Style Sheets and how to use the power of Visual Studio to integrate these rules into your website. And, finally, you have learned how to create consistent, flexible, and accessible navigation for your site.

But all of this was for one page (`Default.aspx`). Copying this code to every page in your site would be, to say the least, a maintenance nightmare. Can you imagine having to update thousands of pages because the user wants a fairly minor design tweak? What you really want is a way to create a reusable template that can be incorporated into every page of your site. This will allow for all pages to look the same throughout your project, while allowing for easier maintenance as your projects mature. In a year or so when you want to redo the entire site, you only need to change the template rather than the coding on every page of your application. With Master Pages, you can do exactly that.

How Did We Get Here?

The idea of creating templated applications is not new. For years, you have been able to use templates for most computer software and applications. For example, it is a fairly common practice to use the templates provided in Microsoft Word to create standard documents such as resumes and fax coversheets. Or, maybe a better example is creating a new PowerPoint presentation. When you create a new presentation, you are given a blank slide with defined areas for the title and subtitle of that particular slide, as shown in Figure 7-1.

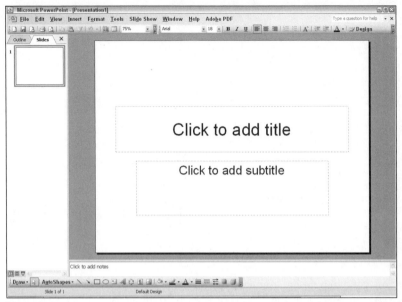

Figure 7-1

However, when it comes to web design, there hasn't always been this easy solution. In the early years, most developers were restricted to using server-side includes to create a templated look to their pages. For example, a developer might create `header.inc` and `footer.inc` files that they would import into each page through code that might look like this:

```
<!--#include file="header.inc" -->

    Hello, world!

<!--#include file="footer.inc" -->
```

This allowed developers to include all of their formatting for the header and footer regions in detached files that were consistently imported to their web projects. That way, if they needed to make a stylistic or structural change, they could just modify one or both of these files to carry the changes to all of the pages that included them.

Many developers still use this approach because it is consistent and reliable. However, with .NET development, there are a few shortcomings. First of which is the fact that this isn't truly a template. You are maintaining at least two distinct files for your "template." These files may, in turn, import several other files. Maintaining this approach can become problematic.

Additionally, you have to be careful about what code you use in the imported files. If, for example, you decide to use ASP.NET coding, you have several new considerations you must take into account. First, you can only have one `@Page` directive in your page. Therefore, if you have three ASPX pages (one for the header, one for the footer, and one for the page that imports the other two), you may have three page directives in the final rendered page. Well, not technically rendered because it won't compile. But you get the idea.

To carry that thought a bit further, you would also have to be careful of what methods and functions you used in those three files. For example, if you had a Button control on the header and content pages both called Button1 that called Button1_OnClick() when they were pressed, your page would not know how to handle this apparent discrepancy. In other words, how would it know which Button1_OnClick method it should go to when you press Button1 in the content page? The answer is that it wouldn't and you would get a runtime error when you tried.

With the introduction of .NET 1.0 and 1.1, developers began experimenting with applying user controls to create a consistent layout for their pages. One way to do this is to create a static ASPX page that provides the layout that you want all of your pages to have and then, when you know where you want the content to go, you place user controls you create to represent what might otherwise be a standalone page. For example, you might create a page called Default.aspx that contained all of the structural and design aspects of your page, including a clearly defined content area. Within that content area you would import user controls (ASCX files) that would provide the content. You might have a user control called ContactUs.ascx that would provide all of the content for a "Contact Us" page. Rather than creating a true page (e.g., something like ContactUs.aspx), you would just load the ASCX file into Default.aspx through implementing the following code (assuming you had a PlaceHolder control on your page called PlaceHolder1):

```
Me.PlaceHolder1.Controls.Add(LoadControl("ContactUs.ascx"))
```

You would, of course, have to have some sort of logic in your page to tell Default.aspx what user control to import. This often would be done through URL querystring parameters.

As you can see, this can get fairly complicated pretty fast. For one, you are loading one page every time and have to have a way of telling that page which control to import. So you, as the programmer, have to remember what Default.aspx?tab=1 is supposed to represent and how that might be different than, say, Default.aspx?tab=12. Using that example, you would also need to have code to determine if the querystring passed to your page is valid (corresponding somehow to a real user control or not) and, if it is not, what to do at that point. This might seem intuitive enough to you when you are creating the first page, but what about in six months when you have to go back and add a new "page"? Or what if you inherit this project and never even touched it in the first place? How long would it take you to understand all of the controls being used and how they get into the page? This could provide a serious headache to anyone tasked with maintaining a website built under this approach.

Another issue is that, when designing the user control, you can't really see how it is going to look in your project until you render it to the browser. In other words, you modify the ASCX file independently of the ASPX page. When you are creating the user control and you look at the Design tab, you will just see the formatting that you have in place for that control. You won't see the header and footer regions of Default.aspx, for example. This makes it a bit more difficult to ensure that the content you are providing in these controls is consistent with the rest of the site. Of course, done properly, this can be controlled through the use of CSS (for the most part), but it is still a nuisance in the coding and design phases of the project.

A better way of creating site templates was needed, and Microsoft provided exactly that with the 2.0 release of the .NET framework: Master Pages. Master Pages provide the first concerted effort by Microsoft to tackle all of the issues brought up so far. A Master Page is a single ASP.NET page that includes the entire structure of your site. This means that, rather than having a page that you use as a template to import a bunch of user controls into (and all of the headaches involved in keeping those user control "pages" programmatically distinguishable through a querystring or similar approach), you have a single template page that can be inherited by all of the pages of your site. You have specific areas of this template that you define as content areas (you can define as many regions as you need). You have the ability to have Button controls on your content page and your Master Page with the same name and same referenced method and still have no conflicts. You do not have issues with conflicting page declarations because there is no page declaration in the Master Page. The coding to import the Master Page is relatively simple and, when done, you can see the full-page rendering (for the most part) in the Design tab of Visual Studio 2005. From an interface perspective, Master Pages might just represent the most important enhancement to the .NET Framework introduced with the 2.0 release.

What is a Master Page?

A Master Page is simply a single page that holds the structure of your website. The files are designated with a `.master` file extension and are imported into content pages through the `MasterPageFile` property of the `@Page` directive of the content pages. They are meant to provide the template that all of your pages use throughout the site. They are not really meant to hold the content of an individual page or even the stylistic definitions of the page. They are meant to provide a blueprint of what your site should look like and then connect that template to style rules set in detached CSS files (as appropriate).

Maybe a clearer example would be the process that an author goes through to write for Wrox Press. When a programmer decides that he wants to write for Wrox, he is given a set of guidelines on how the pages should be formatted. There are specific rules on resolution of images and even font sizes and screenshot formatting. There are also requirements for stylistic usage of headers and even the margins of the pages used to create the manuscript. The editors at Wrox provide the programmer with the guidelines and theme files that he can use in his Windows environment to make the manuscript and all related screenshots look like every other manuscript provided to the publishers. If you stood 10 feet back from the monitor that had a particular manuscript displayed on it, you would be hard pressed to distinguish it from any other manuscript provided. The screenshots all should have the same screen resolution, use the same fonts, and have the same colors. The manuscript should use the same borders and fonts throughout it. However, this is just the shell. Obviously, if you got closer to the monitor, close enough to read the content, you would easily be able to distinguish manuscripts. The programmers fill pages and pages of material with their own ideas, concepts, and examples. They just use the templates and guidelines provided by the publishers as a starting point. In this way, the programmer doesn't have to think about "What font do I use for the header?" or "What colors should I use for the screenshots?" This is already handled by adherence to the guidelines, templates, and themes provided by the publisher. Furthermore, and maybe more importantly, this allows a developer to create a manuscript from different computers without a noticeable change in the look and feel of the final manuscript. On a larger scale, it also allows different programmers from different geographical locations around the world to create a single manuscript that, at least stylistically, flows from chapter to chapter regardless of which actual author created each chapter.

This provides the same principle for programmers in their design of web pages. Time is spent initially to come up with the interface they want for their particular application. Care is given to graphics, style, and layout. Images are created and color schemes are decided on. Style rules are created and stored in CSS files. Areas are defined as content areas that will be filled with, as you might expect, content that comes from the programmer later in the process. There may be some shared properties or functions that would be inherited from the content pages. But, for the most part, the Master Page serves best as a means of defining the structure of the page. Once this stage is completed, a programmer can simply reference the Master Page, and then fill its content areas with the relevant content for a particular page. There is no need to worry about importing user controls or sever-side includes. There is no need to recreate the style for each page. And there is no real concern about creating a consistent layout; all pages that use the Master Page should look the same (or at least similar). Obviously, the programmer would need to have knowledge of what style rules were created, such as what to call the header text division of a page (e.g., < div class="header" > </div>). But once these rules were known, the programmer could just write code/content. This should speed up the process and help create sites that are consistent and, more importantly for the developer, easier to maintain. And, probably most importantly, several coders can work on the same project and create consistent looking pages even though they don't work in the same office or, even, in the same country. As long as there is a shared Master Page that they are all referencing, the final pages will all look the same.

Of course, if you are designing a site for a business or organization, you will need to take into consideration that organization's existing logo and color schemes, if appropriate.

Enough Talk; Time to Code

Okay, now that you have an understanding of what a Master Page is supposed to do and how web development led to its creation, it is time to see how to actually make one work. If you have experience in creating websites but have never used a Master Page as a templating mechanism, you will be pleasantly surprised at just how easy it is to do so.

This chapter will go through the ins and outs of Master Pages before updating the surfer5 book project. Therefore, you should start a new project to practice these new concepts. So, with a new web project open in Visual Studio 2005, click on Website and then choose Add New Item to get the screen depicted in Figure 7-2.

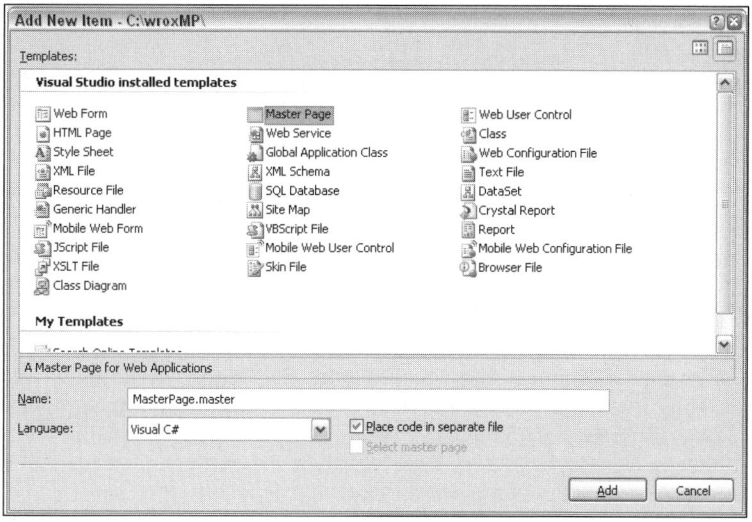

Figure 7-2

You will want to select Master Page, ironically, as the template you want to use for your new item. You can name the page whatever you want, but you should leave the .master file extension. You should choose the language you code in, although this isn't particularly relevant unless you want to do any "under the hood" coding in the Master Page itself. Again, while this is possible and pertinent in some situations, for the most part, this is not relevant for most projects. It should also be noted that the language of the Master Page file will not dictate the language of the content page that inherits it. This just means that you can have a Master Page file that has a language declaration of, say, VB and a content page that inherits it that has a language of C# (or the other way around). To expand on this, you might have a designer who is responsible for creating the look and feel of your projects and is more comfortable with VB.NET. She could easily create the Master Page in VB without any worry about the coding preferences of the rest of the team. Once the VB Master Page is completed, the developers in the group could code against this VB Master Page in their language of choice (VB or C#). Even if there are public properties or methods in the Master Page that are written in VB, C# content pages can access them. This language independence of Master Pages is one of its nicest features.

However, for this example, just choose whatever language you are more comfortable with and click the Add button. This will create a file in your project called `MasterPage.master` that should resemble the following:

```
<%@ Master Language="C#" AutoEventWireup="true" CodeFile="MasterPage.master.cs"
    Inherits="MasterPage" %>

<!DOCTYPE html PUBLIC "-//W3C//DTD XHTML 1.0 Transitional//EN"
    "http://www.w3.org/TR/xhtml1/DTD/xhtml1-transitional.dtd">

<html xmlns="http://www.w3.org/1999/xhtml" >
<head runat="server">
    <title>Untitled Page</title>
</head>
<body>
    <form id="form1" runat="server">
    <div>
        <asp:contentplaceholder id="ContentPlaceHolder1" runat="server">
        </asp:contentplaceholder>
    </div>
    </form>
</body>
</html>
```

There are a couple of noteworthy elements to the default code provided. The first is the @Page declaration or, in this case, the lack thereof. The declaration statement for a Master Page is the @Master declaration. Other than that, though, the declaration looks pretty much identical to the @Page declaration you are probably used to seeing in other pages you may have created previously. There are Language, AutoEventWireup, CodeFile, and Inherits properties, and they are set to intuitive values. In fact, if you compared the @Master declaration to a standard @Page declaration, you wouldn't see any difference except the name of the declaration and the names of the files that are used in the values of the properties just mentioned. They are, in this regard, identical. If you delve into all of the properties available to each, you will see a lot of differences. However, for now, it is sufficient to know that they have some shared properties and that, by default, Visual Studio creates new files with either a @Master or @Page declaration with the same properties in the initial declaration.

The other important thing to notice is the following code in the middle of the file:

```
<asp:contentplaceholder id="ContentPlaceHolder1" runat="server">
</asp:contentplaceholder>
```

This creates the region in the template that will be filled with material from the content pages created by the programmers. Each content page will reference the ID of this placeholder in its code and stick all of the content from that page in this particular region.

It is worth noting that you are not limited to a single placeholder in your Master Page. You can, in reality, set up as many placeholders as you need for your page. However, in practice, you should probably limit the number used to the number you actually need. If you have, for example, 100 placeholders in your Master Page, you are probably not centralizing the content enough and, more importantly, are creating a maintenance headache. One placeholder is the default and around two or three are fairly common to see in practice. If you are using much more than that, you should really evaluate how you are using the Master Page and whether there is a simpler way to handle the content.

However, to see how these placeholders might be used in a project, examine the following code:

```
<%@ Master Language="C#" AutoEventWireup="true" CodeFile="MasterPage.master.cs"
    Inherits="MasterPage" %>
<!DOCTYPE html PUBLIC "-//W3C//DTD XHTML 1.0 Transitional//EN"
    "http://www.w3.org/TR/xhtml1/DTD/xhtml1-transitional.dtd">

<html xmlns="http://www.w3.org/1999/xhtml" >
<head runat="server">
    <title>Untitled Page</title>
</head>
<body bgcolor="navy">
    <form id="form1" runat="server">
    <div>
    <table border="0" width="700">
    <tr>
        <td colspan="2" height="150" bgcolor="gray" valign="middle" align="center">
            HEADER
        </td>
    </tr>
    <tr>
        <td width="150" bgcolor="silver">SIDEBAR</td>
        <td width="550" height="400" bgcolor="white">
            <asp:contentplaceholder id="ContentPlaceHolder1" runat="server">
            </asp:contentplaceholder>
        </td>
    </tr>
    <tr>
        <td colspan="2" align="center" height="20" bgcolor="gray">
            FOOTER
        </td>
    </tr>
    </table>

    </div>
    </form>
</body>
</html>
```

Essentially, you have created a fairly typical layout with a header, sidebar, content, and footer region. For simplicity, this example just uses tables to create the layout. If you were to look in the Design tab in Visual Studio 2005, you should see something that resembles Figure 7-3.

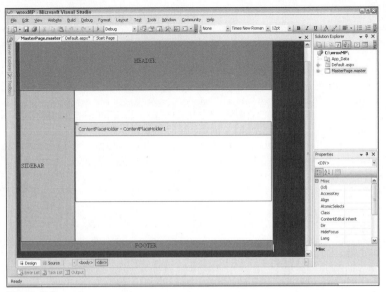

Figure 7-3

You can see that you have created a header and footer region on the top and bottom of the page, respectively, and then created a division for a sidebar and another one for your content. Within your content region, you have the content placeholder control. If you sent this Master Page out to all of your programmers, they could simply reference it and then fill in the content placeholder with their own content for every page they develop.

If you wanted to create separate content placeholders for the sidebar and content areas, you could simply modify the sidebar section of your code to look similar to this:

```
<tr>
    <td width="150" bgcolor="silver">
        <!-- SIDEBAR REGION -->
        <asp:contentplaceholder id="ContentPlaceHolder2" runat="server">
        </asp:contentplaceholder>
    </td>
    <td width="550" height="400" bgcolor="white">
        <!-- CONTENT REGION -->
        <asp:contentplaceholder id="ContentPlaceHolder1" runat="server">
        </asp:contentplaceholder>
    </td>
</tr>
```

This will create a content placeholder called ContentPlaceHolder1 in the content area that will be in the main content area of your page and then a separate content placeholder called ContentPlaceHolder2 that will reside in the sidebar region. The programmer will then have access to both of these regions to put in the appropriate content based on the page he is developing.

You can also, at the Master Page level, set the default content that will go in each of these placeholders. If, for example, you wanted the sidebar to say "this is the sidebar" in the absence of any code on the content page setting the content for this area, you would do this simply by inserting the content between the opening and closing tags of the content placeholder control, like this:

```
<asp:contentplaceholder id="ContentPlaceHolder2" runat="server">
this is the sidebar
</asp:contentplaceholder>
```

When coding the content page that references this Master Page, the developer has the option of setting the content for this placeholder and, if he does, that is what will show up in the final rendered page. If, however, he decides not to set it on the content page for whatever reason, the default content from the Master Page will show up instead.

Most developers think of content placeholders as just a place to store content displayed to the end user in the final rendered page. However, this isn't the only way they can be used. For example, if you place a content placeholder within the <head> region of your page, you can give access to that region at the Child Page level. This means that the Child Page can actually insert links to CSS documents that would be set in the <head> region of the rendered page. So, maybe the Master Page includes a blank content placeholder in the <head> region just below the linked stylesheets. By default, nothing would be added to that section. However, if you needed to, you could fill that content placeholder with a custom CSS document only relevant for that page. This allows for much more flexibility in the design of content pages as your project matures.

For now, however, your Master Page should resemble Figure 7-4 in the Design view.

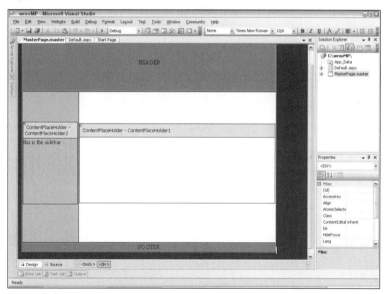

Figure 7-4

Even though you can see the look of the page in the Design tab of Visual Studio, you should not get the wrong impression that you, then, just launch this page in a browser and it will work. That just isn't the case. Master Pages are not meant to be rendered on their own; they are only appropriate to be included as a reference to a valid .NET page. So if, for example, you tried to view this Master Page in a browser, you would see an error similar to the one shown in Figure 7-5.

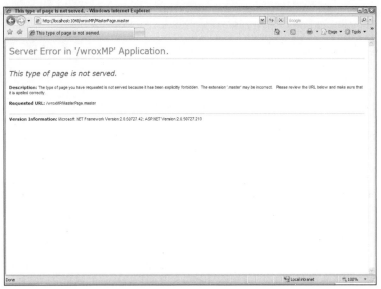

Figure 7-5

Now that you have a Master Page that you are comfortable with, it is time to implement the template in a content page. There are several ways to do this. The first way is to simply add a new item to your project (Website ⇨ Add New Item), which will give you the screen shown in Figure 7-6.

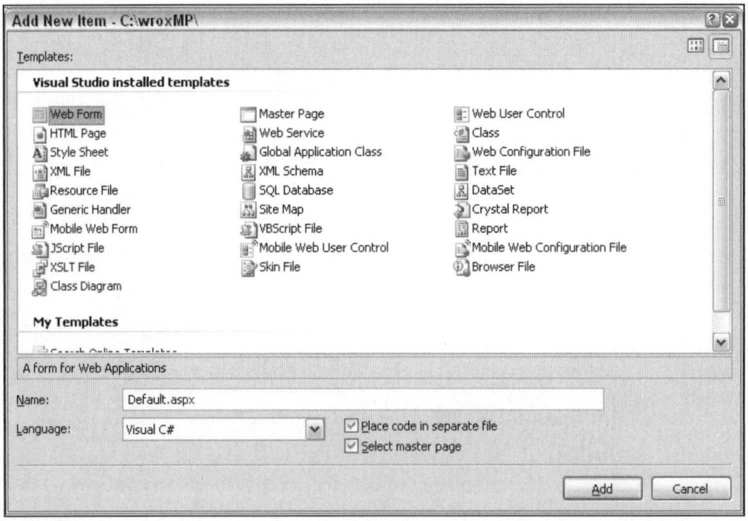

Figure 7-6

As shown in Figure 7-6, you will want to select "Web Form" for your template, as you have probably done in previous projects. However, you want to make sure that you check the option "Select Master page" near the bottom of the screen. Doing so will do two things: it will prompt you to select which Master Page you want to use, and it will also set up your ASPX page to use that particular Master. The former will be done through a screen similar to Figure 7-7.

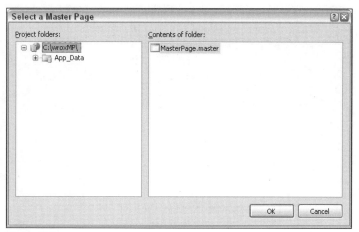

Figure 7-7

This screen shows the Master Pages you have available to you. Essentially, it is a directory browser that only allows you to see Master Pages. In this example, there is only one option: MasterPage.master. Select the Master Page you want to use, and click the OK button. This will generate an ASPX file that is set up to use this Master with code that resembles the following:

```
<%@ Page Language="C#" MasterPageFile="~/MasterPage.master"
    AutoEventWireup="true" CodeFile="Default.aspx.cs" Inherits="_Default"
    Title="Untitled Page" %>
<asp:Content ID="Content1" ContentPlaceHolderID="ContentPlaceHolder2"
    Runat="Server">
</asp:Content>
<asp:Content ID="Content2" ContentPlaceHolderID="ContentPlaceHolder1"
    Runat="Server">
</asp:Content>
```

The first thing you will notice when looking at this file in comparison to an ASPX page that does not use a Master Page is in the @Page declaration. There is a new property here called MasterPageFile that references your new Master Page, MasterPage.master. You will see that the Master Page property value starts with a tilde (~). This simply indicates that the web application will look for the file in the root of the web application or virtual folder. This means that, if you have a web page with this reference sitting in a subdirectory, the web application will look for the Master Page in the root of the web application when it is attempting to render the final page. Removing the tilde will force the application to look for the Master Page in whatever folder the ASPX resides. In many projects this is not that big of a deal, especially if you have all of your .NET files sitting in the root folder. However, it is important to know what the tilde is there for and how it affects your rendering.

The next thing you will notice is, possibly, the sheer simplicity of the page. There is only a @Page declaration and then content placeholders that correlate to the placeholders set up in the Master Page. There is not, for example, a form tag (or any HTML tags for that matter). However, if you browse this page exactly as it is now, you will see something similar to Figure 7-8.

As you can see, all of the HTML tags came through just fine. Along with the form tag and other pertinent formatting and properties, the HTML layout came down from the Master Page into the content page.

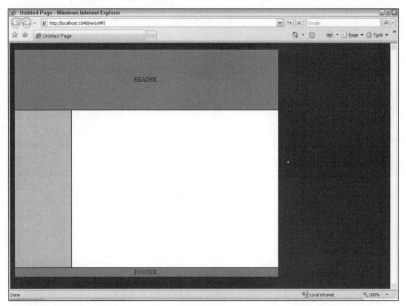

Figure 7-8

But wait, what about the default content in the sidebar? You know, the default content you set in the Master Page for ContentPlaceHolder2? It's not there! Does that mean there is an error in this manuscript? Or is there something that isn't necessarily intuitive going on? Hopefully, you have assumed the latter.

What has happened is that you actually overrode the default value for the way `Default.aspx` is set up. Don't think so? Look at the code again for this content placeholder in `Default.aspx`:

```
<asp:Content ID="Content1" ContentPlaceHolderID="ContentPlaceHolder2"
    Runat="Server">
</asp:Content>
```

Look at what is between the opening and closing tag. Nothing? Well, nothing is what will replace the default content. That isn't to say that the default content will not be replaced; it means that the default content will be replaced with nothingness. To see the default content, just remove the content placeholder code from `Default.aspx`, as follows:

```
<%@ Page Language="C#" MasterPageFile="~/MasterPage.master"
    AutoEventWireup="true" CodeFile="Default.aspx.cs" Inherits="_Default"
    Title="Untitled Page" %>
<asp:Content ID="Content2" ContentPlaceHolderID="ContentPlaceHolder1"
    Runat="Server">
</asp:Content>
```

You will see that the code is exactly the same except that the content placeholder for ContentPlaceHolder2 has been removed. Browsing the new page will yield something similar to Figure 7-9.

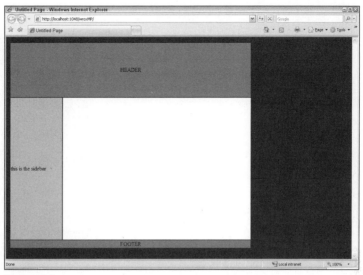

Figure 7-9

Now that the content placeholder for ContentPlaceHolder2 has been removed from `Default.aspx`, the default content comes through. This is an important distinction to remember when setting default content for the content placeholders in your Master Pages. If you create an empty placeholder control on your content page that correlates to a placeholder on the Master Page that has default content set up, the emptiness will override the default content. This allows you to create pages with static content on most pages (as in the left pane of the page used in this example) but gives you the option to set the content to something else if necessary. This makes for an easy way to override some of the facets of a Master Page in the content page that inherits it.

Now, to put content in a particular content placeholder, you need to simply insert the content between the opening and closing tags of that particular content placeholder. For example, modify the page from before to the following:

```
<%@ Page Language="C#" MasterPageFile="~/MasterPage.master" AutoEventWireup="true"
    CodeFile="Default.aspx.cs" Inherits="_Default" Title="Untitled Page" %>
<asp:Content ID="Content2" ContentPlaceHolderID="ContentPlaceHolder1"
    Runat="Server">
this is the content area!
</asp:Content>
```

You now have set up some content for ContentPlaceHolder1, which is reserved for the main content of the page. Browsing this page again will produce a page similar to Figure 7-10.

You now have a page that is filling the content area of the page from the content page, filling the content area of the sidebar with default content, and integrating all of the structural design for the page from the HTML coding in the Master Page.

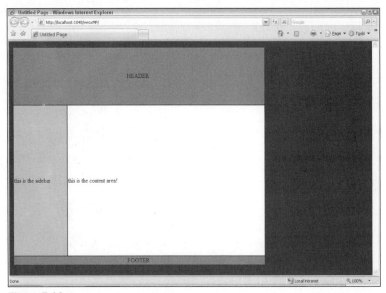

Figure 7-10

As a final thought on this subject, you can toggle back and forth between having content in a Content-PlaceHolder on a content page in the Design view by clicking on the arrow in the upper right-hand corner of the ContentPlaceHolder, as you can see in Figure 7-11.

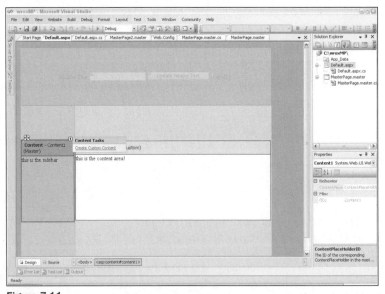

Figure 7-11

If you have a ContentPlaceHolder in the Master Page that you don't have set in the content page, you will see the option shown in Figure 7-11 ("Create Custom Content"). This will add a new ContentPlaceHolder region in the content page that you can now edit. If, however, you have content in that placeholder, your option will change to "Default to Master's Content." Choosing this option will remove the placeholder from the content page and any content that you put there ... without warning. So you need to be careful. If you have set a lot of content in that placeholder and accidentally choose this option, it's just gone.

It is also interesting to note the description of the placeholders in the Design view. Assuming that you still have the sidebar area set to default to the Master Page, its header should read something like "**Content** – Content1 (Master)." This simply means the placeholder has an ID of "Content1," and it is defaulting to the Master. Conversely, in the content area placeholder, its title should be something like "**Content** – Content2 (Custom)." Similarly, this means that the ID is "Content2," and it has custom content (rather than defaulting to the Master).

Partial Classes

One problem that presents itself is how conflicts between same-named controls/classes/whatever in the Master Page and the content page resolve themselves. What if, for example, both implement code in a `Page_Load` event? Or what if both contain a button called `Button1` that fires a `Button1_OnClick` event when pressed? If the Master and Content pages are rendered into one output file at runtime, won't there be conflicts? Errors galore? To resolve this, ASP.NET 2.0 introduced the concept of partial classes.

Partial classes allow classes (and the related events and methods) to span multiple pages. This means that part of the `Page_Load` event will be in the Master Page and part of it will be in its content page. The .NET 2.0 Framework is smart enough to say "this goes with this piece, and this goes with that piece" and prevent the conflicts from ever occurring.

To test this, modify the header region of your Master Page (`MasterPage.master`) as follows:

```
<td colspan="2" height="150" bgcolor="gray" valign="middle" align="center">
   Header Text:
    <asp:TextBox ID="TextBox1" runat="server" />
    <asp:Button ID="Button1" runat="server" Text="Update Header Text"
  OnClick="Button1_Click" />
    <asp:Label ID="Label1" runat="server" Text="" />
</td>
```

You have simply added some text and a TextBox, Button, and Label control. You will also see that the `OnClick` property of the Button control has been set to `"Button1_Click"`. In order to make this work, add the following code to the code for the Master Page:

```
protected void Button1_Click(object sender, EventArgs e)
{
    Label1.Text = TextBox1.Text;
    TextBox1.Text = "";
}
```

This code just fills the Label control with the text that is in the TextBox control and then empties the TextBox control. At this point, you should launch the application and make sure everything works as you would expect it to.

Now, go into the content page and change the page code to resemble the following:

```
<%@ Page Language="C#" MasterPageFile="~/MasterPage.master" AutoEventWireup="true"
    CodeFile="Default.aspx.cs" Inherits="_Default" Title="Untitled Page" %>
<asp:Content ID="Content2" ContentPlaceHolderID="ContentPlaceHolder1"
    Runat="Server">
  Content Text:
  <asp:TextBox ID="TextBox1" runat="server" />
  <asp:Button ID="Button1" runat="server" Text="Update Header Text"
OnClick="Button1_Click" />
  <asp:Label ID="Label1" runat="server" Text="" />
</asp:Content>
```

If you look closely, this is an *exact* copy of the code in the Master Page with the exception that the static text has been changed to "Content Text" rather than "Header Text." The TextBox control is named the same thing. The Button control is named the same thing and has the same OnClick property. Even the Label control has the same ID and properties. Everything is the same.

So, similarly, copy the Button1_Click event from the Master Page code and paste it directly into your content page without modification. In other words, the code in the content page should look exactly as follows:

```
protected void Button1_Click(object sender, EventArgs e)
{
    Label1.Text = TextBox1.Text;
    TextBox1.Text = "";
}
```

Notice that you aren't indicating which Label1 control you are setting the text property for; the same is true for the TextBox1 control. You simply have code referring to the controls in the content page just as you would for any other ASPX page.

Knowing that you will have a big class made up of two partial classes, both containing a Button1_Click event with the same code in each, which modifies the same named controls without distinction between Master or Content, it seems like it should crash. It just shouldn't work. But it does.

Browse your content page and play around with the controls and see what happens. For example, enter "HEADER TEXT" in the header textbox and press the button in that region. This is all contained in the Master Page, and you should see that the text in the Master Page, and only in the Master Page, changes. Now perform a similar experiment using "CONTENT TEXT" as the text for this region. Doing so should create a page that resembles Figure 7-12.

Hopefully, you had similar results and can see the controls, even with the same name and same event handlers, working independently (e.g., not in conflict with each other) on a single rendered page. To see what happens with the rendering, it might be interesting to view the source of the outputted HTML for the page:

```
<!DOCTYPE html PUBLIC "-//W3C//DTD XHTML 1.0 Transitional//EN"
    "http://www.w3.org/TR/xhtml11/DTD/xhtml1-transitional.dtd">
```

```
<html xmlns="http://www.w3.org/1999/xhtml" >
<head><title>
    Untitled Page
</title></head>
<body bgcolor="navy">
    <form name="aspnetForm" method="post" action="Default.aspx" id="aspnetForm">
<div>
<input type="hidden" name="__VIEWSTATE" id="__VIEWSTATE"
    value="/wEPDwUKMTc1NTQ3OTY4MA9kFgJmD2QWAgIDD2QWBAIFDw8WA
    h4EVGV4dAULSEVBREVSIFRFWFRkZAIJD2QWAgIFDw8WAh8ABQxDT05UR
    U5UIFRFWFRkZGT/SKdL82kyg27thzvvkpw5hAI5MQ==" />
</div>

    <div>
    <table border="0" width="700">
    <tr>
        <td colspan="2" height="150" bgcolor="gray" valign="middle" align="center">
            Header Text:
            <input name="ct100$TextBox1" type="text" id="ct100_TextBox1" />
            <input type="submit" name="ct100$Button1" value="Update Header Text"
    id="ct100_Button1" />
            <span id="ct100_Label1">HEADER TEXT</span>
        </td>
    </tr>
    <tr>
        <td width="150" bgcolor="silver">
            <!-- SIDEBAR REGION -->

            this is the sidebar

        </td>
        <td width="550" height="400" bgcolor="white">
            <!-- CONTENT REGION -->

    Content Text:
    <input name="ct100$ContentPlaceHolder1$TextBox1" type="text"
    id="ct100_ContentPlaceHolder1_TextBox1" />
    <input type="submit" name="ct100$ContentPlaceHolder1$Button1"
    value="Update Header Text" id="ct100_ContentPlaceHolder1_Button1" />
    <span id="ct100_ContentPlaceHolder1_Label1">CONTENT TEXT</span>

        </td>
    </tr>
    <tr>
        <td colspan="2" align="center" height="20" bgcolor="gray">
            FOOTER
        </td>
    </tr>
    </table>

    </div>
```

```
<div>

    <input type="hidden" name="__EVENTVALIDATION" id="__EVENTVALIDATION"
  value="/wEWBQL16KKbBQK33sGJAQL197ftDQLc3uCnBAKA4sljxH8gd
  1miEmvDP8poX/i5jMl1JK0=" />
</div></form>
</body>
</html>
```

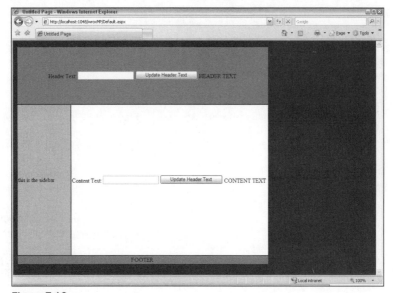

Figure 7-12

Notice what the first button is called: `ct100$Button1`. Now look at the second button; it is called `ct100$ContentPlaceHolder1$Button1`. In essence, the rendering logic of ASP.NET is appending the name of the content placeholder, `ContentPlaceHolder1` in this case, to the name it is using for these controls. Since the first control is located in the Master Page, and therefore outside of the content placeholder, its rendered name does not include the name of the content placeholder. The button in the content area, though, does reside in the content placeholder region and, as such, has that name appended to it. You will also notice that there is no event (i.e., `OnClick`) information on the buttons. This is contained in the encrypted text for the ViewState and is handled server-side.

It just works.

Now there is more going on with partial classes and long discussions could be had, and most certainly already have been had, outlining all the specifics and ramifications of partial classes. However, for this topic, its probably enough for now to say that partial classes are one of the coolest innovations brought in with the .NET 2.0 Framework. And it might even be fair to say partial classes are what make Master Pages possible. Think about all of the tedium that would be involved in making sure that there were no redundant events or methods in the codes for the Master Pages and content pages. What if you wanted to have things happen on the `Page_Load` event that you needed to happen on the Master Page, while still maintaining the ability to have customized `Page_Load` events on each content page that inherits the Master? Or what if you had to try to remember each control used on the Master Page and make sure that you did not reuse it on the content page? Would you resort to some sort of naming schema that incorporated the name of the page into the name of the control? And imagine how much more infinitely difficult it would be if you didn't even code the Master Page but, instead, had to rely on one a designer created for your project? If all of these were issues of consideration for each developer, which they would be without the advent of partial classes, Master Pages would probably not be as popular as they are. Partial classes make Master Pages work.

While it is not necessary to go into a detailed discussion of partial classes for you to understand Master Pages, you may want to get deeper into what they are and how they work. If you would like to expand your understanding of partial classes, you can find out more at the following URLs:

Wikipedia — Partial Classes: `http://en.wikipedia.org/wiki/Partial_class`

MSDN — Partial Class Definitions (C#): `http://msdn2.microsoft.com/en-us/library/ wa80x488(vs.80).aspx`

Passing Data between Master and Child

If you work with Master Pages long enough, sooner or later you will find yourself trying to figure out how to pass data back and forth between the Master Page and its child. There are plenty of reasons for this. Perhaps you want to use a public property, such as a corporate name or slogan, throughout your website but don't want to have to worry about typing it in over and over and risking typing it in wrong. Or maybe the property is likely to change over time and will be used throughout the site, and you don't want to have to go through every page and try to replace the old value with the new one. Perhaps you want to have a method available to some of the content pages but don't want to include it in a subclass for some reason. Or maybe you just want to see if it's possible.

Well, the short answer is that it is definitely possible. The longer answer is that it can be done through several ways, as outlined below.

First Things First

You need to set up something that you want to share. For all examples, you will try to read a public string value that you have set up in your Master Page, which can be set up with the following code:

```
public string myValue
{
    get { return "My Master Page String Value"; }
    set { }
}
```

The set area is not really necessary; it is just there to show good form. What is important here is that you have a public string value in the Master Page that you are setting, when called, to a value ("My Master Page String Value" in this example). Just for reference, assuming that you have the code in your Master Page from the previous example, your code-behind file for your Master Page should now look like this:

```
using System;
using System.Data;
using System.Configuration;
using System.Collections;
using System.Web;
using System.Web.Security;
using System.Web.UI;
using System.Web.UI.WebControls;
```

```
using System.Web.UI.WebControls.WebParts;
using System.Web.UI.HtmlControls;

public partial class MasterPage : System.Web.UI.MasterPage
{

    public string myValue
    {
        get { return "My Master Page String Value"; }
        set { }
    }

    protected void Page_Load(object sender, EventArgs e)
    {

    }
    protected void Button1_Click(object sender, EventArgs e)
    {
        Label1.Text = TextBox1.Text;
        TextBox1.Text = "";
    }
}
```

You will also want to set up a label on your content page that you will fill with the public string value from the Master Page. To do this, modify the code in your content page to look similar to the following:

```
<%@ Page Language="C#" MasterPageFile="~/MasterPage.master" AutoEventWireup="true"
    CodeFile="Default.aspx.cs" Inherits="_Default" Title="Untitled Page" %>
<asp:Content ID="Content2" ContentPlaceHolderID="ContentPlaceHolder1"
    Runat="Server">

    <asp:Label ID="mpLabel" runat="server" Text="" /><br /><br />

    Content Text:
    <asp:TextBox ID="TextBox1" runat="server" />
    <asp:Button ID="Button1" runat="server" Text="Update Header Text"
OnClick="Button1_Click" />
    <asp:Label ID="Label1" runat="server" Text="" />
</asp:Content>
```

You have just added an ASP.NET Label control with an ID of "mpLabel". You will use this label in conjunction with the "myValue" public string property in the Master Page throughout this example.

You will see three ways of passing the data between the Master Page and a Child Page that inherits it. Each example starts from the same base code (the code that you should have to this point). If you make changes in your code for, say, Option 1, you will want to back out those changes before moving on to Option 2 (or Option 3).

Option 1: Just Bring it in

The first example requires the least amount of setup. All you need to do is cast the object returned by the Master Page into the factual object that it is. Once done, you will have access to its public properties and methods. For example, in the code-behind for `Default.aspx` (`Default.aspx.cs`), you can do this through code similar to the following:

```
protected void Page_Load(object sender, EventArgs e)
{
    MasterPage mp = (MasterPage)Page.Master;
    mpLabel.Text = mp.myValue;
}
```

As you can see, you are creating a new object, `mp`, as an instance of your Master Page. Once you do this, you have access to its public members, even in IntelliSense, as you can see in Figure 7-13.

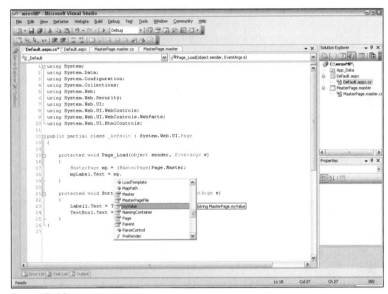

Figure 7-13

It should be noted that the `MasterPage` value used in this example may not be the same as yours. This is the name of the class within your Master Page, as can be seen in the class declaration of your Master Page:

```
public partial class MasterPage : System.Web.UI.MasterPage
```

If you had initially set up your page to use a different name (this was automatically generated for you when you created your Master Page and based on the name of the Master Page file), you would use the name of the class from the Master Page for this value instead. For example, if your class was called `myMasterPage` instead, the code on your content page would look more like this:

```
myMasterPage mp = (myMasterPage)Page.Master;
```

Option 2: Changing Your Class Name

Using the above is probably fine for most examples, but what if you want to change the name of the class you are casting with? That is to imply, without changing the actual name of the class? Perhaps it would be easier to just reference `"myMaster"` as your class instead of the actual class name. This is possible through the `Classname` property of the `@Master` directive of your Master Page.

First, if you made changes to your Master or content pages in the previous option, you might want to revert to the original version for this example. Each option will assume that you have never previously attempted to implement the other options.

By default, the .NET runtime will create a standard class name based on the name of the file. This will be in the format of `ASP.XYZ_master` where XYZ represents the name of your Master Page file. So, in the example up to this point, the name of the referenced class would be `ASP.masterpage_master`. This is long and fairly inconvenient to remember so, in order to remedy that, you need to change the class name that is given to your Master Page.

The first step is to add a `Classname` property to your Master Page directive in your Master Page file as follows:

```
<%@ Master Language="C#" AutoEventWireup="true" CodeFile="MasterPage.master.cs"
    Inherits="MasterPage" ClassName="myMaster" %>
```

In this example, you are setting the value of this property to `"myMaster"`. Save your Master Page and now go into the code behind for your content page (`Default.aspx.cs`). At this point, you should have access to this new class name. For example, go into your `Page_Load` event and start typing out "ASP." and you will see the options that are currently available, including the newly named `myMaster` (see Figure 7-14).

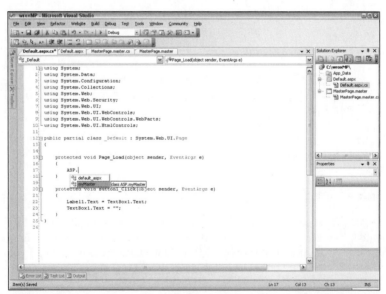

Figure 7-14

So, at this point, you should be able to write the following line of code in your content page without causing any errors:

```
mpLabel.Text = ((ASP.myMaster)Master).myValue;
```

Again, you are casting the returned object to the type that it is (Master) and, in doing so, you are given access to its properties and methods. Therefore, you could have just as easily used the following code, which would be more similar to the code from Option 1:

```
protected void Page_Load(object sender, EventArgs e)
{
    ASP.myMaster mp = (ASP.myMaster)Page.Master;
    mpLabel.Text = mp.myValue;
}
```

Using this option, you are given better names to deal with, potentially, when looking at the drop-down options of classes available. If you have a lot of pages and several Master Pages, it might be difficult to wade through them all and setting the class name to something more intuitive (or easier to find) might buy you some level of comfort. If, however, you only have a few pages and a single Master, this might be overkill. After all, what would changing the name to myMaster buy you? Probably not much. So, depending on the size of your project, this may or may not be a better solution for you.

Option 3: MasterType

Probably the easiest solution to passing variables is to wire your page to go directly to a specific Master Page, setting the Master property of the page for you without having to do any casting. In a default scenario, the Page class exposes a Master property to give developers access to members of a Master Page. If, however, the reference to a specific Master Page is not strongly typed, you have to go through the casting and potentially confusing code to get access to the properties and methods of a Master Page. So it would be easier, obviously, if you had a strongly typed reference to the Master Page. With that reference, you could have direct access to the properties and methods of a particular Master Page through the Master property of the Page class. This can be done with the MasterType directive of a content page.

So, for the example used in the chapter, you would modify the content page to look like so:

```
<%@ Page Language="C#" MasterPageFile="~/MasterPage.master" AutoEventWireup="true"
    CodeFile="Default.aspx.cs" Inherits="_Default" Title="Untitled Page" %>
<%@ MasterType VirtualPath="~/MasterPage.master" %>
<asp:Content ID="Content2" ContentPlaceHolderID="ContentPlaceHolder1"
    Runat="Server">

    <asp:Label ID="mpLabel" runat="server" Text="" /><br /><br />

    Content Text:
    <asp:TextBox ID="TextBox1" runat="server" />
    <asp:Button ID="Button1" runat="server" Text="Update Header Text"
    OnClick="Button1_Click" />
    <asp:Label ID="Label1" runat="server" Text="" />
</asp:Content>
```

As you can see, there is a new MasterType directive immediately following the Page directive. The MasterType directive has only two properties: VirtualPath and TypeName. However, it should be noted that these properties are mutually exclusive. This just means that you can use one or the other, but not both. If you define both properties, you will not be able to compile your page.

So what are these two properties? Well, the easy distinction is that the VirtualPath references the relative location of the page that will generate the strongly typed reference (e.g., "~/MasterPage.master"). With the `TypeName` property, you are simply providing the type name for the Master Page reference (e.g., `"MasterPage"`). The advantage to using the `TypeName` property is that you can actually set the reference to an inherited base class you have set up, for example, in your `App_Code` folder (you will see an example of this later in this chapter). This allows some additional flexibility with this strongly typed reference. However, for this example, it is fine to use the `VirtualPath` reference as shown before.

With your reference in place, you are able to access the public members of your Master Page simply by accessing the `Master` property of the `Page` class. You can see that the public property, `myValue`, is accessible through IntelliSense from the Master Property in Figure 7-15.

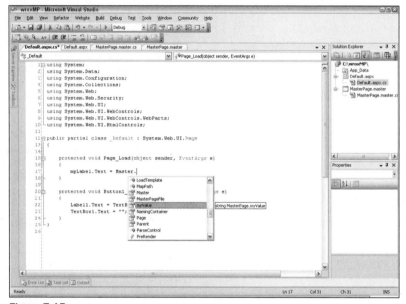

Figure 7-15

So, with that being true, you can set the text of `mpLabel` with the following (much simpler) line of code:

```
mpLabel.Text = Master.myValue;
```

This is, obviously, much easier to read and much easier to code, since there is no casting involved. This means that there is no need to create a new object on your page and cast it to the Master Page class you want to access; this reference is already strongly typed for you via the `MasterType` directive.

Setting the Master Page Globally

If you are creating a web application that will only have one Master Page it ever uses, it may seem like overkill to set the Master Page for every page in the site. If you are only setting the `MasterPageFile` property of the `@Page` directive to the same thing for every one of your hundreds or thousands of pages, why force the property each time? Wouldn't it be easier to just set it in one location and then not worry about it? You can do this by setting up a reference to your Master Page in your `web.config` file with code similar to the following:

```
<system.web>
    <pages masterPageFile="~/MasterPage.master" />
</system.web>
```

As you can see, you just need to set up a `masterPageFile` property in the `pages` element of the `system.web` section of your `web.config` file.

To test this, go back into your content page and take out the `MasterPageFile` property of your `@Page` directive, so that it now looks similar to the following:

```
<%@ Page Language="C#" AutoEventWireup="true" CodeFile="Default.aspx.cs"
    Inherits="_Default" Title="Untitled Page" %>
```

Now run your application. If you have it set up properly, your page should still work and you should still see the page laid out as expected. This means no errors and content that is appropriately placed in the correct areas of the Master Page.

There are a couple of problems with this approach. To see the first error, examine Figure 7-16.

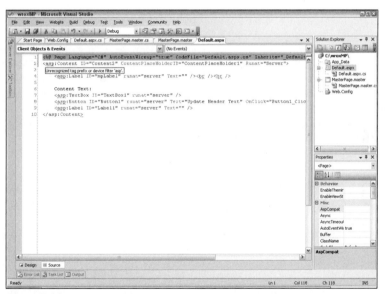

Figure 7-16

You can see that the page that originally showed perfect code now shows several of those nasty red squiggly lines; the first one is highlighted and reads "Unrecognized tag prefix or device filter 'asp'." This same error is going to be true for all of the asp control tags on the page; the last error on the page is complaining that there aren't any "<html>" tags on the page. Why is this happening? Because the page, at this point, doesn't know it is part of a Master Page; it doesn't get this information until it runs.

These error squiggles are annoying, but not terribly counterproductive. However, check out Figure 7-17.

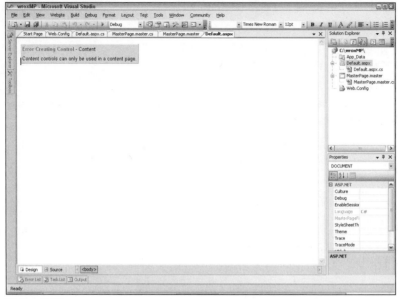

Figure 7-17

This should give pause to you, as a developer. You can no longer see not only the content from the Master Page (which may seem intuitive if you accept that the content page no longer realizes it is associated with a Master Page) but also the actual content of the content page itself. All you see is an error telling you that you can't have a ContentPlaceHolder unless you have a referenced Master Page.

Can you trick it into working? Well, sort of. This is something that probably won't resolve this issue for most developers but may help out a few. If you add back a MasterPageFile property to the @Page directive of your content page and set it to an empty value, you get some remedy. For example, your new @Page directive should now look like this:

```
<%@ Page Language="C#" MasterPageFile="" AutoEventWireup="true"
        CodeFile="Default.aspx.cs" Inherits="_Default" Title="Untitled Page" %>
```

Doing that will change what gets red squiggly lines in the Source view of Visual Studio 2005, as shown in Figure 7-18.

The first error line tells you that this property requires a value, while the second one says that there is no corresponding ContentPlaceHolder1 in the Master Page referenced. This is because it is looking for the Master Page called " ", which is what you told the page it should use. However, with this set, now switch over to the Design view, which should look like Figure 7-19.

As you can see, the content of the page is now viewable. You still can't see the layout provided from your Master Page, but at least you can see the content you are creating for this page.

Figure 7-18

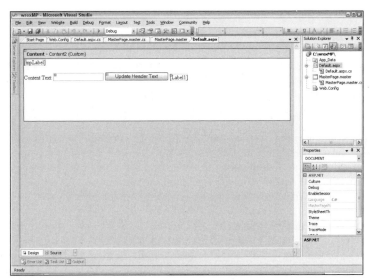

Figure 7-19

However, don't get too happy yet. Don't make any changes and now try to run the page again. You should get the error message shown in Figure 7-20.

This is because the page now believes that its Master Page is '' '', rather than "~/MasterPage.master", which you set in your web.config.

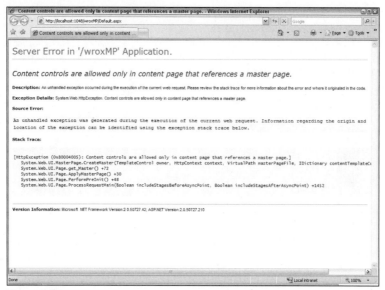

Figure 7-20

This new error partially illustrates the rendering hierarchy of .NET 2.0 in regard to Master Page. It first looks in the web.config to get the Master Page reference and then allows you to overwrite that value on the page itself within the @Page directive. This is done so that you can have a default/global Master Page but still maintain the ability to set a different Master Page for certain files or folders if you need to. While this logic is sound, it provides a problem with this workaround: you are overwriting the web.config Master Page reference with the blank one you are setting on the page.

So, if seeing your content in the Design view is important to you and you still want to set the Master Page reference in the web.config, your options are fairly limited. The only way to do this, really, is to set the MasterPageFile reference to a blank value while you are developing the page and then clear it out before you test or release the page. You could also set the MastePageFile property to the actual Master Page but, if you are doing that, what's the point in setting it globally in the web.config file?

Realistically, if you are setting the Master Page in your web.config, you should probably just limit yourself to working in the Source View of Visual Studio. You will not have any compilation or runtime errors using this approach, and your content pages will inherit their Master Pages as you would expect. Everything will work as you would hope, you will just have some annoying red squiggly lines in the Source view you have to contend with. But overall, your experience will be very similar to one that declares the Master Page in the @Page directive. You just need to realize the limitations of this approach.

Programmatically Setting Master Pages

In many scenarios, you may find it necessary to have multiple Master Pages that need to be set based on criteria that makes sense to your project. Maybe you have a CSS version for text browsers and a tables version for other browsers. Or maybe you have the need for a certain layout for mobile browsers and an entirely different look for other browsers. Or maybe some divisions of your company need to use one Master Page, while others use a different one. Regardless of your reasons, it is likely that you will, at some point, find it necessary to set the Master Page in code. To do this, you need to familiarize yourself with the `Page_PreInit()` event.

In .NET 2.0, a new event was added to the Page lifecycle: `PreInit`. This event is fired off before any other (including `Page_Load()` or `Page_Init()`). The Master Page must be set "in or before the 'Page_PreInit' event" according to a nasty error message you will get if you try to set it in, say, the `Page_Load` event, as shown in Figure 7-21.

Figure 7-21

This is an interesting error message when you consider the Page lifecycle in .NET:

1. `PreInit`
2. `OnInit`
3. `LoadViewState`
4. `LoadPostBackData`
5. `Page_Load`
6. `Control event handlers`
7. `PreRender`
8. `SaveViewState`
9. `Render`
10. `Unload`

On or before the `PreInit` event? Since there is no event occurring before `PreInit`, it seems like the error message should just say "set it in the PreInit event" and that should be it. But, regardless, this is where you are going to play: the `PreInit` event.

So, to set the Master Page, you need to include code similar to the following in the content page code:

```
protected void Page_PreInit(object sender, EventArgs e)
{
    Page.MasterPageFile = "~/MasterPage.master";
}
```

Make sure that there is no <pages> element reference to the MasterPageFile in your web.config or in the @Page directive of your content page (if you have set either of these attributes in the previous sections of this book, you will need to remove them at this point) and then run the application. You should have a page that loads successfully and brings in the Master Page.

This is actually a fairly easy concept to understand, the only possibly counterintuitive thing being the event you must use to set the Master Page. And even that makes sense if you think about it. The Master Page may, and probably will, need to arrange the entire control hierarchy before the page loads. If you wait to set it until the Load() event, it is just too late.

However, like a lot of other things you have seen so far, there are additional considerations if you want to go down this road. . . .

Consideration #1: Design-Time Support

Just as with setting the Master Page in the web.config file, you will have essentially no design-time support for your applications when you set the Master Page programmatically. In fact, if you take out the MasterPageFile property of the @Page directive on your content page, you will have the experience already illustrated in Figures 7-16 and 7-17.

However, unlike the web.config approach, it may actually make sense to set the MasterPageFile property to a real Master Page in your project. In the web.config it didn't make as much sense because you were only using one Master Page for all of your projects. So, if you are setting the MasterPageFile property in the @Page directive of each individual content page, what benefit are you receiving by setting it again in the web.config file?

However, in this scenario, the rules are slightly different. You may very well want to set up a default Master Page that is used by most pages and then reserve the ability to set this to a different Master Page depending on your criteria. So, you set the MasterPageFile to your default Master Page and then, on the relevant pages, you set the Master Page to a different logical file as necessary. This will keep you from seeing the red squiggly lines in your Source view as well as let you see all of the content, including that of the default Master Page, in the Design view of Visual Studio.

To see this in action, create a second Master Page by clicking Website and then Add New Item from the toolbar in Visual Studio. When the Add New Item form appears, select Master Page, set the language to your preference, and name the file MasterPage2.master. This is just for demonstration purposes, so there is no need to add any additional formatting to this particular Master; it will just be a white page with your controls on it. However, you will want to add a second ContentPlaceHolder, since your original has two and, if you switch back and forth between them, you don't want to generate an error because you don't have the same number of content placeholders in your two Masters.

Now, in your content page (Default.aspx), change the MasterPageFile reference in your @Page directive to point to MasterPage2.master. If you have a @MasterType directive, remove it for now (this will be further addressed in the next section, "Consideration #2: the @MasterType directive"). At this point, your code should look similar to the following:

```
<%@ Page MasterPageFile="~/MasterPage2.master" Language="C#"
    AutoEventWireup="true" CodeFile="Default.aspx.cs" Inherits="_Default"
    Title="Untitled Page" %>
<asp:Content ID="Content2" ContentPlaceHolderID="ContentPlaceHolder1"
    Runat="Server">

    <asp:Label ID="mpLabel" runat="server" Text="" /><br /><br />

    Content Text:
    <asp:TextBox ID="TextBox1" runat="server" />
    <asp:Button ID="Button1" runat="server" Text="Update Header Text"
   OnClick="Button1_Click" />
    <asp:Label ID="Label1" runat="server" Text="" />
</asp:Content>
```

In your code behind, you need to remove any of your references that you may have set to get the public property from your Master Page. You should also remove any code you have setting the Master Page, if you have added it based on information earlier in this section. The code behind should look like this:

```
using System;
using System.Data;
using System.Configuration;
using System.Collections;
using System.Web;
using System.Web.Security;
using System.Web.UI;
using System.Web.UI.WebControls;
using System.Web.UI.WebControls.WebParts;
using System.Web.UI.HtmlControls;

public partial class _Default : System.Web.UI.Page
{
    protected void Page_Load(object sender, EventArgs e)
    }
    }

    protected void Button1_Click(object sender, EventArgs e)
    {
        Label1.Text = TextBox1.Text;
        TextBox1.Text = "";
    }
}
```

If you now run the project, your page should look like Figure 7-22.

It may look like it didn't import any Master Page, but it did; it just imported a Master Page that doesn't have anything on it (remember that MasterPage2.master is blank).

Figure 7-22

At this point, go into your code behind and add the following event code for the content page:

```
protected void Page_PreInit(object sender, EventArgs e)
{
    Page.MasterPageFile = "~/MasterPage.master";
}
```

This is setting the Master Page back to the original Master Page. Rerun the project, and it should look like Figure 7-23.

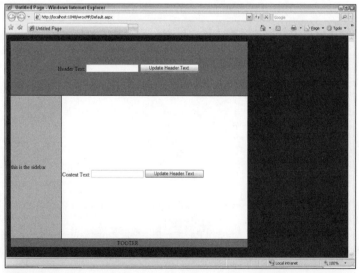

Figure 7-23

This shows that, for one, the code in the code behind works. But it also further illustrates the hierarchy applied in Master Pages. Earlier you learned that setting the Master Page in the web.config could be overridden by setting it in the @Page directive of the content page. Now you have seen that setting the Master Page programmatically overrides the reference set in the @Page directive. So, in the order they are applied, Master Pages are set in the following order:

1. web.config

2. @Page directive

3. programmatically (Page_PreInit() event)

As you have seen, though, the only way to get design-time support for the Master Page is to set it in the @Page directive. Setting it in the web.config or programmatically in the PreInit event will not allow you to see, at a minimum, the Master Page content in the Design view and may actually cause unwelcome errors that prevent you from seeing anything at all in that view.

While it didn't really make sense to set a default Master Page for each content page in the @Page directive for the web.config approach, it probably does for the programmatic approach. So, as outlined in the above steps, you have set up MasterPage2.master as the default Master Page for the project and then, in the PreInit event of the code-behind class, you are setting the Master Page to MasterPage.master. In a real-world scenario, you would probably have some sort of criteria (if/then statements for example) that would determine if you needed to adjust the Master Page reference or not but, even in this mock-up, you can see the noticeable differences in Figures 7-24 and 7-25.

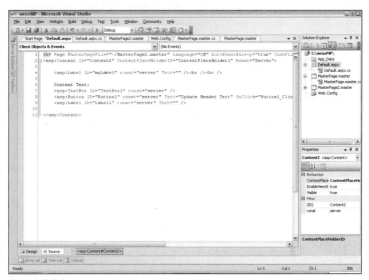

Figure 7-24

As you can see, the red squiggly lines are no longer in the Source view of Visual Studio. There are no errors at this point (feel free to add your own errors as you see fit). You will also see that you are able to view the stuff you have added to the content placeholders in the Design view. In this example, you may think that you aren't seeing the Master Page layout but remember that the Master Page that is set as the default is just a white page holding your content placeholders. So it is, in fact, displaying your Master Page content as well; it's just not very interesting content in this example.

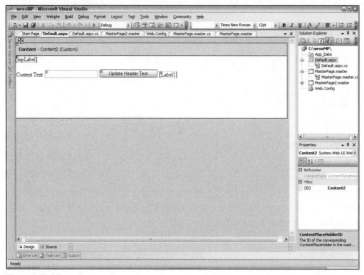

Figure 7-25

Consideration #2: The @MasterType Directive

If you were using the `@MasterType` directive to create a strongly typed reference to your Master Page previously, you will have a problem when you start setting the Master Page reference programmatically. To see this in action, change your content page to reference the original Master Page (`MasterPage.master`) in the `@Page` directive and then add a `@MasterType` directive and set the `VirtualPath` property to the same Master Page, as follows:

```
<%@ Page MasterPageFile="~/MasterPage.master" Language="C#" AutoEventWireup="true"
    CodeFile="Default.aspx.cs" Inherits="_Default" Title="Untitled Page" %>
<%@ MasterType VirtualPath="~/MasterPage.master" %>
```

Now go back into the code-behind of your content page, and change your `PreInit()` and `Load()` events to the following:

```
protected void Page_PreInit(object sender, EventArgs e)
{
    //Page.MasterPageFile = "~/MasterPage.master";
}

protected void Page_Load(object sender, EventArgs e)
{
    mpLabel.Text = Master.myValue;
}
```

In these changes, you are simply changing the code back to the form it was before it was tinkered with in the last section. If you run this, you should see that the page is rendered without errors, and the label in the content area now reads "My Master Page String Value," which was set in the Master Page.

Now, on to breaking it.

Change the `PreInit()` event to read as follows:

```
protected void Page_PreInit(object sender, EventArgs e)
{
    Page.MasterPageFile = "~/MasterPage2.master";
}
```

Now try to rerun the application. It won't be pretty. You should get an error similar to Figure 7-26 as the page is beginning to render.

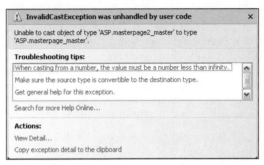

Figure 7-26

If you continue through the error, you will get a very similar error in your browser, as can be seen in Figure 7-27.

Figure 7-27

Remember earlier when you learned about setting the properties of the @MasterType directive? You learned that there were only two properties, VirtualPath and TypeName, which are mutually exclusive. Well, the way you have seen to set this reference, to this point, is what is causing the problem you are now seeing. For the strong type to the Master Page to persist, the reference made in the @MasterType directive must apply to all Master Pages that may end up being set programmatically. This is compounded by the fact that you can't set the properties of the @MasterType directive programmatically. So, if you have the @MasterType directive set to reference MasterPage.master, the application doesn't know how to handle it when you are all of a sudden using MasterPage2.master as your Master Page. And since you can't switch it at runtime, you have a problem.

The best way to handle this is to change the way you are making your reference. What you really need to do is set up a base class that all of your Master Pages will derive from and then set the TypeName property in your @MasterType directive to this class (as opposed to hard-coding the Master Page file in the VirtualPath property).

So, the first step in doing this is to create the base class that you will be using throughout your project. This class will need to inherit from the System.Web.UI.MasterPage class. So, to do this, go to your toolbar in Visual Studio and click on Website and select Add New Item to get the Add New Item screen. Select Class, choose your language preference, and call the file MasterBase.cs or MasterBase.vb (depending on your language). When you press the OK button, you may be prompted to set up an App_Code folder if you don't already have one. Click the Yes button to add the folder, and put your new base class file in that new folder. The default code will look similar to the following:

```
using System;
using System.Data;
using System.Configuration;
using System.Web;
using System.Web.Security;
using System.Web.UI;
using System.Web.UI.WebControls;
using System.Web.UI.WebControls.WebParts;
using System.Web.UI.HtmlControls;

/// <summary>
/// Summary description for MasterBase
/// </summary>
public class MasterBase
{
    public MasterBase()
    {
        //
        // TODO: Add constructor logic here
        //
    }
}
```

You will need to alter the public class declaration so that it inherits the MasterPage class. You will also want to move the public string variable, myValue, from MasterPage.master to the new base class. The class block should now look like this:

```
public class MasterBase : System.Web.UI.MasterPage
{
    public string myValue
    {
        get { return "My Master Page String Value"; }
        set { }
    }
}
```

You now have a public string variable that is a part of the `MasterBase` class you have just created. Now you just need to bring your pages into accord with this new base class.

You need to modify the two Master Pages you currently have so that they have similar class declarations in their respective code-behind files:

```
public partial class MasterPage : MasterBase
```

This would be, of course, the code in the `MasterPage.master` code-behind. This tells the partial class that it should inherit from your newly created `MasterBase` class. Make sure that, if you are in fact using the code-behind model (rather than having your code block written inline) that you do not change the `Inherits` property of your `@Master` directive. When you have a code-behind section for your master file, the `Inherits` property must point to the class that is the code-behind file. That is why you inherit from the new base class at that level rather than in the Master Page itself. If, however, you do not have a code-behind file and are, instead, coding inline, you should change (or add) the `Inherits` property to the base class, similar to the following:

```
<%@ Master Language="C#" Inherits="MasterBase" %>
```

You should repeat this change to every Master Page in your project (at this point, that should only include `MasterPage2.master`).

Now you need to modify your content page, `Default.aspx`, to point to the new base class as well as part of the `@MasterType` directive, which will now look like this:

```
<%@ MasterType TypeName="MasterBase" %>
```

Now to test that everything worked, add or update the `PreInit` event in the code behind for `Default.aspx` to resemble the following:

```
protected void Page_PreInit(object sender, EventArgs e)
{
    Page.MasterPageFile = "~/MasterPage.master";
}
```

Now, launch the application and you should see something resembling Figure 7-28.

Now, go back into `Default.aspx`, and change the PreInit event to use `MasterPage2.aspx`, as follows:

```
protected void Page_PreInit(object sender, EventArgs e)
{
    Page.MasterPageFile = "~/MasterPage2.master";
}
```

Now relaunch the application, and you should see something similar to Figure 7-29.

The interesting thing about this option, if you didn't notice, is that the label has now been set even when using `MasterPage2`. Previously, the label was only populated with the text from the Master Page when you used `MasterPage.master`. This is because the public string variable was only set in that page. But now, since the public string variable is being set in the base class and both Master Pages are inheriting from that base class, both Master Pages produce the text in the label, as they should.

Figure 7-28

Figure 7-29

You will also notice that you didn't need to change any code to set the label in your content page:

```
protected void Page_Load(object sender, EventArgs e)
{
    mpLabel.Text = Master.myValue;
}
```

The reference to your Master Page content is still strongly typed, which means you can access its methods and properties simply by using "Master." The reference persists to the base class (rather than an individual Master Page file) even if you switch back and forth among different Master Pages.

Although seen in a somewhat limited basis, this section provided an overview of base classing, which is a common practice in object-oriented programming that allows for an additional layer of abstraction that can later be extended to an object.

Nested Master Pages

Nesting Master Pages is an interesting concept that is allowed, although only partially supported, with Visual Studio 2005 and the .NET 2.0 Framework. Nesting pages, in its simplest definition, means that you have a Master Page that references a second Master Page. Sound a bit confusing? Well, imagine a scenario where you may have the need for three different, although very similar, templates for developers. Imagine that you want to have the same header and footer for all three and maybe even the same navigation system set up horizontally on the header but, in the content area between the header and footer, you want to allow for a single-column, two-column, and three-column layout. This isn't unheard of for most corporate intranet or Internet sites. Maybe for enterprise data matrix pages (one that just has a lot of data laid out in a matrix that has many columns and rows), developers may want to just have a blank canvas to work with (single-content area). In most other pages, though, the page should have a customized toolbar in a left bar, and the content should be to the right of it (two-column). Still, in a subset of those pages you may want to have specific data highlighted in a third column floated to the right of the content area (three-column). Without nesting, you would have to create three different Master Pages with a lot of overlapping content. All three masters would have the identical code for the header, navigation, and footer regions of the page. If you want to change, say, the layout of the navigation area (e.g., float it to the right rather than to the left), you would have to adjust the code in all three pages. With nesting Master Pages, you are actually creating four Master Pages instead of three. You create a universal Master Page that formats the page for your basic structuring. This would include, in this example, a header region, the site navigation region and controls, and a footer region. It would then contain a content placeholder between the header/navigation and the footer. You would then have three distinct Master Pages that each used that universal master as its own Master Page. In these three masters, you would only have the formatting necessary to fill the content area; no need for <html> or <body> tags, since that should be in the universal Master. You just have the @Master directive with a MasterPageFile property set to the universal Master and a content control that is connected to the content placeholder on the universal Master. Within that content control, you would format each of the three pages to the layout it should represent. In the single-column Master, for example, you would just have content that spread across the entire width of the content placeholder. In the two-column, you would set up a region to the left for the custom navigation and then have the content area floated to the right of it. Similarly, you would split up the content into three distinct regions for the three-column template.

Enough Theory, on to Coding!

This example will probably make more sense if you see it in action. For this nesting example, it would just be easier to start over and not use the other dummy Master Pages created for this chapter. So, in Visual Studio, start a new website and delete the Default.aspx file it includes at start-up (it will be easier to just create a new one later). Now add a new Master Page to your project (Website ➪ Add New Item) called UniversalMaster.master. You can set the language to whatever your preference is and click the

Add button. If you left the "Place code in separate file" option unchecked, your code will look like the following at this point:

```
<%@ Master Language="C#" %>

<!DOCTYPE html PUBLIC "-//W3C//DTD XHTML 1.0 Transitional//EN"
 "http://www.w3.org/TR/xhtml1/DTD/xhtml1-transitional.dtd">

<script runat="server">

</script>

<html xmlns="http://www.w3.org/1999/xhtml" >
<head runat="server">
    <title>Untitled Page</title>
</head>
<body>
    <form id="form1" runat="server">
    <div>
        <asp:contentplaceholder id="ContentPlaceHolder1" runat="server">
        </asp:contentplaceholder>
    </div>
    </form>
</body>
</html>
```

You will want to modify this code to add some style to it (essentially creating header, navigation, and footer regions). Your code might look similar to the following:

```
<%@ Master Language="C#" %>

<!DOCTYPE html PUBLIC "-//W3C//DTD XHTML 1.0 Transitional//EN"
  "http://www.w3.org/TR/xhtml1/DTD/xhtml1-transitional.dtd">

<script runat="server">

</script>

<html xmlns="http://www.w3.org/1999/xhtml" >
<head runat="server">
    <title>Nested Master</title>
<style>
    html{height: 100%;}
    body{height: 100%; margin: 0; padding: 0;}
    #pageWrapper{position: relative; min-height: 100%;
    height: auto; margin-bottom: -25px;}
    #header{width: 100%; height: 50px; background-color: steelblue; color: white;
    font-size: x-large; font-family: Arial Black; text-align: right;
    padding-top: 25px;}
    #navigation{width: 100%; height: 25px; background-color:
    gray; color: white; font-size: small; font-family: Arial;}
    #content{padding: 5px 5px 5px 5px;}
    #footer{width: 100%; height: 15px; background-color: steelblue; color: white;
    font-size: x-small; font-family: Arial; text-align: center;
    padding-top: 5px; border-top: solid 5px gray;}
</style>
```

```
    </head>
    <body>
        <form id="form1" runat="server">
        <div id="pageWrapper">
        <div id="header">Corporate Logo</div>
        <div id="navigation">| Link 1 | Link 2 | Link 3 |</div>
        <div id="content">

            <!-- THE CONTENT WILL GO IN THIS PLACEHOLDER -->
            <asp:contentplaceholder id="ContentPlaceHolder1" runat="server">
            </asp:contentplaceholder>

        </div>
        </div>
        <div id="footer">© copyright 2007</div>
        </form>
    </body>
    </html>
```

This code is presented to show how nested pages work and was specifically targeted at Internet Explorer 7. Therefore, it is possible that this code will not be rendered correctly in all browsers. Again, this code is meant to illustrate nested Master Pages and not necessarily CSS. You may need to tweak the code to make it work in other browsers.

With this code, you can create a content page that will inherit this page. You can do this through the typical way (Website ➪ Add New Item) or you can simply right-click on the Master Page in Solution Explorer and select Add Content Page. You don't need to add any content to the page if you don't want to. Run your project, and you should see something similar to Figure 7-30.

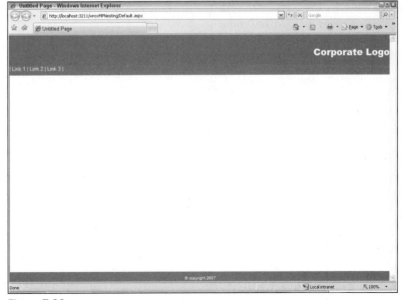

Figure 7-30

This will provide you with the basic shell for your application. What you will want next is to fill up the white area with your other templates. You will want to create two new Master Pages (you don't need to create all three; two will illustrate the intricacies of this approach). So, add the first one (Website ⇨ Add New Item), and call the file OneColumn.master. You will notice that the option Select Master Page is disabled. Don't worry; you will be able to add the other Master Page later. For now, just press the Add button. At this point, without any modifications, your code for this Master Page should resemble the following:

```
<%@ Master Language="C#" %>

<!DOCTYPE html PUBLIC "-//W3C//DTD XHTML 1.0 Transitional//EN"
  "http://www.w3.org/TR/xhtml1/DTD/xhtml11-transitional.dtd">

<script runat="server">

</script>

<html xmlns="http://www.w3.org/1999/xhtml" >
<head runat="server">
    <title>Untitled Page</title>
</head>
<body>
    <form id="form1" runat="server">
    <div>
        <asp:contentplaceholder id="ContentPlaceHolder1" runat="server">
        </asp:contentplaceholder>
    </div>
    </form>
</body>
</html>
```

At this point, you will want to make a few changes in order to make this work. First, you will want to remove any duplicate code (for example, HTML formatting that already exists in the universal Master Page). Doing so will make the code look more like this:

```
<%@ Master Language="C#" %>

    <asp:contentplaceholder id="ContentPlaceHolder1" runat="server">
    </asp:contentplaceholder>
```

You will notice that some of those dastardly red squiggly lines have returned. This is because you have removed all of the references you had set up but have yet to inherit the universal master. In order to remedy this, add a MasterPageFile property to the @Master directive, as follows:

```
<%@ Master Language="C#" MasterPageFile="~/UniversalMaster.master" %>

    <asp:contentplaceholder id="ContentPlaceHolder1" runat="server">
    </asp:contentplaceholder>
```

The red squiggly lines have now shifted from the `<asp:` to the `contentplaceholder` section of the place-holder control. This means that it now recognizes the `asp` tag prefix but a new error has arisen. In a content page, you are not allowed to have any extraneous content. This means that you are not allowed to have formatting/code in any region that is not encapsulated by a content tag. So, in order to fix this final error, change your code once again, to the following:

```
<%@ Master Language="C#" MasterPageFile="~/UniversalMaster.master" %>
<asp:Content ID="Content1" ContentPlaceHolderID="ContentPlaceHolder1"
    Runat="Server">
    <asp:contentplaceholder id="ContentPlaceHolder1" runat="server">
    </asp:contentplaceholder>
</asp:Content>
```

You now have a Master Page that is sitting inside of another Master Page. To see how this will work, you might want to modify this a bit more to add some content that is specific to this Master Page:

```
<%@ Master Language="C#" MasterPageFile="~/UniversalMaster.master" %>
<asp:Content ID="Content1" ContentPlaceHolderID="ContentPlaceHolder1"
    Runat="Server">
    <div style="color: SteelBlue; font-family: Arial Black; font-size: x-large;">
        One-Column Master
    </div>
    <asp:contentplaceholder id="ContentPlaceHolder1" runat="server">
    </asp:contentplaceholder>
</asp:Content>
```

All you are doing here is adding a header. This isn't necessary, but it allows you to visually determine which Master Page you are pulling from in the pages that are inheriting from it.

To see all of this work together, modify your `Default.aspx` to point to the new `OneColumn.master` file, and add a little dummy text in its content placeholder just to see how everything works together. The code might look similar to the following:

```
<%@ Page Language="C#" MasterPageFile="~/OneColumn.master" Title="Untitled Page" %>
<asp:Content ID="Content1" ContentPlaceHolderID="ContentPlaceHolder1"
    Runat="Server">
    Hello, world.
</asp:Content>
```

If you run this page, it should now resemble Figure 7-31.

To break down this example, you can see that the header, navigation, and footer regions are coming from `UniversalMaster.master`, the heading "One-Column Master" is coming from the nested master file, `OneColumn.master`, and the text "Hello, world." is coming from the content page, `Default.aspx`. You have just created a nested Master Page example.

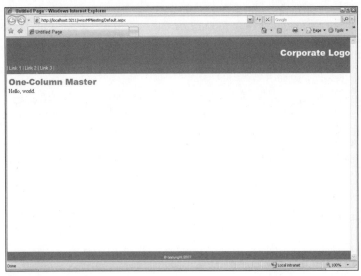

Figure 7-31

To expand this example, create another Master Page in the same manner as before, and call this one
`TwoColumn.master`. Modify its code to look similar to the following:

```
<%@ Master Language="C#" MasterPageFile="~/UniversalMaster.master" %>
<asp:Content ID="Content1" ContentPlaceHolderID="ContentPlaceHolder1"
   Runat="Server">
     <div style="color: SteelBlue; font-family: Arial Black; font-size: x-large;">
        Two-Column Master
     </div>

     <div style="width: 130px; min-height: 150px; background-color: LightGrey;
     padding: 10px 10px 10px 10px; color: SteelBlue; position: static;
     float: left; text-align: center;">
     <asp:contentplaceholder id="ContentPlaceHolder1" runat="server">
     </asp:contentplaceholder>
     </div>

     <div style="position: static; padding-left: 160px; clear: right;">
     <asp:contentplaceholder id="ContentPlaceHolder2" runat="server">
     </asp:contentplaceholder>
     </div>

</asp:Content>
```

You can see that, in this Master Page, you have set up two content placeholders to sit inside of the
content control inherited from the Universal Master Page. These two new placeholders will constitute
the two columns of this particular style and, as such, have CSS rules applied to make them into
two columns.

To see how this looks, create a new content page (right-click on the TwoColumn.master file in Solution
Explorer, and select Add Content Page — it should be named `Default2.aspx` by default). This will create

two content controls in it that reference the content placeholders in the `TwoColumn.master` file. Modify the code to add some content to these controls, similar to the following:

```
<%@ Page Language="C#" MasterPageFile="~/TwoColumn.master" Title="Untitled Page" %>
<asp:Content ID="Content1" ContentPlaceHolderID="ContentPlaceHolder1"
    Runat="Server">
left stuff
</asp:Content>
<asp:Content ID="Content2" ContentPlaceHolderID="ContentPlaceHolder2"
    Runat="Server">

<p style="text-align: justify;">Lorem ipsum dolor sit amet, consectetuer
    adipiscing elit. Morbi elit enim, auctor id, vestibulum eu, aliquam ut, augue.
    Duis at magna. Pellentesque viverra venenatis tellus. Vestibulum at lacus. Ut et
    lectus sed lacus lobortis aliquam. Quisque vitae felis sit amet velit pharetra
    gravida. Nunc scelerisque mi sed massa. Mauris iaculis faucibus massa. Nunc
    dictum, sapien eu adipiscing auctor, ligula risus dictum ipsum, id tincidunt
    tellus nisl in quam. Ut velit tellus, blandit et, luctus nec, congue in, libero.
    Nullam cursus. Donec pharetra. Donec sit amet metus eget enim elementum vulputate.
    Aenean at augue eget tellus pellentesque mollis. Class aptent taciti sociosqu ad
    litora torquent per conubia nostra, per inceptos hymenaeos. Suspendisse id dolor
    tristique quam suscipit commodo. Vestibulum nunc. Vivamus commodo dignissim nulla.
    Curabitur rhoncus, pede a aliquet pharetra, elit pede tincidunt erat, vitae cursus
    ligula elit vel lorem. </p>

<p style="text-align: justify;">Nunc nisl augue, consequat et, pulvinar ac,
    placerat ac, pede. Aenean ante sem, euismod eu, venenatis sed, consequat ut,
    dui. Praesent faucibus, dui id vestibulum ullamcorper, orci diam congue sem,
    varius ultrices justo dolor malesuada nunc. Vivamus interdum, nunc id tristique
    faucibus, diam tortor lacinia arcu, nec interdum est lacus et urna. Mauris
    pulvinar turpis eu tellus. Curabitur vel lacus et elit lacinia molestie. Proin eros
    ligula, adipiscing ac, tincidunt quis, adipiscing sed, massa. Phasellus elit mi,
    malesuada ut, ullamcorper sed, dapibus sed, velit. Integer dolor. Donec
    commodo sollicitudin odio. </p>

<p style="text-align: justify;">Etiam dolor. Cras condimentum posuere felis. Sed
    tincidunt. Etiam id orci. Suspendisse aliquet fermentum neque. Sed cursus, justo
    sit amet adipiscing commodo, velit nisl blandit nibh, quis scelerisque purus leo
    eget nulla. Praesent aliquam pharetra nulla. Suspendisse aliquam tristique nunc.
    Integer augue nunc, sodales nec, sollicitudin ut, hendrerit at, arcu. Morbi mauris
    ligula, auctor in, cursus quis, auctor id, arcu. </p>

</asp:Content>
```

This example just fills in a lot of dummy text to show how the areas will look with a normal amount of text in them.

"Lorem ipsum" text is a standard technique for filling up space with dummy text. It is discussed in Chapter 4.

If you launch this new page, it should look like Figure 7-32.

You have now created two distinctly different Master Pages that inherit the overall structure of your project from a controlling universal Master. Those pages that need to span the entire content window can use `OneColumn.master`. For all other pages, you can use `TwoColumn.master` so that you have an area in which you can put custom content for a sidebar region. Both of these masters, being inherited from `UniversalMaster.master`, will be affected equally when the universal master is updated. If, for example, you decide to add an image to the header or change the colors to an earth-tone schema, the header, navigation, and footer regions would be adjusted, and the content, whether in one or two columns, would still sit nicely between them with no need to modify either of those Master Pages. This is a cool way to solve a fairly typical problem in many Internet and/or intranet web solutions.

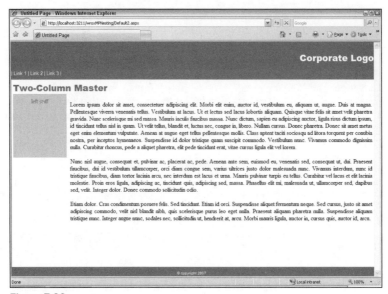

Figure 7-32

No Problems, Right?

Wrong. Nothing comes without a price. And, with respect to nested Master Pages, the hit you take is in the design-time support within Visual Studio 2005. Basically, there is none. If you try to switch to the Design view from one of the content pages (`Default.aspx` or `Default2.aspx` in this example), you will be presented with the error message depicted in Figure 7-33.

Figure 7-33

You aren't even allowed to make the switch and then see the ugly error message in the Design view itself, as was the case with missing `MasterPageFile` references earlier in this chapter. Visual Studio 2005 doesn't even allow you to switch views. You will not get any compilation or runtime errors when using nested Master Pages, and you won't get any red squiggly lines of error in the Source view. You just aren't permitted to go into the Design view when using nested Master Pages in Visual Studio 2005.

But there is hope. The key words for this nuisance are "in Visual Studio 2005." With the next scheduled release of Visual Studio, code-named Orcas, Microsoft promises to fully support nested Master Pages, even in the Design view. In Appendix A of this book, you will see a preview of the latest beta release of Orcas and see some of the features that should be included in the final release, including nested Master Page support. But, for now, you have to live in the Source view.

> *There are examples on the web on how to "trick" Visual Studio into working with nested Master Pages in the Design view. One approach suggests setting the* MasterPageFile *property in the* @Page *directive of the content page to either a valid non-nested Master Page or to just an empty string, and then create a new base class that overrides the* PreInit *event and sets the Master Page at that point. While this will certainly work, it only helps get into the Design view and has other potential inheritance problems, as seen earlier in this chapter. If possible, it is probably safest to just stay in the Source view for now and then rejoice when Orcas comes out.*

One Last Concept

One of the nicer features of Master Pages is that they have mixed level support. This simply means that the language of your Master Page does not dictate the language of your content page, and vice versa. So, if you have a Master Page that has a language of C#, it is perfectly fine to have a content page with a language of VB. This allows for one programmer to be responsible for the templating of a particular web project and to share that template with other developers who can code against it in whatever language they prefer.

To take that a step further, it is perfectly acceptable to have a VB content page that has a TypeName property of its @MasterType directive set to reference a C# base class. So it really is possible to create the framework of the site (the Master Page and its referenced base class) in C# or VB without worrying about how it will be used by the developers who incorporate it into their pages.

Bringing It All Together: Updating the surfer5 Project

You have learned a lot of concepts throughout this book on what Master Pages are and how they can be applied to your projects. It is time to pull some of that information into the book project (C:\surfer5\). With regards to Master Pages, you will want to create, for now, a single Master Page that has a base class set up. This may be overkill for a project with only a single Master, but it allows the site to expand in the future if deemed necessary.

So the first step is to create the Master Base class. For this project, it has been determined that a public string variable should be created called "company" set to a value of "sufer5 Internet Solutions" so that any page wanting to use the company name has easy access to it (which also allows it to be changed throughout the site if the name changes in the future). In order to accomplish this, create a base class in your project called MasterBase.cs (or MasterBase.vb, depending on your language preference), and set it up as follows:

> *Going forward in this and the following chapters, the book project will be using* MasterBase.cs *as the base class. If you choose to use* MasterBase.vb, *you will naturally need to keep this distinction in mind as you work through the rest of the book.*

```
using System;
using System.Data;
using System.Configuration;
using System.Web;
using System.Web.Security;
using System.Web.UI;
using System.Web.UI.WebControls;
using System.Web.UI.WebControls.WebParts;
using System.Web.UI.HtmlControls;

/// <summary>
/// Summary description for MasterBase
/// </summary>
public class MasterBase : MasterPage
{
    public string company
    {
        get { return "surfer5 Internet Solutions"; }
    }

    protected override void OnLoad(EventArgs e)
    {
        Page.Title = "surfer5 Internet Solutions";
    }
}
```

The only thing introduced here is an override function for the OnLoad event that will set the Page Title of any page that inherits this class to "surfer5 Internet Solutions." This will filter down to the content page that inherits the Master Page that inherits this base class. That is just a long way of saying that any content page that uses this base class will have its title set for it. This eliminates the need to set the Title property in the @Page directive of the content page (or to set Page.Title in the Page_Load() event of the content page). By adding this functionality, you are ensuring that the page does not say "Untitled Page," which is what it is set up to say by default (the Title property in the @Page directive is set to "Untitled Page" unless you set it to something else). Just as an aside, if you do set it here, it won't be overridden at the page level. This means that if you do try to set it either in the @Page directive or in the page Load() event, the override here will still win out.

Now you need to create a blank Master Page, called surfer5.master. You will want to add code to inherit from the MasterBase class. At this point, your code for surfer5.master should look similar to the following:

```
<%@ Master Language="C#" AutoEventWireup="true" CodeFile="surfer5.master.cs"
    Inherits="surfer5" %>

<!DOCTYPE html PUBLIC "-//W3C//DTD XHTML 1.0 Transitional//EN"
    "http://www.w3.org/TR/xhtml1/DTD/xhtml1-transitional.dtd">

<html xmlns="http://www.w3.org/1999/xhtml" >
<head runat="server">
    <title>Untitled Page</title>
</head>
<body>
```

```
        <form id="form1" runat="server">
        <div>
            <asp:contentplaceholder id="ContentPlaceHolder1" runat="server">
            </asp:contentplaceholder>
        </div>
        </form>
    </body>
    </html>
```

Similarly, the code behind for `surfer5.master` (`surfer5.master.cs`) should look like this:

```csharp
using System;
using System.Data;
using System.Configuration;
using System.Collections;
using System.Web;
using System.Web.Security;
using System.Web.UI;
using System.Web.UI.WebControls;
using System.Web.UI.WebControls.WebParts;
using System.Web.UI.HtmlControls;

public partial class surfer5 : MasterBase
{
    protected void Page_Load(object sender, EventArgs e)
    {

    }
}
```

You now need to modify the Master Page to bring in all of the HTML formatting you originally set in `Default.aspx`. Your new `surfer5.master` should look like this:

```
<%@ Master Language="C#" AutoEventWireup="true" CodeFile="surfer5.master.cs"
    Inherits="surfer5" %>

<!DOCTYPE html PUBLIC "-//W3C//DTD XHTML 1.0 Strict//EN"
    "http://www.w3.org/TR/xhtml1/DTD/xhtml1-strict.dtd">

<html xmlns="http://www.w3.org/1999/xhtml" >
<head id="Head1" runat="server">
    <title>Untitled Page</title>
    <link href="surfer5_v1.css" rel="stylesheet" type="text/css" />
    <link href="surfer5menu.css" rel="stylesheet" type="text/css" />
    <link runat="server" rel="stylesheet" href="~/CSS/Import.css"
    type="text/css" id="AdaptersInvariantImportCSS" />
<!--[if lt IE 7]>
    <link runat="server" rel="stylesheet"
        href="~/CSS/BrowserSpecific/IEMenu6.css" type="text/css">
    <link href="surfer5menuIE6.css" rel="stylesheet" type="text/css" />
<![endif]-->
</head>
<body>
```

```
        <form id="form1" runat="server">
        <div id="pageWrapper">
        <div id="headerGraphic"></div>
        <div id="navigationArea">
            <asp:Menu CssSelectorClass="surfer5menu" DataSourceID="SiteMapDataSource1"
        Orientation="Horizontal" ID="Menu1" runat="server" />
            <asp:SiteMapDataSource SiteMapProvider="myMenu" ShowStartingNode="false"
        ID="SiteMapDataSource1" runat="server" />
        </div>
        <div id="bodyArea">
        <div id="bodyLeft">Lorem ipsum dolor sit amet, consectetuer adipiscing
elit. Vivamus felis. Nulla facilisi. Nulla eleifend est at lacus. Sed vitae pede.
Etiam rutrum massa vel nulla. Praesent tempus, nisl ac auctor convallis, leo turpis
ornare ipsum, ut porttitor felis elit eu turpis. Curabitur quam turpis, placerat
ac, elementum quis, sollicitudin non, turpis. Ut tincidunt sollicitudin risus. Sed
dapibus risus et leo. Praesent interdum, velit id volutpat convallis, nunc diam
vehicula risus, in feugiat quam libero vitae justo.</div>
        <div id="bodyRight">
            <asp:SiteMapPath ID="SiteMapPath1" runat="server" PathSeparator=" :: " />

            <asp:contentplaceholder id="ContentPlaceHolder1" runat="server">
            </asp:contentplaceholder>

        </div>
        </div>
        <div id="footerArea">&copy 2006 - 2007: surfer5 Internet Solutions</div>

        </div>
        </form>
</body>
</html>
```

You should now have your Master Page completely set up. The only thing left to do is create a content page that will reference this new Master Page. You will want to modify your `Default.aspx` file to look more like the following:

```
<%@ Page Language="C#" MasterPageFile="~/surfer5.master" AutoEventWireup="true"
    CodeFile="Default.aspx.cs" Inherits="_Default" Title="Untitled Page" %>
<%@ MasterType TypeName="MasterBase" %>
<asp:Content ID="Content1" ContentPlaceHolderID="ContentPlaceHolder1"
    Runat="Server">

    <div class="header">Welcome to <asp:Label ID="myCompany"
    runat="server" Text="" />:</div>

 <p>Lorem ipsum dolor sit amet, consectetuer adipiscing elit. Donec elementum
eleifend libero. Fusce tristique tempus nulla. Pellentesque fringilla placerat nunc.
Aliquam erat volutpat. Donec nunc arcu, convallis sollicitudin, gravida eu,
adipiscing ut, eros. Quisque justo mauris, lobortis vel, lobortis et, nonummy
sodales, ante. Suspendisse potenti. Maecenas congue ipsum vitae augue. Sed quis
tortor. Mauris ultricies, turpis ac rutrum tincidunt, diam eros scelerisque dolor,
et auctor metus est sit amet augue. Ut hendrerit posuere pede. Phasellus lacus nisl,
fringilla eget, auctor ut, vestibulum et, neque. </p>
```

```
    <p>Suspendisse eget dui. Suspendisse vel ligula id velit bibendum vestibulum.
Ut bibendum velit eu sapien. Integer nisl. Class aptent taciti sociosqu ad litora
torquent per conubia nostra, per inceptos hymenaeos. Mauris et eros quis eros luctus
ornare. Mauris nec magna a magna cursus fringilla. Vivamus interdum justo scelerisque
sapien rhoncus cursus. Integer arcu neque, semper vel, fringilla vel, iaculis nec,
est. In hac habitasse platea dictumst. Morbi sem arcu, commodo nec, tincidunt
consectetuer, scelerisque quis, nulla. Integer placerat, justo vitae ornare dictum,
nibh felis semper pede, non blandit mauris felis sed dolor. Nunc fringilla
ligula nec ante. </p>

    <p>Proin sodales. Mauris nisi. Fusce ut nisi. Sed id velit nec ante sagittis
tincidunt. Pellentesque sagittis lacus at quam. Suspendisse potenti. Proin
mauris arcu, semper sed, aliquam nec, ultrices hendrerit, odio. Vestibulum gravida.
Cras mi risus, pharetra ultricies, auctor in, tristique sed, nibh. Proin sodales.
Aenean pretium scelerisque tellus. Sed non massa. Pellentesque dictum justo sit amet
lacus posuere scelerisque. Donec eget erat. Praesent vulputate. Cras nonummy.
In sodales est ut quam. Duis et leo. Nam ac odio sed purus gravida vestibulum.
Fusce nonummy orci non nibh. </p>

    <p>Suspendisse in magna. Morbi sit amet diam nec sem varius luctus. Mauris felis
dui, lobortis non, cursus id, cursus nec, diam. Vivamus interdum sollicitudin ante.
Aliquam erat volutpat. Cras nec ipsum. Maecenas fringilla. Nunc aliquam
adipiscing elit. Morbi molestie lectus id felis. Curabitur sem. Pellentesque vitae
nulla. Duis commodo. Duis tincidunt auctor turpis. In hac habitasse platea dictumst.
Aliquam erat volutpat. Aliquam quis metus nec massa feugiat posuere. Nulla congue
molestie massa. Phasellus ut quam vitae urna tempus iaculis. Donec volutpat
diam et felis. </p>

    <p>Duis malesuada odio vel elit. Suspendisse id est. Ut eros. Quisque quis lacus
nec purus tempus porta. Sed nec elit. Ut tempus, purus a mollis sodales, nulla
magna ornare augue, at rhoncus mi dolor in metus. Lorem ipsum dolor sit amet,
consectetuer adipiscing elit. Nunc tempus vestibulum tellus. Sed suscipit, arcu
convallis lacinia bibendum, lectus ante aliquam arcu, sed ornare dui dolor id pede.
Cras vel sem sed nunc laoreet cursus. Duis in enim. Aenean consequat quam
sed orci. Duis tellus. </p>

    <p>Fusce sed leo volutpat neque suscipit accumsan. Nullam non odio. Duis
ullamcorper nunc a elit vestibulum tristique. Pellentesque elementum arcu
facilisis odio pretium cursus. Nam dapibus, urna vitae porttitor vehicula, ipsum
quam interdum nulla, a scelerisque neque velit quis tellus. Sed vitae tellus in
turpis convallis laoreet. Nam feugiat auctor turpis. Aenean sit amet lacus.
Vivamus in diam. Nam ultrices, nulla nec luctus euismod, ipsum leo tempor nunc,
vel faucibus quam elit eget justo. </p>

</asp:Content>
```

The code behind for this file, `Default.aspx.cs`, should now look like this:

```
using System;
using System.Data;
using System.Configuration;
```

```
using System.Collections;
using System.Web;
using System.Web.Security;
using System.Web.UI;
using System.Web.UI.WebControls;
using System.Web.UI.WebControls.WebParts;
using System.Web.UI.HtmlControls;
public partial class _Default : System.Web.UI.Page
{
    protected void Page_Load(object sender, EventArgs e)
    {
        myCompany.Text = Master.company;
    }
}
```

This just imports in the content from the original page and then adds a new label, `myCompany`, to the heading and then imports the text for that label from the Master Page base class.

If you have everything set up, your project, at this stage, should resemble Figure 7-34.

Figure 7-34

You can see that the title bar and the heading in the content area both reflect the code set in the referenced master base class; the header text is from the public string variable and the title bar is from the `OnLoad` override. The page should look, other than those small variances, exactly the same as it did at the end of Chapter 6. What has changed is under the hood. When you get ready to create the next page, you can start with a shell similar to the following:

```
<%@ Page Language="C#" MasterPageFile="~/surfer5.master" AutoEventWireup="true"
    CodeFile="Default2.aspx.cs" Inherits="Default2" Title="Untitled Page" %>
<%@ MasterType TypeName="MasterBase" %>
<asp:Content ID="Content1" ContentPlaceHolderID="ContentPlaceHolder1"
    Runat="Server">
</asp:Content>
```

All you have to do at this point is start filling in the content in the area reserved by the content control, and you will have a page that looks exactly like the initial page . . . just with different content.

Summary

This chapter has been a fairly long one with a lot of potentially new concepts for you. Hopefully, you are leaving it with a pretty good understanding of what a Master Page is and how it provides a solution for an age old problem in web design. You learned the basic covenants of a Master Page and how to set some of the elementary properties of the Master Page. You explored some of the intricacies of trying to pass variables back and forth between content page and master. You discovered the coolness that is nested Master Pages, while also seeing some of their problems. You created a base class that could be inherited into your Master Page to make switching masters programmatically more seamless. And finally, you mastered how to bring all of these concepts into your real-world project, surfer5.

But that is all just technical talk. Hopefully, you learned more than just how to answer questions about Master Pages in an interview. Hopefully, you learned to appreciate the power Master Pages offer and are more familiar with the limitations that are inherent with their use. Maybe you even learned a trick or two about how to get around some of those limitations. But, most importantly, if you haven't really been using Master Pages or have only been using them scarcely, you learned they are a cool tool for development, and you will want to use them in every .NET web project you work on in the future. They are the quintessential tool for making consistent-looking websites. If there was one feature in ASP.NET 2.0 that would be essential for aesthNETics to work, this would probably be it. Now you see why.

8

Themes

If you are a fan of, or can at least relate to, the pirates of old, you can think of this book as a sort of modern day treasure map. With most treasure maps, you might have to go around the palm tree, walk 300 paces to the three-trunk tree, and head south for 150 meters to a spot where the waterfall cleverly hides a cave with the fabled treasure. In the context of this book, however, themes are your buried treasure. Much as with a treasure map, you had to get through several intermediate steps before you were ready to get into making themes, at least successful themes, work. You had to learn about the considerations of web design and standards. You had to obtain a basic working knowledge of graphics and color. You needed to learn what Cascading Style Sheets were and how they can be used in your projects. You had to understand site navigation and the tools in .NET that allow you to make it consistent. And, most recently, you needed to see how to create a standard template using all of the previous ideas and concepts so that you could carry out the overall layout of your site throughout all of the pages that make it up. So now you just need to walk through the waterfall and begin digging ten paces due north; you are finally ready for themes. And, once you open this new treasure box, you will find it filled with CSS, skins, and images that you can apply to all of the pages of your site.

What Are Themes?

Themes are one of the cooler ideas introduced with the .NET 2.0 Framework. With themes, you can create completely skinnable websites. What does this mean? Well, think about many of your Windows applications. For example, think about Windows Media Player. You know how you can go into that application and decide what skin should be applied? Well, first, you probably need to know what a "skin" is. To put it simply, a skin is the design you see when you look at an application. So, to use the Windows Media Player example, one skin may make your player look like the new Windows Vista Media Player while another one may make your player look like, well, buried treasure (look for the "Aquarium" skin for Windows Media Player). So, in many applications, when you apply a skin, you are totally changing the look and feel of the application. Maybe this means that you give it a different background and size. Maybe it means that you completely switch around the location of the standard buttons. Or maybe you even eliminate some components to make the interface more compact. These would all constitute different skins for the same application. And an application that has multiple skins to choose from would be considered a skinnable application.

With ASP.NET 2.0 Themes, you can achieve much the same functionality as skinnable applications. In fact, themes actually have a component called "Skins," which are critical to any well-formed theme. Skins in ASP.NET Themes, though, have a slightly different connotation. In .NET, a Skin file is simply a collection of attributes that you want to make the default for the controls on your page. As an example, you may want to make all of the button controls included in your ASP.NET application have the same border, background color, forecolor, and font styles. You can actually define all of that in your Skin file, which would then be applied to all of the button controls through the ASP.NET Theme. You can also apply theme-specific CSS files and images to your pages as well through very similar techniques.

Using ASP.NET 2.0 Themes, you can, then, create completely skinnable websites. You can, say, have one theme set up for your mobile users that is different from the theme set up for your authenticated users, which is different still from the theme you have set up for your administrators. You can create multiple skins for your site that your users can choose between to decide how they experience your site rather than your doing it for them (well, okay, you're still dictating it to some extent, but at least you are giving them a choice of which dictation they want to follow). You could even create a theme that was set up just for your ADA visitors that got rid of all CSS styling, JavaScript dependencies, and images. You would just put some logic into your site that would decide which theme to apply, either through user selection or through other predefined criteria, and the site would take on that skinned look. With themes, you create the content once and then have it take on various looks, depending on what suits your needs.

But is that it? Is it just a cool way of creating skinnable sites? Does that mean that you need to create multiple skins just to get the benefit of themes? Not in the least. While themes can, and should, harness the style standards of CSS to format your website, they go beyond that. What does that mean? CSS styles HTML; themes not only style ASP.NET controls but also set programmatic defaults for them. So, while any good theme will use the standards of CSS to format the general style of the controls, it will also use Skin files to control things like pagination, sorting, and other attributes of, say, the GridView controls that you typically need to address with each and every GridView control you include in your projects.

To understand this better, think about adding a GridView control to your website. Just by doing so, it would look something like this:

```
<asp:GridView ID="GridView1" runat="server">
</asp:GridView>
```

Now say that you want to add a little style to your GridView. Perhaps you want to have the header have a particular style and then different styles for each of the alternating rows in your grid. Your control might start to look more like this:

```
<asp:GridView ID="GridView1" runat="server">
    <HeaderStyle CssClass="GridViewHeader" />
    <RowStyle CssClass="GridViewRow" />
    <AlternatingRowStyle CssClass="GridViewAlternateRow" />
</asp:GridView>
```

To continue this, though, assume that you want to have pagination set up and maybe the width of the control and some other properties. Your GridView controls now may look something more like this:

```
<asp:GridView ID="GridView1" runat="server" AllowPaging="true" PageSize="10"
    AllowSorting="true" CssClass="GridView" Width="500">
    <HeaderStyle CssClass="GridViewHeader" />
    <RowStyle CssClass="GridViewRow" />
    <AlternatingRowStyle CssClass="GridViewAlternateRow" />
</asp:GridView>
```

You can see how this can continue to get bigger and messier. So assume that you have tens or even hundreds of GridView controls scattered throughout your site, with this same code repeated for every GridView control. Now, in this example, you used CSS to style a lot of this, so much of it would be taken care of in your attached stylesheets should you need to change anything. For example, if all of a sudden you want to turn the header background color from a dark blue to more of a steel blue, you could do that in your CSS. But imagine how frustrating it would be if someone dictated that all multipaginated web grids must allow 15 rows per page instead of the 10 that you have allowed for in this example? You would have to go back and touch each and every GridView control to change that one property. Wouldn't it be better if you could just change that property in one place and it would filter down throughout all of the affected controls? That is where themes and skins come in to play. Using this new technology, you could reduce all of the above code to the following without seeing any difference on your website:

```
<asp:GridView ID="GridView1" runat="server" />
```

All of the header, row, and alternating row CSS references would be made in the skin, so there is no need to type all of that again. In this example, there would be a default skin for the GridView control that would be applied to all GridView controls unless the control was specifically told not to (either by telling the control to ignore the skin settings or to specifically reference a different skin for the GridView control, which you can do through a SkinID attribute of the control). Before themes were introduced in the .NET 2.0 Framework, ASP.NET developers had a very difficult time creating default programmatic and style defaults for the controls they used to develop their sites. CSS is very powerful in what it can do, but can you imagine saying "Hey, CSS, I want the row background color to be light blue but only on alternating rows; in the other rows I want the background color to be white." CSS was never intended for this type of programmatic setting. You can set up the properties for the row and the alternating row in CSS, but you can't just drop a GridView control into your page, make a single reference to a CSS class, and have it be smart enough to tell which style to apply to the first row, or the second row, or the third row, and so on. With themes, you can do exactly that. You just drop a new GridView onto your page, and you are done. All of the row and alternating row styling will be taken care of for you, assuming that you set up your skin to do so.

Furthermore, the other properties of the GridView are taken care of as well. The pagination and sorting stuff? Taken care of. The appearance (or lack thereof) of GridLines? Done. It can all be set in your skin and then inherited in the control.

Don't misunderstand, though. Just because themes enhance what CSS can do for your site this in no way negates the importance of CSS. Themes do exactly that: enhance what CSS can do. CSS is a critical tool and should be used in conjunction with themes. It would be short-sighted to use one or the other and not both. These tools are meant to work together and you should do exactly that. Themes just take CSS to the next level.

Your First Theme!

Now that you have an understanding of the benefit of themes, it's time to create one. You will probably be surprised at how easy it is to do. So, to get started, create a new project just for playing around with themes. For this example, the project will be located in the `C:\Themes` directory. Feel free to substitute your own directory; just understand that this is what will be used for the remainder of this example.

With your project open, right-click on the solution, select Add ASP.NET Folder, and choose Theme, as shown in Figure 8-1.

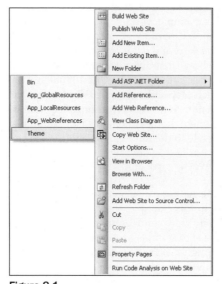

Figure 8-1

Once you do so, you will see a new folder in your Solution Explorer called `App_Themes` and, within that folder, another folder that has a temporary name of `Theme1`, as shown in Figure 8-2.

Figure 8-2

As you can see, the name of this folder is set up so that you can name it whatever you want. In this case, type in the box **myFirstTheme** and press the Enter key.

Be careful of using protected words like "Default" when you are naming your theme. It is possible that using these names will cause you problems when, later, you start trying to set your themes programmatically.

You have now created your first theme entitled myFirstTheme.

Doesn't sound possible? Go into `Default.aspx`, click in an open area of the `@Page` directive, and add a `Theme` property. As soon as you type in the equal sign, you will get a drop-down of available themes for your project, as shown in Figure 8-3.

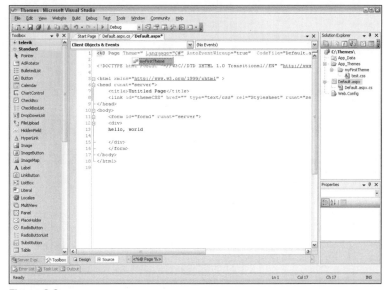

Figure 8-3

Go ahead and select myFirstTheme as your theme. You have now just applied your first theme to a project. Granted, your theme doesn't do anything right now. But, the fact of the matter is, you have created an ASP.NET Theme and applied it to a page. Everything else is just details.

Okay, Time for the Details . . .

Obviously, having a theme that doesn't actually do anything is not helpful in the least. So, in order to make the theme actually do something, you need to add files to the appropriate theme folder. This just means that if you want a file to be added to the myFirstTheme theme, you must add it to that subdirectory under the `App_Themes` directory of your project. The typical files that you would probably include in a theme would include the following:

❑   CSS File

❑   Skin File

❑   Images

Realistically, this is not the extent of the files available for you to include in your theme. If you look at Figure 8-4, you will see the file types that Microsoft believes most suited for themes (you can see these same options by right-clicking on the `Theme` directory and selecting Add New Item. . .).

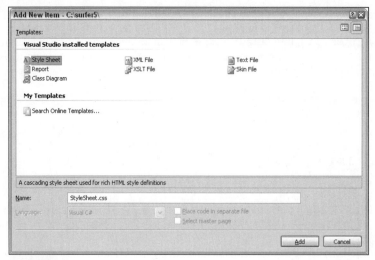

Figure 8-4

As you can see, you have the additional default options of Report, Class Diagram, XML file, XSLT file, and Text File. And, again, these are just the defaults. You can add pretty much any files to this directory as you see the need to include. This is, after all, just a subdirectory of your project. Granted, it is a special type of subdirectory, but it is still a subdirectory.

However, as stated previously, the three main components most developers will use are CSS, skins, and images. Therefore, this chapter is divided among these topics to help you better understand each in more detail.

CSS in Themes

For the first part of this chapter, you will be using CSS. Hopefully, you are already familiar with CSS concepts; for a refresher refer to Chapter 4.

The first thing you need to know about incorporating CSS documents into your theme is that themes handle CSS in a way that is not necessarily intuitive. As you will see, there are some unique behaviors in the way themes apply included CSS documents that limits the power of these CSS documents. You need to take into account this behavior when you start adding CSS documents to your theme. This unique behavior has spawned a lot of disdain for using CSS in themes. In fact, just because of the way themes handle CSS, many developers choose not to use themes at all in the projects they develop. So, as a precursor to a discussion of how to use CSS in themes, it is probably necessary to understand some of this unique behavior. Don't worry, though, as the discussion of CSS in themes continues, you will see a way to work around this behavior, but it is still important to understand it before you get started.

Problem: The Way Themes Apply Included Stylesheets

There are some very real issues when using CSS in themes that will force you to think of different ways of getting around them. Again, this chapter will illustrate one way to get around them, but you can find others just by searching the web.

All of these issues revolve around the fact that you have no control over the way the CSS files are applied to your project. When you add CSS files into your Theme folder, all files are applied to your project in a systematic order (the root is parsed in alphabetical order and then the same is done for each subdirectory in alphabetical order). You don't get to specify which files are applied in which order, and you don't get to specify conditions that apply to some rather than others; they all just get applied in, essentially, alphabetic order. This creates a couple of obstacles:

❑ You are taking the Cascading out of CSS. The first word in CSS is Cascading (Cascading Style Sheets, if you'll remember). The reason they are called cascading is that they are meant to build on top of each other. For example, you might have a main CSS page that has a lot of rules for color and layout and then, perhaps, a set of rules for overrides that you only apply for Internet Explorer browsers. With themed CSS files, this is no longer possible; all of the CSS files in your theme are applied.

❑ You can no longer use Microsoft's Conditional Comments. This point is related to the above, but it deserves its own bullet. In Chapter 5, when you were learning about the CSS Friendly Control Adapters, you saw examples of these conditional comments. For example, you inserted "`<!--[if lt IE 7]>`" to include certain CSS files for Internet Explorer browsers earlier than version 7.0. This insertion allowed you the control to apply CSS files for particular browsers and versions only. Again, since you now can't control which files get applied, this functionality is no longer available if you've put the CSS files in your Theme folder.

❑ You lose control over media types. One of the more ingenious features of CSS files is that you can specify a media type (e.g., print, screen, handheld, braille) that controls the medium that is applicable to a particular CSS file. For example, you might have one CSS file that you would think of as your main CSS rules for the site. However, that probably means that it controls the CSS for the screen version (what a typical viewer will see when visiting your site). In this case, you can set the media type to "screen" so that it is only affects monitor viewing of your page. You might, then, set up a new series of rules for the printable version of your site and, as such, set the media type to "print." This way you have a distinct set of rules for the screen version and an entirely different set of rules for the print version. This is not possible with themes. Again, every CSS is applied. If you have a screen CSS file and a print CSS file in your theme, both will be applied in alphabetical order. You have no control over whether or not a file is applied and, thus, you have no control over what is applied for each media type. Well, you can use media type rules in your CSS file itself (e.g., "`@media print`"), but you can't apply whole files based on a particular media type.

These limitations are very important when you are considering using CSS as part of your theme. However, there are ways to get around them once you come to terms with what the problems are. You will see one such solution in the section entitled "One Solution" in this chapter. But, for now, its enough just to understand what the limitations are so that you can understand the workaround presented in this chapter.

Adding a CSS File to Your Theme

To get started, add a stylesheet called "test.css" to your theme and give it the following formatting:

```
body
{
    background-color: steelblue;
    color: Silver;
    font-size: xx-large;
}
```

Go back into `Default.aspx` and add some dummy text (e.g., "hello, world"). Now run your project and your page should look similar to Figure 8-5.

Figure 8-5

It may be interesting for you to see what code was generated by the .NET 2.0 engine. While in your browser, view the source of the page. It should look similar to this:

```
<!DOCTYPE html PUBLIC "-//W3C//DTD XHTML 1.0 Transitional//EN"
    "http://www.w3.org/TR/xhtml1/DTD/xhtml1-transitional.dtd">

<html xmlns="http://www.w3.org/1999/xhtml" >
<head><title>
    Untitled Page
</title><link href="App_Themes/myFirstTheme/test.css" type="text/css"
    rel="stylesheet" /></head>
<body>
    <form name="form1" method="post" action="Default.aspx" id="form1">
<div>
<input type="hidden" name="__VIEWSTATE" id="__VIEWSTATE"
    value="/wEPDwUJNzgzNDMwNTMzZGQWnrxOLLuhzvowLtiG0obZpuix0A==" />
</div>

    <div>
    hello, world

    </div>
    </form>
</body>
</html>
```

Most of the code will look pretty much as you expected. But look at what was inserted between the closing title and head tags:

```
<link href="App_Themes/myFirstTheme/test.css" type="text/css" rel="stylesheet" />
```

As you can see, there is now a physical reference to the stylesheet you just created. The directory structure to the file has even been filled in for you (`App_Themes/myFirstTheme`). You didn't have to think about it; it was just done for you. This means that all you have to do is create a theme, add a CSS (or whatever) to that theme, set the page theme to your theme, and you are done. There was no need for you to spend the time coding some sort of logic to determine the appropriate path to the CSS file you want based on what theme was applied. No need to set any kind of property, other than the theme, to say that you want to have this CSS applied. It is all done for you. Every CSS file in your theme will be applied to any page that uses the theme without your having to do anything.

Is This a Good Thing?

Like most things ... it depends. For example, you may have no reason to want to have any kind of dynamically set CSS rules. In other words, you may want to apply the same CSS rules (for a given theme) to every person that accesses the site without qualification. If, for example, you work on a corporate intranet and the network policies only allow employees to run IE7 to access the site, you will probably only have one set of CSS rules for your sites. There would be no need, then, to have caveats for mobile devices or for other browsers; the rules that apply to IE7 would be the only ones you needed. In this case, you would not care if all of the CSS documents for your site were applied through a theme because you would apply them to every browser hit to your site anyway.

But what if that isn't true? A really good example would be if you want to keep a truly liquid CSS layout to your page, complete with a footer that sticks to the bottom of your page or the bottom of the content, whichever is more appropriate. If you have tried to tackle this with CSS, you know there is no reliable way of doing this without having different rules set up for different browsers. IE7 doesn't handle the floating commands necessary to pull this off the same way that Firefox does. And, maybe even more frustratingly, IE7 doesn't handle this scenario the same way IE6 does. So, if you want to have this type of layout, you will need to have a way of telling your project which CSS rules to apply depending on whatever criteria you specify.

So how do you do this? Well, out of the box, you don't. That is to say, if you want to apply some rules for some browsers based on some sort of browser detection in your theme, there isn't a way to do this. But that's just it; that example is assuming the use of CSS files or, more specifically, files with a CSS file extension. There is nothing to say that you can't break this rule by not using CSS pages ... exactly.

One Solution

A way to get around the issues involved in the way that themes apply CSS documents to your pages is to create an ASPX page that has a content type set to `"text/css"` that gets applied to your themed page. This solution enables you to integrate the power of managed code (.NET) with the power of CSS. In doing this, you can then manipulate the CSS properties based on determinations you make with integrated .NET code.

To see how to do this, first add a new ASPX page to your project (not your theme; there's no easy way to just add an ASPX page to your Theme folder) called "style.aspx" and specify that you don't want the code kept in a separate file (this is optional but will make it easier to manipulate if you keep everything in one page for this particular use). Go ahead and strip out all of the HTML content of the page and add code to the file to make it resemble the following:

```
<%@ Page ContentType="text/css" Language="C#" %>

<script runat="server">

    protected string browser = "";

    protected void Page_Load(object sender, EventArgs e)
    {
        browser = Page.Request.Browser.Browser;
    }

</script>

body
{
    font-size: xx-large;
<% if (browser == "IE") {%>
    background-color: black;
    color: white;
<%} else {%>
    background-color: steelblue;
    color:silver;
<%}%>
}
```

You should take note of a few things in this code. The first thing is that you set the `ContentType` property of your `@Page` directive to `"text/css"`. This means that the rendered output of this page will be handled as CSS by your browser.

The next thing to see is that you have created a protected string variable called `browser` that you are setting at the `Page_Load` event. In this example, you aren't drilling down to the browser version, but you could do that fairly easily (`Page.Request.Browser.MajorVersion` would return the major version, "7" for IE7, of your browser). Right now, though, it is fine just to know that this is an IE browser as opposed to any other kind.

The last thing to notice is that you have set up CSS rules for the body element of the page referencing your new ASPX CSS page. In that code, you have the font size set equally for all browsers. However, you change the background color and font color of the page based on whether or not the browser is IE (it will be a black page with white font for IE and a steel blue page with silver font for all other browsers).

Now it's time to test out your code. For now, you want to disable the theme reference and then add a reference to the new page. The code of `Default.aspx` should end up looking like this:

```
<%@ Page Language="C#" AutoEventWireup="true"
    CodeFile="Default.aspx.cs" Inherits="_Default" %>

<!DOCTYPE html PUBLIC "-//W3C//DTD XHTML 1.0 Transitional//EN"
    "http://www.w3.org/TR/xhtml1/DTD/xhtml1-transitional.dtd">
```

```
<html xmlns="http://www.w3.org/1999/xhtml" >
<head runat="server">
    <title>Untitled Page</title>
    <link href="style.aspx" type="text/css" rel="Stylesheet" />
</head>
<body>
    <form id="form1" runat="server">
    <div>
    hello, world

    </div>
    </form>
</body>
</html>
```

You are disabling the theme reference in this section so that you do not override the behavior of style.aspx *with the stylesheet you have added for* myFirstTheme. *Later in this chapter, you will see the hierarchy of how CSS documents get applied when linked from your document or Master Page and then also come to the same page from your theme. However, at this point, it is enough to know that, if you included the theme in your* @Page *directive, the properties of the CSS document from* myFirstTheme *would override the properties of* style.aspx.

Again, you have no theme set up for this page but you now have a reference to the newly created style.aspx page that has browser-based CSS rules in it. If you run the page in IE7, you will see a page similar to Figure 8-6.

Figure 8-6

However, if you load the same page in Mozilla Firefox, you will see something similar to Figure 8-7.

As you can see, IE is black and white and Firefox is blue and silver (okay, this probably won't be as evident in the black and white context of the book, but hopefully you can notice a shading difference).

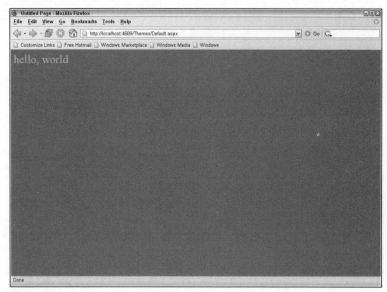

Figure 8-7

What is interesting is that you have, in essence, just conquered one of the most challenging CSS obstacles: CSS constants.

In the world of CSS, there are a lot of times that you want to insert variables into your CSS file so that you can, if necessary, change one or two color variables, for example, and have those colors carried throughout your CSS file (maybe you want to change the color scheme of your page). Many CSS developers would agree that code similar to the following would be nice:

```
$mainColor = SteelBlue;
$secondaryColor = Silver;

body
{
    background-color: $mainColor;
    color: $secondaryColor;
}
```

Obviously, in this particular example, there wouldn't be much benefit to having the variables. However, in a much larger CSS file with many different references to the main colors of your color scheme, having something like this would be invaluable. However, there is no way to really do this within the confines of CSS. If you search for something like "CSS variable" or "CSS Constant," you will get millions of returned records. This is a common problem that developers using CSS face. And, without something like .NET manipulating the CSS, constants just aren't really doable with CSS alone.

So, while this example will continue to grow and get away from the idea of constants, it's probably a good idea to keep this tidbit of information stored somewhere because, whether or not you use themes, if you use CSS, you will want to know this.

Adding Back the Theme

Using the example you have coded so far provides you with a good way of applying browser (or other criteria) based rules to your CSS file. So if, for example, you have a set of layout rules you want applied to all projects that just have the position and dimensions for the different regions or elements of your page, this is a good way to do it.

What if, however, you have some style rules set up in `style.aspx` and some different rules set up in your theme? Who wins if there is a conflict? Well, again … it depends. In this situation, it depends on how you apply your theme.

First, to illustrate the default, add back the `Theme` property to your `@Page` directive, and set it to `"myFirstTheme"` as before. Without making any other changes, run your project again and look at the output in IE7. Unfortunately (perhaps), it will probably look like Figure 8-8.

Figure 8-8

So what happened? Why are you now seeing the steel blue background again? The answer can be seen if you view the source of the page from the browser:

```
<!DOCTYPE html PUBLIC "-//W3C//DTD XHTML 1.0 Transitional//EN"
    "http://www.w3.org/TR/xhtml1/DTD/xhtml1-transitional.dtd">

<html xmlns="http://www.w3.org/1999/xhtml" >
<head><title>
    Untitled Page
</title><link href="style.aspx" type="text/css" rel="Stylesheet" />
<link href="App_Themes/myFirstTheme/test.css" type="text/css"
    rel="stylesheet" /></head>
```

```
<body>
    <form name="form1" method="post" action="Default.aspx" id="form1">
<div>
<input type="hidden" name="__VIEWSTATE" id="__VIEWSTATE"
    value="/wEPDwULLTE0MDkxNzYwNDNkZPoRs+E6QsVq0JGJDvHOD49xfpUz" />
</div>

    <div>
    hello, world

    </div>
    </form>
</body>
</html>
```

If you look at the CSS declarations in the head section of your HTML code, you will see the problem: the theme CSS gets applied after the regularly declared version. CSS rules are applied in the order in which they are declared. So, if you declare a rule in the first called CSS file, it will be overwritten by a conflicting CSS rule in a later declared reference. So, what is happening is that the `style.aspx` CSS rules are being applied first but then being overridden by the `test.css` file in the `Theme` directory.

The CSS Files Rendering Order

Can you fix this? Sure. Again, the problem is in the order the CSS files are being pulled into the project. Calling CSS into your project last is the behavior of themes. Looking for that pesky keyword again, it's `"Themes"`. So, maybe the technical answer to the question of "Can I fix my theme to put the theme CSS file first?" is "No." However, you can use a slightly lesser known way of applying themes: `StyleSheetTheme`.

With a `StyleSheetTheme` reference, you get all of the same power of the theme, it just applies the CSS files in a different order: they go first. This makes the load order of `StyleSheetThemes` and `Themes` follow this basic structure:

❑   `StyleSheetTheme` properties are applied first.

❑   `Control` properties in the page are applied next, overriding `StyleSheetTheme` properties.

❑   `Theme` properties are applied last, overriding control properties and `StyleSheetTheme` properties.

To see this in action, take the `Theme` reference out of your `@Page` directive and add a `StyleSheetTheme` property and set it to your theme, `"myFirstTheme"` and rerun your project. Now, in IE7, your page should look like Figure 8-9.

Now look at the rendered code (view source in your browser):

```
<!DOCTYPE html PUBLIC "-//W3C//DTD XHTML 1.0 Transitional//EN"
    "http://www.w3.org/TR/xhtml1/DTD/xhtml1-transitional.dtd">

<html xmlns="http://www.w3.org/1999/xhtml" >
<head><link href="App_Themes/myFirstTheme/test.css"
    type="text/css" rel="stylesheet" /><title>
    Untitled Page
```

```
</title><link href="style.aspx" type="text/css" rel="Stylesheet" /></head>
<body>
    <form name="form1" method="post" action="Default.aspx" id="form1">
<div>
<input type="hidden" name="__VIEWSTATE" id="__VIEWSTATE"
    value="/wEPDwULLTE0MDkxNzYwNDNkZPoRs+E6QsVq0JGJDvHOD49xfpUz" />
</div>

    <div>
    hello, world

    </div>
    </form>
</body>
</html>
```

Figure 8-9

The theme CSS file is now being applied in between the opening head and title tags, which occurs before the CSS reference you have set up for `style.aspx`. Since the theme CSS gets applied first, its rules are overwritten by the rules in `style.aspx`. This gives you control over which CSS file is applied first or, at least, gives your more control.

> *If you put references in for both* Theme *and* StyleSheetTheme, *it will look like it is only applying the* Theme *parameter. What is actually happening, though, is that it is applying them both. It adds a reference to the CSS before the* Title *tag for the* StyleSheetTheme *and then another one just before the end of the head tag for the* Theme. *So, if you have a referenced CSS file in your code, the HTML will process the StyleSheetTheme CSS, then overwrite that with your referenced CSS page, and then overwrite that with the Theme CSS (which will be the same as the StyleSheetTheme one — it is the same file referenced twice).*

Incorporating style.aspx in Themes

Can you put `style.aspx` in your theme? Yes and No. You can certainly put it in there. You can realistically put anything in there. Will the .NET engine be smart enough to treat the file as a CSS file?

287

Well ... no. You won't get any compilation errors and everything will appear to work; the rules in `style.aspx` just won't be applied. To see this in action, simply drag `style.aspx` into your `Theme` directory, as shown in Figure 8-10.

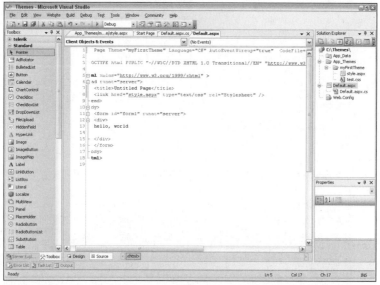

Figure 8-10

You will also notice that, by doing this, you introduced a red squiggly line in your hard-coded reference to `style.aspx`. This is because you no longer have the file sitting in the location it expects: the root. For now, don't worry about that and just launch the application. You should see the same blue page that you saw earlier, and if you view the source of the page in your browser, you will notice that no reference to `style.aspx` has been added. So what you would probably try next is to hard-code the reference to the file directly. For now, pretend that you won't have multiple themes and, therefore, have no need to qualify the link reference in `Default.aspx` to accommodate for different themes. With that assumption, modify your link reference to the following for now:

```
<link href="App_Themes/myFirstTheme/style.aspx" type="text/css" rel="Stylesheet" />
```

Now this should work, right? In theory, if you run the application, the CSS rules in `style.aspx` should now get applied to the page. After all, the only thing you have changed is the location of the file, consequently, the link reference so that it points to the new location. So, run the application again and see what happens.

You will notice that the page is still the steel blue and silver color scheme; no black and white as you had hoped. So maybe it is a conflict in rules between the two sets of CSS rules? To test this theory out, drag `test.css` back to the root of your application. This won't cause any conflicts, since there are no hard-coded references to this file; it is only referenced at runtime through the application of the theme to the page. Now run the application again. You should see the image in Figure 8-11.

Now there is no CSS getting applied to the page. So what is really going on? To see, navigate to the location of the `style.aspx` page in your browser (something like `http://localhost:4689/Themes/App_Themes/myFirstTheme/style.aspx` with a different port number, most likely). If you do this, you will see the image in Figure 8-12.

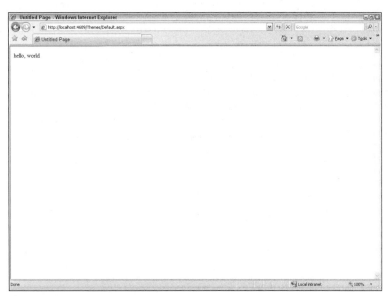

Figure 8-11

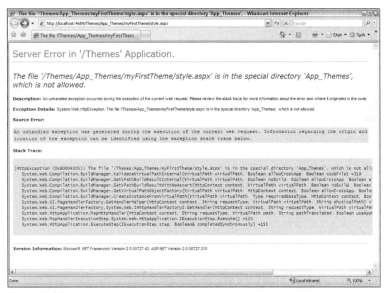

Figure 8-12

Herein lies the problem: ASPX pages in the `App_Themes` directory will not render. This is because `App_Themes` is an ASP.NET special directory and, as such, accessing its files from a web browser is forbidden. Well, that may be a bit misleading. In the other special directories, such as `App_Code`, you can't view any of the contents of any file directly from the browser. With `App_Themes`, however, you can view some files directly (such as images, text files, or CSS files). But even with that expanded functionality, you are forbidden to view ASPX files in the `App_Themes` directory directly from a web browser.

So what does this mean? Well, basically, it means that you can't have an ASPX page act as your CSS page and have it automatically applied from the theme special directory.

So, relative to this discussion, what it the point of `style.aspx`? You can't use it from a `Theme` subdirectory; so this means that `style.aspx` will be unaware of your current theme, right? Well, no, not exactly. You just have to think around the problem. What do you know at this time? You know that you can't put `style.aspx` in your Themes folder; that definitely isn't an option (well, you physically can put it there, it just won't work). You know that you can use `style.aspx` in a nonspecial folder (or at the root) and set conditions in it to apply different CSS rules based on whether the conditions were met. Previously, you used that to determine the browser. But what if you want to determine the theme? Is that possible?

The short answer is, without tweaking the page, you can't really tell the theme of the project. What does this mean? Well, remember, the pseudo-CSS page you have created is, in fact, still an ASPX page. At this point, you have only set the `Theme` at the `@Page` directive of `Default.aspx` (you will learn different ways to apply themes in the next chapter). The theme is only set for that page. So, when `Default.aspx` loads, it brings in the theme information. However, `style.aspx` is not inheriting `Default.aspx`, so, when it loads, it has no idea what the theme is. As written, there is no way to determine the theme applied to the page using `style.aspx`. So, you need to find a way to communicate the theme from `Default.aspx` to `style.aspx`.

Option 1: The Querystring Approach

Maybe the easiest way to pass along the current theme name from the host page to the linked `style.aspx` CSS document is to build a querystring reference to `style.aspx`. What does that mean? Well, in your link reference to `style.aspx`, rather than just linking directly to `"style.aspx"`, link to something like `"style.aspx?theme = myFirstTheme"`. If you do that, you can easily parse the querystring in `style.aspx` to determine the theme and make CSS rule changes directly.

To test this out, you need to make a couple of changes to your pages. First, in `Default.aspx`, you need to update your link reference to get ready to receive the updated querystring reference, as follows:

```
<link id="themedCSS" href="" type="text/css" rel="Stylesheet" runat="server" />
```

You will notice that you have set up an ID field for your link reference, set the `href` to an empty property (this is optional, you could leave it off all together or set it to some existing file), and added a `runat` server property. This link is now ready to be updated by your .NET code. So, in your code-behind, add code to make it resemble the following:

```
using System;
using System.Data;
using System.Configuration;
using System.Web;
using System.Web.Security;
using System.Web.UI;
using System.Web.UI.WebControls;
using System.Web.UI.WebControls.WebParts;
using System.Web.UI.HtmlControls;
```

```
public partial class _Default : System.Web.UI.Page
{


    protected void Page_Load(object sender, EventArgs e)
    {
        themedCSS.Href = "style.aspx?theme=" + Page.Theme;
    }
}
```

This is assuming that you are using a Theme rather than a StyleSheetTheme. If, instead, you are using a StyleSheetTheme, change the line of code setting the querystring to the following:

```
themedCSS.Href = "style.aspx?theme=" + StyleSheetTheme;
```

Now run the application and view the source of the page from the browser. The rendered code, regardless of which approach you used (Theme or StyleSheetTheme) should read like this:

```
<link id="themedCSS" type="text/css" rel="Stylesheet"
    href="style.aspx?theme=myFirstTheme" />
```

As you can see, your link reference now has a querystring parameter of "theme", which is set to the name of your current theme. As the page has a different theme applied, this will automatically update itself.

Now you need to update style.aspx to tell it how to handle the querystring change. In order to do this, modify the code to look more like this:

```
<%@ Page ContentType="text/css" Language="C#" %>

<script runat="server">

    protected string browser = "";
    protected string myTheme = "";

    protected void Page_Load(object sender, EventArgs e)
    {
        browser = Page.Request.Browser.Browser;
        if (Request.QueryString["theme"] != null) { myTheme
        = Request.QueryString["theme"].ToString(); } else { myTheme = ""; }
    }

</script>

body
{
    font-size: xx-large;
<% if (myTheme == "myFirstTheme") { %>
    <% if (browser == "IE") {%>
```

```
      background-color: black;
      color: white;
      <%} else {%>
      background-color: steelblue;
      color:silver;
      <%}%>
  <%} else { %>
      background-color: white;
      color: black;
  <%}%>
  }
```

With these changes, you have added a new protected string variable, "myTheme". At the Page_Load event, you are setting that value based on what is coming in through the querystring parameter "theme". Then, within the CSS rules, you are putting all of the code you had before in a block that is only applied if the theme is set to "myFirstTheme"; all other requests will just get a white page with black text.

Now run the application with your Theme or StyleSheetTheme set to "myFirstTheme", and it should resemble Figure 8-13 in IE7 and Figure 8-14 in Mozilla Firefox. (Note, though, that if you use Theme rather than StyleSheetTheme and you still have test.css in your theme, the hierarchy governing of how CSS is applied will cause test.css to overwrite the CSS rules in style.aspx, which will result in the steel blue and silver color scheme rather than the black and white one illustrated in Figure 8-13.)

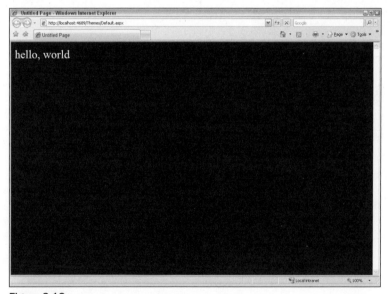

Figure 8-13

Now, remove the reference to your Theme or StyleSheetTheme in Default.aspx and run the application again. This time, your browser experience should resemble Figure 8-15 (IE7) or Figure 8-16 (Firefox).

You can see that, using this approach, you have set up a first criterion to break up the CSS rules based on whether a theme is set, and if a theme is set, you have set up additional criteria to handle IE7 browsers and all other browsers. Again, this is all done by the passing of querystring parameters to style.aspx from the page that references it as a linked stylesheet.

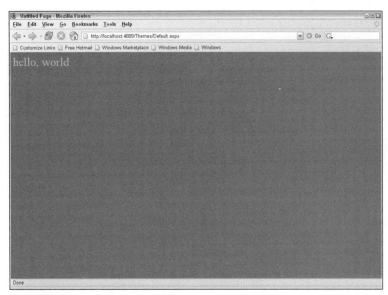

Figure 8-14

Figure 8-15

Option 2: Page Inheritance

Another option for passing the theme name to `style.aspx` is to incorporate a base class to pass the theme name to all pages that inherit it and then inherit that base class in `style.aspx`. This approach is a bit out of order in the grand scheme of the book, since setting your theme in a base class is discussed in the next chapter. However, talking about using the inheritance model for setting the theme in your page is more appropriate in this chapter. This shouldn't be totally foreign to you, since you so how to set your Master

Page through an inherited base class in Chapter 7. To illustrate how this works, this example will assume that you are setting your `StyleSheetTheme` for `Default.aspx` in an inherited base class, which is called `"PageBase.cs"`.

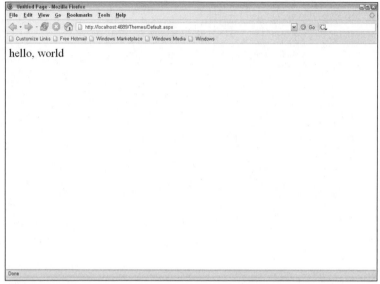

Figure 8-16

The first step to setting this up is to add a new class file to the `App_Code` directory called `PageBase.cs` that looks similar to the following:

```csharp
using System;
using System.Data;
using System.Configuration;
using System.Web;
using System.Web.Security;
using System.Web.UI;
using System.Web.UI.WebControls;
using System.Web.UI.WebControls.WebParts;
using System.Web.UI.HtmlControls;

/// <summary>
/// Summary description for PageBase
/// </summary>
public class PageBase : Page
{
    public override string StyleSheetTheme
    {
        get
        {
            return "myFirstTheme";
        }
        set
        {
            base.StyleSheetTheme = value;
        }
    }
}
```

As you can see, you are overriding the `StyleSheetTheme` property of the page and setting it to `"myFirstTheme"`. You will also want to go ahead and set `Default.aspx` to inherit from this base class by changing the `_Default` partial class to inherit from the new `PageBase` base class, as follows:

```
public partial class _Default : PageBase
```

Now, in `style.aspx`, you will need to make a similar adjustment so that your page will inherit from the same base class, `PageBase`, by modifying the `@Page` directive to include the `Inherits` property, as follows:

```
<%@ Page ContentType="text/css" Language="C#" Inherits="PageBase" %>
```

If you have modified your code to incorporate the querystring approach (Option 1), you will also need to tweak the code that is setting the value for `"myTheme"` to change it from looking for a `querystring` parameter to directly using the `StyleSheetTheme` property. Your version of `style.aspx` should now look like this:

```
<%@ Page ContentType="text/css" Language="C#" Inherits="PageBase" %>

<script runat="server">

    protected string browser = "";
    protected string myTheme = "";

    protected void Page_Load(object sender, EventArgs e)
    {
        browser = Page.Request.Browser.Browser;
        myTheme = StyleSheetTheme;
    }

</script>

body
{
    font-size: xx-large;
<% if (myTheme == "myFirstTheme") { %>
    <% if (browser == "IE") {%>
    background-color: black;
    color: white;
    <%} else {%>
    background-color: steelblue;
    color:silver;
    <%}%>
<%} else { %>
    background-color: white;
    color: black;
<%}%>
}
```

Now try loading `Default.aspx`. Assuming that you put `test.css` back in your theme, you should see something like Figure 8-17 if you're browsing in IE7.

Figure 8-17

It's not necessary to look at this page in any other browser because, if you remember the code, you can tell it isn't working. If viewed in IE7, the page should have a black background and white text. So something isn't working. To see what is going on, you can browse directly to `style.aspx` in your browser; the results of doing so can be seen in Figure 8-18.

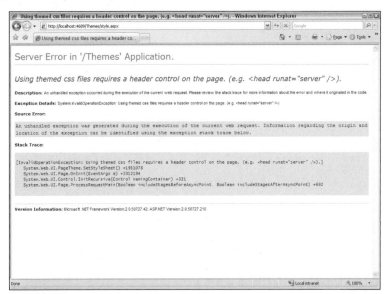

Figure 8-18

This is sort of a strange condition of using themed CSS files, which is what `style.aspx` is. In order for it to work, you have to have a head tag and set the `runat` property to server. You also have to be careful where you set it; it needs to be the last thing on the page or else it won't work. Well, `style.aspx` will technically work (you won't get any errors if you put the head tag earlier in the page); it just won't work as a CSS page in `Default.aspx`.

So, to remedy the solution, you should modify `style.aspx` to look more like the following:

```
<%@ Page ContentType="text/css" Language="C#" Inherits="PageBase" %>

<script runat="server">

    protected string browser = "";
    protected string myTheme = "";

    protected void Page_Load(object sender, EventArgs e)
    {
        browser = Page.Request.Browser.Browser;
        myTheme = StyleSheetTheme;
    }

</script>

body
{
    font-size: xx-large;
<% if (myTheme == "myFirstTheme") { %>
    <% if (browser == "IE") {%>
    background-color: black;
    color: white;
    <%} else {%>
    background-color: steelblue;
    color:silver;
    <%}%>
<%} else { %>
    background-color: white;
    color: black;
<%}%>
}
<html><head id="Head1" runat="server" /><body /></html>
```

As you can see, there is a head tag added as the last line of code in this sample. So that there weren't any squiggly lines, html and body tags were added as well. This really isn't necessary; it just keeps the code cleaner.

> *This example uses the StyleSheetTheme rather than the Theme. This is done to illustrate the final product. Remember, if you use the Theme, your page will load the hard-coded CSS first and then over-write any conflicting rules with the theme CSS. So, in this example, the theme CSS is loaded first as part of the StyleSheetTheme and then any conflicting CSS rules are overwritten with the hard-coded CSS file, style.aspx. The result can be seen in IE7 in Figure 8-19 (Firefox isn't shown in this example, but it works there, too).*

At this point, you have a stylesheet that is, in fact, an ASPX page that can automatically detect what Theme (or StyleSheetTheme) is applied to the pages in your site through a mutually inherited base class and modify the CSS rules accordingly. Further, it can detect what browser is being used and make additional modifications if necessary. This can be a very powerful tool in your web design efforts.

Figure 8-19

Other Options

Of course, these are not the only options available to you. For example, you could use any sort of method to share information between pages to share the theme information with style.aspx. For instance, maybe you want to save the Theme name in a session variable and then check the session variable in style.aspx. This might make the process easier than the querystring approach. There are certainly other ways of doing it as well. The two options provided just illustrate a couple of different approaches you can take when trying to add theme information to your ASPX CSS file.

Pros and Cons to style.aspx

With any "workaround" solution, there are bound to be pros and cons, and with the style.aspx solution, this is no different. There are plenty of reasons to use it, but there are as many reasons to consider not using it. This section will attempt to shine the light on both perspectives.

Pros

There are a multitude of reasons to use the style.aspx approach to address the problems with the ways themes apply CSS documents to your projects, some of which would include:

❑ **Theme specific** — Within this one pseudo-CSS file, you can have different rules for each theme in your project. This allows you a lot more flexibility than using standard CSS files.

❑ **Cascading control** — Since you are hard-coding the reference to style.aspx in the parent page (Master Page or other HTML or ASPX page), you gain back the control over the order in which the stylesheets are applied to your page; an ability lost when applying stylesheets trough themes. Remember, one of the major limitations of themes is that you cannot control the order in which CSS files are applied. It makes sense once you realize that you aren't actually calling the CSS files into your projects yourself; this is done automatically by the .NET engine. So, within that engine, there has to be logic on what order the files get pulled in. With that in mind, the engine brings in CSS files in alphabetical order by directory structure (first the root of the theme gets parsed and CSS files are applied in alphabetical order, then each subdirectory is parsed in alphabetical order and each CSS page in those directories is parsed in alphabetical order). With `style.aspx`, you are hard-coding the order in which the pages should be loaded, so you maintain control of the cascading component of CSS.

❑ **Media control** — With the hard-coded references for `style.aspx`, you gain back the ability to qualify the different styles for different media types. A shortcoming of the automatic inclusion of CSS files in themes is that you can't specify separate CSS files for different media. For example, it is common practice to use media types such as "print" or "screen" to determine what CSS file should be used by the printer or the monitor. With themes, you can't do that; all of the CSS files are applied without consideration for medium. However, since you are hard-coding `style.aspx` through the typical link reference in your page, you can still set the media type.

❑ **No either/or** — This just means that you can put styles that you don't need to tweak through .NET code in the theme and they will be applied for you. You can apply them whether they come first or last with designating `Themes` or `StyleSheetThemes`. Then you can use the logic of the `style.aspx` page to put .NET code into your CSS file to do the tweaking you need. A good mix might be to put things that would apply to everything, such as color, font size, and the like, in the theme and then put things that switch from browser to browser (or media type to media type) in referenced ASPX CSS files. This way, you get the best of both worlds.

❑ **Constants** — This advantage isn't really theme specific, but it is still worth mentioning. As stated earlier, many CSS developers can appreciate having the ability of including constants/variables in their CSS pages that allow them to update many lines of code by changing one flag at the top. With this approach, you can do exactly that. You can set up a string variable at the beginning of the file called something like `"MainColor"` and set it to some hexadecimal color. From there, you can reference `MainColor` throughout your CSS code, and it will automatically bring in your hexadecimal color code. This will keep you from having to type out (or copy and paste) the color reference tens or hundreds of times. And, furthermore, you won't have to find every instance of the reference in your CSS file in a year when you have decided to change the main color for your site. This alone makes approach worth considering, even outside the confines of themes.

❑ **Simplicity** — All of these limitations are well documented if you do much research on themes in ASP.NET 2.0. There are plenty of websites and blogs that discuss each of these limitations in depth. There are also several workarounds documented, some of which will be outlined in the next section of this chapter, that show how you might get CSS to work as you would hope within the limitations of themes. However, many of those approaches are much more technical than just adding an ASPX CSS page and controlling all of these limitations through .NET code. Use themes for CSS when it doesn't matter how it is applied; use the ASPX CSS file when it does. That's pretty simple.

Cons

Obviously, the `style.aspx` solution is not a panacea for themes issues. There are also some very real limitations, such as:

❑ **No design-time support** — Visual Studio doesn't think that this is a CSS file. This has several real limitations. For one, you don't have the availability of Add Style Rule and Build Style Wizards discussed in Chapter 4. You also won't see the affects of the CSS rules you have applied in the Design view of Visual Studio. Finally, probably most importantly, it also means, that you don't get IntelliSense when you are typing out your CSS rules. If you aren't comfortable with CSS, this last consequence alone could be a deal breaker. You have to know the code and Visual

Studio won't tell you if you make a mistake in your CSS rules or property names (e.g., it won't give any error if you try to set a property for the body element called "alwefkljwef"). This can be a bit scary. A way you can get around this is by designing your page in a real CSS file in Visual Studio to get all of the design-time support such as IntelliSense and the wizards. Once you have a set of rules you want to set in the page, you can copy them into the ASPX CSS file and apply .NET code to control the output at that point. This is a bit painful and may make this approach lose a lot of appeal for many developers. It is something that is definitely worth knowing before adopting this approach.

❑ **Defeats the purpose** — It won't be too long before someone reading this will say "well that defeats the whole purpose of themes." But does it? You are still using themes, and you will get into more of what you can do with themes in the next section of this chapter. Granted, you don't have the files sitting in the special `Theme` directory, but they are still affected (potentially) by whatever theme you are applying to the page; you still have theme criteria. This works with the theme; it just overcomes its CSS limitations.

❑ **Potentially messy** — You have to think about all of the code you may have in this ASPX CSS file. You will start off with your `@Page` directive, then get into your .NET code, then get into your CSS rules, which will be augmented with even more .NET code, and then finally have some HTML code at the bottom (if you are using the themed/inheritance approach). There is a lot of code in one file; much of it isn't even CSS. Maintaining the code could potentially be problematic.

❑ **Disassociated files** — This problem isn't really as big of a deal, but it is worth mentioning that you will have files in the root that change with the theme but aren't in the Theme folder. This might be a little too much separation for some developers. Again, this probably isn't that big of a deal, but it is a consequence of this approach.

It is considerably harder to come up with a good reason not to use the `style.aspx` approach for themes than it is to actually use them. The reasons to use this approach are pretty significant and will probably convince many people to at least try this approach. However, the first limitation (the design-time support) is a pretty big consequence. For CSS newbies, this might be too much to overcome. It will truly be up to each developer to decide how well this approach fits in with their needs and expertise level. It will also depend on how much of the project will be impacted by the limitations of CSS handling by ASP.NET 2.0 Themes.

Other Potential Solutions

While the `style.aspx` solution addresses many of the issues related to applying CSS documents through ASP.NET 2.0 Themes, it is not the only solution. This issue has been the topic of many blogs and articles on the web and will continue to be so until Microsoft offers a more permanent solution as part of the .NET Framework.

One example of a really great solution would be to override the behavior of themes by using a custom `VirtualPathProvider` to force the theme to ignore the CSS files found in the `App_Themes` folder. That way, you can put the links to the stylesheets directly in the Master Page and, in doing so, have control over their order and once again have access to media types.

Of course, this means that you are back to hard-coding external CSS references in your Master Page (or other ASPX page). This has its downsides as well. Mainly, you will need to make the link reference dynamic so that it points to the right CSS document for the current theme applied to the page. This may be something as simple as having a variable in the URL path that is reflective of the subdirectory that the theme resides in, which might look something like this:

```
<link href="App_Themes/<%=themeDirectory%>/style01.css"
    type="text/css" rel="Stylesheet" />
```

You can see that there is a variable, themeDirectory, that you can change on the Page_Load event to reflect the current theme. Of course, this assumes that the CSS documents were given the same name in each theme. If not, you would have to change pretty much the entire href property for each applied CSS document.

That isn't meant to negate the custom VirtualPathProvider solution; it is just meant to illustrate that there is no perfect remedy — only different ways of working around the same problem.

To read more about this approach, read "A Resolution to the Problems with Themes, Skins, and Cascading Style Sheets (CSS) — Putting the Cascades back into ASP.NET 2.0 Themes (taking control over CSS Cascades/Load Order, Media Types, and Overrides)" in the "Themes and Skins" category (http://adam.kahtava.com/journal/CategoryView,category,Themes%20and%20Skins.aspx) of Adam Kahtava's blog.

A Final Thought on CSS in Themes

One thing that you need to keep in mind when adding CSS files to your theme in the traditional approach is that any file path reference contained in the CSS is relative to the location of the CSS file. This is not a unique behavior of CSS in themes, but it is something people may not remember when actually getting into the meat of CSS in themes.

For example, assume that you have an image you plan to repeat as a tiling background image for your page. As in the previous example, you will want to add the background image to the theme, so it is only applicable to this particular theme. So, within the Theme folder, you should add a folder (Website ➪ New Folder) and call it images. Within that folder, add a new tiling background image, similar to Figure 8-20, which is called background.jpg.

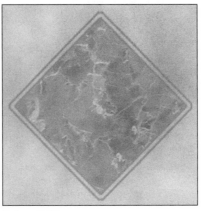

Figure 8-20

At this point, the directory structure of your application should resemble Figure 8-21.

Figure 8-21

Now, within `test.css`, modify your body element rules to include the following:

```
body
{
    background-color: steelblue;
    color: Silver;
    font-size: xx-large;
    background-image: url(Images/background.jpg);
}
```

Now run your application, and it should look like Figure 8-22, with the graphic in the Images folder tiled across the background of your page.

Figure 8-22

Unfortunately, if you move the background image to an Images folder on the root of your application, you can't use the "~" placeholder to indicate that you want to look starting at the root. For example, the following code will not work:

```
body
{
    background-color: steelblue;
    color: Silver;
    font-size: xx-large;
    background-image: url(~/Images/background.jpg);
}
```

If you need to get back to the root, you need to modify the code to look more like this:

```
body
{
    background-color: steelblue;
    color: Silver;
    font-size: xx-large;
    background-image: url(../../Images/background.jpg);
}
```

This may be intuitive to many developers if you are familiar with CSS but, if you are not and you develop your CSS file at the root and then move it into a Theme, you may wonder why it no longer works. Be sure when referencing file paths that you know what you are actually telling the application you want. The application will give you exactly what you ask for, even if it's not what you think you asked for. So just be careful.

The second example, which uses the page "../../Images/background.jpg" *is using a relative URL path, meaning that it is trying to link to a path that is relative to the current position. You could get around this by using an absolute URL path. For example, you could change the* background-image *property to something like* "http://localhost/Themes/Images/background.jpg" *and you wouldn't need to worry about the physical location where the CSS document making this reference resides (in other words, the CSS document can sit at the root of the application, in a Theme folder, or in any other subdirectory, and the reference would always work).*

Skins

After the relative complexity of CSS in themes, you will appreciate one of the more simple features of themes: Skins. Skins are one of the few new file types introduced with the new .NET 2.0 Framework and are only relevant to Themes (or StyleSheetThemes). Skins, as discussed earlier in this chapter, are the component of themes that set the default look and feel, as well as functionality, of the ASP.NET controls you use on your page.

So what does this mean? Well, as shown earlier in this chapter, this means that you can manage all of the properties and attributes of a control with a Skin file. Sure, this means that you can control some design features that are not exclusive to themes, such as height and width and borders, which can be done through CSS alone with a simple `CssClass` reference. But, beyond that, you can add attributes such as `AllowPaging`, `AllowSorting`, and `GridLines`. Even further than that, you can also set all the properties of the `Row` and `AlternatingRow` attributes as well. Whatever you can set in the control, you can template through your Skin file.

However, to get your feet wet with skins, it is probably best to start with something a bit simpler, such as a label control. Creating a label control will show you how the Skin file is created and how it interacts with the controls on your page.

Adding a Skin File

Adding a Skin file to your theme is fairly simple. Click on the Theme folder and then select Website from the toolbar and choose Add New Item... to get the Add New Item Wizard shown in Figure 8-23.

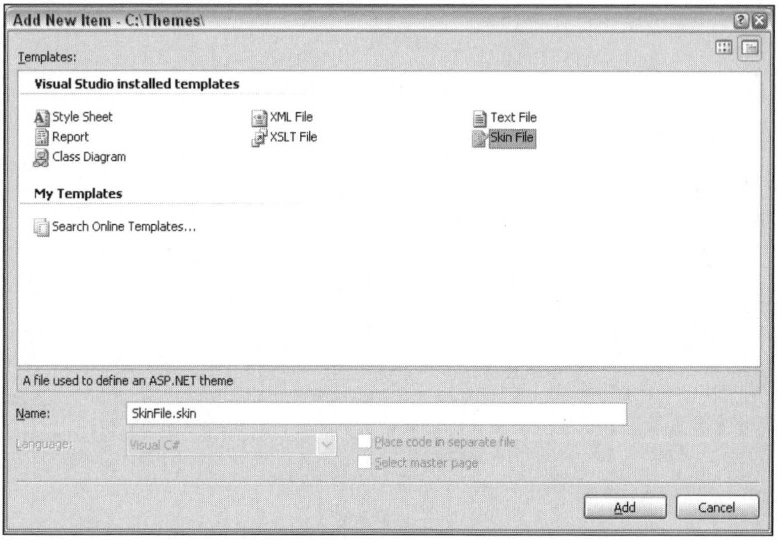

Figure 8-23

Select Skin File from the available templates and, for this example, leave the name "SkinFile.skin." The name, for future projects, is not that relevant. However, it is important that you leave the file extension as "skin" so that the .NET 2.0 engine recognizes it as a Skin file and treats it appropriately.

Once you have added your Skin file, it will look similar to the following:

```
<%--
Default skin template. The following skins are provided as examples only.

1. Named control skin. The SkinId should be uniquely defined because
   duplicate SkinId's per control type are not allowed in the same theme.

<asp:GridView runat="server" SkinId="gridviewSkin" BackColor="White" >
   <AlternatingRowStyle BackColor="Blue" />
</asp:GridView>
```

```
2. Default skin. The SkinId is not defined. Only one default
   control skin per control type is allowed in the same theme.

<asp:Image runat="server" ImageUrl="~/images/image1.jpg" />
--%>
```

These comments provide generic instructions on how to use the Skin file in your project. For this example, though, just erase all of these comments (or leave them in but understand that they won't be included in the rest of the examples in this chapter). To see how a Skin file works, in all its simplicity, add the following code in the skin:

```
<asp:Label
    BackColor="Wheat"
    ForeColor="Olive"
    Font-Size="XX-Large"
    Font-Names="Arial Black"
    runat="server"
/>
```

This code has set up several of the attributes of a label control. Most of them probably are intuitive and are ones that you are accustomed to setting in your projects. However, there are at least two rules that you need to make sure you follow when setting up these properties. The first of which is to make sure that you always include the `runat="server"` property. Failure to do so will result in a compilation error that complains about literal controls in your Skin file when you try to run the project. The second rule to remember is that you never include an ID attribute in the Skin file. This, too, will produce a compilation error stating that you cannot apply the ID property of a control type from the Skin file. This makes sense if you understand that all of the attributes you are setting will be applied to all applicable controls in your project and, thus, you can't rightly give them all the same ID. However, if you are just copying and pasting the control properties you set in an ASPX page into your skin file, it will have an ID property with it, and if you aren't prepared for it, this error will get you.

Now, to see how these settings work, go back into `Default.aspx` and change your code to the following:

```
<%@ Page StylesheetTheme="myFirstTheme" Language="C#" AutoEventWireup="true"
    CodeFile="Default.aspx.cs" Inherits="_Default" %>

<!DOCTYPE html PUBLIC "-//W3C//DTD XHTML 1.0 Transitional//EN"
    "http://www.w3.org/TR/xhtml1/DTD/xhtml1-transitional.dtd">

<html xmlns="http://www.w3.org/1999/xhtml" >
<head id="Head1" runat="server">
    <title>Untitled Page</title>
    <link id="themedCSS" href="style.aspx" type="text/css"
        rel="Stylesheet" runat="server" />
</head>
<body>
    <form id="form1" runat="server">
    <div>

        <asp:Label ID="Label1" runat="server" Text="hello, world" />
    </div>
    </form>
</body>
</html>
```

The only real difference is that you wrapped the text "hello, world" inside of an ASP.NET 2.0 Label control. Now run your application, and you should see that it looks like Figure 8-24.

Figure 8-24

As you can see, you didn't set any properties on the Label control itself; it just used the properties you set in the theme. At this point, there was no need to specify which settings to apply; it just applied the properties of the label settings in your Skin file. This is the basic functionality of skins in themes.

Selectively Applying Skin Attributes

One of the first things you might find yourself asking is "What if I have different formatting needs for a single control?" It's not realistic to expect that one set of formatting rules will apply to every instance of a control in your web application. For example, can you imagine the formatting in the previous example being applied to every Label control in your application? Maybe you want to have some default behavior for your labels but be able to distinguish other labels so that you can format them differently, much akin to the way classes of CSS elements are set up. This can be done by incorporating a SkinID for control and the settings into the Skin file.

To see this in place, first modify your Skin file to resemble the following:

```
<asp:Label
    BackColor="Wheat"
    ForeColor="Olive"
    Font-Size="XX-Large"
    Font-Names="Arial Black"
    runat="server"
/>

<asp:Label
    SkinID="SecondLabel"
```

```
            BackColor="Olive"
            ForeColor="Wheat"
            Font-Size="Medium"
            Font-Names="Arial"
            runat="server"
  />
```

As you can see, you did not do anything to your first settings. However, you did add another label control set of rules with the same properties being set to different values. The other significant difference in these two examples is that the second one uses the `SkinID` property.

Now, to see how this plays out in your project, add the following under the "hello, world" label example:

```
<asp:Label ID="Label2" runat="server" SkinID="SecondLabel">
This is the second line of text.  This is set through the second set of Skin
    control settings.
</asp:Label>
```

You will notice that this example looks very similar, at least in its properties, to the first label being set. However, the difference is that this label has the `SkinID` property set to `SecondLabel` (if you have the `Theme` or `StyleSheetTheme` set at the `@Page` directive, you will see this option in your IntelliSense options after typing in **"SkinID="** in the properties). Running this example will result in Figure 8-25.

Figure 8-25

So, in doing this, you have accomplished two things: first, you have set up the default behavior for all label controls using this theme and, second, you have set up an alternative behavior for controls that is triggered by the `SkinID` property of the control. Both of these are optional. If you don't have any default set of properties set up (all of your control settings in your Skin file have `SkinID`'s applied to them) and you put a Label control on your page without a `SkinID` property set, it won't incorporate any automatic formatting. Also, as seen earlier, you can merely have a default set of rules that will be applied to all label controls. Finally, you could have no settings for a particular control in your Skin files and, thus, no settings would be automatically applied to the properties of the control (this doesn't preclude the control from getting formatting from other sources, such as CSS; it just won't get any formatting from the Skin file).

Solving Conflicts

So what happens if you set properties up in your Skin file and then set conflicting properties in the control on the page? Who wins? Well, as with everything else it seems, it depends. In this case, it depends on whether you are using a Theme or a StyleSheetTheme.

First, to illustrate one scenario, change the properties of the first control to the following:

```
<asp:Label ID="Label1" runat="server" Text="hello, world"
    ForeColor="White" BackColor="Transparent" />
```

If you run this code exactly as written to this point in the chapter, you will get the results shown in Figure 8-26.

Figure 8-26

In this example, even with the limitations of the black-and-white images in the book, you should be able to tell that the background color for the first label went away and the font color changed to white instead of the considerably darker olive. So it would appear that the control on the page wins.

Well, not exactly. Or, maybe more accurately, it depends. There is one key factor that may not have been clear up to this point: you are using a StyleSheetTheme for this project at this time. Look at your @Page directive posted earlier in this section:

```
<%@ Page StylesheetTheme="myFirstTheme" Language="C#" AutoEventWireup="true"
    CodeFile="Default.aspx.cs" Inherits="_Default" %>
```

So, now change the @Page directive to use the Theme property rather than the StyleSheetTheme property, like this:

```
<%@ Page Theme="myFirstTheme" Language="C#" AutoEventWireup="true"
    CodeFile="Default.aspx.cs" Inherits="_Default" %>
```

Now rerun the project, and it should look like Figure 8-27.

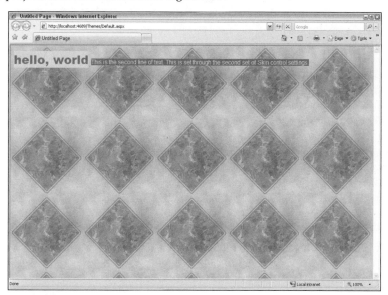

Figure 8-27

As you can see, the label has reverted back to the Skin settings, totally ignoring the properties set at the control in Default.aspx. Well, that isn't exactly accurate either. The control isn't totally ignoring its own settings; it is just allowing the settings in the skin to override the settings on the control itself. If, for example, you had additional properties set on the control that were not in conflict with the skin, they would still be displayed. For example, modify the first Label control to include all of the properties shown below:

```
<asp:Label ID="Label1" runat="server" Text="hello, world" ForeColor="White"
    BackColor="Transparent" BorderStyle="Solid" BorderWidth="5px" />
```

Now rerun the application, and it will look like Figure 8-28.

As you can see, the ForeColor and BackColor properties of the control are being overridden by the settings in the Skin file. The newly added properties, BorderStyle and BorderWidth, are being displayed as part of the control. There is no conflicting properties in the Skin file, so they display as set on the control. Again, this is only true if you are applying the theme settings through a Theme rather than a StyleSheetTheme; if you are using a StyleSheetTheme, the control properties will win out over the ones set in the Skin file.

Turning Off Theming

It is worth noting that you can, if you should so choose, turn off theming for the controls on your page. In fact, you can turn it off at the control level or even at the page level, both of which are done through the EnableTheming property.

Figure 8-28

To turn off theming for the first Label control in `Default.aspx`, modify its code to match the following:

```
<asp:Label ID="Label1" runat="server" Text="hello, world" ForeColor="White"
    BackColor="Transparent" BorderStyle="Solid" BorderWidth="5px"
    EnableTheming="False" />
```

Run your application again (keep the Theme setting in your @Page directive to show how this works), and you will see something more like Figure 8-29.

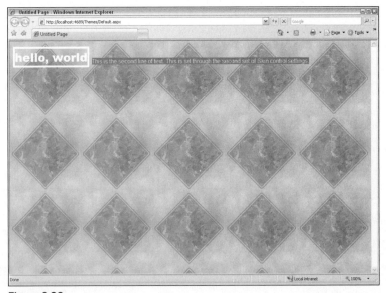

Figure 8-29

If you were running a `StyleSheetTheme`, this would be what you would see without disabling theming on the control. However, it is more interesting if you turn off theming for the entire page, which you can do through the @Page directive, as shown here:

```
<%@ Page Theme="myFirstTheme" EnableTheming="False" Language="C#"
   AutoEventWireup="true"  CodeFile="Default.aspx.cs" Inherits="_Default" %>
```

Now, this assumes that you are only setting the theme at the @Page directive and not in any of the methods shown in Chapter 9. So, assuming that is true, you should see the results illustrated in Figure 8-30.

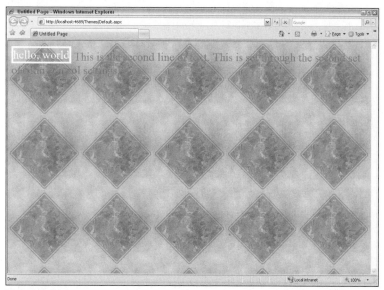

Figure 8-30

What is happening is that the theme is still applying the CSS rules from `test.css` in the theme subdirectory. However, it is not allowing theming to take place on any of the controls. The white border and font for the fist label is set on the control itself (as shown earlier in this section). The silver font and size for the second label are actually rules set up for the body element in the CSS file. None of the attributes from the Skin file are being applied to these controls.

You can, if you so choose, decide to override this behavior at the control level. If, for example, you wanted the second label to be themed, you can enable theming for that one control, as shown here:

```
<asp:Label ID="Label2" runat="server" SkinID="SecondLabel" EnableTheming="True">
   This is the second line of text.  This is set through the second set of
   Skin control settings.</asp:Label>
```

Now, if you run your application again, you will see the results shown in Figure 8-31.

As you can see, the second label once again has the styling of the theme applied to it. This illustrates that `EnableTheming` can be set at the page level or the control level and, if set for at the page level, it can be overridden by setting it at the control level. This gives you potentially more control over the way theming works in your projects.

311

Figure 8-31

Turning On IntelliSense

One of the more questionable decisions made when developing Visual Studio 2005 is the exclusion of IntelliSense from the development environment for Skin files. This has resulted in several different workarounds being developed, including the use of a scratch page (something like scratch.aspx) to build the properties up for the control with the help of IntelliSense and then copying the final control parameters directly into the Skin file. This can be a pain to do and can cause some issues with maintainability, so it would just be better if you had IntelliSense turned on in the first place. With that being said, here are the steps to turn on IntelliSense in your Skin File:

❑ While in Visual Studio 2005, click on Tools and select Options to get the screen shown in Figure 8-32.

❑ Expand the option Text Editor and then click on File Extension (as shown in Figure 8-32).

❑ In the Extension: field, type in **skin**. In the Editor field, select User Control Editor. Click the Add button. This should add a new entry in the listbox of extensions.

❑ Click the OK button to finalize the settings.

Once you have done this, you should have IntelliSense turned on for your Skin files, as you can see in Figure 8-33.

If you look closely at Figure 8-33, you will notice that a new blue squiggly line has been introduced to your Skin file. If you look at the error messages for this project, you will probably also see one similar to the following:

C:\Themes\App_Themes\myFirstTheme\SkinFile.skin: ASP.NET *runtime error: There is no build provider registered for the extension '.skin'. You can register one in the* <compilation> <buildProviders> *section in machine.config or web.config. Make sure is has a BuildProviderAppliesToAttribute attribute which includes the value 'Web' or 'All'.*

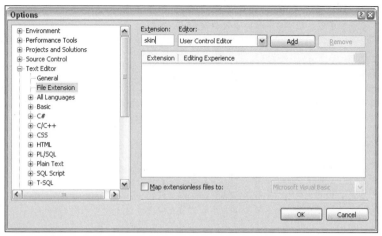

Figure 8-32

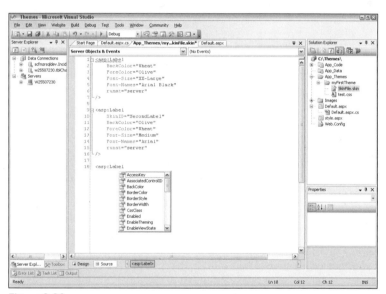

Figure 8-33

Even though it says there is a runtime error, the project will compile without error, and you will not see any runtime error when the project loads. However, if this bothers you, you can fix the problem by adding the following code to the web.config file for your project:

```
<compilation>
    <buildProviders>
        <add
            extension=".skin"
            type="System.Web.Compilation.PageBuildProvider"
        />
    </buildProviders>
</compilation>
```

Adding this code will remove the blue squiggly line in the Skin file and, maybe more importantly, remove the error message from your error listing in Visual Studio.

Final Thoughts on Skins

Even though this chapter only illustrated the Label control, other controls would be handled in exactly the same way. For example, if you wanted to have the properties of a GridView control to be set in a skin, you would just add code similar to the following to your Skin file:

```
<asp:GridView GridLines="None" AllowPaging="True" PageSize="10" AllowSorting="True"
    runat="server" BorderColor="DarkKhaki" BorderStyle="Solid" BorderWidth="2px">
    <HeaderStyle BackColor="DarkKhaki" ForeColor="Khaki" />
    <RowStyle BackColor="Olive" ForeColor="Wheat" />
    <AlternatingRowStyle BackColor="White" ForeColor="Olive" />
</asp:GridView>
```

Once you dropped a GridView control on your page, it would automatically take on all of these settings, including the pagination and sorting parameters, set here. Again, depending on whether or not your enable theming or the method you use to apply the theme (Theme or StyleSheetTheme), you may then be able to modify these properties in the control itself.

Also, note that skins are handled slightly differently than CSS in themes. Skin files must be contained in the root of the Theme subdirectory. This is different than CSS, which can be contained in any subdirectory of the theme. However, with Skin files, if you created a Skins subdirectory to contain all of your skin files, none of them would be applied because the .NET 2.0 engine doesn't go outside of the root to look for Skin files.

However, in the same fashion as CSS in themes, you can (and probably should) have multiple Skin files for a given theme. The way Skin files are used will vary from developer to developer and from project to project. However, it is not hard to imagine that you will want to have many definitions for a Label control for your project, differentiated by distinct SkinID properties. The same might be true for other controls, like the TextBox control. When it comes time to come back and change a single property of a label, it would be much easier to do so if you knew roughly where the controlling rules were set.

So, depending on your project size and the controls you want to manage through your Skin files, it might be a good idea to create a different Skin file for each type of control you want to set and then set all of the rules for each variation of the control you want in that file. For example, you might have a Skin file called something like labels.skin that would contain all of the different rules you have set up for the Label controls of your project. You might then have a different skin file called textboxes.skin that houses the rules for the textboxes in your project.

However, if you plan to manage a lot of controls, this approach may not be practical. Imagine the maintenance headache it might become to try to keep up with a different Skin file for every control available in the .NET Framework. This could be a lot more trouble than it is worth. In that case, you might want to have a default skin that has all of the default settings for all of your controls and maybe a few well-organized skins for any custom skins you may need.

As you continue with skin development, you will find your own best practices. And, most likely, this will shift somewhat from project to project.

Finally, it is worth pointing out one additional quirk of Themes and StyleSheetThemes in Visual Studio 2005. If you are setting your themes using StyleSheetTheme, you have design-time support in the Design view; if you are applying the themes using Theme, you do not. So, if you set all of your attributes in your skins and CSS for your theme and then apply that theme to your project using Theme, you will likely just see a white page with the basic settings for the control. If, however, you switch the setting on the @Page directive to setting the theme by using StyleSheetTheme, you will now see the affects of the theme on the controls on the page. You will not see the affects of the CSS from the theme, but at least you can see how the properties you have set for the control will render (as much as you can tell from the Design view at least — you won't really know until you launch the application and look at it in different browsers, but if you use the Design view for your projects, this is important to be aware of).

Images

There really isn't that much more to images than you have seen already in the previous discussion of CSS and skins in themes. As with those examples, you can have images that are a part of a particular theme that can be applied for that particular theme. Like CSS, these images can reside either in the root or in any subfolder off the root. However, unlike both CSS and skins, images are not automatically applied to anything; they have to be specifically referenced in some capacity. This section will show you some of the more common ways of using images in themes.

Referencing from CSS

As you have already seen, you can reference images from a CSS in your theme. Remember in the previous examples, you had test.css sitting in the root of your theme, myFirstTheme. Within that file, you had the following rules set up:

```
body
{
    background-color: steelblue;
    color: Silver;
    font-size: xx-large;
    background-image: url(Images/background.jpg);
}
```

Since the path of the URL in the background-image rule is relative, you would expect to find background.jpg in an Images subdirectory off the root of the theme, as shown in Figure 8-34.

Figure 8-34

As you have seen previously, this will create the tiled background shown in Figure 8-35.

Figure 8-35

You have seen this example earlier in this chapter, but it is worth reemphasizing, since it is probably one of the most common ways of using images in themes. This is not to say that the practice of setting a tiled background image is the most common use of images in themes. Rather, it is common practice to put images in themes that are used by the theme-specific CSS files. For example, if you had a header region designated in your CSS, as is true with the book project (a little foreshadowing here?), then you might include the CSS in your theme and put the header graphic in an Images subdirectory. That way, the theme-specific CSS and image are both contained in the Theme directory structure.

Integration within a Skin File

A less frequently used approach for incorporating images into your theme would be to use them as part of control rules set up in the Skin file of your theme. To see how this works, first clear out the tiling background of test.css by changing the rules to the following (removing the background-image rule):

```
body
{
    background-color: steelblue;
    color: Silver;
    font-size: xx-large;
}
```

This is because you want to use the background.jpg file as part of a control in a Skin file and, if you don't remove it from the background of the page, you might not see the effect. The fact that the image is included in the CSS and then again in the skin has no consequence; this is purely a stylistic modification.

Now you will want to create a new Skin file (click on the Theme folder in Solution Explorer, and then click on Website on the toolbar and select Add New Item...), and name it `Images.skin`. Within this new file, modify the contents as follows:

```
<asp:Image
    SkinID="backgroundImage"
    ImageUrl="Images/background.jpg"
    runat="server"
/>
```

You have now set up a themed control setting for the Image control that uses a `SkinID` of `"backgroundImage"`. Notice that the `ImageUrl` property is set to a relative path of the Skin file. Again, `background.jpg` is located in an `Images` subdirectory off the root of the theme, which is where `Images.skin` is located.

Now, in `Default.aspx`, add an image control and add a `SkinID` property with a value of `"backgroundImage"`, as shown below:

```
<asp:Image ID="Image1" SkinID="backgroundImage" runat="server" />
```

Now rerun the project, and you will see your project at this point looks like Figure 8-36.

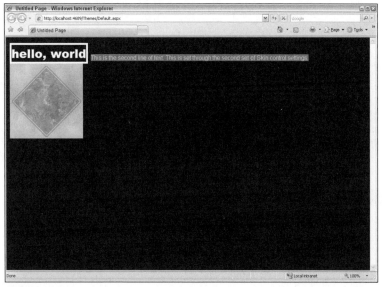

Figure 8-36

As you can see, the image control in `Default.aspx` has incorporated the background image referenced in `Images.skin`, even though the reference in the Skin file only referenced a relative path to the image from the theme. If you look at the rendered output of the page, specifically the image reference, it will look like this:

```
<img id="Image1" src="App_Themes/myFirstTheme/Images/background.jpg"
    style="border-width:0px;" />
```

As you can see, the theme has resolved the URL to the image for you as part of applying the theme. This means that you don't have to spend time thinking of where the files are located in the structure of your project; if it is in the theme, you can just use the relative reference.

One interesting distinction of this methodology as opposed to using it in CSS is that you are allowed to use the "~" special character in the path of the file. For example, you would get the same effect as above if you had used the following code in `Images.skin`:

```
<asp:Image
    SkinID="backgroundImage"
    ImageUrl="~/App_Themes/myFirstTheme/Images/background.jpg"
    runat="server"
/>
```

Knowing this, you are not forced to use images contained in the directory structure of the theme to stylize controls through the skin; you can use images contained in the root directory structure as well (without having to navigate back through directories with the ".." tags). So if, instead of putting `background.jpg` in an `Images` subdirectory off of the root of the theme, you wanted to reference it from an `Images` subdirectory off the root of the entire project, you would modify the code to look like this:

```
<asp:Image
    SkinID="backgroundImage"
    ImageUrl="~/Images/background.jpg"
    runat="server"
/>
```

If you are unfamiliar with the "~" (tilde sign) designation in paths, this is a special character in .NET that tells .NET that you want to begin your path at the application root (or virtual root) regardless of where the reference resides. In the above example, this means that `"~/Images/background.jpg"` *brings the path back to the root of your application, even though the reference is being made from a skin file located at* `"~/App_Themes/myFirstTheme/Images.skin"`.

Hard-Coding a Path to the Theme Image

Remember, when dealing with any objects in a theme, they are just residing in subfolders off the root of your project. So, within your ASPX HTML code, it is perfectly acceptable to just provide a hard-coded reference to the image. For example, you could easily reference the image in the above examples (located in the Images subdirectory off the root of the `myFirstTheme` directory) with the following code:

```
<img id="Image1" src="App_Themes/myFirstTheme/Images/background.jpg" />
```

Notice that this looks remarkably similar to the rendered HTML from the above example. After all, the .NET engine is just translating the paths for you in its conversion of an ASP.NET Image control to an HTML `img` tag. So you could just bypass this process and hard-code in the static reference to the image itself.

If you are within ASPX code, you could also make the reference dynamically by changing the Theme folder with the theme of the page, like this:

```
<img id="Image1" src="App_Themes/<%= StyleSheetTheme %>/Images/background.jpg" />
```

Or, if you are using the `Theme` attribute rather than the `StyleSheetTheme`, your code would differ only slightly and look more like this:

```
<img id="Image1" src="App_Themes/<%= Page.Theme %>/Images/background.jpg" />
```

This code allows you to hard-code a reference to the `Theme` image but keep it dynamic to account for changing themes in your project. The need for this approach to using images in themes probably isn't as great as the need for the other two discussed previously, but this approach is still interesting and may provide some ideas for other ways to use objects in a theme within the pages you create.

Updating the surfer5 Project

With a solid foundation of the concepts and guiding principles of themes, it is time to update the book project, which should be located at `C:\surfer5`. If you are only reading this chapter (or section of this chapter), this is the project that has been updated with the concepts learned in each chapter. At this point, the page has its basic layout (CSS) and graphics. It has its navigation system added through the CSS Friendly Control Adapters and has been templated into a Master Page. It is now time to put the themable components into its first theme.

So, the first step is to open up the project and add a theme called `sufer5BlueTheme` (select the project in Solution Explorer, select Website on the toolbar, choose Add ASP.NET Folder, and then choose Theme).

Adding the Images to Your Theme

Once you have your theme created, you will want to drag the Images folder from the root into your theme, which should make your directory structure resemble Figure 8-37.

Figure 8-37

You want to do this first because all other changes will depend on the images being in place. Plus, this is the easiest step to do, so why not take care of it first?

You may want to fix one thing that probably should have been fixed earlier in the book but really wasn't that big of a deal: move the arrow images that are in the root of the folder into the images subdirectory of your new theme. Those images shouldn't have been in the root anyway so it is a good time to go ahead and clean them up now. Simply drag those two files (`activeArrowRight.gif` and `arrowRight.gif`) into your images subdirectory of your theme before proceeding.

Adding the CSS to Your Theme

Now that the images are added to the theme, it's time to add the CSS. The first step is to create a CSS folder in your theme. This step isn't required, but it will help keep your files separated by purpose so that they are easier to maintain down the road. Once you have created the folder, drag the two browser-independent CSS files (surfer5_v1.css and surfer5menu.css) to the newly created CSS sub-directory of your theme. Make sure you leave surfer5menu IE6.css at root for now, because, if you remember, all CSS files are applied without regard to any criteria you try to set. To elaborate on this example, you cannot specify that this file only comes down for IE6 browsers, which means that you will have to handle that in a different way.

So, at this point, your theme directory should look like Figure 8-38.

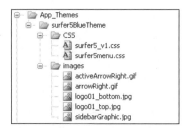

Figure 8-38

You will want to go through your CSS files and update the image paths to reflect the new directory hierarchy environment in which they now reside. For surfer5_v1.css, your code should now look like this:

```
body
{
    padding-right: 1%;
    padding-left: 1%;
    padding-bottom: 1%;
    margin: 0%;
    padding-top: 1%;
    height: 98%;
    background-color: #4d6267;
}
#pageWrapper
{
    width: 700px;
    margin: auto;
    border: solid 1pt #000;
}
#headerGraphic
{
    background-image: url(../images/logo01_top.jpg);
    width: 700px;
    height: 246px;
    clear: both;
    float: none;
}
```

```
#navigationArea
{
    clear: both;
    padding-right: 10px;
    padding-left: 0%;
    font-weight: bold;
    font-size: 0.8em;
    float: none;
    background-image: url(../images/logo01_bottom.jpg);
    padding-bottom: 0%;
    margin: 0%;
    vertical-align: middle;
    width: 690px;
    color: #477897;
    padding-top: 0.3em;
    background-repeat: no-repeat;
    font-family: Arial;
    letter-spacing: 0.04em;
    position: static;
    height: 26px;
    text-align: right;
}
#bodyArea
{
    float: left;
    background-image: url(../images/sidebarGraphic.jpg);
    width: 700px;
    background-repeat: repeat-y;
    background-color: white;
}
#bodyLeft
{
    clear: left;
    padding-right: 10px;
    padding-left: 10px;
    font-size: 0.7em;
    float: left;
    padding-bottom: 10px;
    vertical-align: top;
    width: 126px;
    color: white;
    padding-top: 10px;
    font-family: Arial;
    position: static;
    text-align: center;
}
#bodyRight
{
    clear: right;
    padding-right: 10px;
    padding-left: 10px;
    font-size: 0.8em;
    float: right;
    padding-bottom: 10px;
```

```
        vertical-align: top;
        width: 530px;
        color: #477897;
        padding-top: 10px;
        font-family: Arial;
        position: static;
        text-align: justify;
        overflow: visible;
}
#footerArea
{
        clear: both;
        font-weight: bold;
        font-size: 0.7em;
        float: none;
        background-image: url(../images/logo01_bottom.jpg);
        vertical-align: middle;
        width: 700px;
        color: #477897;
        background-repeat: no-repeat;
        font-family: Arial;
        position: static;
        height: 26px;
        text-align: center;
}
.header
{
        font-size: 1.3em;
        float: left;
        width: 99%;
        color: #FFFFFF;
        font-family: 'Arial Black';
        font-variant: small-caps;
        background-color: #477897;
        padding-left: 1%;
}
```

Similarly, `surfer5menu.css` should look like this:

```
.surfer5menu .AspNet-Menu-Horizontal
{
    position:relative;
    z-index: 300;
}
.surfer5menu ul.AspNet-Menu /* Tier 1 */
{
    float: right;
}
.surfer5menu ul.AspNet-Menu ul  /* Tier 2 */
{
    width: 9em;
    left: 0%;
    background: #eeeeee;
    z-index: 400;
}
```

```
.surfer5menu ul.AspNet-Menu ul li  /* Tier 2 list items */
{
    width: 8.9em;
    border:1px solid #cccccc;
    float: left;
    clear: left;
    height: 100%;
}
.surfer5menu ul.AspNet-Menu ul ul  /* Tier 3+ */
{
    top: -0.5em;
    left: 6em;
}
.surfer5menu li /* all list items */
{
    font-size: x-small;
}
.surfer5menu li:hover, /* list items being hovered over */
.surfer5menu li.AspNet-Menu-Hover
{
    background: #477897;
}
.surfer5menu a, /* all anchors and spans (nodes with no link) */
.surfer5menu span
{
    color: #477897;
    padding: 4px 12px 4px 8px;
    background: transparent url(../images/arrowRight.gif) right center no-repeat;
}
.surfer5menu li.AspNet-Menu-Leaf a, /* leaves */
.surfer5menu li.AspNet-Menu-Leaf span
{
    background-image: none !important;
}
.surfer5menu li:hover a, /* hovered text */
.surfer5menu li:hover span,
.surfer5menu li.AspNet-Menu-Hover a,
.surfer5menu li.AspNet-Menu-Hover span,
.surfer5menu li:hover li:hover a,
.surfer5menu li:hover li:hover span,
.surfer5menu li.AspNet-Menu-Hover li.AspNet-Menu-Hover a,
.surfer5menu li.AspNet-Menu-Hover li.AspNet-Menu-Hover span,
.surfer5menu li:hover li:hover li:hover a,
.surfer5menu li:hover li:hover li:hover span,
.surfer5menu li.AspNet-Menu-Hover li.AspNet-Menu-Hover li.AspNet-Menu-Hover a,
.surfer5menu li.AspNet-Menu-Hover li.AspNet-Menu-Hover li.AspNet-Menu-Hover span
{
    color: White;
    background: transparent url(../images/activeArrowRight.gif) right center
    no-repeat;
}
.surfer5menu li:hover li a, /* the tier above this one is hovered */
.surfer5menu li:hover li span,
.surfer5menu li.AspNet-Menu-Hover li a,
```

```
.surfer5menu li.AspNet-Menu-Hover li span,
.surfer5menu li:hover li:hover li a,
.surfer5menu li:hover li:hover li span,
.surfer5menu li.AspNet-Menu-Hover li.AspNet-Menu-Hover li a,
.surfer5menu li.AspNet-Menu-Hover li.AspNet-Menu-Hover li span
{
    color: #477897;
    background: transparent url(../images/arrowRight.gif) right center no-repeat;
}
```

Updating Your Root Files

You will now need to modify your master page to remove the hard-coding for your CSS files that you have just moved to the new theme folders. Your code for surfer5.master should look like this:

```
<%@ Master Language="C#" AutoEventWireup="true"
    CodeFile="surfer5.master.cs" Inherits="surfer5" %>

<!DOCTYPE html PUBLIC "-//W3C//DTD XHTML 1.0 Strict//EN"
    "http://www.w3.org/TR/xhtml1/DTD/xhtml1-strict.dtd">

<html xmlns="http://www.w3.org/1999/xhtml" >
<head id="Head1" runat="server">
    <title>Untitled Page</title>
    <link runat="server" rel="stylesheet" href="~/CSS/Import.css"
    type="text/css" id="AdaptersInvariantImportCSS" />
<!--[if lt IE 7]>
    <link runat="server" rel="stylesheet" href="~/CSS/BrowserSpecific/IEMenu6.css"
    type="text/css">
    <link href="surfer5menuIE6.css" rel="stylesheet" type="text/css" />
<![endif]-->
</head>
<body>
    <form id="form1" runat="server">
    <div id="pageWrapper">
    <div id="headerGraphic"></div>
    <div id="navigationArea">
        <asp:Menu CssSelectorClass="surfer5menu" DataSourceID="SiteMapDataSource1"
    Orientation="Horizontal" ID="Menu1" runat="server" />
        <asp:SiteMapDataSource SiteMapProvider="myMenu" ShowStartingNode="false"
    ID="SiteMapDataSource1" runat="server" />
    </div>
    <div id="bodyArea">
        <div id="bodyLeft">Lorem ipsum dolor sit amet, consectetuer
    adipiscing elit. Vivamus felis. Nulla facilisi. Nulla eleifend est at lacus.
    Sed vitae pede. Etiam rutrum massa vel nulla. Praesent tempus, nisl ac
    auctor convallis, leo turpis ornare ipsum, ut porttitor felis elit eu turpis.
    Curabitur quam turpis, placerat ac, elementum quis, sollicitudin non, turpis.
    Ut tincidunt sollicitudin risus. Sed dapibus risus et leo. Praesent interdum,
    velit id volutpat convallis, nunc diam vehicula risus, in feugiat
    quam libero vitae justo.</div>
        <div id="bodyRight">
            <asp:SiteMapPath ID="SiteMapPath1" runat="server" PathSeparator=" :: " />
```

```
              <asp:contentplaceholder id="ContentPlaceHolder1" runat="server">
              </asp:contentplaceholder>

          </div>
      </div>
      <div id="footerArea">&copy 2006 - 2007: surfer5 Internet Solutions</div>

      </div>
      </form>
  </body>
  </html>
```

At this point, you have a decision to make. Is the code in `surfer5menuIE6` in need of modification? Does it, for example, need to be modified for various themes that may be applied to it? If so, you may need to do something with it similar to the `style.aspx` code shown earlier in this chapter. However, at least for now, there is nothing in the rules that would necessarily be affected by any of the themes you will be applying; there are only some size rules, essentially, that will show up only for Internet Explorer browsers older than version 7. For this example, it is not necessary to do anything with this file (i.e., it is perfectly fine to leave the file and its reference in `surfer5.master` alone).

The only other thing you need to do is declare the theme for the page. You will get more into setting themes in the next chapter, but for now, you can just declare it in the `@Page` directive of `Default.aspx` and, again for now, it is fine to just use the `Theme` attribute, as shown below:

```
<%@ Page Language="C#" Theme="surfer5BlueTheme" MasterPageFile="~/surfer5.master"
    AutoEventWireup="true" CodeFile="Default.aspx.cs" Inherits="_Default"
    Title="Untitled Page" %>
```

Pulling It All Together

So at this point, you have set up all of the parameters for your theme. So far you have:

- ❏   Created the theme folders in your project
- ❏   Copied the images folder to your new themes project
- ❏   Created a new CSS folder in your themes folder (optional)
- ❏   Copied the browser-independent CSS files to your theme
- ❏   Updated the Master Page to remove references to moved CSS files
- ❏   Updated `Default.aspx` to add the `Theme` attribute to the `@Page` directive.

So now, if your run your project, you should see something that resembles Figure 8-39.

Browser Check

As with any other major (or minor, for that matter) change, you need to make sure that you test the new changes across browsers.

First, check Mozilla Firefox, which can be seen in Figure 8-40.

Figure 8-39

Figure 8-40

You also probably want to check that you haven't messed up anything in Internet Explorer 6, which can be seen in Figure 8-41.

At this point, everything looks good. The page looks correct in IE7, IE6, and Firefox. With this test, you can feel fairly confident that you haven't broken anything, and you are now ready to develop new pages with your theme in place.

Figure 8-41

Summary

With this chapter now behind you, you should feel fairly confident about beginning to incorporate themes into your web projects. You have seen what themes are and learned how to incorporate them into your future projects. You have also seen some of the fairly significant shortcomings of CSS in themes and hopefully found a workaround that overcomes these issues for you. You have seen how to template your ASP.NET controls through the use of skins and have seen how images can be used as part of your theme as well. You have seen how to use this information to update an existing real-world application to a new themed model.

In the next chapter, you will see a little more on how to apply themes to your projects and gain an understanding of the pros and cons of these approaches. At that point, you should have a really good arsenal of aesthNETic tools to take forward into your future .NET web design projects.

9

Applying Themes

At this point in the book, you have been given a fair assessment of what goes into themes, have seen some of the stumbling blocks you may need to consider in planning your theme development approaches, and have hopefully learned to appreciate how powerful themes can be, even with the limitations they do in fact have.

But what have you seen so far in regard to applying themes is very limited. So as not to dilute the concepts of Chapter 8, there was not much mention of the actual application of themes in your projects. In fact, the only way documented was declaring the `Theme` or `StyleSheetTheme` attribute in your `@Page` directive. While it was alluded to that you can apply themes programmatically, nothing concrete was given on how to do this. And, beyond that, no concepts were really discussed or demonstrated. Again, it was with good reason; you needed to get a full understanding of how `Themes` work, how they are different from `StyleSheetThemes`, and which ones you want to use in your projects.

Now that you have a solid understanding of themes, though, it's time to delve deeper into how to actually apply the themes to your projects. Once this is completed, you should have all of the building blocks you need to be comfortable with incorporating themes into all of your future projects.

Before You Begin: Setting the Theme in the Master Page

Before you begin getting into the intricacies of setting your theme throughout your application, it is important to understand one basic covenant: you can't set the theme in the Master Page. It seems that most developers, at some time in their dealings with themes, decide that they need to set the theme in the Master Page. It makes sense, after all, when you think about it. A Master Page is the template that you use to inherit the style and design you have created for your project. A Master Page is inherited by any and every page on your site (theoretically at least). So wouldn't it make sense to set the theme in the Master Page that is already inherited by your page so that you don't have to worry about it at the page level?

The answer is "Yes, it makes sense. That just isn't the way it's set up to happen."

One thing that is for sure is that, as soon as some developers read this section, they will go out to prove this declaration false. Might some of them have workarounds for this? Possibly. But the fact is that Master Pages were not set up to set your theme for you. It would probably make sense if they were, but they weren't. Are there tricks to get around that? Probably. But there are also very legitimate workarounds that will accomplish essentially the same thing (setting the theme in an inherited object or class).

So, that being said, there probably are ways to actually set the Theme (or StyleSheetTheme) directly from the Master Page, but why bother? There are better ways to do it and you will see them in this chapter. Just as importantly, the methods you will be shown here are likely to be more universally understood and widely adopted among developers, projects, and teams you encounter in your career. While striving to prove that themes can, in fact, be set in the Master Page may be a fun personal quest, it might actually prove counterproductive as you try to inject your newfound approach into your projects, since you will probably have to teach everyone on your team how and why you did it, and defend why it is better than the approaches they are more familiar with.

The Default Approach: A Refresher

When first starting out in themes, it is probably easiest to just set the theme at the page level and, more specifically, in the @Page directive. You have seen this throughout Chapter 8, but as a refresher, you can set your theme in the @Page directive with the Theme attribute, similar to the following:

```
<%@ Page Theme="myFirstTheme" Language="C#" AutoEventWireup="true"
    CodeFile="Default.aspx.cs" Inherits="_Default" %>
```

Similarly, you can set the StyleSheetTheme using the StyleSheetTheme attribute of the @Page directive, similar to the following:

```
<%@ Page StyleSheetTheme="myFirstTheme" Language="C#" AutoEventWireup="true"
    CodeFile="Default.aspx.cs" Inherits="_Default" %>
```

Again, this is probably the easiest way to set up your theme. It is the top-level directive on the page, so it is easy to set and doesn't take much thought. Most tutorials on setting themes in ASP.NET 2.0 will probably start with this approach.

There are some other advantages, too. This is one of the only, if not the only, way to get theme support in the Design view of Visual Studio 2005 (well, at least with the StyleSheetTheme — there is no Design view support for themes). In fact, when you start getting into themes and setting them using different approaches, you still may elect to set the theme in the @Page directive just so you can see its effects in the Design view.

However, there are also some fairly significant limitations. For one, you cannot establish any sort of criteria for which a theme is applied. For example, if you want to set one theme for a mobile browser and another for all other viewers, you can't do this at the @Page directive level. Potentially more limiting is the fact that you would have to set the theme on every single page you develop. So, if you have a thousand pages, you will have to set the theme on each and every one of those thousand pages. And, consequently, if you need to change that for some reason, you have to go back and change it a thousand more times. While this is probably the easiest way for new developers to set themes, it is definitely the most constricting and the biggest headache with regard to setting themes up and maintaining them.

Partial Resolution #1: Setting Themes Programmatically

The first issue with setting a theme in the @Page directive is that you can't set it based on any criteria you may need to implement. So, again, if you wanted to have one theme for mobile users and a different one for your other users, you couldn't do that in the @Page directive. What you need to do is set the theme programmatically.

However, as a necessary precursor to explaining how to do this, you have to first decide how you want to apply your theme: through a Theme or a StyleSheetTheme. This decision will, unfortunately, affect how you set your theme programmatically (or how your access the current theme within your code).

Theme

The first discussion will assume that you want to set your theme through a Theme approach. Later you will see how to set your theme through a StyleSheetTheme approach.

For a Theme approach, it is important to become familiar with the Page_PreInit event in the page lifecycle. This is a new event that was introduced in the .NET 2.0 Framework and is the first event you have access to in your code (it fires before the Page_Load or Page_Init events). And, just like Master Pages, themes must be set in the Page_PreInit event if you are going to set them programmatically.

To see how this works, set up a new project (C:\Themes2 will be used for this discussion) with a Default.aspx page that has code similar to the following:

```
<%@ Page Language="C#" AutoEventWireup="true"  CodeFile="Default.aspx.cs"
    Inherits="_Default" %>

<!DOCTYPE html PUBLIC "-//W3C//DTD XHTML 1.0 Transitional//EN"
    "http://www.w3.org/TR/xhtml1/DTD/xhtml1-transitional.dtd">

<html xmlns="http://www.w3.org/1999/xhtml" >
<head runat="server">
    <title>Untitled Page</title>
</head>
<body>
    <form id="form1" runat="server">
    <div>
    hello, world
    </div>
    </form>
</body>
</html>
```

This is just reverting, essentially, to the earliest version of the Themes example in Chapter 8 (just a typical "hello, world" example). Within this new project, create a new theme special folder (App_Themes) and add a new theme to your project by adding a subdirectory to `App_Themes` called `myFirstTheme`. Within that new theme subdirectory, add a new stylesheet document called `StyleSheet.css` with the following rules in it:

```
body
{
    background-color: SteelBlue;
    color: Silver;
    font-size: xx-large;
}
```

The `Theme` attribute for your page is, as you might suspect, part of the `Page` object so, in order to set the theme, you would need to have code similar to the following in your code:

```
Page.Theme = "myFirstTheme";
```

Just to see what happens if you try to set the theme too late in the page lifecycle, try to define the theme at the `Page_Load` event, like this:

```
protected void Page_Load(object sender, EventArgs e)
{
    Page.Theme = "myFirstTheme";
}
```

Now try running your application. If you do, you should get the error shown in Figure 9-1.

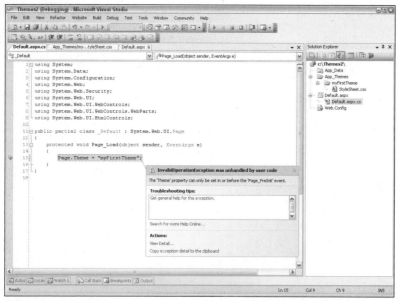

Figure 9-1

The error simply states "The 'Theme' property can only be set in or before the 'Page_PreInit' event." This error message, possibly unlike others you may be familiar with, does not need much explanation.

In fact, it is only stating what has already been said in this chapter: you have to set the theme at the `Page_PreInit` event. So change your code to do this:

```
protected void Page_PreInit(object sender, EventArgs e)
{
    Page.Theme = "myFirstTheme";
}
```

Now, if your run the page again, your page should compile just fine and look like Figure 9-2.

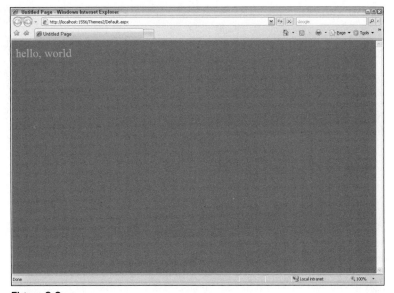

Figure 9-2

This gives you much more control over how the theme is actually set for your page. For example, if you wanted simple browser detection for Internet Explorer that would only apply this theme for IE browsers, you could change your code to something similar to the following:

```
protected void Page_PreInit(object sender, EventArgs e)
{
    if (Page.Request.Browser.Browser == "IE")
    {
        Page.Theme = "myFirstTheme";
    }
    else
    {
        Page.Theme = "";
    }
}
```

Doing so, at least at first, may look as if it didn't do anything. For example, if you load your project to your default browser and that default browser happens to be a version of Internet Explorer, you will see exactly the same thing as in Figure 9-2.

However, if you reload the page in a different browser, say in Mozilla Firefox, you will see that the theme isn't set at all and just looks like a white page with no formatting applied to any elements on the page, as shown in Figure 9-3.

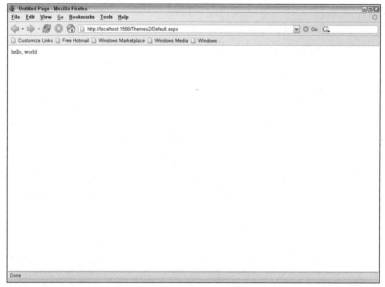

Figure 9-3

The code used to get this result was a little superfluous in that you didn't really need to set the theme to an empty string value for non-IE browsers. It was done just to get you thinking. What if...then...else logic might you implement in your projects to set the different themes? Registered users versus nonregistered visitors? Administrators versus everyone else? Text-based versus GUI (for your accessibility users)? Internet Explorer visitors versus other browsers? Night versus day? Winter versus summer? United States versus United Kingdom? Profile Settings? Once you have control over the actual process of setting the theme, you can set it based on whatever criteria makes sense for your project.

It is also worth noting that, knowing this approach allows you to also use the Theme setting throughout your project as its own criteria. For example, you could use the following code in a Page_Load event to write to the browser what theme is actually set:

```
protected void Page_Load(object sender, EventArgs e)
{
    if (Page.Theme != "")
    {
        Response.Write("<p>Theme: " + Page.Theme + "</p>");
    }
    else
    {
        Response.Write("<p>Theme: No Theme Has Been Set</p>");
    }
}
```

You saw some of this in Chapter 8, but now you can more practically see how you can actually set the theme programmatically using `Page.Theme` in your `Page_PreInit` event.

This may also remind you of one of the limitations of Master Pages: there is no `Page_PreInit` event. This is the reason that you cannot set the theme at the Master Page.

StyleSheetTheme

If you didn't know much about `StyleSheetThemes`, you might think that you could set this attribute the same way you apply the `Theme` attribute to your page. But hopefully you have seen that there are some fairly significant differences between these two approaches, and maybe intuitively these differences carry forward when attempting to set each attribute to your page.

For example, modify the above `Page_PreInit` event to use `StyleSheetTheme` instead of `Theme`:

```
protected void Page_PreInit(object sender, EventArgs e)
{
    if (Page.Request.Browser.Browser == "IE")
    {
        Page.StyleSheetTheme = "myFirstTheme";
    }
    else
    {
        Page.StyleSheetTheme = "";
    }
}
```

When typing this code, you probably noticed that "StyleSheetTheme" came up in IntelliSense after you typed in "Page." (or at least after you typed a few letters of the attribute). Once you finished making the changes, you probably also noticed that no errors came up in the code. But try running the code, and you will get the error message shown in Figure 9-4.

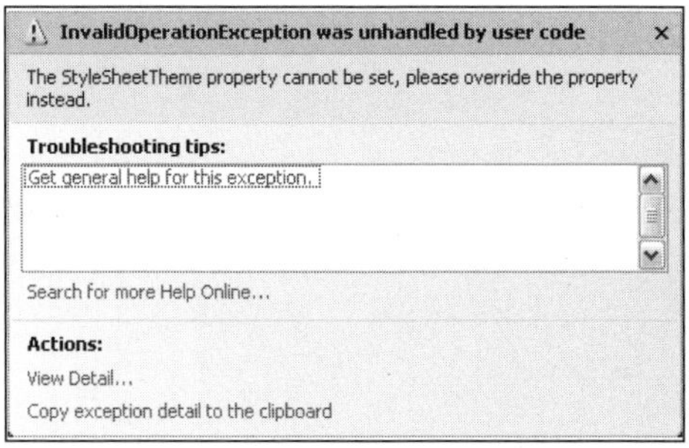

Figure 9-4

Well, as you might have predicted, this shows you that you can't set the `StyleSheetTheme` the same way you set the `Theme`. So how do you set it? As the error message states, you have to override the

StyleSheetTheme property in your page. To do this, you need to incorporate code similar to the following in your code:

```
public override string StyleSheetTheme
{
    get
    {
        return "myFirstTheme";
    }
    set
    {
        base.StyleSheetTheme = value;
    }
}
```

As you may have seen in your experience with .NET coding, you are just overriding a property of your page with code in the page using the get{} set{} accessors. In this case, you are just overriding the StyleSheetTheme property of the page from code.

However, what is potentially more interesting than this is that you aren't incorporating the Page_PreInit event with this approach. This might give you some hope that maybe you have found a loophole in the "no setting themes in Master Pages" rule: you can just override the StyleSheetTheme property in the Master Page.

Unfortunately, you are still out of luck. If you try to do this, you will get the following error message:

Compiler Error Message: CS0115: 'MasterPage.StyleSheetTheme': no suitable method found to override

So, very much like the Page_PreInit event, there is no StyleSheetTheme property available at the Master Page level, which means that this approach won't work either.

Back to the above example — modify your code for your Default page to resemble the following:

```
using System;
using System.Data;
using System.Configuration;
using System.Web;
using System.Web.Security;
using System.Web.UI;
using System.Web.UI.WebControls;
using System.Web.UI.WebControls.WebParts;
using System.Web.UI.HtmlControls;

public partial class _Default : System.Web.UI.Page
{
    public override string StyleSheetTheme
    {
        get
        {
            if (Page.Request.Browser.Browser == "IE")
            {
```

```
            return "myFirstTheme";
        }
        else
        {
            return "";
        }
    }
    set
    {
        base.StyleSheetTheme = value;
    }
}

protected void Page_Load(object sender, EventArgs e)
{
    if (Page.StyleSheetTheme != "")
    {
        Response.Write("<p>StyleSheetTheme: " + Page.StyleSheetTheme + "</p>");
    }
    else
    {
        Response.Write("<p>StyleSheetTheme: No StyleSheetTheme
Has Been Set</p>");
    }
}
}
```

As you can see, you are adding your browser criteria to the get{} accessor of your StyleSheetTheme override to set the theme based on whether the client is an IE browser or not. Running this code should result in the output shown in Figure 9-5 for IE browsers and Figure 9-6 for all others.

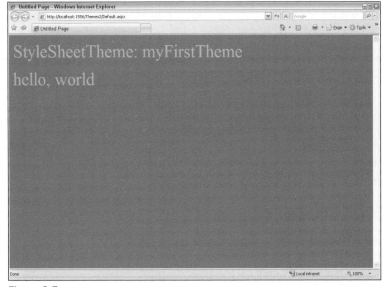

Figure 9-5

Figure 9-6

The Downside to the Programmatic Approach

The idea of integrating programmatic criteria to the application of your Theme logic has some very big advantages. Just by the nature of what you are doing, you are taking back control over the theme and how it gets applied. You can set the theme based on whatever criteria you want to set.

But there is at least one huge downside: the code resides on each page. The logic you have seen in these examples, whether they be for a Theme or a StyleSheetTheme, is set in the code of each and every page of your project. So, imagine a situation where you have a thousand pages on a corporate intranet you are responsible for maintaining. Now imagine that the development of that intranet is distributed across several (or many) developers in different offices located in different cities, states, or even countries. Each page that every developer creates must have this logic in it. Now imagine that your code now needed to break apart a particular version of a browser (i.e., IE was no longer enough, and you now needed to differentiate between IE6 and IE7). What happens then? You have to touch each page to add the new criteria. You have to involve all of the dispersed developers to have them update their pages to include the new logic. This can prove to be a very big hardship for even the smallest of projects but can prove to be outright impossible for a distributed enterprise system maintained by a dispersed group of developers. This approach has some merits, but it's not much better than setting the theme in the @Page directive. For small sites, it might work. But for anything larger, there needs to be a better way. And, if you continue reading this chapter, you will find different approaches that might help you avoid the major downside to this approach.

Who Wins the Rendering War?

So what happens if you set the Theme (or StyleSheetTheme) at the @Page directive on each page but then, on some pages, you introduce logic in the Page_PreInit event to introduce logic for applying the theme to the page; who wins? Will the theme declared in the @Page directive win? Or will the programmatic code in the Page_PreInit event win?

In this scenario, the Page_PreInit wins.

If you want to see this in action, create a second theme called mySecondTheme that has a stylesheet in it with different rules in it (so you can tell which one wins out). For example, add the following rules to your stylesheet document in the mySecondTheme subdirectory:

```
body
{
    background-color: Silver;
    color: SteelBlue;
    font-size: xx-large;
}
```

In the @Page directive, set the Theme attribute to myFirstTheme and then, in the Page_PreInit event, add code to set the theme to mySecondTheme (e.g., Page.Theme = "mySecondTheme";). Browse your project, and you will see that the new theme wins out. This same rule will apply for StyleSheetThemes (the Page_PreInit overrides the settings made in the @Page directive).

Partial Resolution #2: Setting It Globally

One of the major flaws of the approaches illustrated to this point is that you have to set them at each page. With the first approach, you had to hard-code in the Theme or StyleSheetTheme attribute in the @Page directive of every page in your project. With the programmatic approach, you had more control over the way in which the theme is applied, but you still had to code the logic into each page of your project. For many situations, it would be just easier to declare the Theme or StyleSheetTheme once and have it carry through to all pages of your project without any modifications required by the developer(s). In other words, you want to set your theme globally. You can do this in two ways: through the web.config or through the machine.config file.

web.config

If you have a theme that you want to set as either a Theme or a StyleSheetTheme, and you want it to be applied to all pages in a particular project without using any criteria, you can do that in the web.config file. And, for one of the few times in this entire discussion on Themes and StyleSheetThemes, they are identical in this regard. Well, almost identical anyway.

To set a theme up, you simply add an attribute to your web.config file for "Theme" in your pages section, like this:

```
<system.web>
    <pages theme="myFirstTheme"/>
</system.web>
```

Now, to use the similar logic for a StyleSheetTheme, you would only change "theme" to "styleSheetTheme" as follows:

```
<system.web>
    <pages styleSheetTheme="myFirstTheme"/>
</system.web>
```

One thing to remember is that the web.config file is case sensitive, so if, for example, you named this property "StyleSheetTheme", you will get an error and the page will not compile. If you are typing with IntelliSense on, though, it should catch this for you; just be sure that you are conscious of this rule when typing out your properties in your web.config file.

Once you have done this, there is no need to declare the `Theme` logic in the pages for your application. But what happens if you do, in fact, declare the theme on your page? Who wins?

In this instance, the page wins. The `web.config`, then, essentially sets up the default theme for your project that is used by all pages that don't include contrary theme settings.

So if, as in the example above, you declared `"myFirstTheme"` in your `web.config` file, all pages in your project would have that theme applied to them. If, however, you then went into `Default.aspx` and set `Theme` to `"mySecondTheme"` at the `@Page` directive, that page would actually have `mySecondTheme` applied to it rather than `myFirstTheme`. Remembering the logic from the previous discussion, if you then decided just for fun to set the theme back to `"myFirstTheme"` in the `Page_PreInit` event of `Default.aspx`, that would beat out the declaration in the `@Page` directive.

To show this in a more appropriate timeline, at least at this point in the discussion, the order in which `Themes` and `StyleSheetThemes` are applied is:

❏   `web.config` property

❏   `@Page` directive attribute

❏   programmatically set in the `Page_PreInit` event

In a real-world situation, what this really means is that you can set up the default theme for your entire application in your `web.config` but still retain the ability to customize the theme for a particular page if your business needs require it.

Is One Theme a Waste?

This is probably a good time to discuss a question that will inevitably come up with setting the theme at the global level: What's the point of having just one theme? After all, much of the appeal of themes is that you can have the look and feel change based on different criteria. A good example of this might be to have one theme set up for mobile users and another one for all other users. One of the more powerful aspects of themes is that you can change the entire look and feel of a web site like a switch; one second it looks one way, and literally a fraction of a second later it looks entirely different (different colors, fonts, and even layout). So is there really a point to setting the theme globally?

The short answer is that there definitely is an advantage to using a single theme.

The longer answer involves looking at all that is offered with a theme. Sure, to use the mobile theme as an example, you can do a lot of formatting and style differentiation with the media types of CSS files. But, with regard to themes, this is just the beginning. CSS and the standards associated with it are definitely a huge part of any good theme. However, the bigger selling point to a properly created theme is that you can potentially skin all of the ASP.NET controls in the page. You are able to format each calendar view to take on the look and feel of your site. If you want to have a default font size in each TextBox control be 8 pt with a light gray background, you can do that at the theme level. You can set every GridView control to allow pagination with five records per page if you want. Once you have done that, a developer simply drops the control on the page and programs against it in whatever way is appropriate (bind it to a datasource, insert default text, etc.). There is no need to worry about formatting the colors or behavior of the controls; it is defined in the theme.

So, when you think this way, you should be able to easily see the advantage of a well-thought-out theme that is applied globally. It really doesn't matter whether or not you plan on switching themes at any time in the lifecycle of the project. What matters is that you have all of the design elements wrapped up into the page before the developer even begins adding controls. And if you have a project that several developers are working on together, they all have the same look and feel to the controls they use in the page without having to even think about it. They can just work on filling the content with the appropriate material.

That being said, obviously, it takes a while to set up a useful theme. You will have to recognize all of the design elements that need to go into a good web design layout. You will need to create the basic look and feel to the site, including the navigation controls and Master Page. Then you will need to start formatting controls in your theme to go along with that template that you have created. But, once you do that, you can deploy the templated project to your team of developers and they can start dropping in controls and coding against them, and the site will just tie together without their intervention; it will just work.

Now, granted, if your project allows for it, adding multiple themes and the ability to switch between them will give you some real creativity points. But even if you have a single theme for your project, it will be worth the work you put into it.

machine.config

So what if setting the theme globally at the `web.config` level isn't enough? After all, that only affects a single web application. What if you want to affect all web applications on a particular web server? Is it possible to set the `Theme` (or `StyleSheetTheme`) at that level? It is if you set the theme at the `machine.config` level.

What may or may not be surprising is that this is done in exactly the same way you saw in the `web.config` file. Hopefully, this makes sense to you, even if you hadn't thought of it before. The `machine.config` serves essentially the same purpose as the `web.config` file, just at a more global level (storing the configuration parameters that are universal to all applications on a web server rather than just a particular application). Even though a typical `machine.config` has many more parameters in it than you would see in your standard `web.config` file, they are not really mutually exclusive. That is to say that the `machine.config` sets up the universal defaults, and the `web.config` sets up the application defaults that are either not set up at all in the `machine.config` or are just overridden by the `web.config` entries.

So this should give you some insight on what happens if you set up a `Theme` (or `StyleSheetTheme`) in the `machine.config` and then set up a different one in the `web.config` file. As you have probably guessed, the `web.config` overrides the `machine.config`. So, again, you are setting up a global default for all web applications on a particular web server in that server's `machine.config` file. These settings can then be overridden at the application level with the `web.config` file, which can then be overridden at the page level by the `@Page` directive or programmatically through the `Page_PreInit` event. Therefore, the expanded list for the hierarchy of settings for the theme in your websites is:

- ❑ `machine.config`
- ❑ `web.config`
- ❑ `@Page` directive
- ❑ `Page_PreInit` event

This will hold true regardless of whether you are setting your Theme through the `Theme` attributes of the site or its `StyleSheetTheme` attributes; the hierarchy remains constant.

With all of this information, you should feel fairly comfortable in setting your theme in the `machine.config` file:

```
<system.web>
    <pages theme="myFirstTheme" />
</system.web>
```

Again, the `StyleSheetTheme` is set very similarly, as can be seen here:

```
<system.web>
    <pages styleSheetTheme="myFirstTheme" />
</system.web>
```

While the example shown in the `web.config` could very well resemble what is in your `web.config` file, this example is probably not as real world as you would find in your `machine.config` file. When you start looking to set this property in the `machine.config`, you will need to look for the `system.web` section, which will likely be towards the bottom of the file and will probably look something like this:

```
<system.web>
    <processModel autoConfig="true" />
    <httpHandlers />
    <membership>
        <providers>
            <add name="AspNetSqlMembershipProvider"
type="System.Web.Security.SqlMembershipProvider, System.Web, Version=2.0.0.0,
Culture=neutral, PublicKeyToken=b03f5f7f11d50a3a"
connectionStringName="LocalSqlServer"
enablePasswordRetrieval="false" enablePasswordReset="true"
requiresQuestionAndAnswer="true" applicationName="/"
requiresUniqueEmail="false" passwordFormat="Hashed"
maxInvalidPasswordAttempts="5" minRequiredPasswordLength="7"
minRequiredNonalphanumericCharacters="1" passwordAttemptWindow="10"
passwordStrengthRegularExpression="" />
        </providers>
    </membership>
    <profile>
        <providers>
            <add name="AspNetSqlProfileProvider"
connectionStringName="LocalSqlServer" applicationName="/"
type="System.Web.Profile.SqlProfileProvider, System.Web,
Version=2.0.0.0, Culture=neutral, PublicKeyToken=b03f5f7f11d50a3a" />
        </providers>
    </profile>
    <roleManager>
        <providers>
            <add name="AspNetSqlRoleProvider"
connectionStringName="LocalSqlServer" applicationName="/"
type="System.Web.Security.SqlRoleProvider, System.Web,
Version=2.0.0.0, Culture=neutral, PublicKeyToken=b03f5f7f11d50a3a" />
            <add name="AspNetWindowsTokenRoleProvider" applicationName="/"
type="System.Web.Security.WindowsTokenRoleProvider, System.Web,
Version=2.0.0.0, Culture=neutral, PublicKeyToken=b03f5f7f11d50a3a" />
        </providers>
    </roleManager>
</system.web>
```

So, somewhere in that code, you will need to insert the page's attributes (if they don't already exist — depending on how your web server is set up, it may very well already be in place and you will just need to add the `Theme` or `StyleSheetTheme` property).

To locate the `machine.config` file on your web server (or on your local development machine), you should look here:

```
%WINDIR%\Microsoft.NET\Framework\%VERSION%\CONFIG\
```

For example, your system path might resemble the following actual path:

```
C:\WINDOWS\Microsoft.NET\Framework\v2.0.50727\CONFIG\
```

machine.config is Special

One thing to remember about setting the theme in the `machine.config` file is that this is truly a global application setting. When you are setting the theme at the `web.config` level, you are only setting it for a particular web application. However, when you are setting the theme at the `machine.config` level, you are setting the theme for all web applications for the web server. This should make you think "Where does the theme reside?"

The short answer is that it must reside in a location that is accessible to the web application.

So what does this mean? Well, it really can take on a couple of meanings. The first is that it could mean what you have seen up to this point: the theme can be located as part of a particular web application. For example, if you have a theme created in a particular application called `myFirstTheme` as you have done in the past two chapters, you can set the `Theme` attribute to `myFirstTheme` in the `machine.config` and it will work fine in that particular application. The downside to this approach is that, unless you have the same named theme in every web application on your web server, you will run into problems. If, for example, one application does not have `myFirstTheme` set up in it, you will get errors when you try to compile the application.

So what you should take into special consideration in setting themes up in your `machine.config` is exactly where they should reside. The easiest way to ensure that the Theme is available to your web applications is to set it up in a global location accessible by all web applications. Fortunately, the .NET 2.0 Framework is set up with exactly this need in mind. As such, you can create Theme folders in the .NET folder in your Windows directory (similar to the location of the `machine.config` file itself) that will make the theme be accessible. This folder should be:

```
%WINDIR%\Microsoft.NET\Framework\%VERSION%\ASP.NETClientFiles\Themes\%THEME%
```

Notice the final subdirectory of this structure ("Themes")? This folder will likely not exist in your current directory structure, so you may have to add it. Notice that it is called Themes rather than "App_Themes." This is an important distinction to make between themes created within a web application and themes created globally. If you call this folder "App_Themes," the themes you create within that folder will not be accessible to your web applications.

However, other than that, you set up your themes in the same way you would a typical web application. You would need to create a folder within the `Themes` subdirectory for each theme (the folder name would be the name of the theme itself, just as in your web applications) and, within that subdirectory, you would add your theme files (CSS, Skin files, and images).

So, say that you want to create a new theme called `myThirdTheme`, you would create a directory structure similar to the following:

```
C:\WINDOWS\Microsoft.NET\Framework\v2.0.50727\ASP.NETClientFiles\Themes\myThirdTheme\
```

Once you have done this, you now have a new theme available to you in the `machine.config` file, called `myThirdTheme`, that you can set at the global level that will automatically get applied to all web applications on this web server. Granted, you can still override this theme at the `web.config`, `@Page`, or `Page_PreInit` levels, but it is at least set up as a default for all of your applications. You can now fill that directory with CSS, Skin, and Image files that will be automatically pulled down into your applications for you if you don't override the behavior within the application. There is no need to maintain duplicate themes throughout the projects. There is no need for developers to even worry about setting the theme at all. The theme is set up globally and set for them globally; it is just taken care of. This is one of the coolest features of themes.

> The `machine.config` approach was specifically not mentioned with regards to Master Pages in Chapter 7 because they do not work in the same way. While it is possible to set the `masterPageFile` attribute in the pages section of the `machine.config` file, the Master Page must actually reside within the application; you are not allowed to reference Master Pages outside of the application itself. While there are workarounds for this, it would involve setting up the workaround in every application, which seems to defeat the purpose of setting the property globally. Therefore, in a discussion about setting global properties in a machine.config file, it is probably a good idea for themes but not so useful for Master Pages.

The Downside to the Global Approach

Obviously the major downside to this approach is that you are setting the theme in one place without any criteria; thus, you cannot implement global programmatic logic to determine which theme is applied in various scenarios relevant to your project. This is just a long way of saying that you can't introduce any type of decision making into your global themes. You can't say that some themes are applied to IE browsers and a different theme is applied to other browsers; at least globally. You are forced into giving a default theme to every page in a web application or even web server with no logic behind it. Granted, you can override this default behavior at the page level but, in doing so, you are negating the advantage of setting it globally (you are having to reset it at the page thereby doubling the theme-setting logic of your application). For many applications, there won't be a need for multiple themes and, for those applications, this just isn't much of a problem. If, however, you are responsible for one of the projects that does, in fact, require setting the theme based on some criteria, this is a very significant limitation and should be taken seriously before deciding on this approach.

Partial Resolution #3: The Inherited Base Class

When considering how to apply themes, you have seen two distinctly different approaches to setting them outside of the `@Page` directive; both with their own pros and cons. The first was to set the Theme programmatically either through the `Page_PreInit` event (for `Themes`) or through overriding its property accessors (`StyleSheetTheme`). The major advantage to this approach was that could then establish your own business logic in the determination of which theme to apply. However, there was a significant disadvantage as well in that each page still had to have the theme set in its own code. This meant that the logic might not carry through to all pages or, even if it did, you would have to go to each page and change the code if your business criteria for themes changed.

The second approach was setting the theme globally either through the `web.config` or `machine.config` file (or both). The obvious advantage to this approach is that you could set the theme in one location and have it automatically set by default in all of the pages in a particular application or even on an entire web server. The downside to this approach is that you have no real way of introducing any kind of business logic into the methodology of applying the themes. So, if your application needed to apply themes based on different business rules, you would have to override the theme programmatically at the page level. If that is true, it means you are still coding all of the logic on every page (assuming that every page needs to inherit the business logic for setting themes) and, as such, completely negates the advantages of setting the theme globally.

So, with these concepts in mind, it is time to consider a hybrid approach to setting your theme: using an inherited base class. You saw how to do this, at least at a high level, when you were creating Master Page base classes and inheriting them both in the Master Page and as part of the `@MasterType` directive on the page back in Chapter 7. In that example, you were setting properties and variables in a shared base class file, which allowed the information to be passed easily between the two (Master Page and Child).

With regard to themes, though, it is slightly different. In this case, you want to set the programmatic business logic of themes in a base class file and then inherit that base class in each page for your site. What does this afford you? Well, once you have this in place, you can control the logic for setting the theme in each page that inherits the class. So, for example, if you have a site of a thousand pages, if all pages inherit this base class, the logic can be done in one file and affect all. This means that when, inevitably, the logic needs tweaking or a new theme is added, you can adjust the logic in one file and have it ripple throughout your site.

For this reason, this approach can be called a hybrid approach to the two aforementioned alternatives. You get the criteria based logic of setting themes programmatically, while getting the effects of having the theme logic being in one place that is applied to many, if not all, pages in an application. In this way, you get the best of both worlds.

However, like the other approaches, there is still a significant downside to this approach; you have to modify each page at least initially to inherit this base class and/or, maybe more daunting, ensure that all developers of the pages of your application do so. So, while this approach has some definite advantages over the others shown to this point (at least if you need business logic in your application for setting themes), it is still not the perfect solution. But, in regard to setting themes in ASP.NET 2.0, this is probably as close to perfect as you are going to get.

Less Talk, More Code

The first step is to add a new base class to your project. To do this, click on Website on the toolbar in Visual Studio, and select Add New Item. This will give you the screen depicted in Figure 9-7.

As shown in Figure 9-7, name your class `PageBase.cs`, and click the Add button. If you have not set up the ASP.NET 2.0 folder for classes, `App_Code`, you will get the warning shown in Figure 9-8.

Figure 9-7

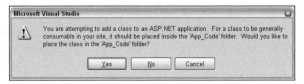

Figure 9-8

You should click the Yes button to proceed with setting up the special folder and adding your new base class to that folder. When the class loads, it should have default code similar to the following:

```
using System;
using System.Data;
using System.Configuration;
using System.Web;
using System.Web.Security;
using System.Web.UI;
using System.Web.UI.WebControls;
using System.Web.UI.WebControls.WebParts;
using System.Web.UI.HtmlControls;

/// <summary>
/// Summary description for PageBase
/// </summary>
public class PageBase
{
    public PageBase()
    {
        //
        // TODO: Add constructor logic here
        //
    }
}
```

The first thing you will need to do is inherit from the `Page` object in your code by modifying the class line to the following:

```
public class PageBase : Page
```

You can also get rid of the default method, `PageBase()`, unless you plan to use it for something else (it isn't necessary for this example, and it just adds more code, so for the rest of this example, that code will be stripped).

Now, within your `PageBase` class, you need to add the `Page_PreInit` event and set the `Theme` to `"myFirstTheme"`, as follows:

```
protected void Page_PreInit(object sender, EventArgs e)
{
    Page.Theme = "myFirstTheme";
}
```

At this point, your base class file, in its entirety, should look like this:

```
using System;
using System.Data;
using System.Configuration;
using System.Web;
using System.Web.Security;
using System.Web.UI;
using System.Web.UI.WebControls;
using System.Web.UI.WebControls.WebParts;
using System.Web.UI.HtmlControls;

/// <summary>
/// Summary description for PageBase
/// </summary>
public class PageBase : Page
{
    protected void Page_PreInit(object sender, EventArgs e)
    {
        Page.Theme = "myFirstTheme";
    }
}
```

Now all that is left to do is strip out any theme-setting logic you have in this application so far (`machine.config`, `web.config`, `@Page`, `Page_PreInit`, or the `StyleSheetTheme` property).

The last step you need to do is inherit the new `PageBase` class in your page, `Default.aspx`. You do this in the same way you inherited the `Page` object in the `PageBase` class earlier. In other words, you just modify the inheritance logic in the page's class declaration, like this:

```
public partial class _Default : PageBase
```

If you have done everything properly, you should be able to run your application and see something similar to Figure 9-9.

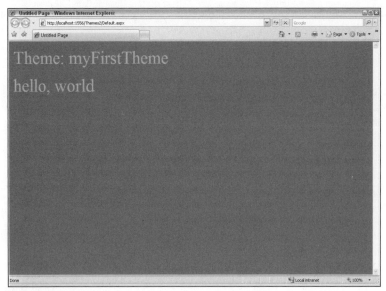

Figure 9-9

Now, if you wanted to instead set the theme through StyleSheetTheme, you would modify your base class file to the following code:

```
using System;
using System.Data;
using System.Configuration;
using System.Web;
using System.Web.Security;
using System.Web.UI;
using System.Web.UI.WebControls;
using System.Web.UI.WebControls.WebParts;
using System.Web.UI.HtmlControls;

/// <summary>
/// Summary description for PageBase
/// </summary>
public class PageBase : Page
{
    public override string StyleSheetTheme
    {
        get
        {
            return "myFirstTheme";
        }
        set
        {
            base.StyleSheetTheme = value;
        }
    }
}
```

Running the application with this code will result in essentially the same thing as in Figure 9-9, except that there won't be any text for the theme name, since the logic on the page is bringing back the value for `Page.Theme`, which is nothing if you are using `StyleSheetTheme` instead.

The Hierarchy of the Base Class

When thinking of setting the theme with a base class, it would be good to know where it fits within the hierarchy of setting themes. In order to understand this, you need to realize what is going on. Using this approach, you are essentially setting global logic in an inherited file. At a slightly more detailed level, you are actually writing code that will be inherited by your page. Since you are writing code, you are really at the programmatic level. As such, you are working at a level akin to the programmatic level of the page itself. With that being said, the hierarchy would be as follows:

- ❑ `machine.config`
- ❑ `web.config`
- ❑ `@Page` directive
- ❑ `Page` base class
- ❑ Programmatically within page (if overrides `Page` base class or if no `Page` base class exists)

The last two items are probably the most interesting. As you would probably expect, the programmatic elements are going to win out against everything else if they are used. But the question becomes "Which one wins if it is declared in both?"

The order shown above isn't entirely accurate. Honestly, it depends on how you use these elements and how you set up the inheritance of the classes for the two elements (the base class and the page class that inherits it). However, a good practice would be to set up the `Page` base class as a default and then allow the page to override the logic in its own code.

For the base class piece, this was already done through the following event code:

```
protected void Page_PreInit(object sender, EventArgs e)
{
    Page.Theme = "myFirstTheme";
}
```

In this case, you have just set up a typical `Page_PreInit` event in code. The trickier part comes in when you want to override this behavior in the page and, unfortunately, the way this works isn't entirely intuitive if you are not already familiar with these concepts. For example, use the same code shown above for `Default.aspx.cs`, but change the `Theme` setting to `"mySecondTheme"`, as follows:

```
protected void Page_PreInit(object sender, EventArgs e)
{
    Page.Theme = "mySecondTheme";
}
```

If you run this now, you will see something similar to Figure 9-10, which might make you think that it worked. However, comment out the line of code that sets `Theme` to `"mySecondTheme"` in `Default.aspx.cs` and rerun the application. You should now see something that looks like Figure 9-11.

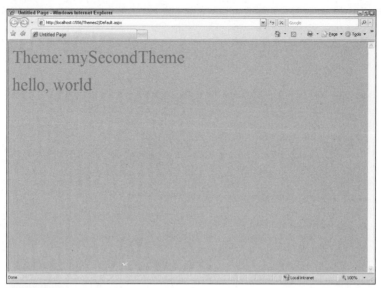

Figure 9-10

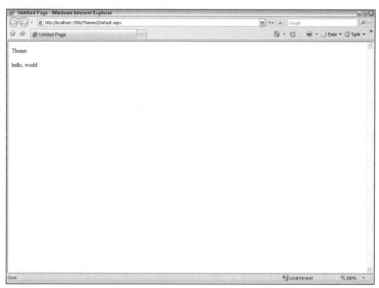

Figure 9-11

You will notice, also, that in Visual Studio, you have now introduced some blue squiggly lines in the `Page_PreInit` event that weren't there before adding this reference to the base class, as can be seen in Figure 9-12.

If you do not see the blue squiggly lines, it is possible that you built the project multiple times. The first time you build the project, it will give you the blue squiggly lines to indicate there is a warning — not an error. Therefore, the next time you build the project, the lines will not appear and the warning will go away. If, instead of "Build Web Site" you select "Rebuild Web Site," you should get the warning message again and the blue squiggly lines should reappear.

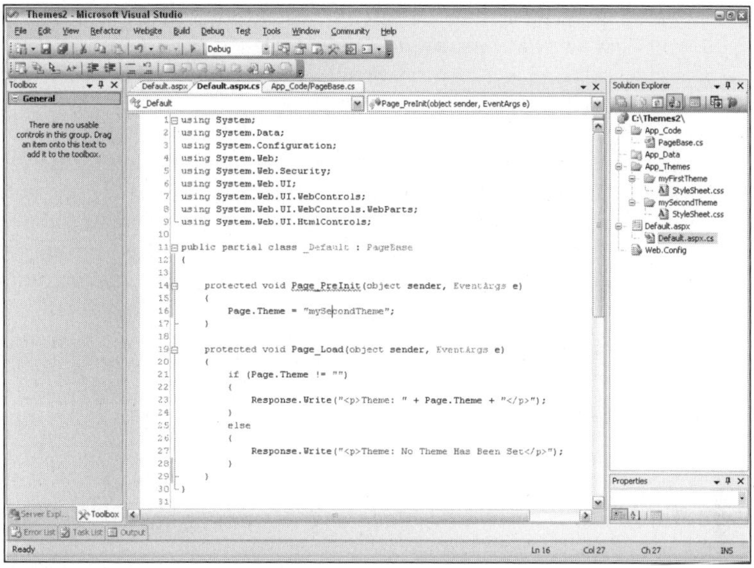

Figure 9-12

So what is going on? Well, the first problem that was seen in Figures 9-10 and is that you are, essentially, hiding the entire `Page_PreInit` event from the base class. An easy way to think about it is that, if you declare it in both places, one is going to win out and the other one is going to be ignored entirely. The way the page is set up, the event at the page level is winning out, so the page is then ignoring the `Page_PreInit` event in its entirety at the base class level.

Is there a way around that? Of course. You just have to call the `Page_PreInit` event in the base class from the `Page_PreInit` event within `Default.aspx.cs`, like this:

```
protected void Page_PreInit(object sender, EventArgs e)
{
    base.Page_PreInit(sender, e);
    //Page.Theme = "mySecondTheme";
}
```

This is taking the variables from page's `PreInit` event ("sender" and "e") and sending them to the base class and triggering the `PreInit` event there. Of course, position is everything, so putting it as the first line of the page's `PreInit` code ensures that the base class runs first and then the lines of code after that call will run on the page level. If you had put the new line as the last line in the page's `PreInit` event, it would fire off last in that sequence and override any conflicting declarations that preceded it.

Is that confusing? Just remember to call it first so that the stuff in the base class will run first and then anything that you need to override in the page you can do after that.

At this point, if you run the application again as-is (the `Theme` declaration commented out in `Default.aspx.cs`), you will see the page with `myFirstTheme` applied. If you then remove the commenting from the `Theme` logic in `Default.aspx.cs`, you will now see the page loaded with `mySecondTheme` applied. So, by doing it this way, you have allowed the base class logic to come into your page as the default but then overridden the values that you needed to (in this case, it is only the `Theme` declaration but, in a real-world situation, this could include other things as well).

Now, on to the squiggly line. In all actuality, this won't cause you many problems. The page will compile, and you won't get any runtime errors. This is, in fact, only a warning and not a true error. But, in order to be a good developer, you probably want to eliminate it. In order to do so, you need to understand what is going on first.

The page recognizes that there are two instances of `Page_PreInit`; one at the page level and one in the inherited base class. The one at the page level is, by default, hiding the one in the base class. This is the behavior you want (the alternative is to overwrite it). The problem is that you haven't explicitly told the page how to handle this conflict. So, in order to make your code cleaner, you need to introduce the `new` keyword into your event in `Default.aspx.cs`, as you can see in the modified code below:

```
protected new void Page_PreInit(object sender, EventArgs e)
{
    base.Page_PreInit(sender, e);
    //Page.Theme = "mySecondTheme";
}
```

Making this small change will take away the blue squiggly warning line, so you no longer need to worry with it. And, with these last few changes combined, you have a clean way of inheriting the `Page_PreInit` logic from the base class and append to it without totally overwriting it in the process if you should so choose.

A Quick Note about StyleSheetTheme

The override logic in the above steps focused on setting the theme through the `Theme` attribute solely and did not touch on setting it through the `StyleSheetTheme` attribute. This is because `Theme` is tricky and `StyleSheetTheme` is easy. With `Theme`, you had to worry about conflicting `Page_PreInit` events, which is somewhat problematic and deserves at least a cursory overview of how the pieces play together.

There is no such conflict with `StyleSheetTheme`. Remember, when setting your theme using `StyleSheetTheme`, you are merely overriding the public property `"StyleSheetTheme"`; there is no need to try to set it within any event or method. Therefore, there is just no need to worry about all of the issues seen with setting the theme in the above example.

To illustrate this, take out all theme-setting logic in your project (including anything in the base class or `Default` page in your project you may have just set). Now go into your base class and add the following code:

```
public override string StyleSheetTheme
{
    get
    {
        return "myFirstTheme";
    }
    set
    {
        base.StyleSheetTheme = value;
    }
}
```

If you run the project, you will see the StyleSheetTheme "myFirstTheme" has been applied to the page. Now go back into Default.aspx.cs and add similar code, but set the returned value to "mySecondTheme", as follows:

```
public override string StyleSheetTheme
{
    get
    {
        return "mySecondTheme";
    }
    set
    {
        base.StyleSheetTheme = value;
    }
}
```

If you run your project again, you will see that the page now has "mySecondTheme" applied to it. No need to worry about conflicts between the two declarations. There is no need to inherit in any logic from the base class because all that is going on there is setting the theme, and that is the behavior you want to override anyway.

This just illustrates that the StyleSheetTheme approach is much simpler in this scenario than the Theme one. Neither one is necessarily better nor worse; StyleSheetTheme is just easier to set in this scenario. That being said, this is just a statement as to which one is easier to set programmatically in your project, which is not the same thing as negating the usefulness of either in the real world. Remember from Chapter 8 that Themes and StyleSheetThemes are different in the way they are brought into your page (StyleSheetTheme comes first and Themes come last). So there are reasons to use either. However, everything else being equal, when you are trying to set a Theme or StyleSheetTheme programmatically through the use of a Page base class, the StyleSheetTheme is easier because it doesn't encounter any of the event conflicts that programmatically setting the Theme does.

Updating the surfer5 Project

Now that you have obtained a fair understanding of the different ways to apply a theme to a project, you can hopefully see some of the pros and cons of each approach and, in so doing, can envision real-world situations where each might be better suited than the alternative. So, with that in mind, it is time to apply the theme to the book project in a better way than at the @Page directive of each page.

As with any project, the way you apply themes will depend on the project needs and resources available. For example, if you think that it would be much easier to just set the theme in the machine.config of the web server, this would be a virtual impossibility if you are hosting your website on a shared Internet hosting account (because they probably won't give you access to tinker with the server's machine.config file). Additionally, if you are only going to have one theme for the entire project, there really isn't much need to go through the complexity of adding a Page base class and having all pages inherit it; you can just set it in the web.config and be done with it. So, when deciding how to apply your theme, you have to take all of these things into consideration. However, in moving forward with the surfer5 project, you should make the following assumptions:

❑   The page will be hosted on some rented space on the Internet (you will not have direct access to the servers).

❑   There will be multiple themes eventually (like, say, in Chapter 10).

❑   There needs to be some sort of logic that will be applied to all pages to determine the appropriate theme.

Knowing this information, what would be the best approach? The first bullet pretty much rules out the `machine.config` approach, since you will probably not have access to that file in the first place. Besides, the fact that there will be multiple themes and requisite logic to switch between the themes rules out that approach. Similarly, this same logic rules out the `web.config` approach.

So, with these requirements, you know that you want to have programmatic logic set up to apply this theme so that the project is set up switch between the multiple themes as the project matures. Since you probably don't want to have to update the logic on each and every page of the project (even though the project will probably be pretty small), the logical choice is probably the inherited base class approach. This way, you can apply the theme for now in a base class that will be inherited by all pages. And, when the new themes are added, you can just make the logic changes in one location rather than all of the pages that have been developed to that point.

So, with that decision being made, open up the project (`C:\surfer5`) in order to implement the necessary changes.

The first thing you need to do is create a new base class (click on Website on the Visual Studio toolbar and select Add New Item), and name it `PageBase.cs`. Once the class has been added, modify its code to resemble the following:

```
using System;
using System.Data;
using System.Configuration;
using System.Web;
using System.Web.Security;
using System.Web.UI;
using System.Web.UI.WebControls;
using System.Web.UI.WebControls.WebParts;
using System.Web.UI.HtmlControls;

/// <summary>
/// Summary description for PageBase
/// </summary>
public class PageBase : Page
{
    protected void Page_PreInit(object sender, EventArgs e)
    {
        Page.Theme = "surfer5BlueTheme";
    }
}
```

Now go back into `Default.aspx` and remove the `Theme` declaration in the `@Page` directive (it was set there at the end of Chapter 8). In the code behind for the page, you will need to inherit from the new base class, `PageBase`. For now, you don't need to touch the inherited `PreInit` event so there is no need to add any of the override event code at this point (just keep it in mind for future reference).

Your code behind should now resemble the following:

```
using System;
using System.Data;
using System.Configuration;
using System.Collections;
using System.Web;
using System.Web.Security;
using System.Web.UI;
using System.Web.UI.WebControls;
using System.Web.UI.WebControls.WebParts;
using System.Web.UI.HtmlControls;

public partial class _Default : PageBase
{
    protected void Page_Load(object sender, EventArgs e)
    {
        myCompany.Text = Master.company;
    }
}
```

You have now taken the logic for applying themes out of the page and put it in the inherited base class that will be inherited by every page in the project (as they are built). If you compile your project, you should see that it now resembles Figure 9-13.

Figure 9-13

This "Updating the surfer5 Project" section was really short because, in all honesty, there wasn't that much to do. The only difference in the project at this point and where it was at the end of Chapter 8 is that the theme has been applied using a different approach. Thus, there really wasn't much you had to change in the project itself. But, with that small change, you are set up continue this theme (and whatever other themes you set up) throughout the rest of the project.

Summary

It is quite possible that, when you started this chapter, you were thinking "Is it really necessary to devote an entire chapter just to setting themes?" Hopefully, after reading the chapter, you will be answering that question with a resounding "Yes!" While some may believe that there really aren't that many ways in which you can apply a theme to a project, once you understand the intricacies of `Theme` and `StyleSheetTheme` and the different ways you can set the project programmatically or globally, you will not be of that mindset.

You should now see that there are many different ways to apply a theme to a project. You can set it as a `StyleSheetTheme` or a `Theme`. Within those classifications, you can set it at the `@Page` directive, program-matically, or globally. Within the realm of programmatically, you can set it at the page level or in some inherited base class. When thinking of globally assigning the theme, you have the option of doing so in the `web.config` or in the `machine.config`.

There are a lot of options for applying the theme.

What is potentially more intimidating is that none of the options is the perfect solution for every project you will ever develop. Each approach has some level of pros as well as some level of cons to it. You can either set it once and forget it or you can have programmatic control over the logic for applying the theme, but you can't really have both (although you can get pretty close).

Hopefully, what you have really gained from this chapter is an appreciation for all of the different ways themes can get into your projects. If you thought of different real-world situations that would be perfect for each solution you read in this chapter, then this chapter met its intended goal. If you thought of new ways you can program with themes or even beyond, then so much the better.

Furthermore, as this chapter closes, you should now feel fairly comfortable with the aesthNETics of web design and feel prepared to pull these ideas and concepts into your own projects. This book started off as a way of talking about themes. However, in order to do that, it was really necessary to talk about all of the design aspects that should, no *must*, be included as part of this approach. Realistically, before you can ever get into themes, you would need to understand basic web design principles, how to create an aesthetically pleasing site using those principles, and how to use the tools in ASP.NET 2.0 to bring these abstract ideas into a tangible reality you can incorporate into your projects and even share among a team of developers. Once you had a template for your page, you could wrap it all up in a complementary theme and apply it in whatever way your business needs are.

In the next chapter, you will create a new mobile theme for surfer5 from scratch and then see how to change the theme as appropriate (when a mobile user views the site). Once you have seen this in place, you will be ready to go forward and create consistent, and hopefully striking, websites using the tools in ASP.NET 2.0 (and maybe a little help from other tools like Adobe Photoshop). You will be an aesthNETics developer.

10

Bringing It All Together — A New Theme

If you have read this book from cover to, well, this chapter, you should have gained an appreciation of the tools you take with you into every project that you can and should implement before you ever write your first connection object to the database of your choice. You first took a high-level look at the basic considerations of web design today, from screen resolution to browser demographics across the web. You have begun to understand some of the meaning behind all of this "accessibility" talk on the web and, maybe, it is no longer just an abstract concept that other developers have to worry about. With that, you began to better understand one of the more hot debates in web design today: the use of CSS vs. tables for web layout. You saw that there are some considerable bumps in your path to full CSS implementation but, hopefully, you also saw some pretty good reasons to consider it. You then started on the basic tenants of your layout, creating your logo graphic and picking the color scheme that would be carried throughout your site.

These first few chapters gave you the prerequisite knowledge of general web design that you would need to start getting into the .NET tools available to take you into the ranks of aesthNETics developers. You learned that, to be a true aesthNETics developer, you need to be more than just someone who knows .NET code. You were given the basic foundation of good aesthNETics with overviews of the concepts of good web design, such as target resolution, color depth, cross-browser support, and accessibility. Those concepts are critical to any web developer but were not specific to .NET. So, after that overview, it was time to put the ".NET" into "aesthNETics." This meant that you needed to get familiar with the inner workings of several of the controls that are available as part of Visual Studio 2005 to help you create consistent, stylish web sites that are easily developed across development teams and hundreds or even thousands of pages.

As a part of this, you learned about the use of the XML-based menu system included in the .NET Framework, which allows you to display, lock down, and localize your navigation system for all of the pages of your site. From there, you learned how to make that navigation system more accessible through freely available control adapters that override the table rendering behavior of the navigation system and, instead, output CSS-friendly equivalents. You then took the basic shell you had at that point and saw how to easily wrap it inside of a Master Page to turn it into a true template that you can use for every page in your site. And, finally, you learned how to mold all of your .NET controls to look and feel the same through the use of themes.

Along the way, you saw some of the shortcomings and quirks of some of these concepts and how to work with those shortcomings or to work around them. You saw how the tools were meant to work, even if that way wasn't necessarily intuitive. You have, at this point, created a consistent look that is ready to be deployed throughout your site. Or have you?

Browser Check

You have seen throughout the book several different times that testing in different browsers is critical for the success of your layout. This becomes increasingly true when you are using CSS for much of the layout and design of your site. With that being said, it is time to look again at the popular browsers and how the book project renders at this point.

With that, examine the site in Microsoft Internet Explorer version 7 (IE7), Microsoft Internet Explorer version 6 (IE6), and Mozilla FireFox version 1.5 (FireFox), as shown in Figures 10-1, 10-2, and 10-3, respectively.

Figure 10-1

Everything looks okay, right? With the browsers you have been using throughout this project, the final layout for your site looks fine.

But what haven't you tested against that you probably should also consider (no fair looking at the title of this chapter)? How does your site look in a mobile browser? To answer this question, examine

Figures 10-4 and 10-5, which show two locations in the same page in a mobile browser. (Figure 10-4 shows the top of the page, and Figure 10-5 shows the view scrolled down to around the middle of the page.)

These images were captured using the Windows Mobile 5.0 Pocket PC Emulator that comes with the Windows Mobile 5.0 SDK for Pocket PC (www.microsoft.com/downloads/details.aspx? familyid=83A52AF2-F524-4EC5-9155-717CBE5D25ED&displaylang=en). This represents one of the most current versions of the Internet Browser for Windows Mobile devices.

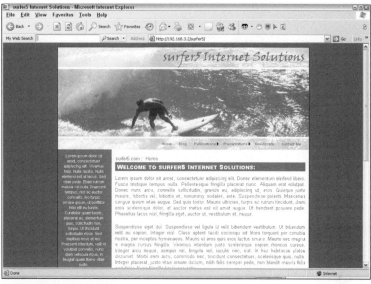

Figure 10-2

Figure 10-3

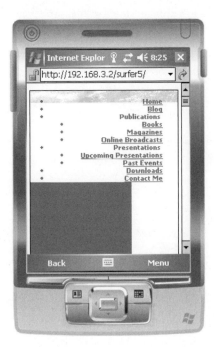

Figure 10-4

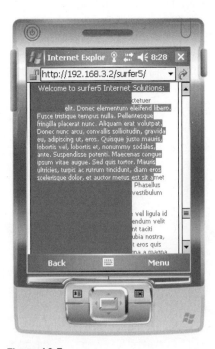

Figure 10-5

As you can hopefully recognize, all of the hard work you set up making a universal template just didn't work out for your mobile users. In the discussion on CSS, it was discussed and illustrated several times throughout the chapter the differences in the way different browsers handle CSS. What wasn't really approached, though, was how differently mobile browsers handle CSS. As you can see by Figures 10-4 and 10-5, mobile browsers handle CSS much differently than any of the other major browsers.

To elaborate on that, though, here is a list of some of the considerations you must take into account when planning on providing content to mobile devices:

❑ Mobile devices can come in various screen sizes. Remember, this can be a mobile phone with an Internet browser (100–320 pixels width) or PDAs (320–640 pixel width). Many devices support their screens displaying in portrait or landscape mode as well. The difference between 100 pixels wide and, say, 640 pixels wide is huge (over six times the amount of screen resolution). This is much more of an issue than typical screen browsers. If you target 100 pixels, your site will look really small in a 640 pixel browser; if you target 640, much of your content may be truncated after the first 100 pixels in the smaller browser window. Therefore, even more so than in screen browsers, a liquid design is crucial.

❑ Because of the limited screen size, you have to reconsider some of your layout options. In the surfer5 project, there is a sidebar that is 150 pixels wide. When that was rendered in the mobile browser, as seen in Figures 10-4 and 10-5, that 150 pixels completely overwhelmed the browser window. Imagine what would have happened had you navigated with a mobile phone that only had 100 pixels width available. So, when taking that into consideration, do you even really need a sidebar at all? If you need the content contained in the sidebar, is there a better way to display it in the limited screen size available? To continue that thought, what other pieces of the page are not really relevant to mobile device users? Are there pieces of your content that you can hide so that less content is provided, making the mobile user able to more easily navigate and read your site? If so, you may want to think about introducing things like display:none rules to begin hiding this content from mobile devices.

❑ There is a serious shift in the way users navigate mobile browsers as opposed to screen browsers. There is no mouse, and in many devices keyboards are optional. Devices rely on a stylus, navigation wheel, or touchscreen for navigating the content in the browser. If your links are images that render really small on the screen and are close together, a person may have a lot of difficultly navigating your site by touchscreen (their fingers may touch two adjacent link images). Related to this, many devices do not support horizontal scrolling (how would you scroll horizontally if you are using a trackwheel?).

❑ If you thought rendering standards were a challenge in screen browsers, you probably need to sit down and relax before trying to tackle mobile browser compatibility. Proprietary browsers in particular follow the specifications and standards of the manufacturer. This means that a Sony mobile device may not follow the same standards that a Motorola device will. To add even more confusion to the mix, the standards aren't even necessarily consistent within a certain manufacturer (two Sony phones may not render information in the same manner). Some of this is getting better, especially with the increased use of third-party browsers (Opera, IE, and so on), and this will hopefully resolve itself over time. But for now, just because you tested your site in your mobile device, that doesn't mean that it will look remotely similar in a different mobile device.

❑ CSS and Style are flaky at best in mobile devices. Using something like @Media does not guarantee that a mobile device will use the media stylesheet. In fact, the mobile device may use both the screen and handheld stylesheet (or neither of them). The most reliable way of differentiating style definitions, which is still not completely consistent, is to use the link tags with specific media properties attached to each. This works most of the time, but not all of the time.

❑   Some devices support font color specifications, and others don't (they may only support black text — a consideration when deciding the background color of your page). Some allow hyperlink markup (changing your hyperlink to be Steel Blue with no underline when they are static and then change to red with underline when the user hovers over them), others just put in default blue underlined text for the for all hyperlinks regardless of what you tell it to do in your CSS.

❑   Mobile devices have much less memory and often have more limited bandwidth than your typical desktop or laptop has. Therefore, if you attempt to provide large images, streaming media, or other large files, your mobile users will lose out.

❑   Many mobile devices butcher tables when they are rendered (if they support them at all). When debating CSS vs. Tables for design, this is another point where CSS wins.

❑   Many mobile device users will switch off CSS and Images to make their browser experiences faster. You need to be prepared to handle that so that the content they see is still acceptable.

So how big of a problem do these issues create?

That, like everything else discussed in this entire book, will depend on your needs. If you are hitting a global audience, maybe mobile browsers aren't that big of a deal in the grand scheme of things. The browser for the examples shown in Figures 10-4 and 10-5 comes through as ''MSIE'' (as opposed to simply ''IE'' for IE6 and IE7) with a version of ''4.01.'' If you look at the statistics for global browser statistics at TheCounter.com, you will see that MSIE 4.x registered less than 85,000 hits of the almost 80,000,000 hits tracked, accounting for only 0.11% of the total. Granted, there are other versions of mobile browsers out there. For example, there are Palm and BlackBerry devices with proprietary operating system and Internet browsing software. But still, on a global scale, the numbers are pretty small.

But is that reason enough to discount the numbers? Probably not. There are more and more people moving to portable devices as their lives get more and more mobile (and as the technology keeps improving). So, even if the number is small now, it probably won't stay that way.

And, again, it also depends on your customers. If you are creating a corporate intranet that many of the directors and officers of your organization will patronize in their daily work, it is likely (or at least possible) many of them will be seeing the pages you create through some sort of mobile interface. And even if those people only account for 2 or 3% of your company, you want to keep them happy. So if you can make them happy with relatively little work on your part, you probably would, right?

So that is what this chapter is going to focus on: the mobile user. This chapter will build up a new theme for the surfer5 project that is specifically targeted at mobile browsers. This theme will be built from scratch to ensure that all pieces are relevant and effective for this particular use. This will include new graphics (created earlier in Chapter 3), new colors, new navigation, a new Master Page, and a new theme to pull all of the pieces together. Some of these things will hopefully serve as a refresher on the concepts and show you a real-world example of how to pull all of these things together.

It should be noted, though, that this chapter will not go nearly as deeply into the concepts presented. It is assumed that you learned these concepts in the previous chapters in this book. This means that concepts already presented will just be dropped into the chapter without much explanation. However, if a new concept is presented, it will be discussed in more detail. For the most part, this chapter serves more as a review than a new learning experience, but there will be a few new concepts.

So, if you are ready to get started, it's time to delve back into the book project one last time in order to add a mobile theme that will allow mobile users to have a comparable, and aesthetically pleasing, experience as other users.

Before You Begin

This chapter is unique compared to the other chapters of this book in that it has a slightly different purpose. In each of the other chapters you learned very specific things about a particular aspect of the aesthNETics approach to web design. In Chapter 2, you learned about general web design considerations; in Chapter 3 you got a crash course in Photoshop. The chapters continued to highlight specific tools available to aesthNETics developers to create consistent and accessible designs for their web projects.

However, this chapter is different in that it aims to show you the entire process of creating a new theme in a summarized version in a single chapter. In this chapter, you will build a new theme from beginning to end and, as part of this, you will end up creating the following pieces (which should be reviews from previous chapters, as indicated in each bulleted item):

- ❏ Consideration of web design considerations for this project (Chapter 2)
- ❏ Modifying your graphic header (Chapter 3)
- ❏ Altering/Creating new CSS rules for this project (Chapter 4)
- ❏ Disabling the CSS Friendly Control Adapters to reenable the standard control behavior (Chapter 5)
- ❏ Creating a new sitemap file and changing your references from the default sitemap file (Chapter 6)
- ❏ Creating a new Master Page (Chapter 7)
- ❏ Creating a new theme (Chapter 8)
- ❏ Changing the base class rules for applying themes to include your new theme and the criteria used to apply themes in general (Chapter 9)

The focus of this chapter, then, is in the review of all of the concepts learned throughout this book in an abbreviated and compiled version. This is not necessarily to say this is the only way to handle the mobility issues already addressed in this chapter. This chapter will show you *a* way to handle mobile device considerations but not *the* way to handle those issues. If you focus too much on whether this is the best way to handle mobile devices in your own projects, you will miss the point of this chapter.

To that end, it is recognized that there are many and varied solutions for mobile devices. However, as discussed earlier in this chapter, mobile devices present many more stumbling blocks than typical screen web projects do. Specifically, there is a lack of standards across the different devices and operating systems. There is varying support for CSS and media types. There are drastically different browser window resolutions and memory and bandwidth considerations.

So what are the pros and cons of the approach shown in this chapter? The pros would include that you can completely modify the HTML markup for the pages served to the mobile browser. This means that if you have images in your Master Page, you don't have to worry about trying to hide them from the browser with something like `display: none` rules (which may or may not work); you can just completely remove the reference. If you no longer want the sidebar, you don't have to worry about sizing it to zero pixels wide or changing the rules for the rendering of the background of the content area (as with the faux column approach); you can just completely eliminate the left sidebar regions of your HTML markup. This ability to modify your HTML markup also has one other added benefit: potentially less code to come down to the mobile device. Take the sidebar example. If you remove all of the reference to the sidebar region of the page, the HTML markup is less in the actual page. But beyond that, you can eliminate the rules for that region in your CSS document. This means that the HTML document and the CSS document can be smaller, which will allow them to render faster in the mobile browser. Finally, you don't have to worry about support of media types within CSS documents or their link references. You have in your new mobile Master Page a link to an external CSS document with no need to provide any media types (which may or may not be supported) because the only users who will use this Master Page will be those using mobile devices. Therefore, there is no need to distinguish some external CSS documents as handheld media-specific, while others are only for the screen media type. There is no need to include the screen version at all, since no screen version will hit this Master Page and there is no need to qualify the link to the mobile CSS document for only the handheld media type. This is the most reliable way of ensuring the proper CSS document is applied for your mobile users.

The obvious downside to this approach is that of maintainability. Using this approach you will not only have a separate external CSS document (which would probably be true for all techniques), but you will also have a different Master Page and an entirely different theme. So what happens when you need to make changes to the way your project looks? You potentially will have to update two different Master Pages and two different themes (and any related skin files, CSS documents, and images). From a maintainability prospective, this is less than ideal. There is the added downside that this solution still may not work for all browsers (but that is not unique to this solution — all mobile solutions will wrestle with this issue).

So what are your options? You could certainly tackle this challenge in a number of different ways. For example, you might try something similar to the following:

- ❑ Adding a new Handheld style using CSS Media Types
- ❑ Adding new navigation Styles (also using media types) and a new Mobile Sitemap
- ❑ Wiring it all up: toggling the Sitemaps, AdapterEnabled based on the `Request.Browser.IsMobileDevice` property

This would certainly be much simpler from a maintainability perspective and would probably be quicker and easier to implement. However, this solution is not ideal, either. For one thing, there are some real problems with using media types when you are using themes, as shown in Chapter 8. Specifically, if you just include your CSS documents in your `Themes` subdirectory, you have no media types available to use (they are all just applied to all browsers). There are ways to get around this (one way was shown in Chapter 8, but there are others). But, even with that being true, there are some serious discrepancies in the ways that different browsers support media types. As already stated, some browsers will apply the CSS documents appropriately based on CSS media type, others will apply all CSS documents (ignoring media types), and still others will apply none of the CSS documents. This approach also sends the exact same HTML markup to the mobile device and, in order to handle hiding certain elements, you have to introduce new code in your mobile CSS document (potentially beefing up the CSS document itself).

So what is the ideal situation? Well, as with everything else you have read about in this book, it just depends. Do you have a definitive list of mobile devices that will be accessing your pages? For example, if your pages are only accessible through your corporate intranet and all mobile devices for the employees in your company use Windows Mobile 5.0, then you can specifically target that platform. If that isn't the case, are you willing to gamble with varying support for media types? Or do you want to take on the additional responsibility of taking on an entirely different Master Page and theme? That is really up to each developer and, as stated in the beginning of this section, is not the focus of this chapter.

This chapter is meant to show you how to piece together an entire theme from beginning to end. In order to do this, a mobile theme was created so that it could accomplish this objective. This is not a statement as to what is ideal for mobile themes; it is just a means to an end (that end being the review of the book concepts spread over more than 300 pages in 9 different chapters).

Step 1: Back to the Drawing Board

The first step is to go back all the way to the beginning and start all over. You have seen how your project looks in the mobile browser and, hopefully, you can appreciate how not much of anything is worth saving for this medium. The logo isn't really showing up, the navigation is reverting back to a lot of full-line cascading list items, the sidebar only serves to hide some of your content, and there isn't nearly the amount of screen real estate, meaning that your 150 pixel sidebar graphic is covering over half of the available screen area.

So now you have to think, what is worth saving? Anything?

The only thing that is worth really saving is the actual content of the page. Everything else needs to be readdressed. The header needs a facelift. The navigation needs some reworking. The sidebar needs to be reconsidered. The content is okay but it needs some formatting changes so that it is actually legible and not hidden by the sidebar.

For the rest of this discussion, you will be starting at the top and working your way down in logical units. The first thing will be the header, then the navigation, then the sidebar, then the content, and finally the footer.

But, before you can even get into that, you need to create the basic shell to start all the formatting changes. You need to create a new template.

Step 2: A New Master

Many themes will not require a new Master Page. After all, for most projects, you just want to change the colors and possibly the layout, most of that can be done within the confines of the original Master Page.

However, this particular theme is different. You will see the differences as the chapter progresses, but there are some conflicts in controls and layout schemas presented in the Master that may be challenging to override with the new theme. At the risk of too much foreshadowing, a good example of this would be the navigation control. With the mobile theme, you may not care as much about having the drop-down appearance and may only want the high-level options presented. This means that you will need to have a totally different SiteMapDataSource control on the page, and that would be hard to do within the confines of the original master.

So, with that being said, add a new Master Page to your project (Website ⇨ Add New Item) and call it "surfer5Mobile.master." Once you have the project open, make sure that it inherits from the `MasterBase` base class you created earlier in the project. For now, this just allows you to share the corporate name among pages, but, for consistency, it is important to inherit this information in your mobile theme as well.

You can go ahead and define the basic areas of the page (e.g., "headerArea," "contentArea," etc.) in the page; it will be formatted later. For now, your code for surfer5Mobile.master will look like this:

```
<%@ Master Language="C#" AutoEventWireup="true" CodeFile="surfer5Mobile.master.cs"
    Inherits="surfer5Mobile" %>

<!DOCTYPE html PUBLIC "-//W3C//DTD XHTML 1.0 Transitional//EN"
    "http://www.w3.org/TR/xhtml1/DTD/xhtml1-transitional.dtd">

<html xmlns="http://www.w3.org/1999/xhtml" >
<head runat="server">
    <title>Untitled Page</title>
</head>
<body>
    <form id="form1" runat="server">
    <div id="headerArea"></div>
    <div id="navigationArea"></div>
    <div id="contentArea">
        <asp:contentplaceholder id="ContentPlaceHolder1" runat="server">
        </asp:contentplaceholder>
    </div>
    <div id="footerArea">&copy 2006 - 2007: surfer5 Internet Solutions</div>
    </form>
</body>
</html>
```

One fundamental difference you will notice between this Master Page and the one created earlier in the book is that there is only one ContentPlaceHolder defined. This is intentional. The sidebar, at least for this application, is mostly just for fluff and serves no real purpose. So, in order to accommodate for the limited screen size, it is being scrapped. The content area, then, will span the entire width of the screen, allowing for a more readable area for your users. This means that you no longer need the second ContentPlaceHolder, so it has been taken out of the Master Page.

The code behind for your new Master Page should resemble the following (again, for now):

```
using System;
using System.Data;
using System.Configuration;
using System.Collections;
using System.Web;
using System.Web.Security;
using System.Web.UI;
using System.Web.UI.WebControls;
using System.Web.UI.WebControls.WebParts;
using System.Web.UI.HtmlControls;

public partial class surfer5Mobile : MasterBase
{
    protected void Page_Load(object sender, EventArgs e)
    {

    }
}
```

The Master Page will be enhanced as the project matures throughout this chapter, but this will get you started.

There are certainly ways to get around the justifications for the Master Page in this chapter. For example, you could programmatically establish the SiteMapData *source within the original Master Page. You could also easily hide the* ContentPlaceHolder *section through CSS or within the* ASP.NET *code. However, you then need to add code to your base class and/or your code behinds to handle these challenges. In the real world, you will have to decide which way makes more sense.*

Step 3: The Mobile Theme

Now it's time to add the mobile theme. Again, just as with the Master Page, you only want to set up the shell at this point. You will want to make sure that everything is wired up correctly before going too far into the new design.

So you just need to add a new theme to your project (Website ➪ Add ASP.NET Folder ➪ Theme) and call your new theme surfer5MobileTheme.

This is enough for now. You have the theme set up and ready to apply to your page in conjunction with your Master Page. It's time to wire it up and see what happens.

Step 4: Wiring It Up

Now that you have your Master Page and theme set up, it's time to put logic into your application to decide which one is applied for each user. Fortunately, you already have the shell for this logic set up in your Page base class, PageBase.cs:

```
protected void Page_PreInit(object sender, EventArgs e)
{
    Page.Theme = "surfer5BlueTheme";
}
```

At this point, you are only applying the theme. However, the Master Page is applied in the same event (PreInit), so it is perfectly logical to introduce code to apply the Master Page as well. You will now need to create criteria for applying the appropriate theme/Master Page. In this case, you want to apply one theme and Master Page if the visitor is a mobile client and the other theme and Master Page combination for all other users.

To do this, you need to modify your logic to something more along the lines of the following:

```
protected void Page_PreInit(object sender, EventArgs e)
{
    if (Request.Browser.IsMobileDevice == true)
    {
        Page.Theme = "surfer5MobileTheme";
        Page.MasterPageFile = "surfer5Mobile.master";
    }
```

```
    else
    {
        Page.Theme = "surfer5BlueTheme";
        Page.MasterPageFile = "surfer5.master";
    }
}
```

The `if` statement is checking to see if the user is, in fact, a mobile user. This is similar to code you used earlier to detect the browser and its associated version. However, you don't really care about what browser or version you are dealing with (at least in this scenario); you only care if the user is a mobile user or not. If the client is a mobile device, you apply the "surfer5MobileTheme" theme and "surfer5Mobile.master" Master Page; all other users will get the "surfer5BlueTheme" and "surfer5.master" combination you have created in the other sections of this book.

So now its time to see if it worked. To do so, load the project back into a couple of browsers and make sure that nothing has stopped working with the implementation of these changes. For example, you can see that the page looks exactly the same in IE7 (see Figure 10-6).

Figure 10-6

For brevity, the other browser screenshots are not included; they should all look the same as they previously did as well.

However, now reload the project in your mobile browser. You should see something that resembles Figure 10-7.

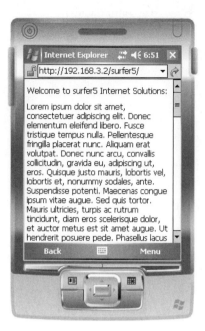

Figure 10-7

To the casual observer, it may appear that the steps outlined have broken something. However, this couldn't be further from the truth. You have created a new mobile framework that is ready for you to fill with a new design. You can tell this worked by the fact that "surfer5 Internet Solutions" is at the top of the page. This is coming directly from the Master Page base class. The text is from the content area, and there is no conflicting sidebar text. You have now set up the mobile shell; you just have to style it.

Step 5: Adding Style

Now that you have the shell set up, its time to add some style. One nice thing about this approach is that you don't have to worry as much about the limitations of CSS in themes with this project. This is because many of the previous problems had to do with setting up conditional rules, media differentiation, and cascading rule conflicts. With this particular theme, none of that is really all that important. You are specifically targeting mobile browsers and, therefore, you don't need the media differentiation or, really, the conditional rules as much. Similarly, the cascading conflicts should no longer be an issue because you will only be applying CSS rules specifically targeted to mobile browsers, which will eliminate this obstacle.

With that being said, it is time to add a CSS file to your theme (Website ➪ Add New Item) and call it surfer5Mobile.css. You will also want to create an "images" subdirectory for your theme and bring in the mobile logo you created in Chapter 3 (logo02_mobile.jpg).

You will need to modify the CSS file to accommodate this new logo. The rules in `surfer5Mobile.css` should, at this time, look like the following:

```
body
{
    width: 100%;
    padding: 0px;
    margin: 0px;
}
#headerArea
{
    height: 75px;
    width: 100%;
    background: #000 url(images/logo02_mobile.jpg) no-repeat;
}
```

This has just set up the page to be 100% of the available screen and then set up the basic properties of the `headerArea` region of your page. Remember that the logo had a size of 75 pixels high and 300 pixels wide. This is the reason that you need to define the height of the region of 75 pixels to ensure that you capture the entire logo. Notice that the background color is set to #000 (black) and that the logo is set to not repeat. This means that the logo will appear exactly one time in the uppermost left-hand area of the region, and any area not covered by the graphic will have a black background. Again, the width is set to 100% so that it will span all the way across the screen.

At this time, it is a good idea to check your style in the browser just to make sure that everything is copasetic. You can see the results of the project enhancements in Figure 10-8.

Figure 10-8

This looks better, but the image isn't exactly right. Again, the dimensions are 75 px high and 300 px wide. As a result, the logo may be a little high but, even if it isn't, it is definitely too wide; you can't even read the entire logo.

Fortunately, this is fairly easy to remedy. Open the image in Photoshop and then select Image on the toolbar and choose Image Size to get the Image Size dialog box. In the Pixel Dimensions area (at the top), change the width to 200 pixels. This should automatically adjust the height to 50 pixels but, if it does not, go ahead and make that change as well. Click the OK button to make the image resize adjustment. Now just resave the image (File ➪ Save), and your logo should be a little more appropriately sized for this theme.

> For this step, you are resizing the graphic image to 200 pixels. This number, however, is a fairly arbitrary setting. The size of 200 pixels was chosen because it should fit inside most mobile device browser windows. Later, it will be part of the header region of your page, and a black background will be used to span the entire width of the browser window. This will have the 200 pixel image sitting to the left side of the screen and then fading into a black background. As long as the browser window is at least 200 pixels wide, the header region of your page will be fully liquid and look like one seamless image.

You will also need to modify your CSS rule for the `headerArea` definition to set the height to 50 pixels rather than 75. Doing so will result in a new look to your mobile theme, as can be seen in Figure 10-9.

Figure 10-9

This fits much better in the mobile browser window. For one, the entire phrase "surfer5 Internet Solutions" fits in the window now. There is also not as much creep on the content area, which means that more content will be viewable to your visitors.

To that end, you need to modify the other regions of your page for your mobile theme. An example of style rules you may want to set up for your theme can be seen below:

```
body
{
    width: 100%;
    padding: 0px;
    margin: 0px;
}
#headerArea
{
    height: 50px;
    width: 100%;
    background: #000 url(images/logo02_mobile.jpg) no-repeat;
}
#navigationArea
{
    width: 100%;
    height: 20px;
    background-color: #000;
    color: #fff;
    text-align: right;
    padding: 1px 1px 0px 1px;
}
#contentArea
{
    width: 100%;
    padding: 10px 5px 10px 5px;
    color: #750001;
    font-size: .8em;
}
#contentArea.header
{
    width: 100%;
    background-color: #BFAB4E;
    color: #750001;
    padding: 5px 0px 5px 5px;
    font-size: .5em;
    border: solid 1pt #750001;
}
#footerArea
{
    width: 100%;
    background-color: #750001;
    color: #BFAB4E;
    padding: 5px 1px 5px 5px;
    font-size: .75em;
    font-weight: bold;
    text-align: center;
}
```

With these rules in place, refresh your mobile browser and it should resemble Figure 10-10.

Figure 10-10

The theme is really starting to come together now. The beginning of the content is easily seen without having to scroll down at all to see it, which is a major plus in and of itself. The content is more logically laid out for the limitations of this browser. The navigation, which will come in next, will go in the black area under the logo. When a user hits this page, then, he will immediately see your logo, your navigation, and your content. This is the experience you want that user to have; not the impossible-to-understand-and-navigate version that came with the default theme. This is definitely progress in the right direction.

Step 6: Adding the Navigation

The final step for this example is to add the site navigation to your new Master Page template and manipulate it to fit the limitations of the mobile browser. So, as a first step, you will need to drag a SiteMapDataSource control and a Menu control onto your Master Page (surfer5Mobile.master). The resulting code should resemble this:

```
<%@ Master Language="C#" AutoEventWireup="true" CodeFile="surfer5Mobile.master.cs"
    Inherits="surfer5Mobile" %>

<!DOCTYPE html PUBLIC "-//W3C//DTD XHTML 1.0 Transitional//EN"
   "http://www.w3.org/TR/xhtml1/DTD/xhtml1-transitional.dtd">

<html xmlns="http://www.w3.org/1999/xhtml" >
<head runat="server">
```

```
        <title>Untitled Page</title>
    </head>
    <body>
        <form id="form1" runat="server">
        <div id="headerArea"></div>
        <div id="navigationArea"><asp:Menu ID="Menu1" runat="server"
    DataSourceID="SiteMapDataSource1" /></div>
        <div id="contentArea">
            <asp:contentplaceholder id="ContentPlaceHolder1" runat="server">
            </asp:contentplaceholder>
        </div>
        <div id="footerArea">&copy 2006 - 2007: surfer5 Internet Solutions</div>
        </form>

        <asp:SiteMapDataSource ID="SiteMapDataSource1" runat="server" />
    </body>
    </html>
```

As you can see, the Menu control should reside within the `navigationArea` area of the page defined earlier. The SiteMapDataSource can pretty much go anywhere on the page; it just serves as a reference to the sitemap file and isn't rendered in the browser.

If you run this page, as it stands, in your browser, it will look something like Figure 10-11.

Figure 10-11

The menu control, unfortunately, looks as bad as the original design (refer to Figure 10-4) and brings back into focus the problems with CSS rendering in a mobile browser. In the original example you could see that the mobile browser wasn't respecting the size rules and, as a result, created a vertical, rather than horizontal, menu. You also saw that the browser rendered out an unordered (bulleted) list rather than the block style you had set with your CSS Friendly Control Adapters. It is also apparent in the original example as well as in this new modified one that there are way too many links to be considered a usable navigation system. This has to do with the fact that you can't have any kind of "hover" activity in your code and, if you think about it, this makes sense. After all, what would trigger the hover? A user hovering his or her stylus over the mobile device? Is there even any way of detecting that? Handheld devices typically don't have mice, so rollovers are useless. This negates the possibility of having hidden menu items that only appear when a user hovers over the parent node. So essentially, you have to show all of the menu items, which means that you probably want to trim the list down a bit.

This means that there are a couple of things that need to be done in order to clean this mess up. The first is to get rid of all of the links that are determined to be irrelevant for a mobile browser (at least for this example). For now, assume that the only links that you want to show your mobile users are Home, Blog, and Contact Me. In the real world, you might reconsider these options, but this will give you a place to start.

So how do you tell your application to only show those three links? There are probably several ways, but for this discussion, you will want to create a second sitemap file that is only for use with mobile browsers and, consequently, has significantly fewer links in it.

With this in mind, you will want to add a new sitemap file to your project and call it `mobile.sitemap`. You can use the original web.sitemap as a guide to par down your options, but it should end up looking like this:

```xml
<?xml version="1.0" encoding="utf-8" ?>
<siteMap xmlns="http://schemas.microsoft.com/AspNet/SiteMap-File-1.0" >
  <siteMapNode roles="*" url="" title="surfer5.com"  description="">
     <siteMapNode url="Default.aspx" title="Home"  description="Main Page" />
     <siteMapNode url="Blog.aspx" title="Blog"  description="Current Blog" />
     <siteMapNode url="ContactMe.aspx" title="Contact Me" description="Contact Me"/>
  </siteMapNode>
</siteMap>
```

As you can see, you are only keeping the parent node ("surfer5.com") and three child nodes ("Home", "Blog", and "Contact Me").

The next step is to set up your project to handle multiple sitemap files. This has to be done in the web.config file. If you have followed this book's project, you probably already have a section in your web.config for your sitemap. You will now need to modify that section to have it bring in your new mobile sitemap file and then set up the default sitemap as your original web.sitemap (so as not to break the other pages). This section should look like this:

```xml
<siteMap enabled="true" defaultProvider="myMenu">
    <providers>
        <add name="myMenu"
            type="System.Web.XmlSiteMapProvider"
            siteMapFile="web.sitemap"
            securityTrimmingEnabled="true"/>
        <add name="mobileMenu"
            type="System.Web.XmlSiteMapProvider"
            siteMapFile="mobile.sitemap"
            securityTrimmingEnabled="true"/>
    </providers>
</siteMap>
```

You still have "myMenu", which you set up earlier, and it is still the default sitemap provider for your application. This will keep the other pages running the same as they always have. However, you have added a new named sitemap, referenced as "mobileMenu" and pointing to "mobile.sitemap", to your providers list to give you the option of bringing in this new mobile sitemap to use instead of the default.

The final step to bringing in this new sitemap is to point the SiteMapDataSource control to this new sitemap in your Master Page. So, in surfer5Mobile.master, change your SiteMapDataSource control to resemble this:

```
<asp:SiteMapDataSource SiteMapProvider="mobileMenu" ID="SiteMapDataSource1"
    runat="server" ShowStartingNode="False" />
```

In this example, you have also trimmed off the starting node just as you did before. This just gets rid of the "surfer5.com" parent node, keeping it from being displayed on the page.

So now, if you load your page again, you will see that the content itself has been cleaned up quite a bit, just by trimming the options down to three, as can be seen in Figure 10-12.

Figure 10-12

This looks much better but still needs some work. Specifically, the navigation system needs some style. Right now, its not a very impressive navigation system and doesn't really tie into the look and feel of the rest of the page.

The problem, though, is the fact that the control is being overridden by the CSS Friendly Control Adapters discussed in Chapter 5 and later applied to the book project in Chapter 6. This overriding behavior is causing the rendering engine to spit out CSS for the Menu control rather than its default behavior of providing HTML tables. This works wonderfully in the other browsers tested but is causing undesirable effects in the mobile browser. It would be nice if you could just turn off the CSS overrides for the mobile version, but, if you remember from the discussion in Chapter 5, the disabling of the adapter overrides is provided only on an experimental basis and this concept is not really supported by the .NET 2.0 Framework.

Well, that just means its time to experiment.

To start this experiment, add the `AdapterEnabled` attribute to your control and set it to false, as follows:

```
<asp:Menu ID="Menu1" runat="server" DataSourceID="SiteMapDataSource1"
    AdapterEnabled="False" />
```

After making this one small change, reload the page in your mobile browser and it should resemble Figure 10-13.

Figure 10-13

At first glance, this may not look like it did much, but you have to really look at it to appreciate what has happened. The bullets are gone. The items have shifted to the left. So what does this mean? This means that you are no longer rendering CSS for this control. It also means that you have the default vertical menu that you would get simply by dropping a Menu control item onto a page (without the CSS Friendly Control Adapters). However, what this really means is that you have gotten back access to the stylistic properties of this control at the control level. In short, this means that you can style the control from the properties of the control rather than relying on CSS.

To see how this works, start playing with the style properties of the control. You will see that their impact will be immediately noticeable in your mobile browser. For example, modify your control to have the following properties:

```
<asp:Menu ID="Menu1" Font-Size="XX-Small" ForeColor="White"
    StaticMenuStyle-Width="130px" StaticMenuItemStyle-HorizontalPadding="5px"
    Orientation="Horizontal" runat="server" DataSourceID="SiteMapDataSource1"
    AdapterEnabled="False" />
```

The major things you did here were to set the orientation to horizontal and add a couple of color and size properties. However, with these simple changes in place, reload your project in your mobile browser to see something similar to Figure 10-14.

Figure 10-14

At this point, you have a styled mobile version of your project that ties into the main theme that you started with but, at the same time, looks distinctly different. You have a completely different layout, different graphics, and even an entirely different sitemap file. You have also disabled the CSS Friendly Control Adapters so that your navigation controls are usable by your mobile clients. You have created an entirely new template that will automatically be applied to your pages if a mobile browser hits your page. That is pretty cool.

So how is this different from the mobile CSS media type? It won't take long for someone to point out that you can shape CSS by media type, including setting certain CSS rules or even entire files only applicable to mobile browsers. So, with that being true, people will wonder why setting up an entirely different mobile theme is so much better than just using the media types of CSS.

Hopefully, as this chapter concludes, you can answer that. With media types for CSS, you can definitely adjust the CSS rules for a page for just mobile browsers. But, as powerful as that can be, it is also very limiting. All of the changes made to this project for mobile browsers would not have been possible merely by adjusting CSS rules. Granted, some of them would have been, but many would not. For example, you have added an entirely new sitemap file that is only used for your mobile browsers and, on top of that, you have removed the CSS Friendly Control Adapters for the Menu control. There just isn't a way to do that through CSS alone. Certainly you probably could have hidden the left sidebar region (well, possibly anyway — CSS is very different in mobile browsers and, as was seen with the child nodes in the menu control, attempting to hide content can have questionable results). You definitely could have adjusted the header graphic and new dimension. In fact, many of the stylistic changes made to this project were done through CSS. However, there are some things that CSS just can't do and that is where the theme steps in. The theme uses CSS for style but then takes over for the programmatic changes required for your project that CSS was never intended to handle.

There are some things in this section that were done merely for illustrative purposes and, as such, may not suit your needs in the real world. For example, it may be possible to create the horizontal menu control formatted exactly the same as the final product using just the CSS Friendly Control Adapters and CSS formatting through an external stylesheet, incorporating the same techniques outlined in Chapter 6 In fact, it might be preferable to try to make the CSS work, since tables aren't very well supported in many mobile devices. And, even if you did revert to the ASP.NET rendering default (overriding the CSS Friendly Control Adapters), as shown in this section, you still would probably prefer to keep your style definitions in an external stylesheet and reference the classes through the CssClass attribute of the menu control. However, for this section, the approach used was included to specifically show you how you might want to turn off the overrides of the control adapter and how, if you did that, you again have access to the properties of the control. This was done not only to review what you learned in Chapter 5 but also to expand upon that to show you that you can, in fact, disable the adapters at the control level if you need to.

Browser Check: A Final Look

So now that all of the changes have been made, it is a good idea to go through and make sure that everything works the way you want it to. First, you need to ensure that all of your original browsers work. You can see examples of this check for IE6, IE7, FireFox, and Netscape in Figures 10-15, 10-16, 10-17, and 10-18, respectively.

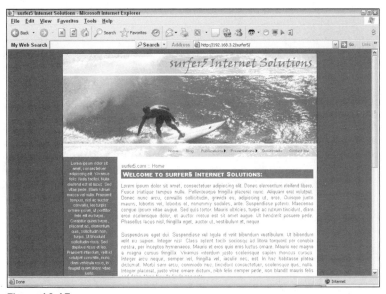

Figure 10-15

As you can see, none of the changes that you have made for this new mobile theme have impacted the visual layout in the other browsers previously tested. This is, obviously, a good thing.

Figure 10-16

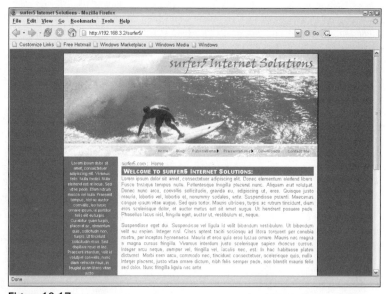

Figure 10-17

So now, just as a final comparison, pull up the mobile version you have been testing against throughout this chapter, as shown in Figure 10-19.

Just for a final test, reload the page in a different mobile browser. You can see how the page now looks on the Pocket PC 2003 operating system in Figure 10-20.

Figure 10-18

Figure 10-19

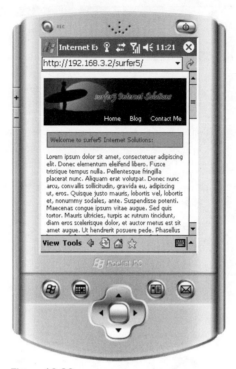

Figure 10-20

In your own situation, you may want to run your application up against other browsers to see how it looks. For example, it might be a requirement for your pages to be BlackBerry-friendly and, therefore, you would run the web page through the BlackBerry browser (or, similarly, maybe the Palm browser). However, this chapter would get terribly long if it included screenshots from every available browser. Even so, with the ones shown, you can see that the final project should work for most users that hit your site. And, since the non-mobile version is built on CSS, it should even be accessible to users with some sort of disability. The site looks good and it works. You are now ready to fill it up with content.

Summary

This chapter provided a working example of a mobile theme that you can apply to the book project. This was done for several reasons. The most obvious reason might seem to show you many of the considerations you need to take into account in your mobile platform planning. The mobile browser discussion at the beginning of the chapter, as well as the steps illustrating how to create a completely new mobile theme, brought to light many of the aspects you should incorporate if and when you decide to target mobile devices in your web project planning. With that being true, it might seem that the point of this chapter was how to plan a good approach to dealing with mobile browsers in your .NET applications.

However, more important than an overview of mobile browser considerations was a review of what it takes to be a true aesthNETics developer. In this sense, you went through all of the steps that a good aesthNETics developer would need to go through in order to create a consistent and aesthetically pleasing web design within Visual Studio 2005. You started off with a blank slate (true, you had a template but it was a busted one with regard to mobile browsers, so you had to start all over). You started with an image, which you tested, saw that it didn't meet your needs, and then resized it to meet your needs. Next, you went through the process of adding a new Master Page and theme to your project and then filling them with the appropriate content and CSS rules and definitions. Finally, you had to take the navigation system into consideration and make adjustments to the way you had previously used the controls to accommodate the mobile browser. With that, you saw how to set up different sitemap files and call them according to your needs. You also experimented a bit with turning off the CSS Control Adapter overrides. In this one chapter, you at least touched on the broad concepts presented in every chapter of this book. And in some cases, as with experimenting with turning off the CSS Friendly Control Adapters, you actually got to expand some of the knowledge you gained in earlier chapters.

Hopefully, at this point, you have the big-picture idea of not just how themes are created and applied to projects but also what adjustments you might make, as an aesthNETics developer, in creating them. A theme is an amazing concept but, without proper planning, it can prove useless. Without the universal building blocks that make up any good website, such as CSS, colors, and accessibility, the themes may not be as appealing to your customers and patrons as you would hope. Beyond these universal building blocks, though, aesthNETics developers need to incorporate .NET-specific tools such as Menu controls, control rendering overrides, and Master Pages, in order to make their themed website stunning, maintainable, and aesthetically pleasing. While this book is not necessarily intended to be a cookbook that you can follow line by line for every project, it hopefully gave you insight into better web design and the use of the .NET tools to help you move in that direction. And, when its all said and done, you should have seen that themes take some work and thought but are well worth it when you are ready to start adding pages to and maintaining them in your project. You are ready to call yourself an aesthNETics developer.

Microsoft Visual Studio Codename "Orcas"

If you are reading this book, and certainly if you are reading this appendix, you have the only truly quintessential tool necessary for being a good developer: you want to learn. Maybe you picked up this book to get a better handle on general design issues for web design and perhaps you wanted to get a better perspective on how .NET can help handle those issues. Maybe you wanted to get a book on themes or Master Pages or maybe even the CSS Friendly Control Adapters. Or maybe (hopefully) someone told you how great this book is and you just couldn't live without it (that is obviously the best scenario). But regardless of your reason, you probably paid money for this book in the hope that you would learn something you didn't already know and have intentions of using the book again as a reference in your future development endeavors. You bought it to learn.

As part of this learning, it is important to understand not only the current state of technology, but also its future. Sure, for the most part, you probably picked up this book because you wanted to learn how to use the tools that are currently in the market for developing .NET 2.0 web projects. And, hopefully, you did exactly that as you read through the other chapters of this book.

But what will serve you best in your career (or hobby) as a programmer is to be prepared for the future. In 1970, Alan Kay, often considered the father of object-oriented programming, said "the best way to predict the future is to invent it." This should be the heart and soul of every dedicated programmer. It's not enough to know where we came from or where we are. It's at least as important, if not infinitely more important, to realize where we are going. And the best of the best can even determine that future.

So how do you prepare for or, even better, decide the future? You find out what's coming out. You start looking at prerelease software and getting up to speed so that, when a product is released, you are already using it to code your projects, not looking for new training on how to use it. You figure out how to use that new technology to jump ahead of the competition. You figure out, in these prerelease versions, what works better and what needs improvements and, if possible, you tell those that are making the future releases so that they can improve it.

With that in mind, it is important to at least have a fair understanding of the technologies coming out in the next few months (the end of 2007). With respect to the tools presented in this book, this means it's time to pay particular attention to the latest offering by Microsoft, Visual Studio's next release, currently codenamed Orcas.

While not necessarily appropriate for a chapter in this book, examination of Visual Studio Orcas certainly warrants discussion. There are so many improvements in this release that it is actually fun to play with the new tools. Things like the inclusion of out-of-the-box support for Microsoft AJAX, LINQ, and a slew of other things will make perfect fodder for many blogs, articles, and books.

However, as it relates to this book, there are a number of enhancements that directly improve things that you may have noticed while working on the projects and examples in the previous chapters. While all of the improvements to Visual Studio could easily take up an entire book, and quite a large one at that, this appendix will try to give at least an overview of some of the improvements that will directly impact the projects and examples in this book.

> *This appendix was written using the most current software available at the time, Visual Studio Code Name Orcas Beta 1 released on April 26, 2007. While the final release, and even any subsequent beta releases, are sure to have a lot of changes and improvements, it is believed that the discussions in this appendix will still be relevant and will probably make the final cut. However, there is no guarantee that this will be true. Inclusion of examples, screenshots, or discussions in this appendix does not mean that the exact same thing will be available in the final version or any version subsequent to Beta 1 (or previous to it). This is, after all, beta software.*

Feels Like Home ... Sort Of

One of the nicest things about this Visual Studio release, which was also true of the 2005 release, is that when you first open it, you are welcomed with a familiar interface (at least if you have used 2003 or 2005), as seen in Figure A-1.

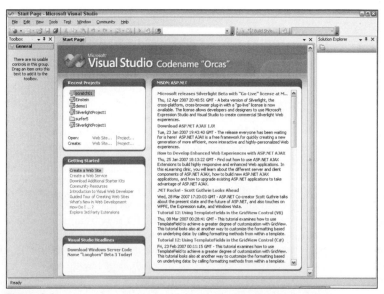

Figure A-1

However, it doesn't take long to take note that things are different. Much different.

For example, examine the screenshot in Figure A-2.

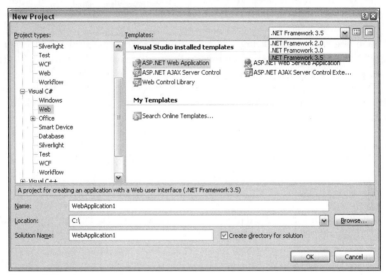

Figure A-2

Notice the drop-down box in the upper-right corner. Your eyes are not playing tricks on you: Orcas allows you to target multiple versions of the Framework.

Well, sort of. It appears that versions previous to the .NET 2.0 Framework are not available. For example, this screenshot was taken from a system that had the following versions set up on it (some of which were installed as part of the Orcas install):

❑ v1.0.3705

❑ v1.1.4322

❑ v2.0.50727

❑ v3.0

❑ v3.5.20404

The computer also had Visual Studio 2003 and Visual Studio 2005 (among other .NET technologies). And, even with that being true, the earliest version you can run up against is .NET 2.0.

Is that really a big issue? Well, it could be. This feature is pretty innovative, but will it be that useful? After all, much of the code people are writing today are still .NET 2.0 core, which will persist through the .NET 3.0 and 3.5 versions. This means, or at least it should mean, that if you have a .NET 2.0 application running on a .NET 3.0 or 3.5 Framework, it will still work.

So, how useful is this? Sure, the Framework you decide may help determine the objects and methods available to you. If you are just writing .NET 2.0, you could just as easily code against the .NET 3.0 or 3.5 Framework and be fine. Similarly, if you are writing something for the new modules and features introduced in 3.0, why would you target the 2.0 Framework?

This feature, while a pretty innovative idea conceptually, doesn't seem to provide that much for the developer. One of the only plausible scenarios where this would come in handy would be in a situation where you were only allowed to code against a .NET 2.0 Framework and you consistently targeted the .NET 2.0 Framework in Orcas to keep you from accidentally using .NET 3.0 functionality that would crash in production.

What might have been nicer would have been to allow you to program back to 1.0 or 1.1. This would allow for easier conversion from those versions to the newer stuff and, as most people already know, there were some fairly big object model changes between those versions. Allowing developers to go back to 1.0 or 1.1 would allow developers to maintain legacy software applications, as well as more current versions, in the same software package. However, since it only goes back to .NET 2.0, that is fairly inconsequential.

That being said, the introduction of this concept may serve to provide this same backwards compatibility as more and more future versions are released. This means that, as the future becomes the present, this enhancement may actually serve as a real benefit to developers. However, in its current iteration, it is little more than a "cool" point.

If you want to switch your target .NET Framework platform in an existing project, you can do that in the Project Property Pages window, as shown in Figure A-3.

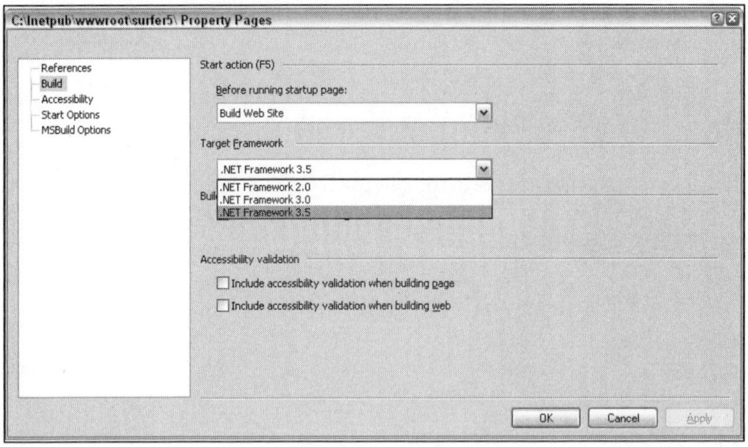

Figure A-3

An interesting related point is that, when opening an existing 2.0 project in Orcas for the first time (you will not see it subsequent times if you select "No"), you will be asked if you want to upgrade it to 3.5, as seen in Figure A-4.

Maybe this is where the potential benefit comes in: you don't have to use Visual Studio 2005 for your .NET 2.0 applications. When VS 2005 was introduced, you couldn't open up 1.0 or 1.1 applications created in VS 2003 without first converting it (or attempting to convert it) to the new .NET 2.0 Framework. This multiplatform targeting, then, will allow developers to ease into the new functionality introduced with the frameworks without forcing them to switch between Visual Studio versions to maintain their existing applications. This will certainly help the transition from 2005 to Orcas, but it is not quite as useful as it might appear on the surface or, possibly, as cool as it could be.

Figure A-4

CSS and Orcas

Here is where some of the real magic of Orcas will start to become apparent, at least with regard to the chapters of this book. Visual Studio has made some remarkable improvements in the way it handles and supports Cascading Style Sheets, and these improvements should really help developers who want to use CSS in their projects. In Visual Studio 2005, there were some pretty nice tools included for CSS development within your projects. However, with the newest set of tools included in Orcas, VS 2005 almost looks amateurish. For any .NET developer wanting to take CSS seriously, these tools are some of the most exciting changes in the latest Visual Studio release.

The CSS Properties Window

To get started with these new tools, you should start a new web in the C:\orcasCSS\ directory as a sandbox to play with the new stuff. For this project, it is not important which version of .NET you target; accepting the default of 3.5 will be fine. When the project opens, you should see something that resembles Figure A-5.

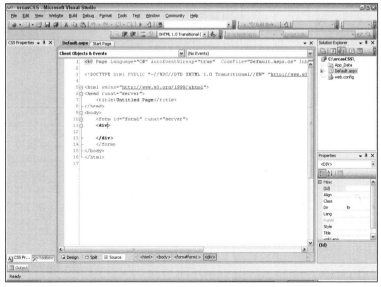

Figure A-5

In this screenshot, you can see that there is a new CSS Properties window to the left of the screen (it is tabbed with the Toolbox window). If you do not see this window, you just need to select View on the toolbar and select CSS Properties, as seen in Figure A-6.

Figure A-6

The problem, at least initially, is that the CSS Properties window, while visible, is disabled. This is one of the "quirks" of at least the beta software that will hopefully be addressed by the final release. In order to enable this view, you have to switch to one of the WYSIWYG views. In previous versions of Visual Studio, this meant switching to the Design view. However, in Orcas, you have an additional option: the Split view. This new Split view allows you to have your source code and your design views both visible at one time.

So, in order to enable your CSS Properties window, switch over to one of the other views. For example, if you switch to the Split view, Orcas should now look like Figure A-7.

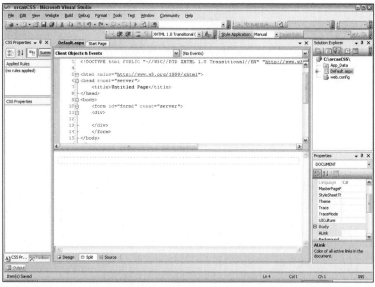

Figure A-7

Okay, so its still not that impressive but be patient; you're almost there.

To start seeing how the CSS Properties window comes into play, modify the `<div>` tag to the following:

```
<div style="background-color: Olive; color: White;">
```

As you start typing in the Source pane, you will notice a new message will appear between the two panes in the Split view, as seen in Figure A-8.

Design view is out of sync with Source view. Click here to synchronize views.

Figure A-8

This is another "quirk" of the beta; the synchronization scenarios have not been finalized and, as such, you must force the two panes to synch up. You can do this in a couple of ways. First, you can simply click on the message. You could also just save the project (e.g., Ctrl-S). You can also use the Synchronize Views command (Ctrl-Shift-Y) in the View menu.

So, whichever ways makes the most sense to you, synchronize your views. Once you do this, you will start seeing how useful this new window is (see Figure A-9).

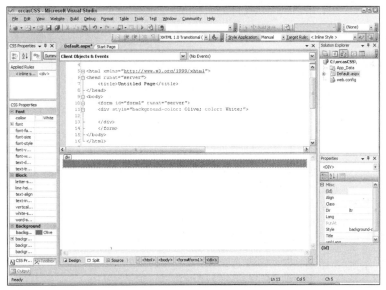

Figure A-9

Maybe at first glance, this might seem like a "nice-to-have" feature that merely displays the properties of the affected CSS. But that is just the surface of it. You can actually set the properties in the window as well. For example, scroll down to the Position section and set the Height and Width each to 200 pixels (if you don't see the scrollbar in your CSS Properties window, you may need to widen your window). You will see a couple of things. First, once you set a property, that property's title is turned to a bold blue font. That might help in some situations when you are trying to quickly find the set properties for a CSS rule. However, the much more powerful functionality is that both the Design and Source views of the Split view are updated automatically (no synching necessary). Your project should now resemble Figure A-10.

Here is an interesting thing to note about this particular feature. If you navigate away from the CSS properties of a particular selector and then come back to them, the properties get reordered so that the ones you have set are at the top. To see this in action, click, for example, the </form> tag of your page in the Source view. Now click back anywhere inside of the division you want to set the properties for (within the <div> tag, the </div> tag, or the space between them), and you will see the properties become viewable again. However, when they come up again, you will see height and width have now been moved to the top of the properties list under Position, as shown in Figure A-11.

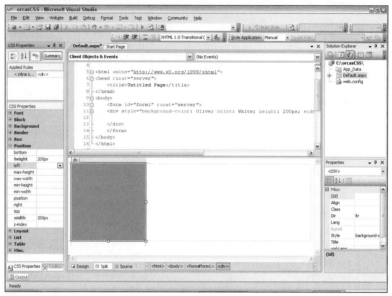

Figure A-10

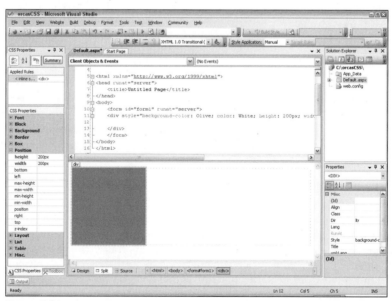

Figure A-11

This actually makes a lot of sense and makes maintaining and updating CSS code much simpler and more intuitive. The properties you have already set are at the top; the ones you have not done anything with are still there but are separated by a logical division. This will prove to be very handy as you start working more and more with CSS.

Adding New Style Definitions

While the ability to modify existing style definitions is very powerful, this is only one of the panes of the CSS Properties window. To start getting really deep into what this new window can do, you have to start looking at the Applied Rules pane. This is probably the most powerful enhancement to the way Visual Studio works with CSS in your projects.

First, right-click on the `<inline style>` line in the listbox (at this point, it should be the only option), and you will see a series of options, as shown in Figure A-12.

Figure A-12

If you select on New Style, you will get the dialog box shown in Figure A-13, which will help you set up a new style.

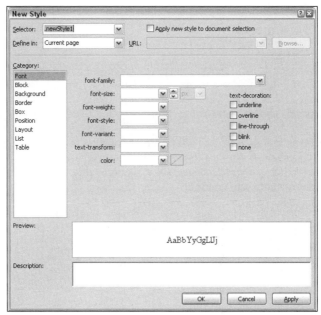

Figure A-13

This is very similar to the Build Style Wizard in Visual Studio 2005. However, this has some very unique functionality incorporated. First, you can set the selector, which means that you can set whether this is an element, class, or ID definition. More impressive is the ability to select where this style rule will get placed. This means that you can place the rules in a style block of the current page, in a new stylesheet that it will create for you or in an existing stylesheet. So, with that in mind, change the settings to resemble Figure A-14.

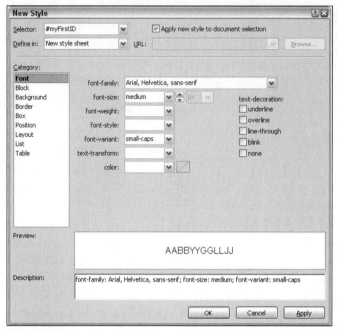

Figure A-14

This is just setting some basic Font properties. However, make sure you check ''Apply new style to document selection'' or you will create a totally new style in a new document that won't be applied to your div selector. It will be created and available; it just won't be used yet. So make sure that you check this option to apply the new rule to the current selector. Click the OK button to continue.

Since you have selected the option to define this new set of rules in a new stylesheet, the application will first create the new stylesheet for you (calling it something like ''StyleSheet.css'') and then it will prompt you to select whether or not you want the new stylesheet linked to your document (you do), as shown in Figure A-15. Click the Yes button to continue.

Figure A-15

When this process is done, you will be taken to the new stylesheet. However, just save that file and close it for now; you will see more about this view later in this appendix. It's time to go back to Default.aspx to see what happened there.

First, add some dummy text ("Hello World") in the division selector just to see the impact of the changes being made. With that, the code should now look like this:

```
<%@ Page Language="C#" AutoEventWireup="true"
   CodeFile="Default.aspx.cs" Inherits="_Default" %>

<!DOCTYPE html PUBLIC "-//W3C//DTD XHTML 1.0 Transitional//EN"
   "http://www.w3.org/TR/xhtml1/DTD/xhtml1-transitional.dtd">

<html xmlns="http://www.w3.org/1999/xhtml">
<head runat="server">
   <title>Untitled Page</title>
   <link href="StyleSheet.css" rel="stylesheet" type="text/css" />
</head>
<body>
   <form id="form1" runat="server">
   <div style="background-color: Olive; color: White; height: 200px;
   width: 200px;" id="myFirstID">
   Hello World
   </div>
   </form>
</body>
</html>
```

You will notice a couple of things. For one, a link for `"StyleSheet.css"` has been added to the HEAD region. You will also see that an ID property has been added for the DIV selector you are working with. Orcas will now look like Figure A-16.

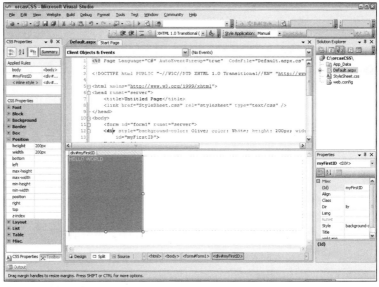

Figure A-16

You will notice that a couple of new entries have been added to the Applied Styles pane of the CSS Properties window. This window is showing you all of the style rules that are impacting this particular selector. In this example, rules for the body element and the myFirstID ID, which come from the new stylesheet have now been added. You can select either of them in the pane, and the rules from those sources will be shown in the properties window below it.

One of the really nice parts of this is that you can actually modify properties in linked stylesheets from this property window just as you saw earlier with the inline styles. When you click on an area of your page, in the #myFirstID section, for example, you will see that there are multiple Applied Rules for that area. If you click on #myFirstID, it will bring up the properties you just set in the new stylesheet. You can now update any of those properties (either updating already set properties or adding new properties to your style definition), and they will be added to your stylesheet for you. If your stylesheet is not already open, Orcas will open it for you and make the changes. This should prove to be a very useful enhancement to the way Visual Studio deals with CSS.

Another way to update the style definitions of a particular selector in a linked stylesheet is to right-click on the listbox option for the rule you want to impact (e.g., "#myFirstID") and select Modify Style from the options. This will bring back the exact same interface as the New Style screen shown earlier in Figure A-14. However, it will now be labeled Modify Style and will have the options preselected that have been set for that ruleset. For illustrative purposes, set the "font-weight" property to "bold" and click the OK button.

You should have seen that the text of "Hello World" have taken on the new bold style rule immediately upon clicking the OK button. If you look at the definitions set up in StyleSheet.css, it should look like this:

```
body {
}
#myFirstID {
    font-family: Arial, Helvetica, sans-serif;
    font-size: medium;
    font-variant: small-caps;
    font-weight: bold;
}
```

As you can see, a new rule for font-weight has been added to the myFirstID ID definition automatically for you.

This means that you can modify the code for your stylesheets without actually opening up the stylesheet at all. If you wanted to, you could maintain all of your CSS rules through the various tools provided in Visual Studio at the page level rather than trying to remember which stylesheet is impacting your selectors and trying to modify them in each of those documents. This can potentially reduce the maintenance headaches that historically come up with maintaining multiple stylesheets for a single project.

CSS Properties Windows Buttons and Settings

Once you are in the CSS Properties window, you will notice that there are several buttons at the top of the window, as shown in Figure A-17.

Figure A-17

You should notice that the first and third buttons are selected by default. This creates the view of the CSS Properties that you have seen so far in this section. The first button, Show Categorized List, keeps the CSS properties grouped by categories. This is why you see sections like Font, Block, and Background in the properties list with related properties listed in each of those sections. This button is actually mutually exclusive with the second button, Show Alphabetized List. As the name implies, selecting this option takes out all of the grouping and sorts the properties in alphabetical order (irregardless of their category). Without changing anything else, this will also keep the properties that are set at the top of the list. This means that all of your set properties are at the top in alphabetical order and then all of the nonset properties follow in alphabetical order.

Remember, this is only true if you haven't changed anything else. This brings us an interesting segue: the "Show set properties on top" option. This option, which is the third button from the left, is what is responsible for the set properties appearing first in your listings and works for both the Categorized and Alphabetized view of your CSS Properties. If you deselect this option, you will see your set properties listed in the normal flow of the view.

The final button, Summary, can be really helpful when you are maintaining existing CSS. When you select this option, the CSS Properties only lists those properties that have been set. So, if you only have the height and width properties set for a particular selector, you will only see those two properties in the CSS Properties window. When you are trying to maintain existing CSS styles in a web project, it makes it much easier to just click on the selector in whichever view you are using (Design, Source, or Split) and then see only the CSS rules being applied to that particular selector. There is no need to sort through a bunch of internal and external stylesheets as well as inline definitions. All of the rules that are applied to a particular selector, and only those rules, will be right at your fingertips. This will make CSS maintenance almost sinfully simple.

Conflicts and Resolution

So what happens in the event you have an area defined, as in the previous example, that has inline styles applied to it as well as ones applied from a linked stylesheet? Or what if your section is actually nested within another section and the same rule is applied by both? That is when you have a potential conflict in rules defined for a particular region of your page. This is where the word "cascading" comes into play in CSS; the styles cascade down to your particular selector. But from an IDE view, can you see what is going on? What is conflicting and who is winning? Previously, no, you couldn't. But with Orcas, you actually can tell.

For example, go back to your previous example where you had the following section set up in your markup:

```
<div style="background-color: Olive; color: #FFFFFF;
    height: 200px; width: 200px;" id="myFirstID">
Hello World
</div>
```

In this example, you have a DIV region set up that has both inline styles applied through the style attribute of the DIV and further styles applied through the linked stylesheet Stylesheet.css through the myFirstID selector. Currently there is no conflict; the properties defined in each are mutually exclusive. But what happens when you try to define the same property in each?

To test this out, go into `Stylesheet.css` and add a definition for "color" and set it to Silver so that the contents of the stylesheet resemble the following:

```
body {
}
#myFirstID {
    font-family: Arial, Helvetica, sans-serif;
    font-size: x-large;
    font-variant: small-caps;
    font-weight: bold;
    font-style: italic;
    color: Silver;
}
```

Now go back to `Default.aspx` and look at the CSS Properties window for `#myFirstID` and look at the color property. (See Figure A-18.)

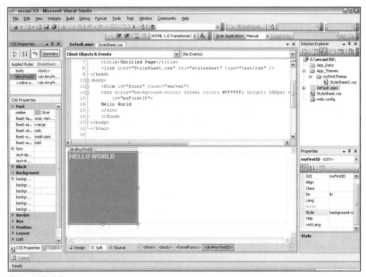

Figure A-18

In Figure A-18, "color" has now been moved to the top of the list of set properties and has the same bold blue font applied to it to indicate it is set in this ID definition. However, notice that it also has a red line through the middle of it. If you hover over it, you will notice that it displays the message shown in Figure A-19.

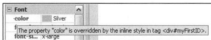

Figure A-19

This is telling you that, even though you are defining the color property in the linked stylesheet, it is going to be overridden by the inline definition being applied to the same region of the page. For this simple example, this might not seem that handy. But when you start getting into nesting selectors and having multiple stylesheets affecting the way any single region on a page displays, it will prove useful to see which ones are being applied to a particular section and which ones are getting overridden. This will prove even more true as you start coming back to projects months later to do basic (or drastic) maintenance and improvements.

Manage and Apply Styles

Besides the CSS Properties window, there are two new windows that can help CSS developers maintain their styles: Manage Styles and Apply Styles. If you do not have these windows already up in Visual Studio, it is a little tricky finding links to enable them. For example, they are not listed with the other available windows (like Solution Explorer or Properties Window) under View on the Visual Studio Toolbar. Rather, they are under a new link on the toolbar: Format.

But that isn't even the trickiest part; Format isn't always an active (or even visible) option on the toolbar. For example, if you have the Toolbox window open and with the focus, you can't see the Format option on the toolbar. If, however, you switch over to something like CSS Properties, Format becomes a new option on the Visual Studio toolbar, as shown in Figure A-20. Hopefully, in future versions, Format will remain active on the toolbar.

Figure A-20

Go ahead and add both of these windows to your project (Format ⇨ CSS Styles and then select both Manage Styles and Apply Styles) to add these windows to your IDE. For the screenshots in this example, both windows will be tabbed with the CSS Properties window, but you don't have to do that in your own project.

Manage Styles

The first thing to look at is the new Manage Styles window, as shown in Figure A-21.

This window acts as a sort of dashboard of the CSS style applied to the open document. There isn't a lot you can actually do directly in the pane; you can just see what is being formatted and from where. As with the CSS Properties window, though, you can add a new style (using the same interface shown earlier in this appendix), and you can attach a stylesheet. The options provide a couple of different ways of viewing the content in this pane (you can, for example, look at all styles applied to the page or only to the currently selected element or selector), but this view is, for the most part, just that: a view.

One interesting feature of this pane, though, is the ability to view all of the code for a particular selector. For example, if you hover your mouse over #myFirstID in the listing under StyleSheet.css, you will see style rules applied through that selector in a familiar-looking ToolTip, as shown in Figure A-22.

If you right-click on any of the selectors, you are presented with similar options that you have seen in this appendix. For example, you can select Modify Style to get the same modify style wizard you saw earlier in this appendix.

It is also worth noting that you cannot see inline styles applied to a particular selector in this view. For example, when reexamining Figure A-21, you will see that there are entries for the body and #myFirstID selectors applied to the page. However, there is no area for showing the inline styles applied. Even if you select the <div> tag in code (in Design view, for example), you still do not have access to the inline styles through this window. This is not necessarily good or bad; it is just interesting that, for some reason, inline style was omitted from this window.

Figure A-21

Figure A-22

But, again, this window is mostly just for managing your styles at a very high level.

Apply Styles

The more interesting of these two new windows is the Apply Styles window, shown in Figure A-23.

The first thing the might jump out at you is that, with this window, you do have access to the Inline styles applied to a particular element (to get this screenshot, the cursor was placed somewhere in the selector region, from `<div>` to `</div>`, in the Source pane of the Split view of Visual Studio).

While this window also has the ability to add a new style or attach a stylesheet to your web document, it has a lot more powerful features than its Manage Styles counterpart, powerful enough that you need to take heed when you start playing with them.

For example, if you accidentally click on the fairly nonthreatening Clear Styles area of the pane, depicted in Figure A-24, you will remove all inline and class style references from the selector (strangely, it leaves the ID reference but removes all other style rules and references). There is no warning; it's just gone. Fortunately, for a lot of reasons besides just this discussion, Visual Studio has a very handy undo function that will get your code references back. But, the first time you clear your style accidentally, your eyes will probably get big and you will wonder what just happened.

Figure A-23

Figure A-24

There are similar options available under the stylesheet and inline areas of the pane. To see them, hover over one of the areas (for example, hover over the `#myFirstID` area under `StyleSheet.css` to see Figure A-25).

Figure A-25

You will notice two things happen when you do this. First, you will see the style rules in a ToolTip again. Second, and more relevant to this discussion, you will notice that a drop-down arrow appears to the right of the region. If you click on the region, you will be presented with the options shown in Figure A-26.

Most of the options should look fairly familiar to you from the CSS properties discussion earlier in this appendix. However, the scary one is the last enabled one (second from the bottom): Remove ID.

If you were to look under the Inline style region, you would see a similar option for Remove Inline Style enabled. You may have noticed this when playing in the CSS Properties window (these options are there, too), but if you didn't take notice of it, you should now. These options do exactly what their name implies: remove the style from the selector.

Figure A-26

However, it's not quite as damaging as what you saw with Clear Styles in this section. This is because, with Remove ID (or Remove Class, if you had a class set up in this project), you are just deleting the reference in the selector and not the supporting code, wherever that may reside. For example, if you were to Remove the ID for #myFirstID in the <div> selector in Default.aspx, this would take out the id reference within the <div> tag but would not touch the code in StyleSheet.css. So, in this way, it doesn't actually delete any style; it just removes the reference in place to a set of style rules. This is a lot less frightening than just deleting the code, but if you select this option just to see what it does, you will probably have a moment of panic when the ID no longer shows up in the view.

However, that being said, there is a function that will actually delete the code in its source location. If you look a little further up in the options in Figure A-26, you will see Delete. Selecting this option will physically delete the style rules from the referenced stylesheet. To continue the example in the previous paragraph, if you had actually selected Delete for #myFirstID rather than Remove ID, the entire code block in StyleSheet.css would have been removed. Fortunately, before it does this, Visual Studio prompts you to make sure this is really what you want to do (as shown in Figure A-27).

Figure A-27

The interesting thing about this is that this function doesn't remove the ID from your selector, which means you may be left with a broken link. For example, if you had selected Yes with this example, all of the style rules would be deleted for #myFirstID in StyleSheet.css, but the <div> tag would still contain an ID reference set to "myFirstID". To complete this deletion, apparently you need to remove the ID (either through the options or manually) separately.

Themes and the New CSS Tools

One thing that is unfortunately missing from the new CSS tools in Visual Studio is the integration of CSS applied through themes with the new CSS Properties window. For example, create a theme called `myFirstTheme`, add a stylesheet called `StyleSheet2.css`, and set up the following rule in that document:

```
body
{
    background-color: Silver;
}
```

Now go to the `@Page` directive of `Default.aspx` and add either a `Theme` or `StyleSheetTheme` reference to `"myFirstTheme"`, similar to the following:

```
<%@ Page Language="C#" AutoEventWireup="true"  CodeFile="Default.aspx.cs"
    Inherits="_Default" Theme="myFirstTheme" %>
```

You would think that, by doing this, you would have access to those rules in the CSS Properties window. However, at least in the Beta 1 release, this functionality is not available. You can compile, recompile, build, and rebuild your project, and it won't become available. You can synchronize views and still nothing. The only way to make it work is to add a hard-coded reference to the stylesheet, completely negating the functionality of themes.

This may get resolved in the final release but, at the time of Beta 1, it isn't there. You have to actually open up the CSS file from the Theme folder and modify it separately there. It would be nice to be able to modify the CSS rules for the Theme CSS file at the page level in the same way you can with linked stylesheets but, at least for now, you can't.

Modifying a CSS Document

If you are in the situation described above (modifying a Theme CSS document), or if you simply prefer to modify your CSS rules at the CSS document level rather than at the page level, you can still do that. The IntelliSense is still available in the document itself and there is still an interface available for a more wizard-style approach to updating the rules. However, this interface has undergone a facelift since Visual Studio 2005 and is noticeably improved, as can be seen in Figure A-28.

The interface, at this point, should look very familiar to you; it is the same one you have used previously in this appendix to create new styles and modify existing style definitions. One of the improvements that you may have noticed before is that the labels for the options you can set are more closely aligned with the actual CSS property names. For example, in Visual Studio 2005, you would set the `font-family` property by going to the Font Name area of the Font tab and change the option for Family (there is another option in this section for System Font). However, in Orcas, you change the option ''font-family'' on the Font tab.

Is this really an improvement? Well, that is a judgment call that is difficult to make. On one hand, the field names on the interface are much more aligned with their property name in CSS. If you ever hope to get really good at manually writing out CSS rules inline or in a stylesheet document, you need to know, or at least be familiar with, the CSS Property names. So getting used to names through the GUI tool might make developers more comfortable with those names and, thus, build up their CSS knowledge and proficiency.

But what about the extreme novice? Being presented with the initial screen with field names like ''font-variant'' and ''text-transform''? What is going to be their reaction? One of the things that was really nice about this tool in Visual Studio 2005 is that it could help bring a total CSS newbie up to a more proficient CSS developer. The interface had field names that were more comfortable to the inexperienced CSS developer; it felt more like a typical style properties interface you might find in some word processor program or other desktop application. The names made sense and were grouped together logically. New CSS folks could play with a more comfortable interface and, as their experience grew, they could start learning the names of the properties by seeing what rules were actually written out in the CSS document when they saved their settings.

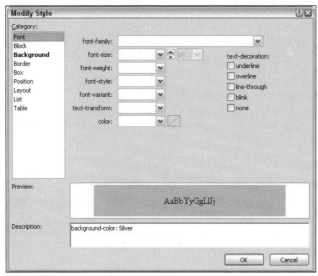

Figure A-28

Seeing how well this new layout and naming schema is accepted among the community will be interesting. The new interface seems more targeted at the moderately proficient CSS developers than the absolute new guys. Maybe most developers will appreciate this change. But there will probably be a significant group that will not be singing its praises. Is this a good thing? Time will tell.

The CSS Outline Window

When modifying a stylesheet directly, you will also notice that the CSS Outline window is still available when you are in a CSS document, as seen in Figure A-29.

If you can't see that window, you may need to click View on the Orcas toolbar and select Document Outline.

This window provides an outline view of your open CSS document, separating the list by whether the selector is an element, a class, an Element ID, or a block. Within each of those divisions you can find all selectors currently defined. For example, you can see that under the Elements division there is only one item listed: body. This is because, in the stylesheet, the body element is the only element defined. You can also see that, under the External IDs division, you have #myFirstID listed.

The nice thing about this feature is that it provides a much abbreviated version of your document so that, when you are looking for a particular set of rules, you can just look through the selector names and, maybe more helpfully, by just the type of selector it is. So if in six months you have to go back and change a rule for the ID "myFirstID," you can just look in the "External IDs" division and then look for the listing for "#myFirstID."

Figure A-29

Once you have located the selector that you want to go to, you can simply click on it in the CSS Outline view, and the navigation system will take you to that set of rules in the CSS document. So if you have, say, a hundred or more CSS selectors defined in one document, you can search through the outline and more easily identify the one you are looking for. At that point, you just click on the name in the CSS outline, and you will be taken directly to the area in the CSS document where that particular selector is defined. This can greatly improve the maintainability of CSS documents, especially those that are particularly long.

However, one thing that has been missing since Visual Studio 2005 and is still missing in the Orcas Beta 1 release is the inclusion of a logical sort order for the selector names in the CSS Outline view, as evidenced by Figure A-30.

As you can see, the selectors are listed in the outline in linear order; the order in which they appear in the document. For example, in the IDs, you have "myFirstID," "aSecondID," and "thirdID." If you were to sort these in alphabetic order, they would be "aSecondID," "myFirstID," and finally "thirdID." However, in the outline view, they are presented in the exact same order that they appear in the CSS document. This means that, if you wanted to find "aSecondID," it would not be in an intuitive order in the outline list and, which might make it more difficult for you to find; especially if you have not seen this document in months (or at all) and don't remember the order in which things were added to the document.

This example is a very small one, but imagine if you had many more selectors defined. If, for example, you have 50 or 60 classes set up, and you need to modify something like "sectionHeader." You would have to look through all 50 or 60 classes in the outline to find that particular class. It would have been much nicer if you had the ability to either sort alphabetically by default or, barring that, force a sort of the outline to put the selectors in alphabetical order. That way, when you are looking for something like "sectionHeader," you know exactly where to look in the potentially long list of classes provided in your outline.

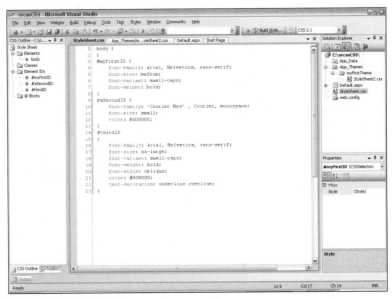

Figure A-30

This section is not advocating for the selectors being sorted in any kind of forced order within the CSS document itself. CSS selectors must remain in a somewhat, if not absolute, order inside of the CSS document. This is because developers rely on the cascading order of CSS files to make them effective. What this section is saying is that the outline representation of those selectors in a given document should be sorted in such an order that a developer can find them. This sort order would have no impact on the CSS document itself. The outline is merely a tool to help you find and easily navigate to different selector definitions in a given CSS document. Since the rules in the CSS document, by their very nature, are going to be out of alphabetic order, it would be nice if the Outline view of that document were sorted in alphabetic order so that you could find them more easily when dealing with hundreds of selector definitions in a single file.

A Final Tip

As you start playing with at least the Beta 1 version of Orcas, you will probably find that you lose your CSS Properties values periodically. This typically happens when you are working in an ASPX page and then switch over to a CSS document. When you go back to the ASPX page, it seems fairly common for the CSS Properties window to just go blank. If this happens to you, you may need to switch to a different WYSIWYG view (e.g., switch to the Design view). Many times, this will bring back the properties immediately. If not, try clicking in a couple of areas on the page while in Design view. Generally speaking, your properties will come back pretty quickly. If nothing works, close down the ASPX page and then open it back up. This is probably just a behavior of the beta installation, but if you see the same thing in your installation, at least you should have a way of getting around it.

So What's Coming Next?

While it may be premature to make a lot of predictions, there is at least one exciting enhancement that should be discussed: CSS hyperlinks. These hyperlinks will show up directly in the markup language of your HTML/ASPX page and will link to the location of the definition, even if that is not in the page itself. The "class=", or presumably the "id=", will be an actual hyperlink. Clicking on the link (or pressing F12 on the underlined link name) will take you directly to the definition itself. This may be at the page level (defined in the HEAD region, for example) or in a linked stylesheet. This should help developers more easily jump to the correct style definition when coding or maintaining a particular web project. Currently, this is scheduled for the Beta 2 release.

Summary of CSS and Orcas

As you can hopefully appreciate, there are some really remarkable improvements planned for to the way that Visual Studio works with CSS documents. This is saying a lot since Visual Studio already offered a lot of really handy tools for CSS manipulation in its prior release. The new tools in Orcas, though, should make CSS developers feel even more at home when doing work in Visual Studio. The improvements include:

❑ CSS Properties window that allows viewing and editing of the CSS properties being applied to a particular area of the page. This tool allows you to edit inline style definitions and linked stylesheets directly in the CSS Properties pane or through a new Modify Style interface. It also allows you to create new style definitions and even new stylesheets.

❑ The new Manage Styles and Apply Styles windows allow you to manage your CSS documents at a high level.

❑ The style manipulation interfaces (Add Style and Modify Style) have been updated from their previous iteration in Visual Studio 2005. The attributes are more logically named in accordance with their CSS property name.

❑ The introduction of new CSS hyperlinks is scheduled to be released with the Beta 2 release. These new hyperlinks will allow you to jump from the markup of a particular page directly to the style definition, even if that is in a linked stylesheet.

However, with these new tools, there are a few limitations to be aware of:

❑ The CSS Properties window does not become enabled until you switch to one of the WYSIWIG views (Design or Split).

❑ The CSS Properties window tends to go blank if it loses focus. You can get it back by going to a different WYSIWYG view.

❑ The synchronization scenarios have not been finalized in the Split view. However, the CSS Properties window does not reflect changes until the views are synched. This means that you have to force a synchronization between the views before the changes will be reflected in the CSS Properties window.

❑ The CSS Properties window does not interact with any theme stylesheets, even if the theme is specifically included through either the Theme or StyleSheetTheme attribute at the @Page directive. You cannot see those settings at all, and any manipulation of the style definitions must be done directly in the CSS page included in the Theme directory.

❑   The CSS Outline view does not sort the selectors in a useful way. Rather than being sorted in alphabetical order, which would allow to easier sift through a long list of items, they are sorted in order they appear in the CSS document. This is not new to Orcas but still warrants inclusion.

When looking at these lists, though, you shouldn't just count them up and say "Well, there are more problems than enhancements." That really isn't a fair comparison. The number of enhancements, when looked at in a summary view, may not seem that long of a list. However, they are monumental enhancements to the way that Visual Studio interacts with and supports CSS. It is also important to remember that most of the limitations are not bugs exactly; they are simply limitations. They did not break any of the functionality of previous versions of Visual Studio; they are only limitations of some of the new enhancements. And remember, this is just a beta release. As such, some of these items may be fixed by the final release. None of these items are what could be considered "show-stoppers"; they are merely things to be aware of as you begin your exploration of Visual Studio Orcas.

Nested Master Pages

When reading through the chapters of this book, you have seen a lot of tools that are specifically targeted towards designing strong web interfaces for your clients. It is the goal of this appendix, though, to show you some of the major improvements to those tools in the Orcas release of Visual Studio. In that regard, you have already seen a slew of improvements to the CSS integration and tools in Orcas. The other major enhancement in the scope of this appendix is nested Master Pages.

Remember in Chapter 7 you created a project (C:\wroxMPNesting) to illustrate the limited support of nested Master Pages in Visual Studio 2005. So, to see the improvements with Orcas, open that project back up. Remember, if you are opening this project for the first time in Orcas, you will be asked if you want to upgrade the project to the new .NET 3.5 Framework (as seen in Figure A-4 earlier in this appendix), selecting either option will be fine for this example.

Open up Default.aspx in the Split view of Orcas, and you will see that it looks like Figure A-31.

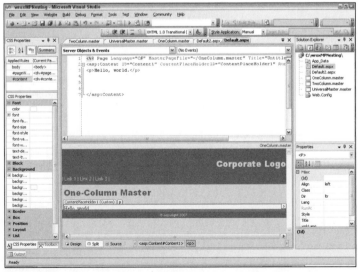

Figure A-31

You can see that you have visual confirmation of what your page will look like. Well, as much visual confirmation as you can have within the IDE of Visual Studio. You will obviously need to test anything you produce in Visual Studio in every browser you plan to support. But at least you can see the basic layout of the page. You can see the blue header, the gray navigation area, and the blue footer area all set up by the universal Master Page (`UniversalMaster.master`). You can also see the heading, "One-Column Master" provided by the One Column Master Page (`OneColumn.master`). Finally, you can see where the content from the actual page, `Default.aspx`, will fall into all of that.

If you open up `Default2.aspx`, which uses `TwoColumn.master` (that inherits `UniversalMaster.master`), you will see Figure A-32.

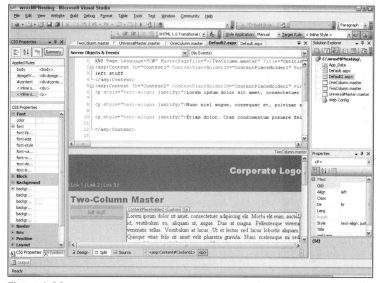

Figure A-32

Again, you can see the header and navigation areas in the Design pane of the Split view (if you scrolled down you could also see the footer) that was defined in the universal Master Page. You can also see the two columns defined in the two-column master (`TwoColumn.master`) file, as well. Finally, you can see the content you are inserting with `Default2.aspx`. This is all viewable in both the Split and Design view.

Just as an aside, look at how many entries there are for the Applied Rules pane in the CSS Properties window. This is for any of the paragraphs in the right-hand column section of the page (the paragraphs with the Lorem Ipsum text). They have style applied from the body element and the `pageWrapper` and content IDs applied from the linked stylesheet. They also have inline style applied to them for the individual paragraph. Interestingly, it also shows the inline style coming down from the `TwoColumn.master` page that positions the content 160 pixels over from the left-hand margin of the page. The real power of the CSS Properties window can be seen more clearly here, but only with some slight modifications.

First, notice that you can see all of the CSS properties set from all sources. However, if you try to edit any of them (besides the inline styles from the current page), you just can't do it. The problem is that you can't modify style defined within the code of a Master Page. This means that, if the style is either defined inline or within the style block in the HEAD region, you can't modify it from a content page. This is true at the content page level but also at the Master Page level that is inheriting a different Master Page. If the code is defined in the markup of the inherited Master Page, you cannot edit it in the CSS Properties window of the content page.

According to Microsoft, the ability to modify style blocks in the Master Page directly from the CSS Properties window of the Content Page is not supported as of Beta 1 but should be included in all future releases (Beta 2 and beyond). So it is possible that by the time you read this, this behavior will have already been fixed in the Visual Studio installation you are working with.

Fortunately, there is a workaround that shouldn't really be a workaround. The workaround is to not define the code in the markup but in a linked stylesheet. The reason this shouldn't be a workaround is because, honestly, this is how you should be working anyway. Defining code inline or anywhere in the Master Page negates many of the advantages of CSS. However, for this dummy project, this wasn't done. So you need to modify the code to make it more like the way it should have been originally created to bring it up to current web standards.

First, modify `Universal.master` to remove the CSS rules. It should look like this after you modify it:

```
<%@ Master Language="C#" %>

<!DOCTYPE html PUBLIC "-//W3C//DTD XHTML 1.0 Transitional//EN"
    "http://www.w3.org/TR/xhtml1/DTD/xhtml1-transitional.dtd">

<script runat="server">
</script>

<html xmlns="http://www.w3.org/1999/xhtml" >
<head runat="server">
    <title>Nested Master</title>
    <link href="StyleSheet.css" rel="stylesheet" type="text/css" />
</head>
<body>
    <form id="form1" runat="server">
    <div id="pageWrapper">
    <div id="header">Corporate Logo</div>
    <div id="navigation">| Link 1 | Link 2 | Link 3 |</div>
    <div id="content">

        <!-- THE CONTENT WILL GO IN THIS PLACEHOLDER -->
        <asp:contentplaceholder id="ContentPlaceHolder1" runat="server">
        </asp:contentplaceholder>

    </div>
    </div>
    <div id="footer">© copyright 2007</div>
    </form>
</body>
</html>
```

Notice that the `<style>` block has been completely replaced and a new link to `"StyleSheet.css"` has been added in its place. All of the definitions provided in the original `Universal.master` should be moved to the new stylesheet. This will make `StyleSheet.css` look like this:

```
body{width: 100%; height: 100%; margin: 0; padding: 0;}
#pageWrapper{width: 100%; min-height: 100%; height: auto; margin-bottom: -25px;}
#header{width: 100%; height: 50px; background-color: steelblue; color: white;
    font-size: x-large; font-family: Arial Black; text-align: right;
    padding-top: 25px;}
```

```
#navigation{width: 100%; height: 25px; background-color: gray; color: white;
    font-size: small; font-family: Arial;}
#content{padding: 5px 5px 5px 5px;}
#footer{width: 100%; height: 15px; background-color: steelblue; color: white;
    font-size: x-small; font-family: Arial; text-align: center; padding-top: 5px;
    border-top: solid 5px gray; clear: both;}
```

For this example, you are only worrying about the two-column layout so you will need to make similar modifications to the TwoColumn.master file. However, the style defined in that page was inline and, therefore, has no class or ID selectors that can be moved to the new stylesheet. In order to remedy this, you will want to modify the code to take out all of the inline style definitions and add new IDs called "TwoColumnLeft" and "TwoColumnRight" while also adding a new class called "PageHeader". Your modified page should resemble the following:

```
<%@ Master Language="C#" MasterPageFile="~/UniversalMaster.master" %>
<asp:Content ID="Content1" ContentPlaceHolderID="ContentPlaceHolder1"
    Runat="Server">

    <div class="PageHeader">
        Two-Column Master
    </div>

    <div id="TwoColumnLeft">
    <asp:contentplaceholder id="ContentPlaceHolder1" runat="server">
    </asp:contentplaceholder>
    </div>

    <div id="TwoColumnRight">
    <asp:contentplaceholder id="ContentPlaceHolder2" runat="server">
    </asp:contentplaceholder>
    </div>

</asp:Content>
```

You will need to move the former inline styles to the new stylesheet under the appropriate selector, as shown below (this is the modified StyleSheet.css file):

```
body{width: 100%; height: 100%; margin: 0; padding: 0;}
#pageWrapper{width: 100%; min-height: 100%; height: auto; margin-bottom: -25px;}
#header{width: 100%; height: 50px; background-color: steelblue; color: white;
    font-size: x-large; font-family: Arial Black; text-align: right;
    padding-top: 25px;}
#navigation{width: 100%; height: 25px; background-color: gray; color: white;
    font-size: small; font-family: Arial;}
#content{padding: 5px 5px 5px 5px;}
#footer{width: 100%; height: 15px; background-color: steelblue; color: white;
    font-size: x-small; font-family: Arial; text-align: center; padding-top: 5px;
    border-top: solid 5px gray; clear: both;}
.PageHeader{color: SteelBlue; font-family: Arial Black; font-size: x-large;}
#TwoColumnLeft{width: 130px; min-height: 150px; background-color: LightGrey;
    padding: 10px 10px 10px 10px; color: SteelBlue; position: static;
    float: left; text-align: center;}
#TwoColumnRight{position: static; padding-left: 160px; clear: right;}
```

411

This is a little cluttered, so you might want to clean it up so that it is easier to read but, hopefully, you can understand what is going on. You have moved all inline styles defined in each of the Master Pages to a linked stylesheet. Doing this means that all style definitions are contained in a linked stylesheet rather than inline in any one (or multiple) pages. Again, this really should have been done in the first place but, with the initial project, this wasn't the focus.

Anyway, now reload `Default2.aspx` in Visual Studio Orcas and see what happens. At first glance, it will probably look like nothing happened. The views all look the same, and the same items are included in the Applied Rules pane of the CSS Properties window. It all looks the same. However, if you go to any of the areas in the Applied Rules pane, including all style rules defined at the Master Page level, you have full access to the properties and can set them as you see fit. This means that you have the ability to view and modify style definitions called in `Universal.master`, `TwoColumn.master`, and `Default2.aspx`. Really, you are only modifying the styles in `StyleSheet.css` and any rules defined inline in `Default2.aspx`. But you have access to certain selectors in `StyleSheet.css` because they are specifically called in the pages inherited by `Default2.aspx`.

This functionality will be increasingly more valuable as you start working with more and more style definition in a multitude of nested Master Pages. You won't have to remember where certain things are defined; you will just open up the content page, and you will have immediate and direct access to the style definitions regardless of where they are defined. This is very cool.

Summary

This appendix is provided for one reason: to begin to give you a glimpse of what is coming with Visual Studio Codename Orcas. There are so many new features and enhancements to the existing IDE, that this appendix can only touch on a few key features. Specifically, the features that mostly directly impacts the projects showcased in the chapters of this book were hit upon. While the amazing new features of .NET 3.0 and 3.5, such as LINQ, WPF, WF, WCF, and Cardspace, are going to drastically improve the way developers use .NET and Visual Studio, it doesn't really impact the projects seen in this book.

The major enhancements to Visual Studio, as it relates to this book, are all of the improvements to the way Visual Studio interacts with CSS. This includes the new CSS Properties window and all of the different ways that this tools interacts with the CSS code of your page. You have seen how these new features work in Beta 1 and seen where they will hopefully be improved a bit before final release. You have also seen how much these seemingly small improvements (it's just one new windows and a couple of interface enhancements, right?) make a dramatic difference in how you will use Visual Studio with CSS in your future web projects.

Make no mistake, the greatest CSS tools in the world will never substitute for a solid understanding of the CSS language. So while these tools are going to change the way .NET developers interact with CSS, you would do yourself a great disservice by letting your entire knowledge of CSS come from what you learn with the tools in any IDE. Go out and learn all you can about CSS; it's going to be the future of the web. And then come back to Visual Studio Orcas, and you will have an even better understanding of how great these new tools are.

You have also seen an improvement in the way Visual Studio handles nested Master Pages. In the previous iteration, it allowed you to create these nested Master Pages without error. However, if you tried to view them in the Design view, you just couldn't. Now you can not only see them in the Design view but you can also see them in the new Split view, which allows you to see the Source and Design views at the same time. Furthermore, you can actually modify the CSS rules brought in by these Master Pages from the CSS Properties window at the content page level. You will find nested Master Pages a lot more useful and easy to maintain when you don't have to switch between three or four pages just to make some stylistic changes to the layout of your entire page. You can now make universal changes that will impact all of your pages, from a single content page.

Sure, there are a couple of things that aren't perfect yet and a few of those things will probably persist through the final release. But even as it works in the beta release, you can hopefully appreciate how much easier much of the work you did throughout this book would have been had you had the power of Orcas to assist you.

If you would like to learn more about Visual Studio Orcas, you may find the following links helpful:

❑ **MSDN: Visual Studio Future Versions** — `http://msdn2.microsoft.com/en-us/vstudio/aa700830.aspx`

❑ **MSDN: Feature Specifications for Visual Studio and .NET Framework ''Orcas''** — `http://msdn2.microsoft.com/en-us/vstudio/aa948851.aspx`

❑ **Scott Guthrie's blog** — `http://weblogs.asp.net/scottgu`

B

An Introduction to Microsoft Silverlight

If you are a web developer, you have probably been tasked with presenting some sort of animated welcome splash page or header area for a web project. Or, if that hasn't happened yet, it probably will at some point in the future. The default solution to this requirement is, generally, to use Adobe Flash. Microsoft has never really offered a web solution for this type of work. They have continually improved their web programming languages (e.g., classic ASP to .NET to the latest .NET 3.5 enhancements) and the tools to develop these technologies, such as the latest Visual Studio products. They have, in the last few years, begun tinkering with interface and design technologies, such as Master Pages and AJAX. Microsoft has even shown a much bigger commitment to CSS and web standards through improvements in its support of CSS in its IDE as well as its Internet browser (which still isn't there but is making progress). But, at least to this point, they haven't dabbled much in providing rich user interfaces on the web. With the introduction of Microsoft Silverlight, though, Microsoft is taking a stab at this market, too.

According to Microsoft, "Silverlight is a cross-browser, cross-platform plug-in for delivering the next generation of Microsoft .NET–based media experiences and rich interactive applications for the Web." If you read anything put out by Microsoft about Silverlight, you will see at least pieces of this phrase somewhere. This might be a little hard to understand, but, essentially, what it means is that they are going to try to compete in the market typically dominated by Adobe Flash. They are trying to provide a canvas to import movies, audio files, and other media content. This canvas will also allow you to draw and animate graphical objects in a very similar, yet easier, way than you did previously with the `System.Drawing` namespace. And, best of all for .NET developers, all of the static code is in the XML-based XAML, and you can add dynamic code through a variety of programming languages, including JavaScript, Visual Basic .NET, and C#. This means that you can, for example, create dynamic flash-like presentations powered by your C# managed code.

In short, Microsoft Silverlight adds the ability to create vector-based graphics, media, text, animation, and overlays to create a new interactive web experience that incorporates the power of .NET managed code with the simplicity of XML design. Visitors to your site, as long as they are using one of the major browsers, will have the exact same experience as any other user (after downloading a small — less than 2MB — plug-in). If Adobe isn't taking this product as a serious competitor, they should. Microsoft has made a very impressive first offering into this market. And, after this appendix, hopefully you will have a decent understanding of what it can do and how you can use it in your own projects.

Prerequisites

This appendix is sort of a stand-alone entity when compared to the rest of this book. This means that you won't really build on the technologies discussed in every other chapter and appendix of this book. Rather, this appendix focuses on an entirely different technology, but one that is, or will soon be, fairly important to web interface designers. Since most of the audience reading this book is probably at least partially responsible for designing the look and feel of the web site projects they work on, this new technology is very relevant to their continuous improvement.

With that being said, the requirements for this appendix are slightly different from any of the other sections of this book.

At a minimum, if you are developing on a Windows machine, you should have the following set up and installed on your system:

- ❑ **Operating System** — Windows Vista or Windows XP Service Pack 2
- ❑ **Browser** — Microsoft Internet Explorer 6, Windows Internet Explorer 7, Mozilla Firefox 1.5.0.8, or Firefox 2.0.x
- ❑ **Hardware** — Intel Pentium III 450 MHz or faster, equivalent processor 128MB of RAM
- ❑ **Development IDE** — Visual Studio 2005 Service Pack 1
- ❑ **Silverlight** — Microsoft Silverlight 1.0 Beta Software Development Kid (SDK)

However, for this appendix, the tools are slightly more forward-looking. To fully showcase the latest and greatest Microsoft has to offer, the operating system, browser, and hardware specifications listed above are used, but the following upgrades are made to the development environment:

- ❑ **Development IDE** — Visual Studio Codename "Orcas" Beta 1
- ❑ **Silverlight** — Microsoft Silverlight 1.1 Alpha Software Development Kid (SDK)
- ❑ **Extra tools** — Microsoft Silverlight Tools Alpha for Visual Studio Codename "Orcas" Beta 1

This environment allows you to have all of the latest Silverlight tools completely integrated in the Orcas IDE. In this appendix, especially in the beginning when setting up new projects, this may provide at least a slightly different experience than if you go with the minimum setup requirements shown at the beginning of this section. However, the basic technologies and usage of Silverlight should still persist. In fact, much (if not all) of the code shown in this appendix would have worked in Silverlight's predecessor, WPF/e.

You can find a full list of system requirements and get the relevant downloads at these locations:

- ❑ **Downloads/requirements** — www.microsoft.com/silverlight/downloads.aspx
- ❑ **Tools/SDKs** — www.microsoft.com/silverlight/tools.aspx

Before you get into the meat of this chapter, it is a good idea to get your development environment completely set up. This means that you need to choose which path you want to take (the minimum requirements or the more advanced tools of Orcas) and get that set up. Again, this appendix will be using the Orcas and Silverlight Alpha setup but you should be able to follow along with the lighter setup as well.

The only other requirement for this appendix is a fair understanding of .NET (C# will be used but should be fairly easily translated to VB) and a willingness, or even eagerness, to learn the newest technologies coming down the pipe.

About the Project

The goal of this appendix is simple: impart enough knowledge to you, the reader, to allow you to begin working with Microsoft's latest web interface enhancement, Microsoft Silverlight. In the planning phase of this appendix, a lot of thought went into what type of project would be good to demonstrate many of the features of Silverlight in an easy to understand and replicate format. One thought was a media player, but the simple ones didn't incorporate that many controls or plumbing under the hood to be a very exhaustive tutorial, and the more complicated ones would be hard to condense into a single appendix.

Because I was determined to create at least one working real-world example from the ground up, I finally decided that building a working clock would cover many of the facets of Silverlight that would be useful to most developers. Specifically, this would include:

- Drawing objects such as lines, polygons, and ellipses
- Importing static images and utilizing the images alpha channel (PNG)
- Generating drawn objects from code (some sort of loop)
- Silverlight animation
- Managing XAML code (the animation) through code

This last bullet was one of the most critical. The clock needed to be able take the current time and set the animation objects within the XAML file accordingly or else you would be left with a glorified stopwatch. This meant that the line object that represented the second hand needed to be set to the exact second of the current time. Similarly, the hour hand needed to be set to the hour and the minute hand to the minute of the current time. On top of that, the exact position of these last two elements needed to be affected by the other hands. In other words, the hour hand needed to point at the appropriate position between two distinct hour ticks based on the number of minutes that had passed so far in that hour (i.e., at 1:30, the hour hand should be halfway between the 1 and 2 hour tick marks on the clock).

Once the project had been defined and the specific goals identified, research was done to see if there were code samples on how to set the animation objects through some sort of code. In doing so, a couple of articles were found with similar examples:

- http://dotnetslackers.com/articles/silverlight/ SilverlightFirstStepsAnalogClock.aspx
- http://msdn2.microsoft.com/en-us/library/bb404709.aspx

Both of these samples were similar in scope to the planned project of this appendix and, as such, both had good ideas that got incorporated into the final text of this manuscript. For example, much of the design of the face of the clock was based on the MSDN article. While not exactly the same, the basic idea of the beveling for the edge of the clock was obtained from reading this article. There was also some code on how to set the current time through the managed code behind the XAML file. However, the formulas for doing this did not seem perfect. For example, there was no accountability for the number of seconds that had passed when positioning the minute hand, which means that at 55 seconds past 12, the minute hand would still be pointing at 12. The formula for the hour hand also seemed a bit strange or, at least, not intuitive. This had some good ideas, but wasn't the perfect implementation either.

The `DotNetSlackers` example was targeted to Silverlight's predecessor, WPF/e, but still had some useful approaches in it. For one, it used polygons for the hour and minute hand, which seemed like a good solution. (The original thought was to use images for the hands but this seemed easier and would illustrate drawn objects better.) It also had drawn tick marks around the clock. However, these tick marks were drawn using JavaScript, which was not within the scope of this project. While JavaScript is powerful, useful, and critical to Silverlight's success, object manipulation was to be done through the code behind if at all possible. This example, too, set the current time but did it through JavaScript. The formulas seemed better than the MSDN example (there is consideration given to the seconds passed when drawing out the minute hand), but not a lot of explanation was given as to how the formulas were derived and, just from looking at them, it might not make sense to a lot of people.

While both had some good ideas, neither implementation seemed ideal. So the book took some inspiration from them, but ultimately a lot of new functionality had to be built for this project. Some specific differences can be noticed:

❑ The current time is set more accurately through the managed code of the project

❑ The tick marks are drawn in the managed code of the project

❑ The background (everything outside of the clock face) has been made transparent

❑ The incorporation of an outside static image and using its alpha channel transparency

There are other sample Silverlight clocks out on the web, some that may incorporate some of these same features. However, the articles listed in this section were the ones that inspired a lot of the content and, if you want to see slightly different ways of creating the clock, you might want to check them out.

The Tick Tock Clock Project

There are so many things that you can do with Microsoft Silverlight that it makes it hard to illustrate all of its functionality in one project. While this project will not cover everything you can do, it will show you many of the most common features that you will probably want to use in a lot of your projects. You will learn, at a minimum, how to do the following:

❑ Create a new Silverlight Project in Orcas.

❑ Draw geometric shapes, such as polygons, ellipses, and lines.

❑ Use gradient and solid fills for shapes.

❑ Import images into your project.

❑ Incorporate basic animation into your project.

❑ Use the managed code behind of your XAML file to set the clock to the correct time.

The final results will be a working analog clock that is set to the current time and keeps the time through animated clock hands for the hour, minute, and second. You may not use this clock in your real project but, when you have it completed, you should be fairly comfortable navigating around the Silverlight tools.

Step 1: Creating Your Project in Orcas

Obviously, the first thing you need to do when starting the project is to actually create it. To do so, while in Visual Studio Orcas, click on File ⇨ New Project on the Visual Studio toolbar. This should give you the dialog box depicted in Figure B-1.

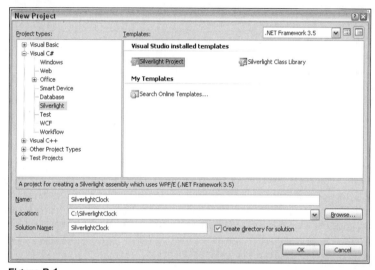

Figure B-1

As you will see, you have a new section under Visual Basic and Visual C# for "Silverlight" with two templates to choose from. For this example, choose Silverlight Project as your template, and give the project a Name and Solution Name of `SilverlightClock` and a location of `C:\SilverlightClock`, as shown in Figure B-1. Click the OK button to create your project. Once you do so, you should have a new project that resembles Figure B-2.

> *If you do not have the same development environment as used in this appendix (Orcas with the Silverlight Tools), you may not get an auto-generated XAML file. If this is the case, you may need to add one by adding a new item. (On the Orcas Toolbar select Project ⇨ Add New Item. When the Add New Item dialog box comes up, select Page and click the OK button.)*

The main things to notice are that you have a `Page.xaml` file with a `Page.xaml.cs` code-behind file attached to it. This is where the majority of the work will be done in creating the clock and its animation. There is also a `TestPage.html` file that has `TestFile.html.js` attached to it. This JavaScript file serves the basic properties of the Silverlight control (e.g., height and width of the control on the rendered HTML page). Finally, there is a `Silverlight.js` file that contains much of the functionality of JavaScript. Therefore, you probably don't want to make many, if any, modifications to this file. If you do need to make changes, it would be a good idea to comment out the line of code you are changing and add the new functionality right before or after that line. That way, if you do break any of the functionality, you can go back to the original version without much effort.

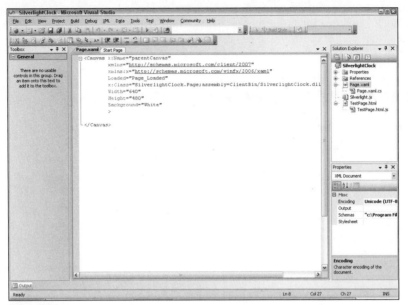

Figure B-2

The filenames used in this appendix are based on the defaults of Orcas. If you are not using Orcas, your default names may be different. For example, in Visual Studio 2005, the main HTML file is called Default.html, *and the XAML file is called* Page1.xaml. *The content of these files should be the same as* TestPage.html *and* Page.xaml, *respectively, but just have different names. If you are not using Orcas, you need to keep in mind the difference in the names throughout this appendix because the default names given by Orcas are what will be used for reference.*

Step 2: Setting Up the Dimensions

This project will be run fairly large so that the details can be seen in the final manuscript. Therefore, the dimensions for this clock should be set to 590 pixels high by 590 pixels wide. These numbers allowed for the clock to take up the entire browser window in IE7 at a 1024 × 768 resolution with a maximized browser window. In your project, this may be too big, but for the remainder of this project, those are the dimensions that will be used.

This means that the clock will be a circle that fits inside of these 590 × 590 pixel dimensions. So, for now, put a placeholder ellipse in your project and fill it with a gray background. You want to do this so that you can see the circle in your rendered project and make sure that it fits in your browser window (or whatever constraints you have for your own project). Page.xaml should be modified to look like this:

```
<Canvas x:Name="parentCanvas"
        xmlns="http://schemas.microsoft.com/client/2007"
        xmlns:x="http://schemas.microsoft.com/winfx/2006/xaml"
        Loaded="Page_Loaded"
```

```
x:Class="SilverlightClock.Page;assembly=ClientBin/SilverlightClock.dll"
        Width="640"
        Height="480"
        Background="White"
        >

  <Ellipse Height="590" Width="590" Fill="Gray"/>

</Canvas>
```

The only thing you added was an `Ellipse` object with a height and width set to 590 and a `Fill` color of `Gray`. Again, these settings are fairly arbitrary, but this will let you see your ellipse to make sure that everything fits in the browser window. If you run your project, the result should resemble Figure B-3.

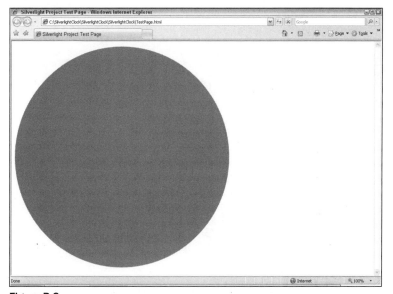

Figure B-3

This appears to work. However, an additional requirement of this project is that clock itself be the only opaque part of the Silverlight object and that everything outside of the clock (e.g., the area outside of the ellipse) be transparent so that you can see the background of your web project.

To test this, modify the code in `TestPage.html` to add a body background color of `"SteelBlue"`:

```
<html xmlns="http://www.w3.org/1999/xhtml">
<!-- saved from url=(0014)about:internet -->
<head>
    <title>Silverlight Project Test Page </title>
    <script type="text/javascript" src="Silverlight.js"></script>
    <script type="text/javascript" src="TestPage.html.js"></script>
</head>

<!-- Give the keyboard focus to the Silverlight control by default -->
```

```
<body onload="document.getElementById('SilverlightControl').focus()"
    style="background-color: SteelBlue;">
    <div id="SilverlightControlHost" >
        <script type="text/javascript">
            createSilverlight();
        </script>
    </div>
</body>
</html>
```

The only thing you have added to the default HTML code was `"style = "background-color: SteelBlue'"'` to the `<body>` tag.

Now, rerun your project to see if the opacity is set properly. Your rendered project should now resemble Figure B-4.

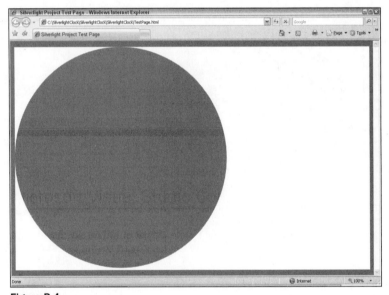

Figure B-4

As you can see, the opacity isn't right yet. There are actually several things you are going to need to change to get the opacity correct.

First, you will notice that the project is spanning the entire widow. This is actually set in the JavaScript file `TestPage.html.js` through the `height` and `width` properties, each set to 100%. You will need to modify these settings to `"590"`, which will make your modified file look like this:

```
// JScript source code

//contains calls to silverlight.js, example below loads Page.xaml
function createSilverlight()
{
    Sys.Silverlight.createObjectEx({
        source: "Page.xaml",
        parentElement: document.getElementById("SilverlightControlHost"),
```

```
            id: "SilverlightControl",
            properties: {
                width: "590",
                height: "590",
                version: "0.95",
                enableHtmlAccess: true
            },
            events: {}
        });
    }
```

You will also want to modify the canvas size defined in `Page.xaml` (it is set by default to 640 × 480; you should change it to 590 × 590). Your `Page.xaml` code will now look like this:

```
<Canvas x:Name="parentCanvas"
        xmlns="http://schemas.microsoft.com/client/2007"
        xmlns:x="http://schemas.microsoft.com/winfx/2006/xaml"
        Loaded="Page_Loaded"

x:Class="SilverlightClock.Page;assembly=ClientBin/SilverlightClock.dll"
        Width="590"
        Height="590"
        Background="White"
        >

  <Ellipse Height="590" Width="590" Fill="Gray"/>

</Canvas>
```

Again, you are just changing the `Width` and `Height` properties to `"590"`. Running the project now will result in the output shown in Figure B-5.

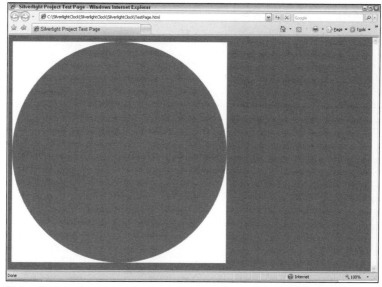

Figure B-5

The project is closer, but you still aren't there. At least the object is now confined to 590 pixels by 590 pixels, and you can see the steel blue background in all other areas of the screen.

However, you still see the white background of the Silverlight object in the areas not covered by the ellipse.

To begin to remove this, you need to adjust the Canvas properties in Page.xaml again to change the Background from "White" to "Transparent," as shown below:

```
<Canvas x:Name="parentCanvas"
        xmlns="http://schemas.microsoft.com/client/2007"
        xmlns:x="http://schemas.microsoft.com/winfx/2006/xaml"
        Loaded="Page_Loaded"

x:Class="SilverlightClock.Page;assembly=ClientBin/SilverlightClock.dll"
        Width="590"
        Height="590"
        Background="Transparent"
        >

    <Ellipse Height="590" Width="590" Fill="Gray"/>

</Canvas>
```

However, if you run the project again, you will see the same thing you saw earlier in Figure B-5; the white corners are still there. This is because there are two things getting in the way. The first is the background color of the Silverlight canvas, which you just fixed. However, the other is the background color of the Silverlight object itself, which is, unfortunately hard-coded to white (there is no property in your method calls or XAML file to fix this by default).

So how do you fix this? If you look back at the file TestFile.html.js, you can see that its contents are basically a function call to create the Silverlight object. Currently, there are only a couple of parameters listed in the parameters section of that function call (width, height, version, and enableHtmlAccess). To clear the background, you need to add two new parameters: isWindowless and background.

The Windowless property of the SilverLight object, set by the isWindowless parameter of the create-Silverlight JavaScript function, tells the Silverlight object if it should run as windowless or windowed control. Without getting too much into what that means, the most important thing to know for this example is that, if you set it as windowless, you can include an alpha value for the background color. This means that you set the background color to an eight-character color setting; where the first two characters represent the alpha level and the other six represent the hexadecimal color setting you want to use. For this example, you want the alpha level to be zero (meaning it is completely transparent), so the six characters that come after that are fairly irrelevant. However, just to have something there, you can put in the hex color for white (FFFFFF). Your modified TestFile.html.js should look like this:

```
// JScript source code

//contains calls to silverlight.js, example below loads Page.xaml
function createSilverlight()
{
    Sys.Silverlight.createObjectEx({
        source: "Page.xaml",
```

```
        parentElement: document.getElementById("SilverlightControlHost"),
        id: "SilverlightControl",
        properties: {
            width: "590",
            height: "590",
            version: "0.95",
            enableHtmlAccess: true,
            isWindowless:'true',
            background:'#00FFFFFF'

        events: {}
    });
}
```

If you now run your project again, you should see the results shown in Figure B-6.

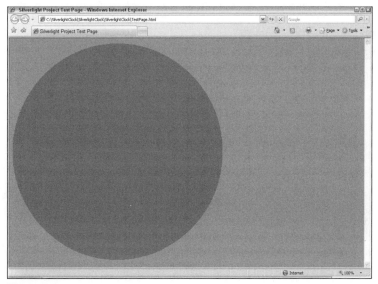

Figure B-6

So, at the end of this section, you now have a Silverlight object rendering on your page within the size limitations you have set (590 × 590) and a completely transparent background (only things added by you in your code will show). You are now ready to begin drawing your clock.

Step 3: Drawing the Clock

One of the things that were specifically excluded from the pared down Silverlight (as opposed to its big brother, WPF) is any kind of 3D modeling. As such, if you want to try to include any kind of 3D effect, you are going to have to try to play around with some of the settings.

To this end, what you want to do with this clock is try to create a sort of bevel effect to the outside of the clock face. To do this, you want to create a gradient fill from a light color to a dark color in the original ellipse and then, inside of that ellipse, draw a smaller ellipse with an opposite gradient fill (filling from dark to light). This will give the appearance of a small bevel around the edge of your clock.

425

This will be accomplished in a way that is very familiar to you if you remember the layers discussion from Chapter 3. You will create a layer that has one gradient fill, then you will put another layer on top of that one that is slightly smaller and with a gradient effect that goes in the opposite direction. Finally, you will put one more layer on top of that that is a solid color that will serve as the clock face.

So, the first step is to modify the `<Ellipse>` definition to break up the tag, as follows:

```
<Ellipse Height="590" Width="590" Fill="Gray"></Ellipse>
```

If you are familiar with XML formatting, this should make sense to you. What you are doing with this is opening up the ability to add more properties for the `Ellipse` object you have just drawn. However, before you start doing that, you want to take out the `Fill` attribute and add a `Stroke` property. You will take care of the fill through a linear gradient fill in the next step. As for the stroke, you want to add a small border around the ellipse just to set it apart. Your modified ellipse code should look like this:

```
<Ellipse Height="590" Width="590" Stroke="#000000" StrokeThickness="3"></Ellipse>
```

Notice that you also added a `StrokeThickness` attribute. This will determine the thickness of the line that is drawn around your ellipse object.

The final step for this ellipse is to fill it in with a linear gradient fill. This can be done with code similar to the following:

```
<Ellipse Height="590" Width="590" Stroke="#000000" StrokeThickness="3">
  <Ellipse.Fill>
    <LinearGradientBrush StartPoint="0,0" EndPoint="1,1">
      <GradientStop Color="#eeeeee" Offset="0"/>
      <GradientStop Color="#444444" Offset="1"/>
    </LinearGradientBrush>
  </Ellipse.Fill>
</Ellipse>
```

The first addition, `Ellipse.Fill`, just sets up the fill properties of its parent `Ellipse` object. Within that setting, you are adding properties for your `LinearGradientBrush`. The only properties set directly in the `LinearGradientBrush` declaration are the `StartPoint` and the `EndPoint`. To better understand what this means, refer to Figure B-7.

With any given drawing object, the coordinates are set up exactly as they are shown in Figure B-7. It is not relevant to the specific height and width of the object; they are always referred (with respect to the `LinearGradientBrush` at least) in either a zero or a one or any number between the two. For example, you can have a coordinate of (0.283, 0.875), you just can't go below zero or above one. Well, technically you can. Doing so, though, will take the reference point off of the image. So if you have a starting point of (10,10) and an ending point of (1,1), you won't have any effect shown because the entire effect is taking place outside the canvas of the object.

So if, for example, you wanted to have a horizontal gradient fill, you would have a starting point of (0,0) and an ending point of (1,0). However, for this example, you want to have a diagonal gradient fill with a starting point of (0,0) and an ending point of (1,1). This will make the gradient go down the diagonal line from the upper-left corner of the image to the bottom-right corner.

Next, with the `GradientStop` properties, you are saying what colors make up the gradient fill. There is no limit to the number of stops you can make, but you should use at least two. After all, it isn't much of a gradient effect if there is only one color involved.

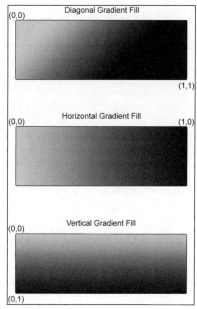

Figure B-7

For this example, you are creating a gradient that is very light gray (#eeeeee) in the top-left position and fades to a darker gray (#444444) in the bottom-right corner. The offsets are saying at what point, zero to one, that these colors occur. For this example, you want the light color to start at the zero position and the dark color to be at the end of the gradient, or the one position. Again, you can go over 1 or less than 0, you will just be dealing with the space outside of the canvas. You won't get an error and, if you start playing with these settings, you will see that the gradients are affected (if you set the second stop to 10 rather than 1 the entire ellipse will look almost white because the gradient is so gradual that you can't see it).

With these settings in place, rerun your project. It should now look like Figure B-8.

As you can see, you now have an ellipse with a black border around it and a gradient fill.

The next step is to include a contrasting ellipse within the existing one. This means that the new ellipse should lie on top of the existing one, be slightly smaller than the existing one (so that you can see the gradient effect from the existing one), and have an opposite gradient fill (going the opposite direction).

To do this, you can copy and paste the existing ellipse code and make the following adjustments:

- Adjust the `Height` and `Width` of the ellipse to 550 pixels. This will provide a padding of 20 pixels between the two ellipse objects (allowing 20 pixels of the original ellipse to show on the outside of this new ellipse).

- Adjust the `StrokeThickness` to 1 to make a less defined line between the two ellipses.

- Move the new ellipse over from the upper-left position by 20 pixels on both the x- and y-axis. You make this adjustment with the `Canvas.Left` and `Canvas.Top` attributes of the `Ellipse` object; `Canvase.Left` moves the object over on the x-axis and `Canvas.Top` moves the object over on the y-axis.

❑ Reverse the `StartPoint` and `EndPoint` settings for the `LinearGradientFill` settings (set `StartPoint="(1,1)"` and `EndPoint="(0,0)"`).

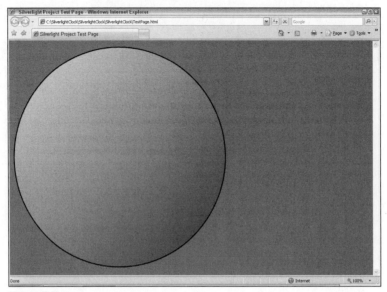

Figure B-8

Making these changes should make the code for your second ellipse resemble the following.

```
<Ellipse Height="550" Width="550" Stroke="#000000" StrokeThickness="1"
  Canvas.Left="20" Canvas.Top="20">
  <Ellipse.Fill>
    <LinearGradientBrush StartPoint="1,1" EndPoint="0,0">
      <GradientStop Color="#eeeeee" Offset="0"/>
      <GradientStop Color="#444444" Offset="1"/>
    </LinearGradientBrush>
  </Ellipse.Fill>
</Ellipse>
```

You need to ensure that this code comes after the original ellipse. Failing to do this will result in this ellipse being hidden by the larger ellipse. If you have all of your code set properly and in the right order, your project should now resemble Figure B-9.

Next, you want to add the actual clock face to your drawing. This should be a third oval that is a solid color that is slightly smaller than the second ellipse and is offset from the top-left corner of the canvas enough to center the object within the other ellipse. Using the same theories that applied to the second ellipse, you should add a third ellipse directly after the second ellipse. The code for this new ellipse should resemble the following:

```
<Ellipse Height="520" Width="520" Stroke="#000000" Canvas.Left="35"
  Canvas.Top="35" Fill="#333333" />
```

This code just creates the ellipse with a height and width of 520 pixels and offsets its upper-left corner by 35 pixels on both the x- and y-axis. If you now run the project, it should resemble Figure B-10.

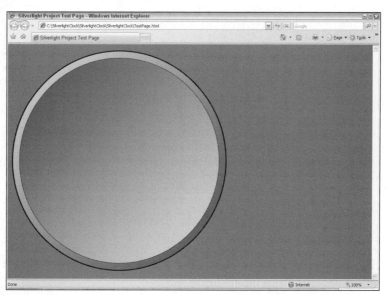

Figure B-9

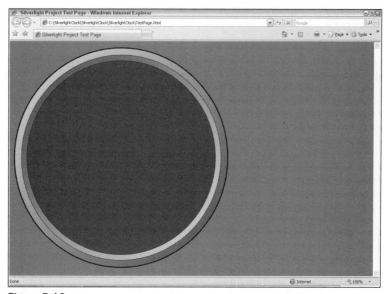

Figure B-10

The final element of the clock face for this project is to add an image to the background to brand the clock. For this example, you will want to import a file similar to the one used in this example. The example for this project uses a PNG image that is 200 pixels wide and 171 pixels high. The image has a transparent background whereas everything that is not part of the logo is completely transparent. Since Silverlight fully supports PNG and its alpha-transparency, this means that the same transparency seen in the PNG image will be brought into the Silverlight object.

The name of the file used for this example is `wrox_logo.png` and the code to bring it into the Silverlight project is:

```
<Image Source="images/wrox_logo.png" Canvas.Left="195" Canvas.Top="209.5"/>
```

The basic parameters of this code should look fairly familiar to you if you have coded HTML before. You are starting off with `Image`, which is akin to `img` in HTML, and adding a `Source` attribute, which is very similar to the `src` attribute of the `<img>` tag in HTML. Actually, that is all that you would need to bring in your image. However, this image should be centered within the drawn object you already have on your canvas.

To get the settings for how far over you need to move this, you need to do a little math. You know that the image is 590 pixels by 590 pixels. This means that the exact center point of the object is (295, 295). So, to center your image on the x-axis, you need to move over the center point (295 pixels) and then back up half the width of the image (200 pixels). This means that you need to subtract 100 pixels (again, half the width of the 200 pixel wide image) from the center x-coordinate of the image. This means that you need to move the image 195 pixels over on the x-axis. Similarly, you need to back the image back half of its height from the center of the y-axis. Since the image is 171 pixels high, this means that you need to subtract 85.5 pixels from the 295 pixel center point of the y-axis. This results in a y-axis adjustment of 209.5 pixels.

As with the ellipse objects in this project, you need to ensure that you place the code properly in your XAML file. If the code for you image occurs before any of the ellipse objects, it will be covered up by those ellipse objects. Therefore, you need to make sure that you put your code after the last ellipse object in your XAML code. If you have everything placed in the right order and set to the proper values, your project should now resemble Figure B-11.

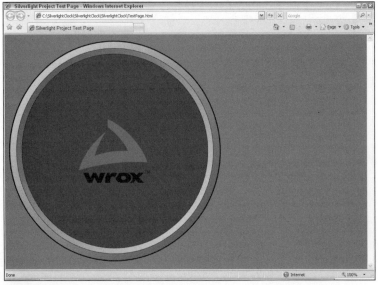

Figure B-11

At this point, you have the basic background image for your clock drawn, and your XAML file should resemble the following:

```
<Canvas x:Name="parentCanvas"
        xmlns="http://schemas.microsoft.com/client/2007"
        xmlns:x="http://schemas.microsoft.com/winfx/2006/xaml"
        Loaded="Page_Loaded"

x:Class="SilverlightClock.Page;assembly=ClientBin/SilverlightClock.dll"
        Width="590"
        Height="590"
        Background="Transparent"
        >

  <Ellipse Height="590" Width="590" Stroke="#000000" StrokeThickness="3">
    <Ellipse.Fill>
      <LinearGradientBrush StartPoint="0,0" EndPoint="1,1">
        <GradientStop Color="#eeeeee" Offset="0"/>
        <GradientStop Color="#444444" Offset="1"/>
      </LinearGradientBrush>
    </Ellipse.Fill>
  </Ellipse>

    <Ellipse Height="550" Width="550" Stroke="#000000" StrokeThickness="1"
    Canvas.Left="20" Canvas.Top="20">
      <Ellipse.Fill>
        <LinearGradientBrush StartPoint="1,1" EndPoint="0,0">
          <GradientStop Color="#eeeeee" Offset="0"/>
          <GradientStop Color="#444444" Offset="1"/>
        </LinearGradientBrush>
      </Ellipse.Fill>
    </Ellipse>

  <Ellipse Height="520" Width="520" Stroke="#000000" Canvas.Left="35"
   Canvas.Top="35" Fill="#333333" />

  <Image Source="images/wrox_logo.png" Canvas.Left="195" Canvas.Top="209.5"/>

</Canvas>
```

Step 4: Adding the Tick Marks

Now that you have the basic shape and design of your clock face, it is time to add some tickmarks around the face to designate the time. The basic requirement for this will be 60 small tick marks used to indicate the minute and second and then 12 larger tick marks used to indicate the hour; each versions of the tick marks will be spread evenly around the clock face. The 12 larger tick marks will occur at the same location as 12 of the 60 smaller tick marks. When this occurs, the larger tick marks should completely hide the smaller ones so that only the larger ones are visible. The end result of this process should resemble Figure B-12 (although the smaller tick marks may not be easily detected in a black and white book).

There are several ways you can accomplish this requirement. Based on what you have seen so far, you could draw a line in your XAML file for, say, the 12 o'clock position, and then copy and paste that line 59 times to make all of the small tick marks and then adjust all 59 new marks to have a different start and end point (after you figured out what the starting and ending points would be for each of the 59 new lines) so that they aren't all just lined up at the 12 o'clock position. You could then repeat that procedure for the 12 larger tick marks. You could certainly do that, but it would be a very time-consuming and frustrating process.

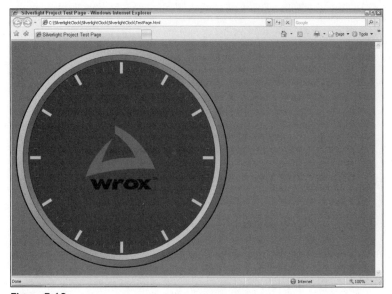

Figure B-12

It would be better to draw these lines programmatically so that you don't have to even really think about their position. In this regard, there are at least two viable options: You can do it client-side through JavaScript, or you can do it through managed code, such as C#. There can certainly be arguments made for using either method. However, generally speaking, the managed code will run faster, especially when you start looping through records. Granted, with only a total of 72 loops (60 for the smaller tick marks and then 12 more for the larger ones), there may not be that noticeable of a performance difference.

However, since this book is focused on .NET, and since there may be a small performance improvement with managed code, this example will focus on the managed code solution.

You should also understand that this example will focus on one way to do this that works. There are certainly others. Again, you could go to JavaScript. But beyond that, you could probably find a different way to accomplish this same task within C#. But this way works and, if you like it, it will work for you in other similar capacities in the future.

The first thing you will want to do is set up the wiring for this job. One way to do this is to add a new canvas object in your XAML code and, from that canvas, call a method from the code behind (that you will need to set up as well). You will need to place the canvas object after the other drawing objects you have already created for this project so that anything happening with that canvas will go on top of the other drawn objects; remember that the objects are rendered in linear order.

So, with that in mind, add the following code to `Page.xaml` after your other objects (but still within the parent canvas):

```
<Canvas Name="TickMarks" Loaded="TickMarks_Loaded"/>
```

As you can see, you have added a new canvas object with just two attributes: Name and Loaded. You will need to have the Name attribute set so that you can refer to this object from your managed code. The Loaded attribute allows you to put in a method call for when this object is loaded. In other words, every time this canvas object gets loaded, Silverlight will call the "TickMarks_Loaded" method. However, at this point, no such method exists, so you will need to add it.

To add a new method to this project, you should expand your XAML file in Solution Explorer. When you do so for `Page.xaml`, you should see that it has an attached code-behind file called `Page.xaml.cs`. Open that file and it should look like this:

```
using System;
using System.Windows;
using System.Windows.Controls;
using System.Windows.Documents;
using System.Windows.Ink;
using System.Windows.Input;
using System.Windows.Media;
using System.Windows.Media.Animation;
using System.Windows.Shapes;

namespace SilverlightClock
{
    public partial class Page : Canvas
    {
        public void Page_Loaded(object o, EventArgs e)
        {
            // Required to initialize variables
            InitializeComponent();
        }
    }
}
```

So far, the only method in your code behind is `Page_Loaded`, which you should already be familiar with from your previous experience in coding .NET applications. This method just calls the Initialization stuff when the XAML page loads.

You will need to add the new method, `TickMarks_Loaded`, within the partial class for the page. For now, it is okay to just leave an empty method, as follows:

```
public void TickMarks_Loaded(object sender, EventArgs e)
{
}
```

The cool thing is that you now have the functionality wired up to call managed code directly from your XAML file. Granted, it isn't doing anything right now, but the functionality is in place to allow you to write custom code to shape your XAML file. This is one of the really nice features of Silverlight.

As mentioned earlier, there are a couple of ways to code in the lines in your code behind. However, this can get a bit tricky. If you code in a new line object in the code, draw it, and then rotate the canvas a certain degrees and draw the line again, only the last line shows up. The way that the code behind deals with graphic objects is a bit tricky.

The easier way is to create a dummy line object in your XAML and then use that code in code behind to add that same line over and over again. Perhaps it sounds like the same thing, but there is at least one small difference: this works.

So the first step in adding your line objects is to create the line object in your XAML file, like this:

```
<Line X1="295" Y1="50" X2="295" Y2="60" Stroke="#777777"
    StrokeThickness="1"></Line>
```

The attributes X1 and Y1 are setting up your first coordinate (295, 50), and X2 and Y2 are setting up your second coordinates (295, 60). This means that you are moving from the 50-pixel mark to the 60-pixel mark on the y-axis at the 295 pixel point of the x-axis. The end result of that is that you have a 10-pixel line going straight up and down the x-axis, as seen in Figure B-13.

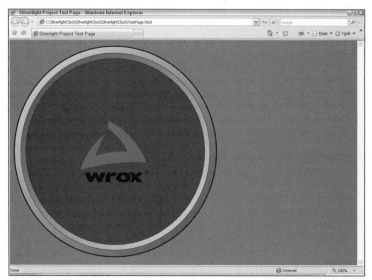

Figure B-13

If you have trouble seeing this line in the black-and-white context of the book, there is a small grayish line at the 12 o'clock position of the clock face. The color was determined by the Stroke attribute of the line object (#777777) and its width was determined by the StrokeThickness (1) attribute.

When this is automated, you are going to want to take that line and then rotate around the clock face and redraw it at different angles. So now you need to get the rotation piece in place as well. You can do this by modifying your line code to the following:

```
<Line X1="295" Y1="50" X2="295" Y2="60" Stroke="#777777" StrokeThickness="1">
  <Line.RenderTransform>
    <RotateTransform CenterX="295" CenterY="295" Angle="90"/>
  </Line.RenderTransform>
</Line>
```

With this code, you have set up a RenderTransform property with a RotateTransform setting. If you have done any graphics coding in the old System.Drawing namespace (or its predecessor, Graphics Device Interface, or GDI), you are at least familiar with these terms. Basically, with this code, you are setting up a rotation of the Line object that encapsulates it (e.g., the RenderTranform occurs between the <Line> and </Line> tags).

Within the RotateTransform, you need to set up a couple of properties. The first two, CenterX and CenterY set the axis point to rotate around. For this example, you want to rotate the line around the central point of the clock, which is also the central point of the Silverlight object. Since you know from earlier in this chapter that the clock is 590 by 590, the central point is (295, 295). If the clock had been 640 × 480, you would have set the CenterX to 320 and the CenterY to 240 to rotate around the center point of those dimensions. But, since the clock is 590 × 590, you need to set both the CenterX and CenterY to 295.

The only other setting you need to make is the Angle attribute. For illustrative purposes, this was set to "90", which results in what you will see in Figure B-14.

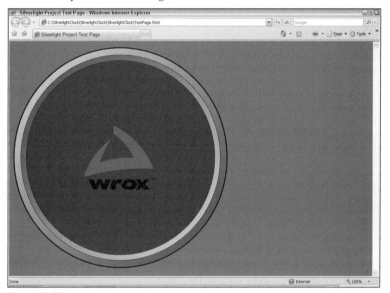

Figure B-14

Again, if you can't see the line because of the nature of the printed manuscript, the 10-pixel line has now moved to the 3 o'clock position. At this point, you have all of the code you need to make 59 more lines (with a little tweaking of course).

What you will be doing is taking that code and inserting it 60 times, all at different angles. The first thing you need to do is update your TickMarks_Loaded method to include the variables you will be using in this step:

```
public void TickMarks_Loaded(object sender, EventArgs e)
{
    Canvas parentCanvas = (Canvas)this.FindName("TickMarks");
    string xaml = "";
    float angle = 0;
    Line line = new Line();
}
```

435

The first line is grabbing the `TickMarks` canvas that you have already added since this is the object that all of your lines will be drawn to. The next variable, `xaml`, will hold the string representation of your XAML code for the line you just created. The next variable, `angle`, will be used to store the angle of the current line being drawn (this will be modified as you rotate around the clock). The final variable, `line`, holds the actual Line object that you will be adding to the canvas.

To test the approach you will be taking, you will want to add a new line using this method. The first step is to modify the `Line` object from your XAML code so that it fits in your string variable. To do this, you want to make it all one line of code (take out the carriage returns) and insert a backward slash (\) in front of any quotation marks (so that the quotation marks will not break your string variable). You might want to do this in something like Notepad so that you can play with it without breaking anything else (copy the XAML code into a text editor before copying it again to the code behind). Your code should look something like this:

```
<Line X1=\"295\" Y1=\"50\" X2=\"295\" Y2=\"60\" Stroke=\"#777777\"
    StrokeThickness=\"1\"><Line.RenderTransform><RotateTransform CenterX=\"295\"
    CenterY=\"295\" Angle=\"90\"/></Line.RenderTransform></Line>
```

You now want to add that string into your method and replace the hard-coded angle with a placeholder for the angle property. Your method should now resemble the following:

```
public void TickMarks_Loaded(object sender, EventArgs e)
{
    Canvas parentCanvas = (Canvas)this.FindName("TickMarks");
    string xaml = "";
    float angle = 0;
    Line line = new Line();

    xaml = "<Line X1=\"295\" Y1=\"50\" X2=\"295\" Y2=\"60\" Stroke=\"#777777\"
    StrokeThickness=\"1\"><Line.RenderTransform><RotateTransform CenterX=\"295\"
    CenterY=\"295\" Angle=\"" + angle + "\"/></Line.RenderTransform></Line>";
}
```

Now, to make this actually render a line, you need to add two lines of code following the XAML entry:

```
public void TickMarks_Loaded(object sender, EventArgs e)
{
    Canvas parentCanvas = (Canvas)this.FindName("TickMarks");
    string xaml = "";
    float angle = 0;
    Line line = new Line();

    xaml = "<Line X1=\"295\" Y1=\"50\" X2=\"295\" Y2=\"60\" Stroke=\"#777777\"
    StrokeThickness=\"1\"><Line.RenderTransform><RotateTransform CenterX=\"295\"
    CenterY=\"295\" Angle=\"" + angle + "\"/></Line.RenderTransform></Line>";
    line = (Line)XamlReader.Load(xaml);
    parentCanvas.Children.Add(line);
}
```

Since you didn't change the angle from zero when the variable was instantiated, this will draw a line at the zero position, as shown in Figure B-15.

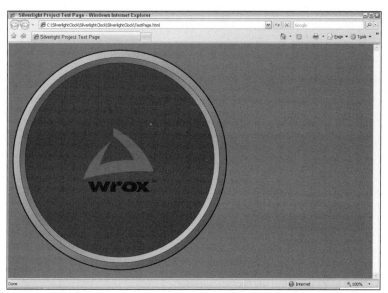

Figure B-15

You should be able to see two lines: one at the 12 o'clock position and one at the 3 o'clock position. The 12 o'clock line was drawn from your `TickMarks_Load` method, while the 3 o'clock position was drawn from the hard-coded version you still have in your XAML code. At this point, you no longer need your XAML entry, so you can delete that line in `Page.xaml`. As for the `TickMarks_Loaded` method, you need to now set your new functionality into a `for` loop that will iterate 60 times and draw a new line at a new angle each time. To do this, you should modify your method to look like the following:

```
public void TickMarks_Loaded(object sender, EventArgs e)
{
    Canvas parentCanvas = (Canvas)this.FindName("TickMarks");
    string xaml = "";
    float angle = 0;
    Line line = new Line();

    for (int x = 0; x < 60; x++)
    {
        angle = x * (360 / 60);
        xaml = "<Line X1=\"295\" Y1=\"50\" X2=\"295\" Y2=\"60\" Stroke=\"#777777\"
StrokeThickness=\"1\"><Line.RenderTransform><RotateTransform CenterX=\"295\"
CenterY=\"295\" Angle=\"" + angle + "\"/></Line.RenderTransform></Line>";
        line = (Line)XamlReader.Load(xaml);
        parentCanvas.Children.Add(line);
    }
}
```

With these additions, you are iterating through your code 60 times and updating the angle with each iteration. As you can see with this example, you need to update the code by the equivalent of 360 degrees divided by 60 lines. You could have just as easily written this code as:

```
angle = x * 6;
```

If you run your project again, it should now resemble Figure B-16.

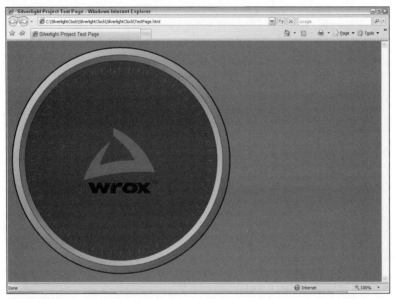

Figure B-16

You should now be able to see 60 little lines drawn all around the clock face. On top of those lines, you want to draw 12 more that are thicker, longer lines to designate the hours. To do this, you want to copy and paste your original `for` loop and modify the `xaml` variable to increase the size of the line. Your updated `TickMarks_Loaded` method should look like this:

```
public void TickMarks_Loaded(object sender, EventArgs e)
{
    Canvas parentCanvas = (Canvas)this.FindName("TickMarks");
    string xaml = "";
    float angle = 0;
    Line line = new Line();

    for (int x = 0; x < 60; x++)
    {
        angle = x * (360 / 60);
        xaml = "<Line X1=\"295\" Y1=\"50\" X2=\"295\" Y2=\"60\" Stroke=\"#777777\"
StrokeThickness=\"1\"><Line.RenderTransform><RotateTransform CenterX=\"295\"
CenterY=\"295\" Angle=\"" + angle + "\"/></Line.RenderTransform></Line>";
        line = (Line)XamlReader.Load(xaml);
        parentCanvas.Children.Add(line);
    }

    for (int y = 0; y < 12; y++)
    {
        angle = y * (360 / 12);
        xaml = "<Line X1=\"295\" Y1=\"40\" X2=\"295\" Y2=\"70\" Stroke=\"#CCCCCC\"
StrokeThickness=\"8\"><Line.RenderTransform><RotateTransform CenterX=\"295\"
CenterY=\"295\" Angle=\"" + angle + "\"/></Line.RenderTransform></Line>";
```

```
        line = (Line)XamlReader.Load(xaml);
        parentCanvas.Children.Add(line);
    }
}
```

The major things you should change after you copy and paste the new `for` loop are bolded in this code example. Specifically, you want to change your Y1 to `"40"` and your Y2 to `"70"`. This will make your line 30 pixels long, rather than 10 with the smaller marks. You also want to change the stroke color and thickness to further set these tick marks apart.

If you rerun your project now, you should see the image in Figure B-17.

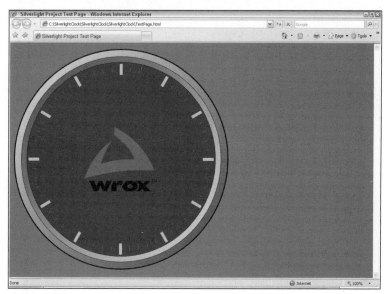

Figure B-17

So, with your new code in place, you now have all of your tick marks in place for your clock. It's time to add the hour, minute, and second hands, animate them to move around the clock, and then, finally, set your clock to the proper time. But first things first: Its time to add the clock hands.

Step 5: Adding the Clock Hands

Before you can worry about animating the clock hands or setting them to the proper time, you need to actually draw them first. For this, you will want to draw three "hands." The first one will be the second hand. This can be a long line that extends past the hour and minute hands on both ends. Cosmetically, it should have rounded ends just so that it looks better than squared-off ends. This line can be added with the following code (make sure that you add this after the `TickMarks` canvas):

```
<Line Name="SecondHand" Stroke="#1D2BF2" StrokeThickness="5" X1="295" Y1="50"
    X2="295" Y2="340" StrokeEndLineCap="Round" StrokeStartLineCap="Round"></Line>
```

You should set the `Name` property even though you will not be referencing that later in your code; it's just a good practice to get in. The X1, X2, Y1, and Y2 coordinates should look familiar to you from the tick marks example; these are just drawing a line that extends through the center axis of the image through the tick marks. You have also added StrokeStartLineCap and StrokeEndLineCap attributes and set them both to "Round" (the options are Flat, Square, Round, Triangle). The colors are fairly arbitrary but, in this example, it is set to a purplish color that will go along with the other hands (that will all be blue-based).

If you run the project at this point, you should see something similar to Figure B-18.

Figure B-18

At this point, the second hand isn't that impressive; it's just a line. However, as the project matures, you will see how this becomes the second hand of your clock.

The next step is to add the minute hand. For this image, you will want to draw a triangle that points just under the large tick marks and extends slightly below the center axis of the clock. This can be done through the Polygon drawing object, as shown here:

```
<Polygon Name="MinuteHand" Stroke="#0E528C" StrokeThickness="3" Fill="#167ED9"
    Points="295,90 310,315 280,315"></Polygon>
```

This object has many of the settings you are already familiar with, such as Name, Stroke, StrokeThickness, and Fill. In fact, the only new attribute is the Points property. This attribute allows you to enter as many sets of points (two numbers separated only by a comma); each set separated by a space. This example uses three points, (295, 90), (310, 315), and (280, 315), to draw a triangle that will be used as your minute hand. If you run your application again; it should resemble Figure B-19.

It might be hard to see in the book, but in your project, you should be able to see that you have created a triangular image that will serve as the minute hand and that the second hand extends below and above it (although the part that extends above is really hard to see when the image is static).

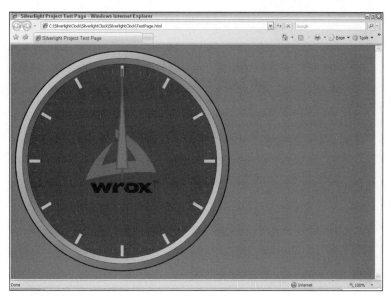

Figure B-19

You now want to repeat the same process to create the hour hand. You can use the following code for this:

```
<Polygon Name="HourHand" Stroke="#0E1573" StrokeThickness="2" Fill="#1A27D9"
    Points="295,140 310,310 280,310"></Polygon>
```

You can see that this is almost exactly the same code as the MinuteHand example. The same attributes are being set; they are just being set to slightly different values. The points, for example, are still drawing a triangle through three points, the triangle is just smaller (the tip is slightly farther down the x-axis, and the bottom side is slightly higher on the x-axis).

If you run the example at this point in the project, it should resemble Figure B-20.

As before, it will probably be hard to see the different hands in the book figures. However, in the project you are building, you should be able to tell that there are three different hands (even if the distinction is slight). The fact that the images look so similar won't be a big issue as the project gets life (the hands will always be moving). However, at this point, especially in the book, it will probably be a little hard to notice the distinction. If you look closely, you can see that the minute hand extends above and below the hour hand and that the second hand extends above and below both other hands. For now, this is good enough.

As a final touch, you might want to have a small center cap that sits on the center-axis of the clock to show where the rotation is occurring. This can be a small ellipse object that sits on top of the hand objects and can be something as easy as the following:

```
<Ellipse Name="ClockCenter" Canvas.Left="289" Canvas.Top="289" Height="12"
    Width="12" Fill="#000000"/>
```

Figure B-20

This will just add a 12 pixel by 12 pixel black ellipse to the center of your clock (you have to back off half of the ellipse size, or 6 pixels, from the center x- and y-coordinates or 295 pixels to make sure that the image is centered on the center axis of the image). Adding this center cap will result in Figure B-21.

Figure B-21

You are ready to start making the hands move.

Step 6: Animating the Clock Hands

At this point, the hands of your clock are in place, but they are static. You will want to add some animation to them to move them around the face of the clock.

To begin to see how to do this, you will want to modify your second-hand code to include a `RotateTransform` property that is similar to the code you used earlier in this chapter for the tick marks:

```
<Line Name="SecondHand" Stroke="#1D2BF2" StrokeThickness="5" X1="295" Y1="50"
    X2="295" Y2="340" StrokeEndLineCap="Round" StrokeStartLineCap="Round">
  <Line.RenderTransform>
    <RotateTransform Name="SecondHandRotation" CenterX="295"
    CenterY="295" Angle="90"/>
  </Line.RenderTransform>
</Line>
```

This should be very familiar to you if you have been following this chapter to this point. The only thing you are doing is rotating the line 90 degrees around the center axis of the clock. If you run the project, it should now look like Figure B-22.

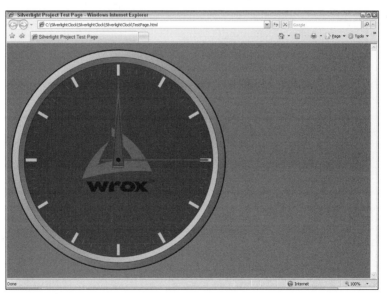

Figure B-22

Now that you have the rotation object in place, you will want to animate it. This can be done through a `DoubleAnimation` set up for the line with the following additions to your code:

```
<Line Name="SecondHand" Stroke="#1D2BF2" StrokeThickness="5" X1="295" Y1="50"
    X2="295" Y2="340" StrokeEndLineCap="Round" StrokeStartLineCap="Round">
  <Line.RenderTransform>
    <RotateTransform Name="SecondHandRotation" CenterX="295"
  CenterY="295" Angle="90"/>
  </Line.RenderTransform>
```

```
   <Line.Triggers>
     <EventTrigger RoutedEvent="Line.Loaded">
       <BeginStoryboard>
         <Storyboard>
           <DoubleAnimation Name="SecondHandAnimation"
  Storyboard.TargetName="SecondHandRotation"
  Storyboard.TargetProperty="Angle" From="0" To="360" Duration="0:1:0"
  RepeatBehavior="Forever"/>
         </Storyboard>
       </BeginStoryboard>
     </EventTrigger>
   </Line.Triggers>
 </Line>
```

The first thing you are doing is setting up a trigger that will force the encapsulated code. In this example, you want the trigger to be when the line is loaded. So, in your EventTrigger, you set the attribute RoutedEvent to Line.Loaded. Again, this will tell your Silverlight application to run the encapsulated code when this particular line object is loaded.

The next few lines are setting up your storyboard. The storyboard encapsulates one or more animation objects. There really aren't any properties you need to set for BeginStoryBoard or StoryBoard; you just need to have them in place.

The next section, DoubleAnimation, is where the magic takes place. DoubleAnimation sets up an animation to run from one point to another point over a certain duration. This can mean moving from one point to another point within your canvas. This could mean going from one percentage of opacity for an image to another (fading in or fading out). However, for this example, it is used to rotate the angle of SecondHandRotation from 0 degrees to 360 degrees. Therefore, you need to set the following properties as part of your DoubleAnimation:

❑   **Name** — you need to set this because you will reference it later in code. You can set this to whatever you want but, for the examples in this chapter, SecondHandAnimation will be used.

❑   **Storyboard.TargetName** — This is the object in your XAML code that you want to target. For this example, you want to target the RotateTransform object for your Line, called SecondHandRotation.

❑   **Storyboard.TargetProperty** — This is the property of the object defined in Storyboard. TargetName that you want to manipulate. In this example, you want to modify the angle of the rotation, so you need to target the Angle property.

❑   **From** — set this to "0"; you want to modify the angle starting at zero degrees.

❑   **To** — set this to "360"; you want to modify the angle ending at 360 degrees (full circle).

❑   **Duration** — this property is set in the following format: "hours:minutes:seconds". Since you want the duration to occur over one minute (one full rotation of the second hand around the clock), you need to set this property to "0:1:0", which translates to zero hours, one minute, and zero seconds.

❑   **RepeatBehavior** — set this to "Forever" so that the animation continues after it does its initial loop.

If you run the project again, you will see that the second hand is now moving around the clock at the correct rate (takes one minute to go from the 12 o'clock position back to the 12 o'clock position).

You will want to repeat these same steps for your minute and hour hands. The code for these two objects should now look like this:

```
<Polygon Name="MinuteHand" Stroke="#0E528C" StrokeThickness="3"
   Fill="#167ED9" Points="295,90 310,315 280,315">
  <Polygon.RenderTransform>
    <RotateTransform Name="MinuteHandRotation" CenterX="295"
  CenterY="295" Angle="90"/>
  </Polygon.RenderTransform>
  <Polygon.Triggers>
    <EventTrigger RoutedEvent="Polygon.Loaded">
      <BeginStoryboard>
        <Storyboard>
          <DoubleAnimation Name="MinuteHandAnimation"
  Storyboard.TargetName="MinuteHandRotation" Storyboard.TargetProperty="Angle"
  From="0" To="360" Duration="1:0:0" RepeatBehavior="Forever"/>
        </Storyboard>
      </BeginStoryboard>
    </EventTrigger>
  </Polygon.Triggers>
</Polygon>

<Polygon Name="HourHand" Stroke="#0E1573" StrokeThickness="2" Fill="#1A27D9"
   Points="295,140 310,310 280,310">
  <Polygon.RenderTransform>
    <RotateTransform Name="HourHandRotation" CenterX="295"
  CenterY="295" Angle="90"/>
  </Polygon.RenderTransform>
  <Polygon.Triggers>
    <EventTrigger RoutedEvent="Polygon.Loaded">
      <BeginStoryboard>
        <Storyboard>
          <DoubleAnimation Name="HourHandAnimation"
  Storyboard.TargetName="HourHandRotation" Storyboard.TargetProperty="Angle"
  From="0" To="360" Duration="12:0:0" RepeatBehavior="Forever"/>
        </Storyboard>
      </BeginStoryboard>
    </EventTrigger>
  </Polygon.Triggers>
</Polygon>
```

You are essentially setting up the same properties for these objects that you did for the line; the major difference being the duration. For example, for the minute hand, you need to set the duration to one hour (e.g., "1:0:0") and the hour hand to have a duration of 12 hours (e.g., "12:0:0"). Setting these attributes this way will cause the minute hand to make a full trip around the clock in an hour and the hour hand to do a full trip in 12 hours, as you would expect.

If you compile your project and let it run for a little while, you should now see something similar to Figure B-23.

Obviously, with this static image, it is impossible to see the animation occurring. However, you can see that the hour, minute, and second hand have all moved at their own pace and are at different positions on the clock face. This indicates that the animation is in place properly and working as it should . . . for a stopwatch. Now you need to set your clock to actually reflect the current time.

Figure B-23

Step 7: Setting the Time

The final step for this project is to make the time for your clock be reflective of the actual time. In order to do this, you need to go back to your managed code in the Page.xaml.cs file.

In order to set the time, you will need to use some of the same functionality you saw earlier when drawing the tick marks. You will need to create a new method for setting the current time and then grab certain objects in your canvas (the animation objects) and change a property for each one.

The first step is to set up your new method in your Page.xaml.cs file:

```
public void SetCurrentTime()
{
}
```

Within your new method, you will want to set the variables that you will want to use throughout this process:

```
public void SetCurrentTime()
{
    Canvas canvas = (Canvas)this.FindName("parentCanvas");
    DateTime date = DateTime.Now;
    int seconds = date.Second;
    int minutes = date.Minute;
    int hours = date.Hour;
}
```

As before, you are setting up a canvas object in code. However, unlike the tick marks example, you are grabbing the parent canvas, called parentCanvas, to use throughout the steps. You are also getting the current date and, from that, deriving the current seconds, minutes, and hours and storing those in an `int` variable.

The next step is to perform some math to get the angles for each of the clock hands:

```
public void SetCurrentTime()
{
    Canvas canvas = (Canvas)this.FindName("parentCanvas");
    DateTime date = DateTime.Now;
    int seconds = date.Second;
    int minutes = date.Minute;
    int hours = date.Hour;

    float secondAngle = seconds * (360 / 60);
    float minutesAngle = (minutes * (360 / 60)) + (secondAngle / 60);
    float hoursAngle = (hours * (360 / 12)) + (minutesAngle / 12);
}
```

The seconds formula is the easiest to understand. You are taking the total number of seconds and figuring out how much of the total rotation that amount constitutes. Each second warrants 6 degrees of rotation (360 degrees total divided by 60 increments — one for each second of time).

The second and third formulas are a bit more complicated. They both start with the same basic approach (figuring out the amount of the total rotation the number represents). For example, with the minutes, you need to figure out how much of the total rotation is warranted by the number of minutes you are at. However, for both of these formulas, you also need to take into consideration the other hands on the clock. For example, if the time is 1:55 PM and you set the hour hand to point directly to the 1 o'clock position, it will not move very far in the five minutes it takes to get to 2 PM. Therefore, when the time switches to 2 o'clock, the hour hand will still be pointing at the 1 o'clock position. Therefore, you need to add the percentage of time that has elapsed between the current hour position (1 in this example) and the next one (2 for this example). To continue this example, if it is 1:55, 55/60 of the hour has elapsed and you need to adjust the hour hand by that amount.

At this point, you have all of the angles that the hands needed, so you just need to adjust the animations from your XAML to reflect these new angles. In order to do this, you need to adjust your method to add each of these angles to your XAML code:

```
public void SetCurrentTime()
{
    Canvas canvas = (Canvas)this.FindName("parentCanvas");
    DateTime date = DateTime.Now;
    int seconds = date.Second;
    int minutes = date.Minute;
    int hours = date.Hour;

    float secondAngle = seconds * (360 / 60);
    float minutesAngle = (minutes * (360 / 60)) + (secondAngle / 60);
    float hoursAngle = (hours * (360 / 12)) + (minutesAngle / 12);

    DoubleAnimation secondRotation = (DoubleAnimation)canvas.FindName
    ("SecondHandAnimation");
    secondRotation.From = secondAngle;
    secondRotation.To = secondAngle + 360;
```

```
    DoubleAnimation minuteRotation =
    (DoubleAnimation)canvas.FindName("MinuteHandAnimation");
    minuteRotation.From = minutesAngle;
    minuteRotation.To = minutesAngle + 360;

    DoubleAnimation hourRotation =
    (DoubleAnimation)canvas.FindName("HourHandAnimation");
    hourRotation.From = hoursAngle;
    hourRotation.To = hoursAngle + 360;
}
```

With each of these three code blocks, you are first finding the appropriate DoubleAnimation object on your canvas. Once you do that, you are setting the To attribute to the appropriate angle and then setting the From angle to that same angle plus 360 degrees. This will give the animation a full rotation starting at the appropriate angle for the given time.

The final step is to actually call this new method. The easiest way to do this is to just do a method call from the existing Page_Loaded method:

```
public void Page_Loaded(object o, EventArgs e)
{
    // Required to initialize variables
    InitializeComponent();

    SetCurrentTime();
}
```

If you now run the project, you should see that it now resembles the current time, as shown in Figure B-24.

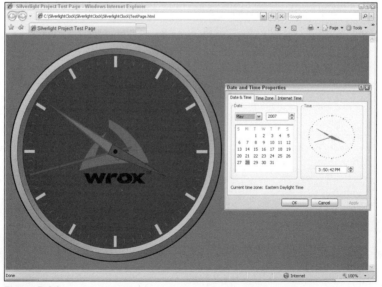

Figure B-24

As seen in Figure B-24, both the Silverlight clock and the Windows System Clock are set to 3:50:42 PM. You can see that the minute hand is almost to the 51 position (because it is 42 seconds into the 50th minute) and that the hour hand is almost at the 4 o'clock position (because the minute is in the 50th of 60 positions).

And, with this final code addition, you have a completely working clock!

The Clock Project Code

With all of the tinkering with all of the pages, it might be nice to see what the code for the finished project looks like. This section will just provide a final copy of all of the pages created as part of this project.

Page.xaml

```xml
<Canvas x:Name="parentCanvas"
        xmlns="http://schemas.microsoft.com/client/2007"
        xmlns:x="http://schemas.microsoft.com/winfx/2006/xaml"
        Loaded="Page_Loaded"
        x:Class="SilverlightClock.Page;assembly=ClientBin/SilverlightClock.dll"
        Width="590"
        Height="590"
        Background="Transparent"
        >

<Ellipse Height="590" Width="590" Stroke="#000000" StrokeThickness="3">
  <Ellipse.Fill>
    <LinearGradientBrush StartPoint="0,0" EndPoint="1,1">
      <GradientStop Color="#eeeeee" Offset="0"/>
      <GradientStop Color="#444444" Offset="1"/>
    </LinearGradientBrush>
  </Ellipse.Fill>
</Ellipse>

  <Ellipse Height="550" Width="550" Stroke="#000000" StrokeThickness="1"
  Canvas.Left="20" Canvas.Top="20">
    <Ellipse.Fill>
      <LinearGradientBrush StartPoint="1,1" EndPoint="0,0">
        <GradientStop Color="#eeeeee" Offset="0"/>
        <GradientStop Color="#444444" Offset="1"/>
      </LinearGradientBrush>
    </Ellipse.Fill>
  </Ellipse>

<Ellipse Height="520" Width="520" Stroke="#000000" Canvas.Left="35"
  Canvas.Top="35" Fill="#333333" />

<Image Source="images/wrox_logo.png" Canvas.Left="195" Canvas.Top="209.5"/>

<Canvas Name="TickMarks" Loaded="TickMarks_Loaded"/>

<Line Name="SecondHand" Stroke="#1D2BF2" StrokeThickness="5" X1="295"
  Y1="50" X2="295" Y2="340" StrokeEndLineCap="Round" StrokeStartLineCap="Round">
```

```xml
      <Line.RenderTransform>
        <RotateTransform Name="SecondHandRotation" CenterX="295"
CenterY="295" Angle="90"/>
      </Line.RenderTransform>
      <Line.Triggers>
        <EventTrigger RoutedEvent="Line.Loaded">
          <BeginStoryboard>
            <Storyboard>
              <DoubleAnimation Name="SecondHandAnimation"
Storyboard.TargetName="SecondHandRotation" Storyboard.TargetProperty="Angle"
From="0" To="360" Duration="0:1:0" RepeatBehavior="Forever"/>
            </Storyboard>
          </BeginStoryboard>
        </EventTrigger>
      </Line.Triggers>
</Line>

<Polygon Name="MinuteHand" Stroke="#0E528C" StrokeThickness="3"
Fill="#167ED9" Points="295,90 310,315 280,315">
  <Polygon.RenderTransform>
    <RotateTransform Name="MinuteHandRotation" CenterX="295"
CenterY="295" Angle="90"/>
  </Polygon.RenderTransform>
  <Polygon.Triggers>
    <EventTrigger RoutedEvent="Polygon.Loaded">
      <BeginStoryboard>
        <Storyboard>
          <DoubleAnimation Name="MinuteHandAnimation"
Storyboard.TargetName="MinuteHandRotation" Storyboard.TargetProperty="Angle"
From="0" To="360" Duration="1:0:0" RepeatBehavior="Forever"/>
        </Storyboard>
      </BeginStoryboard>
    </EventTrigger>
  </Polygon.Triggers>
</Polygon>

<Polygon Name="HourHand" Stroke="#0E1573" StrokeThickness="2"
Fill="#1A27D9" Points="295,140 310,310 280,310">
  <Polygon.RenderTransform>
    <RotateTransform Name="HourHandRotation" CenterX="295"
CenterY="295" Angle="90"/>
  </Polygon.RenderTransform>
  <Polygon.Triggers>
    <EventTrigger RoutedEvent="Polygon.Loaded">
      <BeginStoryboard>
        <Storyboard>
          <DoubleAnimation Name="HourHandAnimation"
Storyboard.TargetName="HourHandRotation" Storyboard.TargetProperty="Angle"
From="0" To="360" Duration="12:0:0" RepeatBehavior="Forever"/>
        </Storyboard>
      </BeginStoryboard>
    </EventTrigger>
  </Polygon.Triggers>
</Polygon>
```

```
    <Ellipse Name="ClockCenter" Canvas.Left="289" Canvas.Top="289"
    Height="12" Width="12" Fill="#000000"/>

</Canvas>
```

Page.xaml.cs

```csharp
using System;
using System.Windows;
using System.Windows.Controls;
using System.Windows.Documents;
using System.Windows.Ink;
using System.Windows.Input;
using System.Windows.Media;
using System.Windows.Media.Animation;
using System.Windows.Shapes;

namespace SilverlightClock
{
    public partial class Page : Canvas
    {
        public void Page_Loaded(object o, EventArgs e)
        {
            // Required to initialize variables
            InitializeComponent();

            SetCurrentTime();
        }

        public void TickMarks_Loaded(object sender, EventArgs e)
        {
            Canvas parentCanvas = (Canvas)this.FindName("TickMarks");
            string xaml = "";
            float angle = 0;
            Line line = new Line();

            for (int x = 0; x < 60; x++)
            {
                angle = x * (360 / 60);
                xaml = "<Line X1=\"295\" Y1=\"50\" X2=\"295\" Y2=\"60\"
    Stroke=\"#777777\" StrokeThickness=\"1\"><Line.RenderTransform><RotateTransform
    CenterX=\"295\" CenterY=\"295\" Angle=\"" + angle + "\"/>
    </Line.RenderTransform></Line>";
                line = (Line)XamlReader.Load(xaml);
                parentCanvas.Children.Add(line);
            }

            for (int y = 0; y < 12; y++)
            {
                angle = y * (360 / 12);
                xaml = "<Line X1=\"295\" Y1=\"40\" X2=\"295\" Y2=\"70\"
    Stroke=\"#CCCCCC\" StrokeThickness=\"8\"><Line.RenderTransform>
    <RotateTransform CenterX=\"295\" CenterY=\"295\" Angle=\"" + angle + "\"/>
```

```
        </Line.RenderTransform></Line>";
                line = (Line)XamlReader.Load(xaml);
                parentCanvas.Children.Add(line);
            }
        }

    public void SetCurrentTime()
    {
        Canvas canvas = (Canvas)this.FindName("parentCanvas");
        DateTime date = DateTime.Now;
        int seconds = date.Second;
        int minutes = date.Minute;
        int hours = date.Hour;

        float secondAngle = seconds * (360 / 60);
        float minutesAngle = (minutes * (360 / 60)) + (secondAngle / 60);
        float hoursAngle = (hours * (360 / 12)) + (minutesAngle / 12);

        DoubleAnimation secondRotation =
(DoubleAnimation)canvas.FindName("SecondHandAnimation");
        secondRotation.From = secondAngle;
        secondRotation.To = secondAngle + 360;

        DoubleAnimation minuteRotation =
(DoubleAnimation)canvas.FindName("MinuteHandAnimation");
        minuteRotation.From = minutesAngle;
        minuteRotation.To = minutesAngle + 360;

        DoubleAnimation hourRotation =
(DoubleAnimation)canvas.FindName("HourHandAnimation");
        hourRotation.From = hoursAngle;
        hourRotation.To = hoursAngle + 360;
    }

    }
}
```

TestPage.html

```html
<html xmlns="http://www.w3.org/1999/xhtml">
<!-- saved from url=(0014)about:internet -->
<head>
    <title>Silverlight Project Test Page </title>
    <script type="text/javascript" src="Silverlight.js"></script>
    <script type="text/javascript" src="TestPage.html.js"></script>
</head>

<!-- Give the keyboard focus to the Silverlight control by default -->
<body onload="document.getElementById('SilverlightControl').focus()"
    style="background-color: SteelBlue;">
    <div id="SilverlightControlHost" >
        <script type="text/javascript">
            createSilverlight();
        </script>
```

```
        </div>
    </body>
</html>
```

TestPage.html.js

```
// JScript source code

//contains calls to silverlight.js, example below loads Page.xaml
function createSilverlight()
{
    Sys.Silverlight.createObjectEx({
        source: "Page.xaml",
        parentElement: document.getElementById("SilverlightControlHost"),
        id: "SilverlightControl",
        properties: {
            width: "590",
            height: "590",
            version: "0.95",
            enableHtmlAccess: true,
            isWindowless:'true',
            background:'#00FFFFFF'
        },
        events: {}
    });
}
```

Silverlight Considerations

When thinking about implementing Silverlight into your web projects, you would do yourself and your patrons a favor to weigh whether it meets the needs of the visitors to your site. For one, there is a client-side plug-in required to see anything at all. This file is touted as less than 2MB but, even at that size, this could be a burden to users with slower connections or without the rights to install plug-ins on their system (if they are locked out of installing new software as part of corporate network system security, for example). If they can't install the plug-in or choose not to because of its size, then they can't see your content.

More than that, though, is the issue of accessibility. As you probably remember from discussions on accessibility in Chapter 2, there is an increasing movement to make web pages today accessible to all users of the Internet. Because of that, newer technologies like AJAX are being scrutinized since they are not accessible to all people (screen readers do not recognize that new content has been placed on the page because no page header was sent to the browser).

So how accessible is Silverlight? Right now, not very. First and foremost, it is completely dependent on JavaScript. Granted, this chapter focused on the managed code to make programmatic changes to the way Silverlight operates (such as drawing the tick marks or setting the current time). But how was the Silverlight object instantiated in the first place? It was called by a JavaScript function. And remember that the basic foundation of Silverlight is contained in the linked `Silverlight.js` JavaScript file. If you turn off JavaScript in your browser, your clock project will look like Figure B-25.

453

As you can see, you can't see anything. There is no clock. There is no warning message. There is nothing. Silverlight just doesn't work.

And remember, also from Chapter 2, that JavaScript is not an issue just because of the accessible standards. Many people, whether because of corporate security settings or personal preference, have JavaScript disabled. And, if JavaScript is not enabled, Silverlight doesn't work.

Microsoft has openly stated that they plan to address accessibility in future releases. However, as of the Alpha 1.1 release of Silverlight, it has not been addressed. They remain optimistic that it can be addressed because the code in XAML is text-based and, as such, should be easy to translate for text readers. However, this work has not been done yet and, thus, Silverlight just isn't accessible. Will it be? Hopefully. But you need to understand, at least in its current iteration, it isn't accessible. And this is something to take seriously as you plan whether you are going to integrate Silverlight in your future projects.

Figure B-25

Summary

Silverlight is an exciting new tool for .NET developers that can completely revolutionize the way websites are designed. It has the ability to provide rich multimedia interfaces, while harnessing the power of .NET managed code. You can draw vector-based graphics and include animation and interaction that is fully supported across a wide variety of browsers. You finally have the power to do multimedia programming generally done by other programs right from the Visual Studio IDE that you are already comfortable with. The language is XML-based XAML with a .NET code behind. This will let you start experimenting with design features you may have avoided before, while not forcing you out of your coding comfort zone.

There are some limitations or, at least, considerations you need to look at when going to this platform. There is a plug-in that is almost 2MB that all users will have to have installed to see your new design skills. And, more importantly than that, Silverlight does not currently meet accessibility standards. Hopefully the accessibility issue will be addressed as the Silverlight project matures, and maybe the plug-in will become less and less of a problem as more users install it or, possibly, as it comes to be packaged with some browsers. But, at least in the infancy of Silverlight, these are things you need to keep in mind.

However, even with these limitations, Silverlight is one of the most exciting enhancements to web development Microsoft has offered. Beyond what was shown in this chapter, there are separate programs that allow designers to design projects (e.g., Microsoft Expression Studio) and then ship the design to developers to wire in the .NET power, and the product of Expression perfectly integrates into Visual Studio. This is brave new ground for Microsoft, and it is fun to be a part of the ride.

Index